D1035627

AMERICAN POLITICAL HISTORY
AS SOCIAL ANALYSIS

ৡ৶ *Twentieth-Century America Series*

140021

American Political History as Social Analysis

ESSAYS BY

SAMUEL P. HAYS

973.072
———
H 425

THE UNIVERSITY OF TENNESSEE PRESS

KNOXVILLE

Alverno College
Library Media Center
Milwaukee, Wisconsin

ꜱ Twentieth-Century America Series

DEWEY W. GRANTHAM, GENERAL EDITOR

Copyright © 1980 by The University of Tennessee Press, Knoxville. All rights reserved. Manufactured in the United States of America. First Edition.

Clothbound editions of University of Tennessee Press books are printed on paper designed for an effective life of at least 300 years, and binding materials are chosen for strength and durability.

Library of Congress Cataloging in Publication Data

Hays, Samuel P
    American political history as social analysis.
    (Twentieth-century America series)
    Includes bibliographical references and index.
    1. United States—Politics and government—
20th century—Collected works. 2. History—Study
and teaching (Higher)—United States—Collected works.
3. History—Statistical methods—Collected works.
I. Title.
E743.H35   309.1'73   79-17567
ISBN 0-87049-276-4

For graduate students at the State University of Iowa and the University of Pittsburgh whose ideas contributed heavily to the essays in this volume.

Contents

I.
INTRODUCTION

THE essays in this volume represent a series of steps in an evolving process of thought by which I have sought to reconstruct patterns of historical change in the United States. This objective was not my original intention, nor was it, for many years, a consciously formulated goal. It was rather the result of an accumulation of ideas emerging from reading, research, classroom teaching, and the direction of graduate research. Since the essays are in a sense autobiographical rather than systematic, at the suggestion of Dewey Grantham—the editor with whom I have worked in preparing the volume—this introduction has been written to provide a personal explanation of the concepts and experiences which shaped my writing.

It will readily be apparent that my intellectual environment has been heavily influenced by colleagues and, especially, by graduate students. The dedication of the book is not made lightly. My own thinking has been so closely interwoven with ideas and insights acquired in graduate seminars or discussions with individual students that I often find it difficult to separate my writings from theirs. These ideas, of course, were not part of an orderly, planned process; they simply arose in the normal course of interaction between teacher and student, often as a result of my persistent posing of suggestions and questions in the form of assigned reading or seminar discussion. Without this "ebb and flow" of ideas, the intellectual evolution represented in the following pages would have been severely limited.

I

ALTHOUGH the first serious research I undertook—the investigation of the conservation movement during the Progressive Era—grew

out of no profound intellectual inquiry but only a personal interest
in the subject, this as well as subsequent work was undoubtedly influenced by previous experiences. First of all, I felt a deep sense of
roots in family and community tradition in southern Indiana where
I grew up; twelve of my great-great-grandparents and thirteen
great-great-great-grandparents had lived, died, and been buried
there. These personal ties with the past were clearly felt then and
still remain. They gave rise to an active interest in family genealogy
and an extensive high school hobby of identifying and transcribing
gravestone inscriptions, which has remained to the present day. My
first use of the United States manuscript census returns in the 1940s
was for genealogical rather than more general historical research.

This continuing enthusiasm for family history, or "genealogical
reconstitution" (to paraphrase the Cambridge demographers), long
remained a latent influence on my historical thinking, but it particularly reinforced my interest in patterns of life in the grass-roots
community, the examination of social change through the family,
and the differential role of tradition and change in social institutions.
When I later investigated these subjects, they made sense in terms
of family and community involvements established much earlier.

Second, from the outset I have had a persistent desire to reconstruct the larger context of history. This involved a significant
change in direction while I was an undergraduate. I had originally
decided to major in philosophy, and while its constant process of
intellectual construction and reconstruction was highly intriguing, I
found it far too abstract and remote for my liking. In history I
found a similar opportunity to construct in large fashion, but here
there was a greater emphasis on the concrete human context. Suf-
fering from the customary aversion to high school history, I had
harbored no thoughts of emphasizing history in college; but as a
junior I took a European history survey and became more than interested. What I particularly enjoyed in three seminars at Swarthmore College, where the weekly assignment was to read widely in
secondary sources and reconstruct a historical problem, was the constant task of bringing together diverse aspects of a subject into a
single whole—and this experience in turn has shaped my image of
the task of the historian. History is a large jigsaw puzzle of which
one has the outlines and some (often mighty few) of the pieces; the

task is to fill in the gaps with as much concrete evidence as possible, but with imaginative reconstruction when necessary.

Third, I came into graduate work in history fresh from an undergraduate major in psychology and with the clear notion, although the precise reasons for it were not clear, that the latter would be highly useful in historical inquiry. One might chalk this up to a built-in bias toward focusing such inquiry on people rather than on their artifacts, which is an implicit theme of the essays. Far more important, however, was the heavy emphasis at Swarthmore on gestalt psychology, the perspective of which I adopted. Henceforth every situation of human behavior became immediately transformed into a cognitive context: How did this particular individual or group of individuals perceive the world, and how could that perception be understood in terms of the particular world of experience upon which they sought to impose order?

Although I had studied some depth psychology, I became highly suspicious of psychoanalytical explanations of history because they seemed extremely slippery and vague. This predisposition has continued and is seen in an aversion to the noncognitive psychological explanations of history popular in recent years, such as "status revolution," the attempt to dismiss ethnocultural factors in human life as secondary, irrational, and "soft," or the argument that much social and political behavior accompanying modernization can be ascribed to irrational actions resulting from alienation. The persistent psychological theory which underlies much of the social theory of these essays has its origins in the perspective of gestalt psychology.

Finally, a distinctive political relationship to the past is implicit in these essays. I have never considered history as a context which one uses to work out personal values or contemporary political choices. For many this is a crucial element of their work as historians. My own relationship to the past is to look upon it as a challenging field for detective work and as a maturing experience which generates satisfactions from the encounter with a variety of people and human circumstances. I have not sought out the past to decide what values, personal or political, to support in the present or to reinforce these values, and I have never considered the historical inquiries in which I engaged to be directly relevant to those choices. My decision to be a conscientious objector in World War II came not out of reading history but out of personal, existential choice. And so have other political involvements. Hence, I have been rather indifferent to the direct role which my historical writing plays in current political issues.

A more distinct indirect relationship between past and present is evident in this book, however. I have been heavily concerned with what appears to be a rather primitive level of self-understanding which Americans have about their politics, and I have looked upon teaching and writing as a small effort to advance that understanding. The opinion persists among many students and adults, and often among faculty as well, that political life is a contest between the good and the bad, the rational and the irrational, the knowledgeable expert and the unknowledgeable citizen—themes which are as prevalent today as they were in the Progressive Era. Administrative and judicial politics, as well as party and legislative politics, seem too often beyond the ken of most people. If there is a mission within these pages, it is to emphasize the realities of power in American political life and the institutional value choices which are made. The relationship of past to present is one of sensitizing people to their contemporary surroundings rather than providing direct answers to current problems.

Some of the essays in this volume have more direct political relevance than others. I have been especially intrigued by the impact of the article on municipal reform, which has had as much political as intellectual influence. Students for a Democratic Society, for example, reprinted it. However, the questions I have pursued as a historian have been far more closely connected with an evolving set of ideas about social change than with an agenda for social reform. I have been unwilling to accept the adjustment implications of modernization theory because they seemed to obscure the obvious persistent elements of inequality in condition and power amid social change, and I have been suspicious of the ideologies of many so-called radical social movements because their romantic attachment to populism often obscured the structure and dynamics of political inequality.

II

MY first formative experience with specific historical ideas came in undertaking the research and writing for *Conservation and the Gos-*

pel of Efficiency.[1] It would be an exaggeration to say that before then, during course work at Harvard, I had any clear notions about American history, the concepts which it involved, or even the importance of particular problems for research. These courses I had dutifully absorbed as an interesting intellectual exercise, but they did not set my mind in motion imaginatively. The dissertation subject itself reflected a personal interest in conservation, part of which resulted from the association with farming in earlier life but most of which arose from three years of work in forestry in western Oregon, as a conscientious objector, during World War II. When my adviser, Frederick Merk, suggested that I apply for a Harvard fellowship which permitted work on a subject concerning Theodore Roosevelt, and that the history of conservation would be such a fit subject, my dissertation topic was determined.

The research and writing, however, were another matter. I do not recall how fully I accepted the notion that something called "progressivism" constituted a popular revolt against the "interests." But since I recall that the evidence began to rearrange views held earlier, I suspect that the idea was there, even though held lightly. A new formulation began to emerge quite early in the research, so that during the summer of 1951, after some six months of work, I became convinced that conservation had been rooted primarily in the experiences, perceptions, and reactions of scientists and technicians. What especially appealed to me was the view that science and technology in this case were not inert and disinterested activities; their practitioners had intensely held opinions as to how decisions should be made. This established some perspectives which have influenced me profoundly ever since—a belief that administrative politics was more important than party and legislative politics, that the political process lay far deeper than the formal aspects of political life in the values of individuals as they evolved nonpublic undertakings, and that there was a drive and dynamic in empirical inquiry which was one of the major impulses of modern American politics. The research also established a larger context of centralization and decentralization in American political processes, as I contrasted the tendencies of conservationists to bring resource matters into one framework of decision making and the tendencies of their oppo-

1. *Conservation and the Gospel of Efficiency: The Progressive Conservation Movement* (Cambridge, Mass. 1958).

nents to maintain a more open set of options to reflect the views of users at a more regional level. That perspective spilled over into a number of later writings.

The impact of the above on my later historical work was somewhat limited. However, it did help to shape the approach to a new foray into research during my first year of teaching—an examination of the recent history of agricultural politics. As time went on, however, I became less interested in the book for the subject matter of conservation itself and more for the structure and processes of American political life which it outlined. I became concerned that the book "typed" me as a conservation historian when, in fact, it was part of a developing interest in the nature and distribution of political power generally. Increasingly I came to look upon it as an example of "systematization" in American political life. I was able to define the meaning of the book more explicitly when it was republished in 1965 in paperback with a new introduction, and when Allan Bogue asked me to write a short piece on the theme for a book he was coediting, *The West of the American People*.[2] Readers can decide for themselves the degree to which these concepts became more self-conscious with time.

During my first few years of teaching at the Universities of Illinois and Iowa, I became absorbed in agricultural politics in the twentieth century, examining political forces at local and regional levels. I was increasingly impressed with the role of the farm cooperative in national economic politics. Several facts began to emerge: that Herbert Hoover had tried to integrate cooperatives into a single, nationally directed marketing system, while Franklin D. Roosevelt had agreed to fund them as autonomous local and regional units; that the more highly controlled system of farm supply-demand and price manipulation which developed in the 1930s was a direct product of politically organized economic forces at the grass roots—farmers, bankers, ginners, processors—rather than of Roosevelt, Henry A. Wallace, or the New Deal; that the farm political forces which Ezra Taft Benson led during the Eisenhower administration were simply the more elaborate evolution of the entire farm cooperative movement for which he had served as executive of its

2. "Conservation and the Structure of American Politics: The Progressive Era," in Allan G. Bogue et al (eds.), *The West of the American People* (Itasca, Ill., 1970), 612–21.

main organization in the 1920s; and that the evolution of the farm cooperatives in the late nineteenth and early twentieth centuries was typical of one of the major elements of modern national economic politics.

These observations propelled me in a variety of directions. First, I became impressed with Herbert Hoover as a systematizer *par excellence*, linking his engineering background, his World War I experience, and his agricultural policies to a political process which placed a premium on centralized direction and control. Second, I became more interested in the economic politics of agriculture as it was reflected in the farm cooperative movement. In particular I focused on the Iowa scene, examining in detail the movement which led to the organization of the Farmers Grain Dealers Association of Iowa. A master's thesis on the subject by Curtis Cowle clarified much of the picture. It described the change from fitful starts toward organization in the late nineteenth century to effective economic and political strength in the twentieth. I was struck especially by the fact that such organizations not only reduced the costs of marketing, but served as an instrument of political power. I was equally impressed by the way in which organizational power was translated into support for attorneys to press farm interests in railroad rate matters in Washington before the Interstate Commerce Commission. Here was the grass-roots basis for national economic politics very similar to that exercised by resource users in conservation matters.

The reader will readily discern the connection between the above and the chapter in *Response to Industrialism* entitled "The Organizational Revolution."[3] Tracing the development of farm cooperatives led me to the conclusion that they were very similar to trade unions and trade associations in their origins, their form of organization, and the direction of their political activities. I did no research into trade unions, and that part of the argument rested entirely on secondary sources. But the work with farm cooperatives did lead to some investigation of trade associations, especially as it pertained to railroad regulation. Examination of the role of cooperatives in railroad politics created a picture of close cooperation between them and urban shippers. A study of hearings leading up to

3. *The Response to Industrialism, 1885–1914* (Chicago, 1957), 48–70.

the Hepburn Act revealed the deep involvement of industrial and commercial shippers in perfecting railroad regulation. By the time of writing the *Response*, I had developed more fully the concept that these economic groups represented a general form of political organization, nonparty and extra-party in character, and a new influence in the entire political order. That section in the *Response* represented an attempt to formulate such a view.

In the mid-1950s I conducted an inquiry into voting patterns in the late nineteenth and early twentieth centuries, a topic which subsequently became a major preoccupation. I recall that even in the 1952–53 academic year, while at the University of Illinois, I calculated countywide voting percentages for Illinois and compared and contrasted the votes in the primaries and general elections of 1910 and 1912. After 1953 I extended the study to the counties of the five states of the eastern Midwest and to elections in the nineteenth as well as the twentieth century. Especially dramatic, in my thinking, were the shifts in voting, countywide, in Michigan and Wisconsin between 1892 and 1896, shifts which indicated extremely sharp Republican gains in the lumbering and mining counties and large Democratic gains in south central Michigan. I then constructed congressional party composition in each election since the beginning of Congress and prepared graphs which indicated that most of the sharp breaks came in off-year elections. Amid all this, Lee Benson's initial writing on voting behavior was exciting and influential.[4] I began to identify voting changes in the 1890s as constituting one of the major shifts in voting patterns in American history and to focus on the depression of 1893 as the immediate source of the change, on the Republican party as the beneficiary of discontent, and on William McKinley as a candidate particularly attractive to newer immigrant and working-class voters.[5]

Over the last few years of the 1950s these voting analyses achieved considerable more depth for the state of Iowa. Using a simple Frieden calculator, Dan Potts, my research assistant, computed precinct votes for every county in Iowa from the earliest returns to 1920, and for some dozen or more urban counties for the years up

    4. Lee Benson, "Research Problems in American Political Historiography," in Mirra Komorovsky (ed.), *Common Frontiers in the Social Sciences* (Glencoe, Ill., 1957), 113–83.
    5. *The Response to Industrialism*, 46–47.

to the late 1950s; I then tried to relate these to demographic variables. I do not recall where or when the ethnocultural characteristics of voters began to strike me as important, but very early on I was searching for data that might illuminate them. It all stemmed from the practice of ranging precincts in a township from highest Republican to lowest and then looking at local history sources to determine population distinctions. Carroll County, Iowa, especially fascinated me, as it has many others. It was traditionally the most Democratic of Iowa counties, and yet it involved two distinct voting patterns, one heavily Democratic and German in the north and west, and the other heavily Republican and Yankee in the south and east. County after county was tackled in this fashion, and during a graduate seminar a half-dozen studies in depth were made, all revealing the importance of ethnic and religious characteristics.

The analysis took several different turns. One was to identify precincts in terms of ethnocultural composition and then to graph their voting patterns at one election or over a long period of time. George Daniels used this technique, with great success, to analyze German voters in the 1860 election in a seminar paper for Allan Bogue.[6] The trends in voting for different ethnocultural groups provided distinctive patterns of analysis. Especially impressive was the way in which Scandinavian voters, traditionally strongly Republican, reduced their Republican support sharply in 1918 after William Lloyd Harding, governor of Iowa, had issued a proclamation declaring it illegal to speak a foreign language in Iowa. At the next election they bounced back to their Republican loyalties. A second approach was to analyze the relationship between prohibition referenda and both election data and demographic data. The results were striking, revealing the similarities in voting among German Catholics and Lutherans and the strong connection between prohibition votes and party voting. In some counties which had experienced little immigration, moreover, the precinct pattern of prohibition votes in the nineteenth century was similar to that of party voting in the mid-twentieth century. I was especially struck by the differences in voting behavior among Germans; Presbyterian, Reformed, and Evangelical Germans as well as German Methodists

6. George H. Daniels, "The Immigrant Vote in the 1860 Election: The Case of Iowa," *Mid-America* 44 (1963), 142–62.

voted far more Republican than did Lutherans and Catholics. This set in motion a fascination with German subcultures in the United States which has continued to the present.

The results of these inquiries appeared in several publications while I was at the University of Iowa, especially in some brief sections in the *Response* concerning the elections of the 1890s and in "History as Human Behavior," which was published in the *Iowa Journal of History* in 1959.[7] For the most part, however, these inquiries have been pursued more effectively by graduate students. Sam McSeveney began his study of voting in Connecticut, New York, and New Jersey while I was still at Iowa. Paul Kleppner carried the Midwestern analysis much further in a wide variety of historical materials besides voting data and developed the distinction in terms of pietistic and ritualistic modes of values. John Allswang, who completed an M.A. degree with me at Iowa and then came to the University of Pittsburgh, carried this type of analysis to the city, as did Bruce Stave, who completed a dissertation on Pittsburgh politics. Samuel Lubell's *The Future of American Politics* had deeply influenced several of us, and Joseph Huthmacher's work on Massachusetts made an equal impression. One other dissertation, by Roger Peterson, reflected this line of thought; it examined the early roots of ethnocultural voting patterns by focusing on the years between 1845 and 1870 in Pennsylvania. Peterson emphasized especially the realignment of the early 1850s and extended the argument of Lee Benson that the emergence of the Republican party had more to do with ethnocultural factors than with the Kansas-Nebraska Act.[8]

Far more important than the specific focus on ethnocultural factors in voting, however, these inquiries added an important "grassroots" dimension to my historical thinking. Before then I had been

7. "History as Human Behavior," *Iowa Journal of History* 58 (1960), 193–206.

8. Samuel T. McSeveney, *The Politics of Depression: Political Behavior in the Northeast, 1893–1896* (New York, 1972); Paul Kleppner, *The Cross of Culture: A Social Analysis of Midwestern Politics, 1850-1900* (New York, 1970); John M. Allswang, *A House for All Peoples: Ethnic Politics in Chicago, 1890-1936* (Lexington, 1971); Bruce Stave, *The New Deal and the Last Hurrah: Pittsburgh Machine Politics* (Pittsburgh, 1970); Samuel Lubell, *The Future of American Politics* (New York, 1952); J. Joseph Huthmacher, *Massachusetts People and Politics, 1919-1933* (Cambridge, Mass., 1959); Roger Peterson, "The Reaction to a Heterogeneous Society: A Behavioral and Quantitative Analysis of Northern Voting Behavior,' 1845–1870: Pennsylvania as a Test Case," Ph.D. diss., Univ. of Pittsburgh, 1970; Lee Benson, *The Concept of Jacksonian Democracy* (Princeton, 1961).

principally concerned with national policy; both the conservation book and the inquiries into agricultural policy were in that vein, and my course in recent American history at Iowa concentrated mainly on the New Deal and the evolution of national policy then as well as in the Progressive Era. This emphasis was to remain, but now added to it was a focus on the individual in the smaller context of life in the community, along with a strong sense of the role of ethnicity and religion. From that time on I was deeply interested in the historical problems that focus on the immediate human context —the community and community change, religion and religious values, migration and mobility, education and the family. These concerns did not all emerge full-blown simultaneously, of course. But the voting studies were the first exploration into the field, and once the importance of this level of human life and historical inquiry had become fixed in my mind, a string of questions followed.

These three research forays—into conservation, agricultural politics, and voting behavior—gave rise to a three-layered context for thinking about political life in recent America. On the one hand, politics focused inevitably on national affairs and national patterns of political forces. On the other, it also inevitably involved the choices and preferences of people within the more immediate context of their daily lives and experiences. What became particularly striking was that these two different levels of political life did not have to be logically consistent with one another; what might be crucial in understanding patterns at one level would not be at all directly relevant to another. The organizational patterns of farm cooperatives, labor unions, and trade associations seemed to constitute a middle level between the other two, with a range of activities and ties which was much larger than the context of voting and smaller than the national focus of politics.

This three-layered approach was first articulated in a piece written for the *Political Science Quarterly* in 1965, originally presented as a paper at the 1964 meeting of the American Historical Association.[9] The major thrust of the argument was to establish an alternative to the presidential synthesis of American political history which had been so ably critiqued by Thomas Cochran and later by Lee

9. "The Social Analysis of American Political History, 1880–1920," *Political Science Quarterly* 80 (1965), 373–94.

Benson.[10] My aim was not to set forth a well-developed theory but rather to suggest a setting for future work—to point out that American politics cannot be considered simply as nationally focused events, but as events and human activity at different vertical levels. In some fashion, then not at all clear, the three levels had to be interwoven. I was especially convinced that efforts to look upon state and local politics as simply national politics writ small, or national politics as local politics writ large, were unsatisfactory. I disagreed with the perennial attempts to write of "progressivism in the states," as if it were simply one phenomenon at different political levels. All this crystallized a decade of evolution in historical thinking and foreshadowed a variety of future writings.

The Response to Industrialism, although it incorporated some of the themes already recounted, was written before this sense of vertical layers had been fully formulated. That book reflects a different set of concepts which grew out of the same experiences and which have had an equally profound effect. For while the concept of layers placed special emphasis on patterns of political relationships at any one time, on structure, the *Response* is built far more around concepts of change. It is concerned with the various ways in which individuals and groups reacted to the vast changes brought about by industrialism, and it played a major role in establishing the theme of change and reaction to change in my thinking. The *Response* reflects the dual contexts of structure and change which have been repeated in subsequent writings.

At this time I find it far more difficult to understand the evolution of the *Response* than the origins of the series of forays into conservation, organizational activity, and voting behavior. The book was written in 1956 and grew out of the course in recent American history which I had taught since the fall of 1953, as well as a course in American economic history begun some time later. Many specific aspects of the book, among them those already mentioned, are clear. But the idea of "response" is a different matter. One source of the theme was a growing belief that many political movements, traditionally thought to be innovative in the sense that the terms "progressive" or "liberal" implied the unfolding of new stages of

10. Thomas C. Cochran, "The Presidential Synthesis in American History," *American Historical Review* 53 (1948), 748–59.

long-run historical changes, were in fact reactions to innovation rather than elements of innovation themselves. The book considered farm and labor movements in the late nineteenth century in this light and analyzed the views of Henry George and Edward Bellamy in a similar context. There were elements of these ideas in the conservation book, where both the middle-class support for conservation and the views of Theodore Roosevelt are seen as characteristic of the less industrialized past. But all this does not seem to account for the general idea of "response."

The *Response* does reflect, however, a great dissatisfaction with the "people versus the interests" theme so common in traditional historical writings about the Populist and Progressive eras, and a desire to root political and social change in a reaction not simply to the corporation but to industrialization in all of its facets. This belief arose because an attempt to recapture the experience and response in politics led back to an initial confrontation not with the corporation but with varied facets of change in human life. Throughout all of the inquiries undertaken before writing the *Response*, that viewpoint seemed to persist. A political phenomenon could be understood best by focusing on the people involved, observing the circumstances in which they lived and thought, and examining their ideas and behavior as a reaction to that situation. From this vantage point the *Response* does not reflect an attempt to apply modernization concepts or some other theory of social change to recent American history, but the persistent infusion of a perspective in which the reactions of people to their circumstances are the major focus of attention. Building up from this type of question led initially to the insistence upon industrialization, i.e., broad social and economic changes, rather than the corporation itself as the focal point of reaction. Only later did this develop further into more elaborate concepts of social change; only later, for example, did I prefer the concept "modernization" to "industrialization."

In retrospect the *Response* appears to be overwhelmingly experimental in nature and to contain a minimum of conceptualization. It seems somewhat tentative and loose, lacking the more sharply defined categories of response to change which I would now prefer. More important, however, the deficiencies of the *Response* lie in its failure to develop a clear statement of the evolving patterns of urban-industrial America to which responses occurred and which would provide an opportunity to observe the points of interaction between change and the reaction to change. The initial chapter of the book, "Industrialism Under Way," was merely a backdrop to what came later and, as I recall, was written last precisely to establish this setting. This weakness has become especially striking as time has passed, and writing along these lines in the future will require a fuller elaboration of the innovative forces in American society. A number of articles in this book, to which reference will be made later, represent attempts to establish those innovative forces more fully. Despite all this, the *Response* added a context of political change to that of political structure, two interwoven themes which became a permanent and integral part of my historical thinking.

III

As an outgrowth of my own research and the direction of graduate theses, three particular aspects of twentieth-century American history began to occupy my interest in the late 1950s while I was at the University of Iowa. The first was the internal politics of the Republican party in Iowa, including Old Guard, Cumminsite, and Bull Moose factions; the second was the impact of World War I on American life; and the third was the movement for reform in municipal government in the early twentieth century. All three set in motion research and ideas that accompanied me to the University of Pittsburgh and were heavily influenced by an urban setting.

Examination of the Republican party took several forms. One was a direct analysis of the argument of George Mowry concerning Progressive party leaders in California, an M.A. thesis carried out by Dan Potts and later published in *Mid-America*. This work was the first of a number of pieces of research which rendered the "status revolution" arguments of both Mowry and Richard Hofstadter untenable.[11] The Potts thesis also led to another M.A. essay by David Carey on similar political leadership at the local level (in Burlington, Iowa), which found some significant distinctions among Republican factions and reinforced the notion that political life was

11. E. Daniel Potts, "The Progressive Profile in Iowa," *Mid-America* 47 (1965), 257–68.

quite different at different levels of the political order; these levels could not safely be lumped together.[12]

Following another tack in Republican party analysis, I examined the peculiarities of the voting base of Old Guard and Cumminsite support. The strength of the two groups was especially striking in the primary contest between Senator William B. Allison and Governor Albert B. Cummins in 1908. A plot of that countywide vote, which Leland Sage published in his biography of Senator Allison, led me to undertake a more intensive examination of the voting base and to discover a peculiar association of non-Yankee ethnics in the Republican party, especially Germans and Scandinavians, with the Cummins movement. I began to interpret the intraparty quarrel as an effort of groups long submerged by the Yankees in the party to have their day. This view was more fully confirmed in my mind when a study of the factional leaders who gathered around Cummins in the 1890s and the early twentieth century demonstrated the same ethnocultural source. This basis of intraparty factionalism was underlined further when I read David Brye's dissertation on Wisconsin politics, which explored the roots of the La Follette movement and put forth a similar argument.[13]

The Cummins movement had other sources as well, namely, in the drive for economic growth and development by particular sections or economic groups in Iowa to which the Old Guard, tied to a previous era of railroad development, did not adequately respond. I found that Cummins was a major spokesman for business groups in the state which favored the Hepburn Act and demanded more effective regulation of railroad rates. I also found that his concern for a lower tariff stemmed from an interest of many Iowa industries in reciprocity, so that they could tap new markets in Canada and Latin America. This reinforced my notion that the demand for railroad regulation was not just farmer-based but also grew out of the desires of shippers, many of them industrialists, to obtain the rates desirable to stimulate regional economic growth.[14] It also estab-

12. David J. Carey, "Republican Factionalism in Burlington, Iowa, 1906–1908," M.A. thesis, State Univ. of Iowa, 1960.

13. David Brye, "Wisconsin Voting Patterns in the Twentieth Century, 1900–1950," Ph.D. diss., Harvard Univ., 1973.

14. See material in *The Response to Industrialism*, 55–56. The argument was elaborated in detailed and much more convincing fashion by Richard Vietor, whose seminar

lished in my mind the view that the Insurgent tariff argument was not simply a matter of Western agricultural consumers pitted against Eastern industrial producers; it reflected the drive by Midwestern regional industry for growth and development. What especially crystallized my views on tariff policy was a detailed examination in a seminar paper of the correspondence of Senator Jonathan Dolliver, which demonstrated that while advocating lower tariffs for some products he also fought to keep or raise tariffs on products of "infant" Iowa industries.

An examination of the Bull Moose contingent in the Iowa Republican party focused on some altogether different situations. Here was a distinct group of people tied up with distinct social changes. One such change was the drive to promote Iowa agricultural development, especially activities associated with the Country Life Movement—a coalition of individuals and business interests which included agricultural experts at Iowa State College, the Iowa Bankers Association concerned with farm mortgages, railroads with a stake in hauling farm commodities, and mail-order houses interested in rural free delivery. Close connections could be found between Theodore Roosevelt's espousal of the Country Life Movement and a host of developments not simply in rural life per se but in professional and urban-based economic groups which had a stake in a reversal of the downward trend in rural population and prosperity. The above themes were developed in an M.A. essay on the Iowa Progressive party by Richard Sias, and I found them to apply also in Illinois, where leaders of the Illinois Bankers Association were ardent Progressives. I became especially intrigued with the Good Roads Movement as a prototype of the entire phenomenon of town- and city-based promoters reaching out to penetrate the countryside and organize it from central places. All of these investigations were instrumental in arousing my interest in a regional focus to economic, social, and political life—an interest which came to be articulated more fully in later years.

This work on Iowa Republicans, the first research and thinking about a political party which I had undertaken, helped to shape a

paper on the drive for railroad regulation (Univ. of Pittsburgh, 1971) was published as "Businessmen and the Political Economy: The Railroad Rate Controversy of 1905," *Journal of American History* 44 (1977), 47–66.

particular and continuing view of party analysis. The social, economic, and perceptual context within which parties operate is fundamental to an understanding of them. That context had to be reconstructed in some independent fashion so that the impulses of the larger social order could be seen working through parties. I began to be disillusioned with analyses of purely party phenomena, such as legislative voting, campaign pronouncements, and platforms by themselves, and with the arguments based on that information and applied to the larger society by many party historians. Instead I began to contend that the patterns of the larger social order had to be reconstructed in and of themselves, and those impulses had to be followed into lines of political action. "Political impulses" included types of action different from parties and legislatures. Functional groups and corporate systems were forms of political action along with parties. Political history should be concerned with many human impulses and values arising from the general society, not just with those that happened to become reflected in the formal political party.

A shift in academic setting from Iowa City to Pittsburgh in the fall of 1960 provided an entirely new and different context for my historical work. The city began to emerge as a convenient framework within which research could be designed. Graduate seminars used Pittsburgh materials for social research, and this in turn added a forceful urban slant to previously established lines of thinking. There was no sudden break in my ideas or interests, and in fact one can consider the post-1960 articles as the elaboration of general historical ideas seen within two contexts—that of the region or state (which was the focus in Iowa City) and that of the city (which was the focus in Pittsburgh). I did not come to consider urban history as a distinct field in itself, but rather as a peculiarly useful setting in which to examine some general social and political patterns and processes.

The move to Pittsburgh yielded another highly important influence. As the History Department at the University of Pittsburgh developed, the major categories of historical interest became not traditional countries and chronological periods, but different types of human activities and social processes over time. We sought to stress common aspects of human life in a variety of periods and geographical locations, rather than in distinctive national contexts. We wanted to discover what was common to urbanization, economic development, religion, the impact of modernization on rural life, migration, regional organization, the family, ethnicity, working-class people, and political behavior in different times and places, and what differentiated them because of their distinctive backgrounds. This approach fostered many fruitful discussions among the faculty, both in formal faculty-student seminars and in informal conversations. Although its specific impact is difficult to assess, this departmental setting provided an enormously stimulating atmosphere for historical thinking.

One interest which carried over directly from Iowa to Pittsburgh was the examination of structure and change in the context of World War I. The war provided an opportunity to examine a variety of questions which the inquiries of the 1950s had opened up. Because of the time-period limitation of the *Response*, none of this appeared there, but relevant fragments appeared in later articles.

The war, first of all, was a major occasion for the acceleration of centralization in decision making outlined in *Conservation and the Gospel of Efficiency*. This possibility first struck me as I examined the reaction of farm cooperatives to the U.S. Railroad Administration and found that the efficiencies established by that government body so completely disrupted the established patterns of traffic and the influence of shippers in the regulatory process that the latter violently objected to continued federal control. They were an important influence in ending that control by means of the Transportation Act of 1920. This seemed to be another example of the tension between centralizing and decentralizing forces outlined in the conservation book. Austin Kerr most ably developed the entire subject in the context of railroad regulation; he completed an M.A. thesis on the subject at Iowa and extended it at Pittsburgh into a doctoral dissertation, later published.[15]

Reaction to the war also presented some real possibilities for examining political life at the grass roots and especially through the elections of 1918 and 1920. Some forays into this subject at Iowa convinced me that voters began to rebel against the Wilson admin-

15. K. Austin Kerr, "Shipper Groups and the Transportation Act of 1920," M.A. thesis, State Univ. of Iowa, 1960; *American Railroad Politics, 1914–1920* (Pittsburgh, 1968).

istration in 1918, that the anti-Democratic reaction of 1920 was merely a continuation of trends begun in 1918, and that this swing had much more to do with the adverse effect of the war in 1917 and 1918 than with the reaction to the League of Nations. The anti-Railroad Administration politics of 1918 first led me in this direction, but examination of party activity and voting confirmed it. A quick survey of Democratic candidates for the Iowa state legislature in 1918 revealed a dramatic decline in the number of races in which they ran, certainly reflecting their gloom about prospects. Some brief calculations of party makeup of several state legislatures from 1914 to 1922 convinced me that the drop in Democratic support was a more widespread phenomenon.

An M.A. thesis by John Schou outlining these trends for Iowa extended the analysis to a variety of effects of the war on Iowa people and their reactions in 1918 and 1920,[16] and a later doctoral dissertation at Pittsburgh by Joseph Makarewicz did the same for Pennsylvania.[17] One aspect of the reaction loomed fairly large—the response to food rationing, a significant element of which was the eastern European immigrants' objection to being required to purchase corn meal—a food fit only for horses—in order to secure wheat flour. This emphasis was confirmed in a personal way when I went through several boxes of letters belonging to my father, who had been a food administrator in Harrison County, Indiana, during the war. The letters described the constant surveillance of sugar and flour purchases and intense hostility on the part of the consumer. My father had frequently told me that the biggest mistake of his life had been to think that he could launch a political career by starting out as a local food administrator; it had made him highly unpopular.

Several aspects of these inquiries into World War I policies had further consequences. One was an examination of the role of Arch Wilkinson Shaw in the war effort. Shaw had been a professor of marketing at Harvard Business School and had written extensively about his belief that the greatest inefficiency in the American economy during the early twentieth century was in the field of distribu-

16. John T. Schou, "The Decline of the Democratic Party in Iowa, 1916–1920," M.A. thesis, State Univ. of Iowa, 1960.
17. Joseph Makarewicz, "The Impact of World War I on Pennsylvania Politics With Emphasis on the Election of 1920," Ph.D. diss., Univ. of Pittsburgh, 1972.

tion. During the war he had an opportunity to apply his concepts to wartime economic affairs. What was more revealing was to follow the pages of the journal he edited, *System*, in which he outlined a variety of ways in which every aspect of business could be systematized. This not only brought the words "system" and "systematization" more sharply into focus in my thinking but also convinced me that the dramatic ideas and activities of Frederick W. Taylor were far less important than a multitude of social processes at work in "system" after "system" in the nation in both private and public life, which added up to the creation of a network of centrally directed patterns of organization. This built extensively upon ideas in the conservation book and served as a bridge between them and later writing on systematization, such as the introduction to *Building the Organizational Society*, edited by Jerry Israel.[18]

Equally significant in my thinking was an examination of the statistical work carried out during the war. I came upon the activities of the Statistical Board, its related agencies, and Wesley Mitchell, found close connections between them and leaders of the earlier conservation movement, and traced them into the social research activities of the 1920s in connection with the National Bureau of Economic Research. I found similar patterns in the role of Robert Brookings during the war, of efficiency experts in municipal government before the war, and of the Brookings Institution thereafter. All this extended even further my notions about organized system and efficiency and began to develop some ideas about the dynamics and drive of those systems, particularly the role of intensive empirical inquiry as an underlying condition for system control.

Although I never used the war as a major context for examining changing patterns of social, political, and economic structure in the United States, the outlines of such a work were there. They indicated the way in which the war provided an occasion for the rapid acceleration of processes of system development long at work in the economy and the society, and for their incorporation into government in a far-reaching manner.[19] From that point on I began to

18. "The New Organizational Society," in Jerry Israel (ed.), *Building the Organizational Society: Essays on Associational Activities in Modern America* (New York, 1972), 1–15.
19. An excellent analysis of this process for women workers during the war has been

view the centralization found in the conservation movement in larger terms, as a persistent process of systematization which ran deeply through private and public affairs. An undergraduate seminar in the fall of 1970, entitled "The Evolution of Technical Systems in Modern America," provided an opportunity to think through the topic more extensively.

A second subject which carried over from Iowa to Pittsburgh was Progressive Era municipal reform. I became interested in this subject initially while examining twentieth-century politics in Iowa, especially the movement for a commision form of government in Des Moines. The initiative for this development seemed to come largely from the Chamber of Commerce and dominant business and professional leaders in the city. On moving to Pittsburgh I examined reform in the municipal government there in 1911 and came to the same conclusions. In that case social registers provided an opportunity to locate the reform leaders more precisely. Initially I prepared a paper on the subject—pertaining only to a revision of Lincoln Steffens' views about municipal reform in Pittsburgh—which was given at a meeting of the American Historical Associaion in December 1962.[20] A talk in 1963 at the University of Washington, Seattle, on the more general subject of municipal reform in the Progressive Era brought together Des Moines and Pittsburgh data and a number of secondary writings. While there I examined municipal reform in Seattle and found similar evidence. All this gave rise to a considerably modified version of the argument which appeared in the *Pacific Northwest Quarterly* in 1964.[21]

As time went on more implications of the argument took shape. Even prior to the municipal reform article, I had examined the characteristics of city councilmen for several decades prior to the changes in Pittsburgh government in 1911 and for a similar time thereafter, in order to discover a major shift in their occupational background. Similar data, with similar conclusions, were prepared for the Pittsburgh School Board. Through the work of Joan Miller,

completed by Maurine Greenwald, "Women, War and Work: The Impact of World War I on Women Workers in the United States," Ph.D. diss., Brown Univ., 1977.

20. "The Shame of the Cities Revisited: The Case of Pittsburgh," in Herbert Shapiro (ed.), *The Muckrakers and American Society* (Boston, 1968), 75–81.

21. "The Politics of Reform in Municipal Government in the Progressive Era," *Pacific Northwest Quarterly* 55 (1964), 157–69.

an M.A. student at Roosevelt University who came to the University of Pittsburgh for doctoral study, a focus on the candidate choices made by reformers was undertaken. Her M.A. thesis had used handbooks in which the Chicago Municipal Voters League made recommendations to voters among city council candidates in Chicago.[22] I found similar material for Pittsburgh, and later another M.A. student at Pittsburgh obtained the same for Cleveland. All the evidence supported the view that "reformers" preferred candidates who were of higher occupational and educational background, as well as white Anglo-Saxon Protestants.

As a result of the above, I began to place special emphasis on the organizational rather than the socioeconomic quality of the reform movement. I was particularly fascinated by the shift from ward to at-large elections. Reform involved not just a set of socioeconomic choices, but a rejection of small-scale in preference for large-scale organization. I began to link the processes of reorganization in urban, economic, social, and political life to shifts from smaller- to larger-scale systems. There were important socioeconomic aspects to the change in which people from upper levels sought to transfer power toward themselves from people at lower levels. But this could not be explained purely in socioeconomic terms. A levels-of-organization dimension to the problem was required as a separate vantage point of inquiry. The long-term process of social change which this involved, I felt, was bound up with the reorganization of urban life over a long period. As time has gone on, this aspect of municipal reform has loomed much larger than the socioeconomic element.

This interest gave rise to some new explorations into urban life and government, all intended to elucidate these organizing and reorganizing processes. I particularly wanted to know whether precise connections could be made between levels of organization in governmental structure and economic or professional life. Several graduate seminars focused on this problem. Students found that business life could be organized in a hierarchy depending upon its scale,

22. Joan S. Miller, "The Politics of Municipal Reform in Chicago during the Progressive Era: The Municipal Voters' League as a Test Case, 1896-1920," M.A. thesis, Roosevelt Univ., 1966.

from small to intermediate to large, varying primarily with the geographical extent of the market, and that organized business efforts, through boards of trade and chambers of commerce, could be arranged in the same fashion.[23] Involvement with municipal reform increased markedly as the scale of economic activities was enlarged. A similar scale could be fashioned for professionals, doctors, architects, and schoolteachers, ranging from those preoccupied with small-community affairs to those involved in citywide affairs.[24] Such inquiries indicated a direct relationship between scale of professional activities and degree of involvement in municipal reform.

These investigations gradually were extended to earlier and later periods as I explored further patterns in scale of organization. One seminar paper, for example, dealt with the shift from citywide to ward representation in 1833.[25] I studied the involvements of city councilmen and school board members throughout the history of Pittsburgh from the earliest time to the present. This approach gradually led me to a perspective on urban history which emphasized processes of centralization and decentralization and the tension between them as the city grew. One crucial aspect was some notion of periodization, of stages in which either one or the other tendency dominated or a particular balance was achieved between them. This formulation was initially presented at the Conference of the Australian–New Zealand American Studies Association held at LaTrobe University in Melbourne in August 1970, and it was published later in the initial issue of *Urban History*.[26] The article is, in many ways, a digestion of a considerable number of graduate seminar papers completed at the University of Pittsburgh based upon social research on the city. Another summary of this research and thinking, more specifically focused on Pittsburgh's history, was

23. Mary Young, "The Pittsburgh Chamber of Commerce and Allied Boards of Trade in 1910," seminar paper, Univ. of Pittsburgh, 1966; Frank Lukaszewicz, "Regional and Central Boards of Directors of Pittsburgh Banks in 1912," seminar paper, Univ. of Pittsburgh, 1966.

24. Ross Metzger, "The Medical Profession and Urban Reform in Pittsburgh, 1890–1920," seminar paper, Univ. of Pittsburgh, 1966.

25. John Dankosky, "Pittsburgh City Government, 1816–1850," seminar paper, Univ. of Pittsburgh, 1971.

26. "The Changing Political Structure of the City in Industrial America," *Journal of Urban History* 1 (1974), 6–38.

published in the *Magazine* of the Western Pennsylvania Historical Society in late 1974.[27]

Examination of World War I and municipal reform gave rise to some modified views about the relationship between the prewar Progressive Era years and the 1920s. To what extent were the 1920s, in the form of "normalcy," a reversal of past policies? Did the "progressive" impulses of the prewar years continue to be strong? These persistently debated questions seemed to have missed the mark, I felt, because the continuity of long-run social and organizational processes gave a unity to the years 1897-1929; the very impulses historians had labeled "progressive" were in fact the same forces, evolved further, which in the 1920s they had labeled "conservative." The Progressive Era organizational drives in the city which made for municipal reform and those in the region that made for rural and regional improvement, typified by such groups as the chambers of commerce, set the tone of the 1920s. Institutions during World War I such as the Councils of National Defense seemed to gather together many of the political forces which in prewar years were called "progressive" to give them new life in a new format in the following years. This argument remains as a major unifying theme concerning political patterns between 1897 and 1929.

IV

By the late 1960s several essays began to take on more explicitly the theme of social and political structure. This was not a new departure, for the structural context of American politics had been implicit in the initial conservation book as well as in later writings, but it now became more elaborate and more forcefully stated. A major impetus in this direction was provided by Robert Merton's article on "locals and cosmopolitans."[28] The idea of a community-society dimension in historical analysis probably did not take root in my mind without earlier predispositions, and yet those origins are dif-

27. "The Development of Pittsburgh as a Social Order," *Western Pennsylvania Historical Magazine* 57 (1974), 431–48.

28. Robert K. Merton, "Patterns of Influence: Local and Cosmopolitan Influentials," in Merton (ed.), *Social Theory and Social Structure* (Glencoe, Ill., 1949), 387–420.

ficult to pinpoint. By establishing a more articulated pattern of social structure, it provided an effective context for relating both
large-scale organizing processes and grass-roots human activities. It
also suggested a direction of change, of cosmopolitanizing forces
developing amid more local forces, gradually overcoming them and
creating a new pattern of social order. It crystallized themes which
had been implicit but not well developed in the *Response*. This
concept, which seemed to bring together a number of ideas into
a single whole, is the subject of "Political Parties and the
Community-Society Continuum," written in 1967.[29]

These new formulations also triggered investigation of a number of new problems, one of which was mobility. Mobility had
never entered my thinking seriously in previous years, and I am not
sure from what quarter the first interest arose. I was aware of the
work being done on vertical mobility by Stephan Thernstrom, Stuart Blumin, and Clyde Griffin.[30] In the 1960s a student in one of
my seminars had undertaken what is now a typical study of out-
migration from a Pittsburgh community, a study which had found
a positive relationship between persistence and property ownership. But the theme of mobility seemed to involve much more than
that, and several strands began to emerge.

Late in the 1960s I became interested in geographical mobility
as a general phenomenon of social discontinuity and argued that it
had to be approached by placing all types of migration in a single
systematic and comparative context. The westward movement, migrations from Europe, rural to urban migration, movement from
the central city to the suburbs, and the intercity movement from
suburb to suburb were all different instances of a similar process. I
was struck by how much selectivity there had been on the part of
historians in studying geographical mobility; migrations embedded
in folk culture were emphasized, and others were virtually ignored.
One could ask the same questions about each of these migrations:
who migrated, what happened to people in the process of migration, how were they received in the host community? Oscar Hand-

29. "Political Parties and the Community-Society Continuum," in William N. Chambers and Walter Dean Burnham (eds.), *The American Party Systems: Stages of Political Development* (New York, 1967), 152–81.

30. See this and other work in Stephan Thernstrom and Richard Sennett (eds.),
Nineteenth-Century Cities: Essays in the New Urban History (New Haven, 1969), 165–208.

lin's *The Uprooted* obviously influenced these questions, and his book had long served as a major point of departure for my thinking about immigration from Europe. I was pleased to see the historical research then being done on migration, but at the same time I found my own ideas taking a particular direction.

I was especially dissatisfied with the growing implication in migration studies that individual movement could be divorced from social context. An assumption was developing that the heavy rates of out-migration from communities and cities constituted an atomizing process often labeled "social disintegration." This was the explicit contribution of an article by Peter Knights and Stephan Thernstrom which appeared in 1971, based on their Boston data.[31] It seemed to lead to a concept of personal social "alienation" that constituted a general pattern of social response. All this seemed far more connected with the contemporary psychological needs of the reader, both professional historian and student, than with the elaboration of an explicit theory of historical change. I was struck by John Modell's statement in his review of Peter Knights's book on Boston that those of his students who had a distinct aversion to quantitative evidence in history were highly receptive to Knights's highly quantitative statement of atomized human movement because, feeling alienated themselves, they could identify with it.[32] My concerns on this matter were presented at a conference on urban geography and history at York University in 1972, in which I argued that geographical movement took place within persistent social patterns and that by focusing only on movement and not on the persistent patterns the entire process was misunderstood.[33]

I pursued two lines of thought regarding mobility. The first was based on the notion that every community had persistent and mobile elements and that the persistent ones contributed a structured pattern to that community despite a great deal of movement in and out of it. In this view I was much influenced by studies done by two

31. Stephan Thernstrom and Peter R. Knights, "Men in Motion: Some Data and Speculations About Urban Population Mobility in Nineteenth Century America," *Journal of Interdisciplinary History* 1 (1970), 1–35.

32. John Modell, book review of Peter R. Knights, *The Plain People of Boston, 1830-60: A Study of City Growth,* in *Historical Methods Newsletter* 6 (1972), 26–33.

33. "Social Structure in the New Urban History," paper presented to the Conference on Historical Urbanization in North America, York Univ., Toronto, Jan. 24–26, 1973.

fellow historians at the University of Pittsburgh, each of whom was examining this question—Walter Glazer for mid-nineteenth-century Cincinnati and Robert Doherty for five towns and cities in Massachusetts in the first half of the nineteenth century.[34] This led to the conviction that by focusing only on individual movement and not on the comparative analysis of urban social structures, modern geographical mobility studies were extremely one-sided and deceptive.

The second notion, also heavily influenced by Glazer and Doherty, focused on the role of life cycle in mobility. Mid-twentieth-century census data emphasized heavily the direct relationship between migration and age; there seemed to be no reason to doubt a similar pattern for earlier years, and the research by Glazer, Doherty, and Laurence Glasco on Buffalo seemed to confirm it. All this gave rise to a working theory about the relationship between mobility and social structure, namely, that geographic mobility represented not a "breakdown" in the social order but a transition point in a shift from one pattern of shared values, one pattern of social structure, to another. Young people who had high migration rates were participating in transition years between a pattern in a previous generation and one in a succeeding generation. Geographical movement generally was an occasion for a break in historical continuity and the focal point for change in human values, aspirations, and preferences.

I became equally interested in vertical mobility. Here again I was impressed with the efforts of Stephan Thernstrom to work out the process in Newburyport, Massachusetts, and I began to explore the problem in other works, especially in sociology. I was drawn more to the pattern of structure rather than the process of mobility, at least as defined by Thernstrom and others. They appeared to wish to answer the question as to what extent "opportunity" had existed in the United States. This seemed to me to be rather limited. I became more interested in the resulting patterns of social structure which vertical mobility generated and the relationship between the process of mobility itself and that structure. I spelled out

34. Walter Glazer, "Participation and Power: Voluntary Associations and the Functional Organization of Cincinnati in 1840," *Historical Methods Newsletter* 5 (1972), 151–68; Robert Doherty, *Society and Power: Five New England Towns, 1800–1860* (Northampton, Mass., 1978).

these concerns in a long review of Thernstrom's second book, *The Other Bostonians*, in the *Journal of Social History* in 1976.[35]

Two ramifications of this line of thought began to emerge as crucial concepts. First was the view that despite increases in the total output of goods and services per capita, and despite improvements in conditions at all levels of the social order, the distribution of wealth and income—the shape of the curve—had not apparently changed very much throughout the course of American history. I was struck by the way in which the argument about change was modified considerably when quantitative data were translated into qualitative description. What seemed to Thernstrom to be "little" vertical mobility could be seen by other scholars as "much." What one described as "relative equality" could be described by another as "relative inequality." When the upper 10 percent of rural wealth holders owned 30 percent of the wealth, was that relative equality or relative inequality? When that 30 percent owned by the upper 10 percent increased to 70 percent in cities, did that mean that by contrast the rural wealth owners displayed a condition of "equality"? I began to develop the view that at no time in American history could one speak of "relative equality," that the only sensible conclusion was that a continuous pattern of inequality had obtained and that the only significant changes were from one degree of inequality to another. I came to look upon the "equality-inequality" alternative not as sound social description, but as an infusion of ideology into the descriptive process and one which should give way to a focus on different patterns of inequality.

This approach to the problem was reinforced when I began to think of vertical mobility as a differentiating process. The persistent fact arose: some moved up and others did not. The differences were partly due to social differences in which the conditions for vertical movement were more abundant for some than for others. But within each level of occupation and affluence there were variations; again, some moved up and others did not. All this resulted in a process of differentiation between individuals. The same process could be observed for geographical mobility from rural communities, as some remained and some left. I began to look upon mobil-

35. *Journal of Social History* 9 (1976), 409–14.

ity studies generally as focusing on the process of differentiation. The knotty question to be unraveled was why individuals differed within a group at the same "level of opportunity." Differentiation led to the constant creation and re-creation of inequalities as some moved up and others did not, a concept which was reinforced by the knowledge of downward mobility and the idea of "net mobility" which first impressed me on reading Stuart Blumin's doctoral dissertation.[36] I began to think of the term "equal opportunity" as, in fact, the equality of opportunity to become unequal, and to consider differential mobility as creating persistent patterns of vertical social structure.

All this led, finally, to a growing interest in the concept of psychological mobility. I cannot say just how this developed. It crystallized with the reading of Daniel Lerner's book *The Passing of Traditional Society*, especially his chapter on the Turkish peasant.[37] But that argument took hold, I feel sure, because of a desire to understand the process of mobility. What it focused on was the change in the human mind, in one's perception of the world, in an understanding of the available alternatives, and in one's capacity to empathize with other people in other places who represented those alternatives. I was searching for some way of thinking about the manner in which people in similar social circumstances responded differently to circumstances "out there." The question clearly implied some difference in the way that larger world of possible alternatives was perceived; although Lerner's concept of psychological mobility did not explain it, it at least provided a set of ideas through which the problem could be defined and explored. From this time on my thinking on mobility involved an attempt to weave together concepts of geographical, vertical, and psychological mobility.

As a result of this trend of thought, I began to focus on social differentiation in order to understand the process by which variation evolved in people's values, attitudes, and circumstances. An interest in social differentiation had arisen earlier in one particular context, the analysis of the upper class; the materials used in exam-

36. Some of this material was published in Stuart Blumin, "Mobility and Change in Ante-Bellum Philadelphia," in Thernstrom and Sennett, *Nineteenth-Century Cities*, 165–208.

37. Daniel Lerner, "Modernizing Styles of Life: A Theory," in *The Passing of Traditional Society* (Glencoe, Ill., 1958), 43–75.

ining the sources of municipal reform had led me to observe a wide range of upper-class phenomena. A graduate seminar on the subject in 1965, with topics chosen from Pittsburgh, generated a variety of studies of upper-class communities, ethnic upper classes, and particular economic groups, such as bankers. These papers highlighted the variation within the upper class, the fact that it was not homogeneous—that the process of vertical movement, upward and downward, gave rise to fine gradations from bottom to top within the group. This reinforced the notion of differentiation throughout the vertical social order.

Several directions of analysis of the upper class were heavily influenced by graduate student research papers. One, a comparative study of the nineteenth-century iron and steel upper class in six cities by John Ingham,[38] emphasized the problem of continuity and discontinuity within this group as well as layers within it; Ingham's work has appeared in article form and recently in a book. A second was a seminar paper, a comparative study of different upper-class levels in Pittsburgh by George Bedeian; this was a computer analysis of three upper-class registers, each reflecting a different level of strata within the group and giving special focus to the distinction between "old" and "new" upper classes as of the first decade of the twentieth century.[39] A third was a study under the direction of Walter Glazer by Joseph Rischel, who traced descendants of the Pittsburgh upper class as of 1840 through several generations.[40] I was particularly struck by Rischel's calculation of downward mobility, as in each successive generation approximately one-third of the children did not sustain the upper-class level of their parents.

By the early 1970s, however, I began to use many more phenomena as focal points through which to examine social differentiation. Social history had come to include the study of ethnicity and race, religion, family, women, and education; hardly an aspect of human life could remain apart from analysis. All of these facets seemed to be brought together by a common role in the process of differentiation amid social change. Ethnicity especially attracted

38. John Ingham, *The Iron Barons: A Social Analysis of An American Urban Elite, 1874-1965* (Westport, Conn., 1978).

39. George Bedeian, "Social Stratification Within a Metropolitan Upper Class: Early Twentieth-Century Pittsburgh as a Case Study," seminar paper, Univ. of Pittsburgh, 1974.

40. Joseph Rischel, "The Founding Families of Allegheny County: An Examination of Nineteenth Century Elite Continuity," Ph.D. diss., Univ. of Pittsburgh, 1973.

me. I was intrigued by the enormous impact of forces of social transformation on ethnic traditions, the drama of the tension between tradition and modernity, between localism and cosmopolitanism. Three studies by doctoral students were especially influential, one of ethnic politics in Erie, Pennsylvania, by William Garvey, another of changes in the German ethnic community in Pittsburgh by Nora Faires, and a third of the Pittsburgh Irish community by Victor Walsh.[41] All three emphasized differentiation within particular ethnic groups in terms of subcultures, the analysis of which, I became convinced, was the most important method of examining the impact of social change on ethnic groups. A brief article in the *Pitt Magazine* expressed my thinking on that score.[42]

The connection was clear between my interest in ethnicity and my earlier interest in the social bases of popular voting, which stressed ethnocultural factors. This connection also led to an interest in the history of religion which arose during the voting studies and continued thereafter. I was especially drawn to the variations in religious values that were represented not by denominations but by phenomena which cut across them. Increasingly this took the form of a distinction between traditional and modern values in religion and investigation of the impact of evangelical religion in the nineteenth century on traditional religion within the various Protestant denominations. It also involved the impact of "modernism" in the twentieth century, first on Methodists, Presbyterians, and Congregationalists, then on Catholics, and finally on Missouri Synod German Lutherans. My thinking on this question was sharpened by reading the work of Charles Glock and Rodney Stark, especially their book *Religion and Society in Tension*,[43] and was developed considerably by conversations with Linda Pritchard, a graduate student, as she worked out a doctoral dissertation on evangelical religion and social change in the mid-nineteenth century.[44]

I became interested in education while tracing the centraliza-

41. William Garvey, "The Ethnic Factor in Erie Politics, 1900–1970," Ph.D. diss., Univ. of Pittsburgh, 1973; Nora Faires, "The Germans in Pittsburgh in 1860," seminar paper, Univ. of Pittsburgh, 1972; Victor Walsh, "Class, Culture and Nationalism: The Irish Catholics of Pittsburgh, 1870–1883," seminar paper, Univ. of Pittsburgh, 1976.

42. "The Ebb and Flow of Ethnicity in American History," *Pitt Magazine* 29 (1973), 9–15.

43. Charles Glock and Rodney Stark, *Religion and Society in Tension* (Chicago, 1965).

44. Linda Pritchard, "Sectarian Movements in Western New York and the Upper Ohio Valley, 1840–1860: A Study in Social Change," Ph.D. diss., currently under way.

tion of school authority in the city during the first third of the twentieth century, a task that I pursued during my work on municipal reform. One seminar research paper which stimulated my thinking was by William Issel on the role of teachers in educational politics in Pittsburgh during the municipal reform era.[45] This now extended to education as a setting for social differentiation, especially differentiation in perspective associated with psychological mobility. This approach was reinforced by a number of the more contemporary works on value changes associated with education. The University of Pittsburgh Archives of Industrial Society had gathered some detailed materials on the Pittsburgh school population for the nineteenth century, and these provided an opportunity for a much more precise description of differentiation within primary and especially secondary education. The records were secured through the initiative of a doctoral student, Carolyn Schumacher, who then wrote a dissertation on the nineteenth-century Pittsburgh school population.[46] The data demonstrated that a rather high percentage of Pittsburgh's young people attended high school, but few graduated because they wished to secure only that training required for white-collar jobs. The data also indicated the varying proportions of students who came from families of different ethnic backgrounds and occupational levels. This created the impression of a persistent process of social differentiation arising from the varied involvements of individuals in the opportunities of the wider world, and at a time when high school attendance was voluntary rather than compulsory.

Several studies in the history of women confirmed this context. I did little research on this subject, but the work of two doctoral students influenced my thinking. Jay Kleinberg completed a dissertation on the role of working-class women in Pittsburgh in the nineteenth century, not as factory workers but as individuals performing tasks in the family and in community activities.[47] She de-

45. William Issel, "The Pittsburgh Teaching Profession and Its Politics, 1900–1912," seminar paper, Univ. of Pittsburgh, 1964.

46. Carolyn Schumacher, "School Attendance in Nineteenth-Century Pittsburgh; Wealth, Ethnicity and Occupational Mobility of School Age Children, 1855–1865," Ph.D. diss., Univ. of Pittsburgh, 1977.

47. Susan J. Kleinberg, "Technology's Step-Daughters: The Impact of Industrialization Upon Working-Class Women, Pittsburgh, 1865–1890," Ph.D. diss., Univ. of Pittsburgh, 1973.

veloped considerable insight into ethnocultural and socioeconomic variations, the role of widows and young women as well as wives, the patterns of sickness and death, and the use of new technologies in the home. She was able to place working-class women within the larger context of variations in community setting, household work, geographical area and social class. The other student, Marguerite Renner, completed a seminar paper on the social bases of various women's organizations in the late nineteenth and early twentieth centuries, finding socioeconomic and local-cosmopolitan dimensions specific to particular voluntary organizations.[48] These more detailed analyses of the social role of women were influential in my thinking about the history of women in particular and social differentiation in general.

Finally, much of this seemed to focus on the family as providing an opportunity to examine in more detail the history of education, religion, ethnicity, and women. I consolidated my thoughts on the subject in an introduction to a new edition of *Homestead, The Households of a Mill Town*, the volume from the old Pittsburgh Survey, in which I concluded that the book was a case study in the history of women and the family instead of a community history.[49] I also wove into this concern for family history some of my long-standing interest in family genealogy, as I began to argue that the best context in which social differentiation could be examined was the reconstitution of families over generations. In this way, for example, one could describe the specific patterns of out-migration from a given place or changes in social characteristics in generational sequence from an initial point in time. My interest in this was stimulated by the practice of requiring undergraduate students to prepare four-generation family genealogies in order to observe the process of social change and social differentiation within their own families. The question always arose: Why did some great-grandchildren turn out so differently from others? The question itself emphasized heavily the process of social differentiation. My thoughts on the problem appeared in a three-part article, "History and Genealogy: Patterns

48. Marguerite Renner, "A Study of Women's Participation in Voluntary Organizations," seminar paper, Univ. of Pittsburgh, 1971.
49. "Homestead Revisited," In Margaret F. Byington, *Homestead: The Households of a Mill Town* (Pittsburgh, 1974), xvii–xxxiv.

of Change and Prospects for Cooperation," which appeared in *Prologue* during 1975 and is included in these selections.[50]

A considerable number of implications of these various strands of inquiry into social history appeared in an article, "A Systematic Social History," in *American History: Retrospect and Prospect*, edited by George Billias and Gerald Grob in 1971.[51] It both crystallized previous thinking and expressed a variety of concerns in social analysis. It brought together an interest in social structure and in social change, which seemed to link several stages of development in my thinking. My analysis of social change was strongly influenced by the various inquiries into mobility, especially psychological mobility, and by the varied content matter of social history which provided a vast range of settings within which to examine both structure and change. A later synthesis on the more specific subject of value change amid modernizing tendencies in American history, entitled "Modernizing Values in the History of the United States," appeared in *Peasant Studies* in the spring of 1977 and is included here.[52]

V

THUS far I have described the evolution of my thinking about American history, the problems defined for inquiry, and the patterns in accordance with which American history should be reconstructed. All of this was heavily infused with a persistent interest in problems of historical data and method; I was concerned, too, with the matter of curriculum content. Thus, it is appropriate for this volume to contain some articles about the setting and resources for historical inquiry. There is a close relationship in my thinking between the problems of how one should go about historical discovery and the evolution of historical concepts.

My interest in social phenomena in history and the relationship between society and politics required, above all, social data. In or-

50. "History and Genealogy: Patterns of Change and Prospects for Cooperation," *Prologue* 7 (1975), 39–43, 81–84, 187–91.
51. "A Systematic Social History," in George Athan Billias and Gerald N. Grob (eds.), *American History: Retrospect and Prospect* (New York, 1971), 315–66.
52. "Modernizing Values in the History of the United States," *Peasant Studies* 6 (1977), 68–79.

der to reconstruct the lives of people in particular settings and do it broadly, as an antidote to the overemphasis on national events and prominent individuals, masses of data about individuals were necessary; otherwise, elementary social description was impossible. I had not been particularly aware of the existence of such data and their potential use prior to the mid-1950s, save for the federal manuscript census which I had used since 1947 for personal family genealogical research. Analysis of voting patterns made me much more aware of the possibilities; the search for data to associate with voting patterns opened up an astoundingly rich new world of historical materials. For several years, therefore, preoccupied with the discovery of data which could be utilized for social description, I gathered a wide range of such materials, in printed form, for my own personal use and for the Library at the University of Pittsburgh.

One of the objectives of the Archives of Industrial Society, established in the University of Pittsburgh Library in 1964, was to gather quantifiable material for social research by students and faculty. On two occasions I wrote articles to describe the range of such materials as part of a growing interest among a number of historians in quantitative social description. One essay, "Archival Sources for American Political History," was an outgrowth of a paper read in 1964 at the joint meeting of the Society of American Archivists and the Mississippi Valley Historical Association and later published in *The American Archivist.* The other, "The Use of Archives for Historical Statistical Inquiry," published in *Prologue* in 1969, was a paper given at a conference on statistical research held in 1968 at the National Archives.

At the same time, I became extremely interested in the computerization of such data to facilitate ready manipulation for historical research. Early in the 1960s I joined with Lee Benson, Allan Bogue, Murray Murphy, and political scientist Warren Miller to promote the computerization of county-level election data at the Inter-University Consortium for Political Research at the University of Michigan. Through grants from the National Science Foundation, a very high percentage of theoretically extant county returns was recovered for elections between 1824 and the present for the races of President, governor, congressman, and U.S. senator. This was computerized by the ICPR. In the summer of 1965 the consortium sponsored a seminar at Ann Arbor in which historians were brought together in order to encourage use of the election data being computerized and in which I participated as an instructor. The possibilities of historical research arising from the use of these and other quantitative data were described in a paper, "New Possibilities for American Political History: The Social Analysis of Political Life," which was presented during the meeting of the American Historical Association in 1964 and was published in a compilation, *Sociology and History: Methods*, edited by Seymour Lipset and Richard Hofstadter. It is one of the articles in this volume.[53]

At the same time, as chairman of the History Department at the University of Pittsburgh I promoted the development of a Pittsburgh data bank within the Social Science Information Center. We began to computerize the Pittsburgh manuscript federal census for the nineteenth century, and finished those for 1850, 1860, 1870, and 1880. To this gradually will be added other quantitative data sets. This greatly facilitated student and faculty research and especially underlay the ability of graduate students to complete significant social research using Pittsburgh as a case study; some of this work has already been mentioned. It led to the conviction that history departments should take on the responsibility of computerizing such data for their own geographical regions; the cost is far too great to be undertaken by a national foundation, private or public, and the project can be completed only through small increments of funds and time allocated at the local and regional level. A paper on historical computer research was presented at a conference on computers and the humanities at Purdue University in 1965 sponsored by the IBM Corporation; it was published as a chapter, "Computers and Historical Research," in a book edited by Samuel Bowles, *Computers in Humanistic Research.*[54]

As a result of these writings and activities, the University of Pittsburgh History Department and I became associated in the minds of many members of the profession with quantitative historical research. Publication of the *Historical Methods Newsletter* by

53. "New Possibilities for American Political History: The Social Analysis of Political Life," in Seymour Martin Lipset and Richard Hofstadter (eds.), *Sociology and History: Methods* (New York, 1968), 181–227.

54. "Computers and Historical Research," in Samuel Bowles (ed.), *Computers in Humanistic Research* (New York, 1967), 62–72.

the department added to the connection. Although this impression was partly accurate, it was also misleading. Both I and others in the department were more concerned with the conceptual implications of social research, which were taken up much more slowly by the profession, than with quantitative data and techniques themselves, which were adopted rapidly. I was far less preoccupied with ever more precise refinement of detail and technique than were many scholars in the social research movement and have always been more concerned with conceptual ramifications. This larger concern and divergence in view is evident as early as the writing of "New Possibilities," which stressed the content of conceptual thought as much as techniques of statistical manipulations or the possibilities of "scientific history." This is not to say that the interest in quantitative data diminished over time, but only that the directions which others took I did not find especially productive.

Three of these tendencies especially disturbed me. One was the apparent willingness to select problems for investigation on the basis of the availability of quantitative data capable of intensive statistical manipulation, rather than on the basis of their conceptual importance. Increasingly, I began to question the value of the results of much quantitative research, feeling that while it was technically accurate, it was not overly relevant conceptually. At the same time, I was disturbed by the limited approach to the implications of statistical research. Of all quantitative work yet done in American history save for economic history, studies of popular voting have had the greatest impact on historical thinking. In the hands of some scholars, these studies merely raise the question of the strength of the statistical correlation between "socioeconomic" and "ethnocultural" factors in voting. In my mind, voting studies have led to a host of further problems—those associated with the role of "grassroots" patterns of life, social differentiation, the persistence of ethnic tradition in a modernizing society, value differentiation in religion, and the history of the family. I have already described the link between such tendencies in my thinking with the earlier forays into voting analysis. Concern with quantitative technique alone has tended to freeze the historical imagination as firmly as presidential history or biography did in years past.

A second concern was the confusion between "technique" and

"method." The emphasis on data gathering and manipulation was persistently called an aspect of historical method. In my opinion, however, such an emphasis actually obscured methodological problems, which were the crucial elements in linking data on the one hand and concepts on the other. Historical method deals with procedures of analysis, with ways in which evidence is juxtaposed in patterns so as to raise questions and establish relationships. It is concerned with comparative methods of inquiry, with sorting out parts from wholes, with the discovery of similarities in patterns over space or time. Rules of inductive logic are far more important in guiding such inquiry than are statistical techniques. Worthwhile research can be carried out and significant contributions to historical conceptualization can be made with evidence at either a crude or a refined level of quantitative precision. Not to be aware of this possibility, as is reflected in the persistent confusion of two quite different problems implicit in the misleading use of the term "method" when it refers to "technique," only limits sharply the range and significance of historical inquiry. I elaborated on this point briefly in a review of several books on quantitative techniques, "Historical Social Research: Concept, Method, and Technique," for the *Journal of Interdisciplinary History* in the winter of 1974.[55]

Finally, I also became concerned with two significant tendencies among the majority of practitioners of quantitative research—especially those who were prone to call themselves "hard quantifiers"—one to cast their work in the context of the possibility of "scientific explanation" and the other to define research in terms of historical case studies which test social theory generated in the non-historical social sciences. According to the first, sufficient quantitative data and the appropriate techniques make possible a "scientific history." But I found the process of historical synthesis far more complex than such an approach would permit and was always more intrigued with the reconstruction of patterns, based upon as thorough and systematic a social description as possible, within the larger context of social structure and social change. This called for the use of quantitative data for that description wherever they were available, but also for the use of qualitative data and "imaginative

55. "Historical Social Research: Concept, Method and Technique," in *Journal of Interdisciplinary History* 4 (1974), 475–82.

reconstruction" where appropriate. I preferred to use the terms "social analysis" and "social research," as the reader of these essays will observe, and to avoid the implications of the term "scientific history." One might well describe my predisposition as one of pursuing "informed speculation," a procedure which seems far closer to the real world of historical inquiry and far less pretentious than an assertion of the possibility of "scientific explanation."

The term "social science history" conveyed another tendency, that of using historical data and acceptable statistical techniques to demonstrate the validity of concepts generated in the social sciences, especially sociology, political science, and economics. The reason for this choice, it seemed to me, was to be able to maintain a stance of being "scientific," which meant, largely, achieving statistical accuracy—a goal associated with the "advanced" sectors of those disciplines. Once again I was concerned, however, with the irrelevance of studies conducted in this spirit. I was defining problems in terms of long-run social change, that is, from the context of history itself, and not from that of the nonhistorical social sciences. Formulations generated imaginatively out of the historical setting itself became far more powerful as the starting point of inquiry than concepts from the "other" social sciences. I felt that historians could derive innumerable topics for inquiry from their own work in examining long-run social change, topics that they would miss if they simply hitched their intellectual wagon to those "other" disciplines. Reading in the social sciences simply sparked my imagination to delve into facets of history not before observed; it did not lead me to formulate precise theories and then seek to test them with historical data. On this score, too, I thought that many of the new practitioners of "social science history" were becoming narrow and rigid in their views, expressing my concerns in a review of the first meeting of the Social Science History Association, published in the *Historical Methods Newsletter* in June 1977.[56]

There were important implications in all this for teaching and curriculum at both the graduate and undergraduate levels. As an outgrowth of my interest in quantitative research on popular voting, and my work with the Inter-University Consortium on Political

56. "The First Annual Meeting of the Social Science History Association," *Historical Methods Newsletter* 10 (1976), 39–42.

Research, I contributed a piece, along with one by Lee Benson, to the *Newsletter* of the American Historical Association in June 1966 called "Quantification in History: The Implications and Challenges for Graduate Training."[57] This called for special training programs at the graduate level to locate and develop data, to sample and manipulate them. At the same time, however, I also called for training in "research design," which would emphasize methods of linking data and concepts. Even in this case, then, one can observe both an interest in quantification and a larger concern for making sure that the use of data was firmly connected to significant research problems through effective design. Today I would make this even more explicit.

The quantitative aspect of the graduate training program at the University of Pittsburgh took on a particular twist. We made no extra efforts to secure personnel specialized in quantitative techniques in order to teach such courses—partly because a general feeling for the usefulness of quantitative work pervaded the department, but also because there was a more overriding concern with the relevance of historical problems. My own approach was first to immerse students in a variety of social research problems through case studies organized in terms of their conceptual relevance, and thereby to interest them in a problem which could be considered conceptually significant. Invariably this involved social analysis, which, in turn, required social data. At that point students usually recognized the need for the use of quantitative material and for sufficient knowledge of statistics and computer techniques to manipulate data effectively. This often was provided in the form of ad hoc "minicourses" or informal instruction offered by personnel of the Social Science Information Center, of which the History Department was a leading participant.

With such an approach doctoral work had to be justified not in terms of its quantitative content and statistical accuracy, but in terms of its conceptual relevance. At the same time, however, it produced graduate students who, although they were adept at statistics and the use of computers, were not very anxious to teach such subjects and preferred to teach content- or problem-oriented

57. "Quantification in History: The Implications and Challenges for Graduate Training," *AHA Newsletter* 4 (1966), 8–11.

courses. Frequently the department received inquiries regarding candidates for openings in which the major description of the position was that of "quantifier." We had few students who wished to go under that label. Such requests seemed to indicate that the profession as a whole had become as myopic about social inquiry in history as had some of its "hard quantifier" practitioners, being unable to visualize the conceptual implications of important developments in historical social inquiry and being mesmerized by the emphasis on quantitative techniques. Yet this emphasis in graduate training paid off as a significant number of students made important contributions to conceptual problems in American history, with a firm quantitative base; few could be described as making purely technical contributions.

Training in the use of quantitative data and techniques could be organized effectively at the undergraduate level once a ready data bank was at hand. The Pittsburgh manuscript census permitted this by providing a subject-matter content which was "close to home"; based upon it, seminars in urban historical analysis were developed for undergraduate students. My own interest, however, turned more to the conceptual implications of social inquiry, which I attempted to work out in undergraduate as well as graduate courses. Some aspects of this were included in a paper, "History and the Changing University Curriculum," presented at the annual meeting of the Organization of American Historians in Chicago in 1973 and printed in *The History Teacher* in 1974; it is a part of this compilation.[58]

In this paper I summarized several ways in which my interest in historical social inquiry had been translated into undergraduate, even freshman survey, courses. I had become dissatisfied with many of the innovations in teaching then under way which, it seemed to me, were highly superficial, relying solely on new techniques of presentation (such as visual media) but based on highly traditional conceptual content. I had also become dissatisfied with the "problems" approach, in which students were confronted with the debates over historical questions in which professional historians were engaged. All this, in my mind, precluded the really exciting in-

58. "History and the Changing University Curriculum," *The History Teacher* 8 (1974), 64–72.

quiries into history which were emerging as a result of social analysis and which were conceptual in character. My emphasis on contexts of human experience as a focal point of inquiry, and the larger concepts of social structure and social change, seemed to provide a very different approach. I had organized courses along these lines and felt that they enabled the student to get closer to the realities of the past and to draw more effective connections between the past and the present.

Just as, in research, history could be organized around the human contexts of life within which processes of change were observed, so could the courses taught to undergraduates, and even to high school students, for that matter. Such human contexts were closer to the "real-life" situations which students experienced and thus provided a greater opportunity to involve them imaginatively in the past. The problem was to activate the student's imagination; the validity of a curriculum depended upon its "imaginative potential," its ability to stir the student's mind to shift from the current context of human experience to one in the past. I was especially interested in the use of comparative analysis for this purpose and the reconstruction of personal family genealogies by students as a process of generating such comparisons. The reader might well regard the article on "History and Genealogy," already referred to, as a spin-off from my concern with teaching and curriculum as well as research.

These interests in training and teaching were intimately connected with interests in research and writing through their common conceptual base. One can observe throughout this extended introduction a journey in the historical imagination, a description of the way in which the implications of one discovery stimulated the formulation of a new problem. This process of historical imagination came, in my view, to be the key element in successful teaching. A student's mind, like that of a professional historian, could well become confined and rigid far too early as a result of narrow technical training and work. Significant discoveries come through disciplined imagination. All too often the tendencies in modern systematic inquiry in the natural sciences, the social sciences, and the humanities have been toward narrower and narrower definitions of problems, more refined and more technical manipulations, and more limited visions. We come to know more and more about less and less. If there is a theme in these twenty-five years of historical activities and inquiry, it is the affirmation of the creative potential of the disciplined historical imagination. The essays reprinted here might well provide a modest testimony to the usefulness of that conviction.

II.

THE SOCIAL ANALYSIS OF POLITICAL HISTORY

THE five essays in this section constitute programmatic statements of the directions which historical inquiry into the nature of society and politics should take. They were written over a period of slightly more than a decade and display both a continuity of interest and an elaboration of concern. The perspective from which they were written remains essentially the same, but the themes are elaborated and extended.

The articles emphasize the "human situation," people in their different settings. They reflect an attempt to ferret out the experience, understanding, values, and actions of people rather than to be restricted to the formal aspects of history. By the time of "New Possibilities" there is an explicit statement of the need for a "situational" context; "A Systematic Social History" extends this concern to an emphasis on variation as a central focus for historical description. There is a persisting emphasis on the patterns of human relationships as a major task for description and analysis, and on the larger ordering of those patterns in terms of structure and change. The essay on urban history expresses a specific concern for structural analysis of the city. A recurrent theme is the problem of both the smaller human situation and the larger elements of the social order.

A second topic is the interrelationship between society and politics. On occasion this is spelled out explicitly, such as the search for the social roots of particular political phenomena—the ethnocultural sources of popular voting behavior, for example—and on occasion there are assertions of the peculiar potential of political and social history for providing larger historical synthesis. While the first three essays reveal the results of concern with more formal political phenomena and work backward to the social context from that starting point, the last two represent an attempt to work more explicitly with social historical materials apart from their connections with political life. While many of the themes of "A Systematic Social History" are similar to those of "New Possibilities," thus representing a continuity of concern and thought, their application to social history involves some new twists, such as the outline of major patterns of social structure.

One can observe a third continuing line of thought in these five essays: the way in which inherited historical ideas in the form of "liberal history" are considered inadequate to contain either the new information that is being accumulated or the new questions being asked. All of the essays in this volume express considerable frustration with "cultural lag," the gap between inherited ideas and new knowledge. Prevailing historical concepts and especially "liberal history," later called "reform history," seemed incapable of incorporating either new research results or new questions. A new set of concepts was needed—a new synthesis, capable of integrating the substantive results of research and formulating their implications in terms of new problems for definition and inquiry. The articles express the excitement of the contemporary ferment in historical social inquiry and the frustration caused by the gap between inherited historical ideas and approaches on the one hand, and emerging work and understanding on the other.

These articles establish a general climate of historical inquiry rather than explicit theories. Although they are liberally sprinkled with concepts and with specific examples of substantive research, their role is more one of pointing out limitations of past historical work and setting a tone for new approaches. They formulate general directions rather than establish firm historical concepts; they affirm imaginative possibilities rather then demonstrate established conclusions. They reflect a period of ferment in which the new types of social data and new sets of historical questions were working a profound effect on inherited historical ideas and modes of inquiry and analysis. They seek to direct some of this renewed energy toward the "social analysis of political history."

[1]

*History as Human Behavior**

THE study of history in both high schools and colleges, it seems to me, suffers from a lack of emphasis on the vital human quality of the past. It is concerned traditionally with the formal and outward aspects of events, and not with human experience, understanding, values, and action. This problem is the central theme of this paper. I hope primarily to suggest a number of ways in which we might approach more closely the human side of the past. By this I mean not simply ways of enhancing the "human interest" factor in history, but ways of systematically studying human experience and behavior so that solid and concrete generalizations emerge. My argument is that if we could develop this approach to history we would not only have a more significant story to tell, but would also arouse greater interest on the part of both high school and college students.

I

PERHAPS the best example of formal history is the traditional political history which abounds in our textbooks. Here the major focus of organization centers on presidential administrations: nominating conventions, campaigns, cabinet meetings, the administration's legislative program and its treatment by Congress. This approach has been called "presidential history." Its main justification is not that it conforms to any major movements or changes in American society, but that it follows the rather accidental fact of our four-year presidential terms. It provides little room for an emphasis on political experience and behavior, nor does it give more than a brief in-

*This paper, read before the meeting of the Iowa State Education Association on Nov. 6, 1959, courtesy of the Iowa State Historical Department/Division of the State Historical Society.

sight into the ebb and flow of activity lying behind the outward events.

Economic history suffers from the same attention to the outward and formal, and the lack of attention to the dynamics of change. In most of our history books we learn about the rise of corporate combinations in the late nineteenth and early twentieth centuries. We describe the legal forms involved—the trust and the holding company—and we relate the number and size of combinations. But rarely do we go into the forces behind this. Rarely do we analyze the economic processes which led to the rise of such large combinations of capital. If we did this, we would spend less time talking about the number and size of combinations, and more about the way in which cheap transportation created, for the first time, a national market; the way in which a national market created, for the first time, intense competition for that market; the way in which producers all over the country tried to protect themselves against competition; and the way in which all economic segments of the nation began to take up collective effort to exercise control over market conditions. These economic processes are far more important than are figures about the number of combinations.

It is precisely this formal approach to history which makes history unsatisfactory to many students. Those who seek an analysis of human society often fail to find it in history and go elsewhere. These views stem from conversations with a great number of students about both their high school and their college history courses. I have come to the conclusion that the more a history course touches the human content of the past the more challenging and satisfying it is to the student. Those courses which are dull and boring seem to consist of memorization of the outward and formal facts of history; those which are more exciting involve a treatment of human experience, human understanding, and human values.

In my own teaching I have observed that the closer one approaches the human situation the more interest rises. I do not mean this in terms of the popular definition of "human interest," such as the last words of Nathan Hale, or the stock market manipulations of Jim Fisk and Jay Gould, or the illegitimate offspring of Grover Cleveland, or Coxey's army. I mean simply the systematic description of human experience, of the universal human situations faced by people in the past and faced by students in the present. I find, for example, that students react very positively to such a book as that by Oscar Handlin, *The Uprooted*, an account of the immigrant in America told from the point of view of the immigrant, an analysis of his experience of being uprooted from a traditional and stable European culture and abruptly entering a more mobile and traditionless society. Handlin's major contribution is that he sees history from the inside out. And this I think challenges students and captures their imagination, because all of us inevitably see life from the inside out.

Both of these general concerns point, it seems to me, in one direction—that history must be considered more in terms of human behavior. The reason that much of history is formal and unsatisfying is because the units of history we write and talk and teach about do not consist of types of human experience, thought, and behavior. By changing to this focus we can make history more meaningful from the point of view of the disinterested analyst, and also from the point of view of the student who will inevitably find some contact between his own experience and that of the past.

II

ONE important way in which we could make this change in focus is to shift attention from top-level affairs to grass-roots happenings. Most of our history is a description of events at the center of national politics, economic affairs, or intellectual life. This is true, for example, of the "presidential history" approach; it focuses on the activities of the office of the President and of Congress. This kind of history is easy to write because materials for it are usually available in a central place. And it is easy to teach because it is a simple way of giving a single focus to history. It is easier to talk about one President than about fifty governors; it is easier to describe the ideas of a few thinkers than of a large number of people. Yet, at the same time, it provides only a partial and limited view, and the limitations of the view can readily be realized once one focuses his attention closer to the grass roots, to the state, the county, or municipal level. Evidence from this level indicates that top-level history not only leaves out many aspects of the past but often leads to the wrong conclusions.

Consider, for example, the period from 1877 to 1914. According to the traditional approach in history, the major development of the time was the so-called "trust" issue, the growth of business combinations, their influence in politics and government, and the reaction against them on the part of many segments of the community. Most of the chapters in our textbooks for this period are organized around some phase of this question, and evidence from the local or state level is selected to illustrate this national focus. The history of Iowa in the early twentieth century, for example, involves the Progressive revolt within the Republican party, described primarily as a reaction against railroad domination of Iowa politics, and considered to be merely another illustration of a national political trend.

But if one looks at evidence from grass-roots history for its own sake, and not as an illustration of national trends, he frequently comes to an altogether different conclusion. For example, an examination of the precinct voting patterns in Iowa from 1885 to 1918 shows that the matters which most aroused voters, which determined party affiliations, and which filled the local newspapers were not connected with the "trust question" but were largely cultural in nature. They were such questions as the use of foreign language, Sunday observance, and above all prohibition. Defined in terms of how people voted, which is about as close to the grass roots as one can get, the "trust question" was relatively unimportant, but the prohibition issue was of vast importance. Party differences in voting patterns were cultural, not economic, in nature. If one can argue that a single issue was more important than any other issue in Iowa between 1885 and 1918 it was prohibition.

But prohibition was more than an issue; it was the most specific aspect of a general conflict between patterns of culture in Iowa which dominated the political views of the people of the state for many years. One of these cultural patterns we can call, for want of a better term, Pietism. It stressed strict standards of behavior derived from Puritan sources, especially Sunday observance, and prohibition of gambling, dancing, and, above all, drinking alcoholic beverages.

It was evangelistic; it exhorted individuals to undergo a dramatic transformation in their personal lives, to be converted, and it sought to impose these standards of personal character on the entire community by public, legal action. But there were others, whose pattern of culture was altogether different, who resisted these views. They came from a different cultural background, and their religion consisted more of a sequence of rituals and observances through which one passed from birth to death, with the primary focus of religion being the observance of those practices. For many of them Puritan morals meant little; Germans, for example, were accustomed to the continental Sunday of relaxation in beer gardens or to using wine for communion services.

These cultural differences divided groups in Iowa, and the voting patterns follow, to a remarkable degree, the differences in cultural patterns. On the one hand were the native Americans, from English and Scotch extraction, the Norwegians and Swedes, and the German Methodists and Presbyterians. On the other hand were the Irish, Bohemian, and German Catholics and the German Lutherans. In county after county in Iowa the persistently strong Republican precincts from 1885 to 1914 are predominantly from the first group, and the persistently strong Democratic precincts are from the second. Consider, for example, the precincts in Carroll County, Iowa. The eastern tier of townships, Jasper, Glidden, Richland, and Union, all strong native American (77, 84, 83, and 91 percent, respectively, in 1880), between 1887 and 1914 averaged 33, 26, 34, and 33 percent respectively for the Democratic gubernatorial candidate. In the northwestern part of the county, on the other hand, four townships, Kniest, Wheatland, Roselle, and Washington, all heavily German (91, 78, 95, and 80 percent, respectively, in 1880) and all heavily Catholic, over the same period of time and for the same race averaged 82, 83, 80, and 73 percent Democratic. In displaying real distinctions in voting patterns, Carroll County is typical of most Iowa counties.

These were persistent distinctions, and they led frequently to the importance of such issues as prohibition and woman's suffrage, which was part and parcel of the prohibition movement. In some elections they produced rather violent shifts in voting sentiment. In fact, one can argue that the only violent shifts in voting behavior came when such issues were present. The most striking of these was the gubernatorial election of 1916 when the Republican candidate, William Lloyd Harding, was an avowed "wet" and the Democratic candidate, Edwin T. Meredith, was "bone dry." This reversed the traditional roles of the parties; as a result many traditionally Democratic precincts voted heavily Republican, and some traditionally Republican precincts voted Democratic. There was no gubernatorial election up to the depression of 1929 which stirred voters so deeply.

When one begins to examine grass-roots behavior through election data at the precinct level or through local newspapers, one sees immediately that it was this kind of issue that stirred people deeply, that determined their political attitudes. It was far more important than the trust issue. By using this approach one feels that he is approaching more closely the human content of politics. It is becoming increasingly clear to me that very little of our top-level politics is understandable unless one knows the grass-roots context in which to place the top-level events. And basically what this means is that we have to examine what people feel and think and experience, and see their political action as a product of those inner events.

III

A second important shift in thinking that we must undergo concerns our notion of the significance of the role of government in American life. No phenomenon has more preoccupied historians of recent America than has this one. But it is usually treated in such a way as to obscure rather than to illuminate the meaning of an increasing role of government. We have especially failed to distinguish between government as an end in itself and government as a means to an end. All instances of increased federal functions and all movements in that direction are considered by historians to be a part of the same historical trend, while all tendencies opposed to such federal functions are of a different development. "Presidential history" confirms this approach, for the ideology of top-level political battles is usually cast in terms of the desirability of more or less government. But these categories obscure the most important question, namely, what are the purposes to which government is put? History, it seems to me, should be organized around the goals of human action, not the techniques, around the ends rather than the means.

There are many cases in recent American history in which two tendencies, both of which increase the role of government and therefore appear to be of the same historical trend, may involve different and contradictory goals and therefore be of quite different historical movements. Consider, for example, railroad regulation. The Hepburn Act establishing effective railroad regulation was passed in 1906. During the First World War the United States government operated the railroads under the United States Railroad Administration. After the war there was a debate over whether or not the railroads should be returned to their private owners. The debate culminated in the Transportation Act of 1920, by which the roads were returned. This act, it has been argued, was a reversal of past trends; the logical extension of the spirit of the Hepburn Act would have been continued government ownership. The Transportation Act of 1920, on the other hand, was merely a part of the dominant private enterprise philosophy of the postwar era, of "the return to normalcy."

This reasoning is logical if one considers the problem purely as one of distinguishing between more or less government action. But the whole question becomes more complex when one asks: who wanted what and why? What groups were involved in the passage of both the Hepburn Act and the Transportation Act of 1920? Evidence concerning this problem discloses that the very groups which wanted more regulation in 1906 and fought for the Hepburn Act opposed continued government operation in 1920 and wanted the railroads returned to their private owners. In terms of the groups involved and their goals, then, the Transportation Act of 1920 with continued private ownership was not a reversal but a continuation of the tendencies behind the Hepburn Act. And if public ownership had become a reality, it would have been a sharp departure from the recent past.

The major force behind railroad regulation consisted of the organized shippers of the country, who wanted lower rates and better services. Although farmers constituted the voting support for the movement, the drive was led by merchants and manufacturers who shipped via railroad and who were organized in the Interstate Commerce Law Convention. After the passage of the Hepburn Act these groups used the machinery of the Interstate Commerce Commission to their advantage. Up until the First World War they were able to prevent attempts by both railroad owners and railroad labor to raise rates. But once the United States government took over the railroads and operated them, these advantages were lost. The powers of the Interstate Commerce Commission were suspended, and as a result the shippers lost a powerful friend at court. The railroads were placed in the hands of leaders in the industry who were brought into the Railroad Administration, and for the first time since the Hepburn Act the roads received substantial rate increases, and labor, in turn, received substantial wage increases. The shippers were unable to protest, for their machinery of appeal no longer existed. It was little wonder, therefore, that following the war shippers asked that railroads be returned to their private owners and that the powers of the Interstate Commerce Commission be restored. These were provided in the Transportation Act of 1920.

These events are easily traceable if one examines as evidence the ideas and actions of the groups themselves which wanted railroad control. In Iowa the two most active of these groups among farmers, for example, were the Farmers Grain Dealers Association of Iowa, a statewide trade association of farmer-owned grain cooperatives, and the Corn Belt Meat Producers Association, an organization of car-lot shippers of cattle and hogs. Both were concerned with sales problems, and both used railroads heavily for shipping. The proceedings of their conventions and the correspondence of their executive secretaries provide abundant evidence of their shipping problems and of their dissatisfaction with the operations of the United States Railroad Administration. And yet, strangely enough, while historians have written much about such general farm organizations as the National Grange, the Farmers' Union, and the American Society of Equity, they have barely mentioned either the Grain Dealers or the Meat Producers. The reason, it seems to me, is because they cannot be readily used as a local illustration of a nationally defined top-level political problem. And yet examination of their situation and their views on the state level helps enormously to redefine the character of national politics.

Government can be viewed most effectively by the historian if it is considered not as an end in itself, but as the context within which political struggles take place. All political groups in society contend for the control of the advantages which government has to offer: a shifting of the tax burden, positive financial aid, legal aid to restrict individual action where private groups cannot do so, or restrictions on competing groups. No one group seems to have a monopoly on the desire for positive government or for its elimination. The railroads, for example, were grateful for the stabilization of rates which the Interstate Commerce Commission provided. Consequently, the understanding of any particular government function must rest upon an analysis of the circumstances which give rise to that function, the groups which demand it, and the ends which will be served through it. And the categories in which we organize history must be in terms of those circumstances, groups, and goals, rather than the fact of government itself.

IV

An excellent opportunity for undertaking a grass-roots approach to history is provided by the use of election statistics. But this involves a different approach to the analysis of elections than we have used in the past. Elections are dealt with rather extensively in a "presidential history" approach, but usually only in terms of who won or who lost and by what percentage of the vote. Such an analysis is extremely limited and yields very little understanding. It would be far more important to know how much change in voting sentiment had occurred since the last election, not just what percentage of the votes a winning candidate received. For the major fact in any election for the historian is change, and the amount of change usually determines the importance of the problem for study.

A "presidential history" approach may completely distort this whole question by emphasizing only the shift from one political party to another, while frequently the most important changes in voting sentiment occur without a change in party dominance. Suppose, for example, that the Democrats won the presidential election of 1948 by 50.1 percent of the vote, and suppose that the Republicans in 1952 won also by 50.1 percent. A complete change in party would have involved a change in Republican voting strength of only two-tenths of a percentage point. Suppose, further, that Eisenhower won in 1956 with 60.1 percent of the vote. This victory involved no change in party, but an increase in 10 percentage points, or 50 times the shift in vote between 1948 and 1952. Which is the more important election? Where is the turning point? A "presidential history" approach would place the break at 1952, but in terms of voting change it would be 1956.

Many important shifts in voting behavior can be obscured not only by a "presidential history" approach, but also by failing to extend the analysis down to the grass-roots level. For example, Herbert Hoover won the presidential election of 1928 by a landslide margin. But one of the most significant facts of the election is that despite Hoover's victory, Al Smith, for the first time in the twenties, and perhaps for the first time since the Civil War, won for the Democratic party a majority of the votes in the nation's twelve largest cities. The Democrats had been gaining in the metropolitan areas in the early 1920s and by 1928 had won a slight majority. These facts have been brought out only in very recent years. They were hidden by the overall election returns. But they point to the highly significant fact that the Democratic party was gaining strength in crucial areas of the country prior to the Depression, and they open up a whole new understanding of the impact of cultural factors in politics in the twenties.

One could give many examples of the possibilities of going behind the results of a single election to see changes in political behavior, but perhaps a few drawn from Iowa politics would be most appropriate. Consider, for example, political changes since 1950 in the state and specifically in Des Moines. Politics in Des Moines since the early Depression has revolved primarily around socioeconomic factors, with the lower income groups constituting the center of strength of the Democratic party, and the upper income groups the Republican party. The line of division is very clear geographically; that part of Des Moines west of Harding Road is strongly Republican, and that part to the east is strongly Democratic.

Gubernatorial elections between 1946 and 1956 revealed this split in party majority very clearly, but they also revealed that while the Democratic candidates gained steadily in the county as a whole over that period, they gained most in the lower income areas east of

Harding Road. On the other hand, they lost ground in the higher income areas to the west. For example, between 1946 and 1956, five of the precincts west of Harding Road, of the highest socioeconomic level, registered a Democratic loss of 19 percentage points, while six to the east of the lowest socioeconomic level registered a Democratic gain of 23 percentage points. The trend, therefore, has been in opposite directions. This is somewhat unusual in elections, for it is more typical for the trend to be toward or away from a party in the same direction in all precincts, with a variation in the degree of the trend from precinct to precinct. A shift in opposite directions at the same time indicates a sharp and unusual cleavage of political interests.

Much of the same kind of problem can be illuminated by examining the voting behavior of precincts in Cedar Rapids since the Depression of 1929. Here there are three major groups of voters. In the southwest part of the city are voters of Bohemian descent who have been traditionally Democratic. To the east and northeast are voters of native American descent, for the most part, of middle and upper socioeconomic levels, and traditionally Republican. To the northwest are working-class groups largely of native American extraction; these were strongly Republican up until the Depression of 1929, largely because of the cultural issues of nationality, language, and custom which were sharp in Cedar Rapids during that time. But the Depression produced a greater concern for economic issues and led to this northwest area of the city voting less and less like the northeast and more and more like the southwest. It has voted Democratic in gubernatorial races since 1944.

In both Des Moines and Cedar Rapids, therefore, one can observe a gradual shifting of political alignments around socioeconomic differences. These factors are obscured merely by observing the party strength for the entire county. They can be brought out by examining the returns at the precinct level, which greatly add to our understanding of political behavior.

One type of election which sharply reveals the social and economic structure of a community is the so-called "nonpartisan" municipal contest. Stripped of the restraining influence of party discipline, these elections frequently bring out in full force latent intracommunity tensions. Contests over the commission form of government, the so-called Des Moines plan, in Iowa in 1908 are excellent cases in point. In Des Moines, Cedar Rapids, and Davenport the plan was pushed forward by the business and professional classes of the community on the one hand, and by native American moral reformers on the other in order to secure political power in municipal affairs and to carry out the various policies that they desired. In each city, however, major elements of the working-class and immigrant communities vigorously opposed the plan because they interpreted it as a device to deprive them of political influence and to institute such policies as prohibition, which they opposed. In Des Moines workingmen succeeded in defeating the "businessmen's slate" of candidates for the first commission government. In Cedar Rapids, the South-end Bohemian population fought, though unsuccessfully, the commission plan as an attempt by the inhabitants of "piety hill," the northern and eastern sections of the city, to secure control of municipal affairs. And in Davenport the Germans, fearing strict enforcement of anti-liquor laws, succeeded in defeating the proposal to inaugurate a commission government. Precinct and ward voting data in these contests, when related to nativity, religious, and income factors, clearly bring out the forces involved in the election and the persistent cultural and socioeconomic structure of the entire community.

Much, then, can be gained by using election returns as a device for studying political behavior and changes in that behavior. Perhaps the greatest opportunity this approach can provide in an overall way is to give us a systematic method of dividing up the units of political history in terms other than presidential administrations. One can construct an index of political change by computing the percentage strength of a particular party in each election, for example, the Republican presidential vote, and plotting it on a graph. Or one can secure an index which reveals change every two years, rather than at four-year intervals, by plotting the party strength in Congress (congressional popular voting statistics are not yet compiled in usable form). Such a graph would provide a rough outline of political change, somewhat as a business cycle does for economic change.

This kind of graph reveals several broad trends: (a) from 1874 to 1894 a stalemate between the two parties, with the Democrats winning four of five presidential elections by popular vote, but the Republicans winning three of the five by electoral vote, and with the Democrats winning the House of Representatives eight out of ten times and the Republicans controlling the Senate seven out of ten times; (b) 1894-1910, a period of Republican dominance; (c) a Democratic rise beginning in 1906, reaching a peak in 1914, and declining to a low point in 1920; (d) a Republican rise beginning in 1916, reaching a high plateau from 1920 to 1928, and declining to a low point in 1936; (e) a Democratic rise, beginning in 1924 in the cities, reaching a high point in 1936, and declining to a low point in 1946. These units of political history, it seems to me, are much more appropriate than are presidential administrations. It is curious that many problems which these units pose, such as the reason for the shift from stalemate between 1874 and 1894 to Republican dominance for sixteen years, have never been answered by historians primarily because the questions have never been asked. The value of developing units of voting behavior for study, then, is primarily one of bringing to our attention questions which have heretofore been obscured.

V

EACH of these examples—the importance of cultural issues as opposed to the trust question, the analysis of the role of government as a means to an end, and the possibility of using election data to define problems in history—involves a refocusing of attention from the outward formal aspects of history toward the level of human behavior. Each constitutes an attempt to categorize history in terms of types of human experience, types of human understanding of the world, types of human values, and types of resulting human action. This is a group analysis of society in which one sorts out events in history in terms of social organization and behavior. It offers, it seems to me, a much fuller, a more satisfying, and a more provocative approach to the study and writing of history.

There are several factors, however, which make this approach difficult to undertake at the present time. One is the simple fact that few historical studies and many fewer textbooks are written from this point of view. Most texts are organized in a formal, descriptive style, often from the point of view of "presidential history." On the college level most texts have chapters on presidential administrations, with a few on economic or social history sandwiched in between. There is little attempt to integrate all this around patterns of behavior. High school texts, for the most part, follow the same general pattern.

On the other hand, there is considerable reading material which does have a different slant and which can be used. One which I have already mentioned is Oscar Handlin's *The Uprooted.* A book which provides a good picture of the role of cultural groups in political life is Samuel Lubell's *The Future of American Politics.* Two excellent studies of state political life which touch the grass roots closely are V. O. Key, *American State Politics,* and Gordon Baker, *Rural Versus Urban Political Power.* An excellent case study of the goals implicit in public action is Stephen Kemp Bailey, *Congress Makes a Law,* a study of the political forces behind the Full Employment Act of 1946. The movements behind the Interstate Commerce Act of 1887 are examined in Lee Benson, *Merchants, Farmers and Railroads.* These, of course, are only a few of a number of books which provide a slant toward history more in terms of human behavior.

But there is a far more important roadblock which grass-roots history faces, namely, the difficulty in resisting prevailing public assumptions about what ought to be taught in history courses. A behavioral approach immediately raises questions involving group differences in society, differences between ethnic, religious, or socioeconomic groups. And in our society it is not considered legitimate to talk about such differences; instead we are expected to paint a picture of a unified, all-community spirit to support a kind of community patriotism and loyalty. Every community resists introspection into its own social, economic, and political structure, and equally resists history which examines the same questions.

For example, would teachers in Carroll, Allamakee, Winneshiek, or Jones counties, in Davenport, Cedar Rapids, or Des Moines feel free to delve into the whole range of cultural and economic differences which have long existed there and which throughout the years have determined the course of politics? How freely does one in Davenport discuss in the classroom the full implications of cultural conflict represented by the different names "Cork Hill" and "Sauerkraut Hill" which used to describe the Irish and German areas east and west of Brady Street? How freely in Des Moines does one talk about the political differences between Grand Avenue and the downtown area, especially the "bottoms" at the junction of the Des Moines and the Raccoon rivers, and the way in which urban reform for over sixty years has pitted upper-class business and professional people against lower-class laboring groups? How freely can one in Carroll County discuss the religious and cultural differences between the Anglo-Saxon, Protestant eastern tier of townships and the remaining German Catholic townships? Or how freely in almost any small town can one discuss the "pecking order" among the churches, or the community hierarchy of power and control, in the face of the ideology that the community is one big happy family? Two sociologists, Arthur J. Vidich and Joseph Bensman, have done just that in a study called *Small Town in Mass Society*. Their approach would be useful in examining any Iowa small town, past or present, but it brings to light factors in social structure and human behavior which community boosters usually do not appreciate.

And yet the attempt to skip quickly over such fundamental human features of history only does the study of history a disservice, and in my view is one reason why history frequently repels rather than attracts students. Most students know first hand the realities of social and community life, enough to know what is legitimate to talk about and what is not. To obscure these realities in history and social studies courses is to earn a reputation for talking about the unimportant and to court a pose of hypocrisy in the eyes of students. The more we refuse to get down to the human level of history at the grass roots, the more history will be looked upon as dealing only with the formal and the outward and will be shunned. The more we explore the realities of human life, on the other hand, the more students will look upon history as a significant study worth their time and effort.

[2]

The Social Analysis of American
Political History, 1880–1920 *

IN recent years the analysis of American political history in the decades from 1880 to 1920 has undergone considerable innovation. Historians have, for example, used statistics more than in the past, investigated new subject-matter areas, and promoted to some degree the crossbreeding of history and the social sciences. Far more than that, however, they have become increasingly concerned with examining the patterns and processes of political change, and thereby have asked new basic questions and developed new frameworks of analysis. Following Professor Thomas C. Cochran's critique of the "presidential synthesis" in 1948,[1] historians have increasingly shifted their focus from the episodic and the formal to the underlying uniform patterns of political life. They have become, in other words, more thoroughgoing social analysts. Here I wish to examine some specific aspects of this trend and to elaborate briefly on some of its implications.

I

THE social analysis of history, it should be emphasized at the outset, does not involve a concern for a particular "social" subject matter which can be distinguished from political, economic, or constitutional history. On the contrary, it refers to a particular way of looking at all aspects of the past, a focus on the structure and processes of human relationships. Society, the assumption runs, is a network

*This essay reprinted with permission from the *Political Science Quarterly* 80 (September 1965): 373–394.
1. Thomas C. Cochran, "The Presidential Synthesis in American History," *American Historical Review* 53 (1948), 748–59.

of human contacts in which there are uniform and persistent patterns. The most important aspects of these persistent relationships are their structure and the processes by which that structure changes. For the social analyst the crucial questions concern human institutions and the types of organization of economic, social, political, and intellectual life that develop and change over time. These, it is emphasized, are to be described and analyzed not in terms of the formal statements which institutions produce such as laws, constitutions, newspaper editorials, annual reports, speeches, or official press releases, but in terms of the types of human interrelationships which are inherent in those institutions. My concern here, then, is not with social facts as a separate type of data, but with social analysis as a particular set of questions which can be asked of every type of data that involves human relationships.

More specifically I am concerned with the social analysis of politics, of those human activities which involve the distribution of power throughout society. Political life consists of many economic, social, cultural, and ideological facets, which must be incorporated into historical analysis not simply as new elements which influence formal political institutions, but as factors which lie outside those institutions and form an even broader system of political life. Leadership in the educational, religious, and economic world, for example, is as much a political fact as leadership in party politics or public administration, for it is a crucial feature of decision making and the distribution of power. The social analysis of political life, therefore, requires that the definition of politics be greatly broadened; it requires that the historian move from the formal aspects of political institutions to the structure and processes of every type of public human relationship.

In political history the emphasis on social analysis has affected most greatly conceptions of the structure of politics, that is, of the distinct groupings of people in political life, their ideas and practices, and the relationships among these groupings. For many years historians have divided political groups in the decades around the turn of the century between the business community on the one hand, and its mass-supported opponents, chiefly farmers, workers, and small businessmen, on the other. Political differences centered on the problem of control of the business community and the role of parties, legislation, and court decisions in that struggle. Whole periods of political history have been classified on the basis of whether the business community or its opponents dominated the era and people and events in terms of whether they were bound up with one or the other side of that struggle. For want of better terminology, I will refer to this viewpoint as the liberal framework, a term which will be used here in a purely descriptive sense, referring only to the view of history outlined above and below, and without further connotations.

The liberal analysis assumed a highly moralistic and rationalistic political structure. Political life involved divisions not between well-defined economic and social groups, but between a mass, undifferentiated, equalitarian "people" or "public," held together by common cosmic forces of morality and reason and limited cultural and economic groups which sought special power and influence. That conflict, moreover, was unnatural and transitory, the prelude to eventual harmony rather than a permanent manifestation of a fundamental structure of industrial society. Progress came not through the victory of one group over another, but from the elimination of group conflict through the activation of the cohesive forces of morality and reason as education increased and as right-thinking and right-feeling people arose to positions of power.

It seems clear now that this analysis consisted primarily of an elaboration of contemporary ideology rather than of generalization from evidence concerning political practice, that historians mistook the self-conceptions of an age for an accurate description of its political system. But an equally important source for it lay in the predominance of the assumptions of social science in history. Social science is essentially reformist. Political science and economics, for example, visualize ideal systems which should be created through private or public action. The resulting conception of political forces consists of those making for ideal systems on the one hand, and partial "selfish" influences working against them on the other. Thus to understand the politics of tariff making, the historian must rely on studies by political economists, for whom the forces consist of those wishing to create an ideal system of free trade and those who would prevent this by "selfish" action. For municipal reform political scientists provide studies which describe conflicts between independent rational voters and more limited group power, represented by the "machine," which interferes with that process. By relying on such studies for his analyses, the historian has absorbed a normatively defined political structure, highly moralistic and rationalistic in tone, rather than one growing out of evidence concerning patterns of human relationships.

This framework historians are discovering to be increasingly confining, because newer evidence concerning underlying social patterns and processes is inconsistent with it. An increasing amount of social, rather than ideological, analysis has produced evidence of a far more complex and varied political structure. The most explicit and widely acknowledged example is the current view that social reform did not spring from but was often opposed by the urban masses.[2] But the implications of other research are equally significant. For example: the source of commission and city manager movements lay primarily in the upper business and professional classes;[3] railroad regulation arose from competition among rival commercial centers more than from a struggle between farmers and railroads;[4] conservation involved a political conflict between the consolidating tendencies of science and technology and the varied needs of resource users rather than a popular revolt against corporations;[5] industrial towns of the 1870s were often controlled by workingmen, and not always by the new industrial elite;[6] ethnic and cultural issues, such as prohibition, language, and Sunday observance, determined voting attitudes more often than did questions of corporation con-

---

2. George E. Mowry, *The California Progressives* (Berkeley and Los Angeles, 1951), 86–104; Richard Hofstadter, *The Age of Reform* (New York, 1955), 131–269.

3. Harold A. Stone et al., *City Manager Government in Nine Cities* (Chicago, 1940); Frederick C. Mosher et al., *City Manager Government in Seven Cities* (Chicago, 1940); Harold A. Stone et al., *City Manager Government in the United States* (Chicago, 1940); James Weinstein, "Organized Business and the City Commission and Manager Movements," *Journal of Southern History* 28 (1962), 166–82.

4. Lee Benson, *Merchants, Farmers and Railroads: Railroad Regulation and New York Politics, 1850–1887* (Cambridge, Mass., 1955).

5. Samuel P. Hays, *Conservation and the Gospel of Efficiency* (Cambridge, Mass., 1959).

6. Herbert Gutman, "An Iron Workers' Strike in the Ohio Valley, 1873–74," *Ohio Historical Quarterly* 68 (1959), 353–70; "Trouble on the Railroads, 1873–1874; Prelude to the 1877 Crisis," *Labor History* 2 (1961), 215–36.

trol;[7] labor joined business to oppose lower tariffs and railroad regulation not from fear of business but from convictions of self-interest.[8]

The implication of evidence such as this, let me emphasize, is not to modify value judgments about political movements, but rather to change fundamental and value-free conceptions of political relationships. That one should praise rather than condemn the "robber barons" involves little progress in historical understanding, but only a moral reclassification of events within a traditional analytical framework. The designation of leaders such as Theodore Roosevelt and Woodrow Wilson as more "conservative" than "progressive" equally accepts rather than questions traditional assumptions concerning political structure. The argument here presented is that this set of assumptions, the liberal framework, has become of dubious usefulness, formal and confining for historical analysis, rather than conducive to the imaginative exploration of social patterns and processes. Exercising considerable power over the definition of historical problems, that framework has instinctively turned historians from many significant aspects of political life. More recent social analysts, however, find these views increasingly to be a "steel chain of ideas," the assumptions of which they must break through in order to delve into a wider range of political phenomena. Here I wish to review several examples of this trend.

II

DURING the last decade and a half the analysis of leadership has undergone a marked transition from an almost exclusive concentration on individual biography to a greater interest in collective biography. Cases in point are studies of the backgrounds of business leaders by William Miller[9] or Gregory and Neu;[10] of railroad leaders

7. Samuel P. Hays, "History as Human Behavior," *Iowa Journal of History* 58 (1960), 193–206.

8. Walter Poulshock, "Pennsylvania and the Politics of the Tariff, 1880–1888," paper delivered before the Pennsylvania Historical Assoc., Oct. 20, 1961.

9. William Miller, "American Historians and the Business Elite," *Journal of Economic History* 9 (1949). 184–208.

10. Frances W. Gregory and Irene D. Neu, "The American Industrial Elite in the 1970's; Their Social Origins," in William Miller (ed.), *Men in Business* (New York, 1954), 193–211.

by Cochran;[11] of the Philadelphia elite by E. Digby Baltzell;[12] of reform groups by Chandler and Mowry.[13] In the same general vein is the treatment of the patrician liberals of the post–Civil War era, which in its latest version Ari Hoogenboom has dealt with in the specific context of civil service reform.[14] Of unquestioned value, these studies provide a broader base from which to generalize about leadership, its recruitment, its status, its ideology, its impact.

The most influential of these studies, those by Chandler and Mowry, describe the old middle-class, Puritan, native-American, educated background of Progressive party leaders and develop the argument that this background shaped the peculiar nature of Progressive reform. This analysis has played a crucial role in several recent works on the Progressive era and in the elaboration of newer cultural interpretations of modern America.[15] But these collective biographies are deficient in method, and the reasoning based upon them is faulty in logic; they illustrate both the dangers and the advantages of this technique of analysis.

In the first place, the Chandler-Mowry studies were not comparative. They tell us who Bull Moose leaders were, but fail to investigate if and how they were different from other, for example, Old Guard leaders. Evidence is now available that in at least one important state, Iowa, both Progressive party leaders and Cummins Insurgents were just like their rivals in background.[16] If this is the case generally, one can no longer explain the peculiar behavior of reformers in terms of a background not peculiar to them. There can be no doubt of the crucial importance of the crisis facing older America in an urban-industrial society. But it produced varied reactions, some of which, for example prohibition and the defense of small-businessmen merchants threatened by the revolution in dis-

11. Thomas C. Cochran, *Railroad Leaders, 1845-1890* (Cambridge, Mass., 1953).

12. E. Digby Baltzell, *Philadelphia Gentlemen* (Glencoe, Ill., 1958).

13. Alfred D. Chandler, Jr., "The Origins of Progressive Leadership," in Elting Morrison et al. (eds.), *The Letters of Theodore Roosevelt* (Cambridge, Mass., 1951-54), VIII, Appendix III, 1462-64; George E. Mowry, *California Progressives*.

14. Ari Hoogenboom, "An Analysis of Civil Service Reformers," *The Historian* 23 (1960), 54-78.

15. Richard Hofstadter, *Age of Reform*; Henry May, *The End of American Innocence* (New York, 1960); George E. Mowry, *The Era of Theodore Roosevelt, 1900-1912* (New York, 1958).

16. E. Daniel Potts, "The Progressive Profile in Iowa," *Mid-America* 47 (1965), 257-68.

tribution, found expression in Old Guard politics. The question to be answered is, What special segment of older America did reform attract?

There is a second problem as well. Can one describe an entire movement by the characteristics of its top-level leaders? What of its voting base, the associated private movements, or local leadership? One analysis of local leadership found that the backgrounds of the two Republican factions were just the reverse of those suggested by Chandler and Mowry.[17] Reformers were far more immigrant, less educated, more non-Protestant, and more working-class than was the Old Guard. Such evidence suggests that a broad political movement involves different levels of activity from the top down to the grass roots, and that leadership evidence from one level does not necessarily describe the entire movement.

Collective biographies, rightly approached, have much to offer. They can, for example, pinpoint the historical sequence of leadership groups and the process by which one elite fuses into or clashes with a succeeding one. Robert Sharkey has delineated a fairly clear line between older, mercantile, low-tariff, sound-money leaders and the newer industrialists, expansionist in finance and high-tariff advocates.[18] Ari Hoogenboom has found the same two groups on opposite sides of the fence in civil service reform.[19] These reflect a growing body of evidence which sets off an earlier elite bound up with commercial America from a rising industrial elite which looked at public affairs in a new way.

Several decades later the "rule-of-thumb" speculative industrial entrepreneur gave way to the systematizer and efficient expert.[20] The new leadership appeared in many forms: the Taylor Society, conservation, the Municipal Research Bureau, and the city manager movement; the efficiency movement in the public schools; vocational education; welfare capitalism and the scientific personnel movement; or the less formal innovations seen through the pages of

17. David Carey, "Republican Factionalism in Burlington, Iowa, 1906–1908," M.A. thesis, State Univ. of Iowa, 1960.

18. Robert Sharkey, *Money, Class and Party* (Baltimore, 1957).

19. Hoogenboom, "Civil Service Reformers."

20. Loren Baritz, *The Servants of Power* (Middletown, 1960); Hays, *Conservation*; Dwight Waldo, *The Administrative State* (New York, 1948), 3–61, trace different aspects of the efficiency movement.

a journal such as Arch Wilkinson Shaw's *System*. Such movements reflected the rise of men who thought in terms of systematic analysis and manipulation, who viewed earlier entrepreneurs with scorn, and who sought, with persistent success, to redirect the values and goals of American society. This new elite was highly attractive to patricians and intellectuals. While many in both groups had rejected the materialism and brashness of the new industrial elite, they found in the tendencies toward rationality and systematization an acceptable outlet for their talents, and thereby became reconciled to the very business community which earlier they had abhorred.

Collective biographies can also provide insight concerning the perplexing problem of the relationship between leadership and following. Why and how does an elite secure support for its political goals? This problem arises for the post–Civil War era in the fact that the industrial elite commanded broad political support. Why should this be when the "people and the interests" supposedly occupied opposite sides of the political fence? Various corrupt practices, we have answered, prevented voters from expressing their own convictions. Thus, the urban workingman supported McKinley in 1896 because of threats and coercion. Newer evidence, however, suggests an alternative explanation, that political leaders allied with the industrial community provided a strong positive attraction for many voters. Oscar Handlin has emphasized such a role for the urban political machine in the life of the immigrant. Two recent papers at historical association meetings have stressed that McKinley and the tariff were positive symbols for urban workers who blamed the depression of 1893 on the Democrats.[21] Voting data, moreover, suggest that Anglo-Saxon Republican voters of Calvinist and Wesleyan descent looked upon their party not as an organization of corrupt political buccaneers, but as an instrument of "great moral ideas," as one of them put it, which rid the nation of slavery and stood for the defense and extension of evangelical Protestant morality. Perhaps the political leadership of the industrial elite depended as much upon its identification with particular culture patterns as upon its economic achievements.

21. Samuel T. McSeveney, "The Politics of Depression: Popular Voting Behavior, 1893–1896," paper delivered before the Mississippi Valley Historical Assoc., Apr. 20, 1961; Poulshock, "Politics of the Tariff."

By the same token, how did reform leaders secure political support? The implication of recent research is that reformers were not responding to an upwelling of popular demands, but, rather, that they faced an indifferent or even hostile public, and therefore were preoccupied with the problem of securing a following. Perhaps this explains why reformers seized upon prohibition, one of the few mass movements of the early twentieth century which sprang irresistibly from the grass roots and swept political leaders before it. Working within the context of reform as an outgrowth of mass protest, historians have assumed that no special problem was involved in relating reform leadership and grass-roots attitudes. With the knowledge, however, that reform sprang from upper socioeconomic groups and met frequent mass opposition or indifference, this problem is brought into sharp focus.

III

HISTORIANS have frequently stressed that understanding American politics depends upon an analysis of developments at the middle and grass-roots levels. More recently, social analysts have argued that our political life uniquely involves the vitality of the middle levels of politics, which provides a degree of stability, a sense of participation, and a measure of fluidity absent in political systems where the elite and the mass face each other directly.[22] In the evolution of this middle level lay some of the most significant changes in American politics in the Age of Reform.

One such development concerns the rise of organized economic groups. With recovery from depression in the late 1890s, economic organizations grew rapidly and began to constitute a system of politics with a life of its own, independent of the party system. Since liberal historians, however, have condemned these organizations as an interference with more legitimate political processes or with desirable policies, there has been little attempt to understand their natural evolution or their role in political life. Some recent studies have utilized a more satisfactory approach, for example, those of

22. William Kornhauser, *The Politics of Mass Society* (Glencoe, Ill., 1959), for example.

the background of railroad regulation by George Miller, Lee Benson, and James Doster.[23]

Studies such as these emphasize the role of trade and business groups in "reform" movements, and suggest that they were even more characteristic sources of political change in the Progressive era than were farm and labor organizations. After 1897 trade associations grew rapidly, especially in distribution, where a veritable revolution, similar in impact to the earlier transportation revolution, displaced many merchants. Even more important were the opportunities for economic expansion which came with the upswing of 1897 and gave rise to community economic growth spearheaded by business groups organized in local chambers of commerce. One has the impression of a significant increase in associated commercial and industrial endeavor nurtured by the increased opportunities for economic expansion.[24]

Much political activity of the early twentieth century sprang from the demands of these trade groups. The Hepburn and Mann-Elkins Acts came about primarily through the efforts of organized trade associations and chambers of commerce. Pure-food laws were shaped to a great extent by small merchants who complained that packaged foods, mass distributed by such firms as the National Biscuit Company, deceived the customer. Chambers of commerce invariably sparked reforms in municipal government and played a large role in the Country Life Movement. The drive to strengthen the Sherman Antitrust Act came largely from trade associations whom its enforcement affected most adversely and who sought to perfect the act by emasculating it to legalize their own price-fixing devices. Finally, commercial groups who sought markets in Canada and Latin America spearheaded the movements for lower tariffs and reciprocity. This political revitalization of the nation's middle-level economic groups was an especially important force in Midwestern Insurgency and its southern counterparts.

23. George Miller, "Origins of the Iowa Granger Law," *Mississippi Valley Historical Review* 40 (1954), 657–80; *Railroads and the Granger Laws* (Madison, Wis., 1971); Benson, *Merchants, Farmers and Railroads*; James F. Doster, *Railroads in Alabama Politics, 1875-1914* (Montgomery, Ala., 1957).

24. Robert Wiebe, *Businessmen and Reform* (Cambridge, Mass., 1962).

A second significant expansion of activity at the middle levels of politics was the shift in decision making from local communities to states and municipalities. The systematization of public affairs in industrial society involved the increasing absorption of centers of political initiative and decision making from local to higher levels, the atrophy of township and ward units as centers of political life, and the growth of state and municipal activity. Politics, in other words, underwent a process of centralization, a process of which many aspects of "reform" were an integral part.

One focal point of this development lay in municipal government reform, of which the crucial element was not so much the democratization of politics as the shift from ward to citywide elections for city councils. This reduced both the influence of ward organization and the participation of the average citizen in both ward and city affairs. On the other hand, the citywide election of councilmen gave greater influence to those centralizing and consolidating tendencies within the community and especially to business and professional leaders. The centralization of decision making, which greater efficiency in municipal affairs required, and which was also demanded for a citywide focus for such matters as street and other public works construction, often depended upon the centralization of the system of representation.

A more specialized example of the same process lay in the transfer of control over urban schools from the ward to a citywide school board. The urban elementary school lay primarily under the jurisdiction of a locally elected school board, as it did in rural areas, composed of a representative cross section of the community's occupational groups. Educational reformers were shocked at the thought of permitting bartenders, oculists, and barbers supposedly ignorant of the details of education to guide the growth of an increasingly professional school system. In their minds the only solution was to consolidate control in a central board which would be responsive to professional educators rather than to laymen.[25] Business groups, concerned with cost and tax problems, heartily approved. The shift in jurisdiction, therefore, permitted a different group of people or-

---

25. Lila Ver Planck North, "Pittsburgh Schools," in Paul Underwood Kellogg (ed.), *The Pittsburgh District Civic Frontage, VI, The Pittsburgh Survey*, 217–305, esp. 247–48.

ganized on a citywide level, business and professional groups, to exercise more control.

Of the same order as these trends in urban politics were shifts from township and county authority to the state. School consolidation and good roads are cases in point. Organized formerly on the township level, encompassing relatively small geographical areas and under the control of township officials, these activities became absorbed into larger statewide units, covering the entire state and under the control of state officials. Both were crucial elements of the Country Life Movement, in which Theodore Roosevelt took such a great interest and which attracted many to him in the Bull Moose campaign.

The good roads movement, for example, involved a conception of an intercity system as a single network of transportation. Formerly each community had planned its own roads to connect individual farmsteads to local schools, churches, and market towns. When a larger system was formulated which attempted to link cities over a wide area, a new approach arose. Now roads cut through farms, instead of going around them, serving the requirements of the larger system. The transportation needs of the entire state gave rise to a statewide rather than a local perspective and therefore a more centralized authority. It was just such a shift in focus which rural inhabitants feared. Conflict arose over the power of the state highway commission to establish and enforce standards of construction and maintenance. As its power grew, the power of local officials diminished. The location of decision making had shifted to the middle levels of political organization.

IV

A number of historians have stressed from time to time that we must examine politics from the vantage point of the grass roots. For this purpose, our greatest dividends will come most quickly through analysis of voting data and the association of that data with social, economic, and cultural factors. The pioneering work done by V.O. Key, Samuel Lubell, and Lee Benson in this field opens up enormous possibilities.[26] Two large types of questions can be explored.

26. V.O. Key, "Secular Realignment and the Party System," *Journal of Politics* 21

First, what are the major changes in political sentiment, and how can they be explained? Second, how do groups on the opposite side of the political fence differ?

Voting data can define changes in political behavior so that less emphasis is placed on the outcome of particular contests and more on the patterns of political attitudes and the shifts in those patterns. The politics of the 1890s is a case in point. For many years we have focused on the election of 1896; we have asked, Why did Bryan lose? But two major observations are now compelling a reformulation of the problem. One is that the most important long-run change in political sentiment between the Civil War and the First World War was the shift from the even balance between the parties form 1874 to 1894 to sixteen years of one-party Republican domination. The second is that the election of 1894 witnessed what appears to be the sharpest shift in voting sentiment during the entire period from 1874 until the First World War. These two facts prompt one to argue that the question as to why Bryan lost is less important than those of why the long-run shift in voting sentiment and why the sudden rise in Republican fortunes. The significance of this "revolution" in voting patterns has been pointed out by W. Dean Burnham, Samuel Lubell, and Lee Benson.[27] Burnham, for example, wrote, "In 1892 the Republican two-party percentage of the membership of the House of Representatives rose to 37.0 percent, while in the violent G.O.P. overturn of 1894, the proportion of Republican members rose abruptly to 70.7 percent."[28] A number of doctoral dissertations in progress involve an analysis of this dramatic shift, and a paper at the Mississippi Valley Historical Association meeting recently examined the apparent close relationship between the depression of 1893 and the sudden rise in Republican strength.[29] It therefore appears that the analysis of voting behavior

---

(1959), 198–210; and "A Theory of Critical Elections," *Journal of Politics* 17 (1955), 3–18; Samuel Lubell, *The Future of American Politics* (New York, 1952); Lee Benson, "Research Problems in American Political Historiography," in Mirra Komarovsky (ed.), *Common Frontiers in the Social Sciences* (Glencoe, Ill., 1957), 113–83.

27. Lee Benson, *The Concept of Jacksonian Democracy* (Princeton, 1961), 128–31; W. Dean Burnham, *Presidential Ballots, 1836–1892* (Baltimore, 1955), 154–56; Duncan McRae and James Meldrum, "Critical Elections in Illinois," *American Political Science Review* 54 (1960), 669–83.

28. Burnham, *Presidential Ballots*, 155.

29. McSeveney, "Politics of Depression."

is radically altering our approach to the politics of the eighteen-nineties.

A second long-run change in political sentiment is the rise in Democratic strength in the first fifteen years of the twentieth century. Using the party composition of congressional delegations as a measure of change, Democratic support began to rise in 1906, persisted through 1908 as the party, despite Taft's victory, increased its legislative strength, reached a congressional majority in 1910 and a peak probably in 1914. The end of this Democratic majority came with the First World War, but the cause for its development is not so clear. The most important single fact seems to be its concentration in a group of states from Illinois on the west to New York and New Jersey on the east. Between 1904 and 1910, for example, the Democrats gained ninety-two seats in the House, of which sixty-two came from those six states: Illinois, Indiana, Ohio, Pennsylvania, New Jersey, and New York. Ohio and Indiana, the centers of the movement, increased their Democratic strength respectively from one to sixteen out of twenty-one, and from two to twelve out of thirteen. The location of the focal point of the shift rules out its relationship with Insurgency and the timing, that it began before 1909, rules out its peculiar connection with Taft's policies in 1909 and 1910. It may be that, as in Ohio, Democratic increases were associated with prohibition.[30] The problem remains yet unexamined and unsolved, but the use of voting data to define it as a significant focus of interest inevitably draws attention to shifts in voting patterns at the grass roots.

Voting data can also establish more precisely the distinctions between political contestants, parties, factions within parties, or the opposite sides of a nonpartisan issue. Precinct returns for the gubernatorial race in Iowa between 1887 and 1918, for example, demonstrate that differences between and within the two major parties were overwhelmingly ethnic and cultural.[31] Republican precincts were distinctively Methodist, Presbyterian, Quaker, and United Brethren among native American groups, and German Presbyterian, German Methodist, Reformed, and Scandinavian

---

30. Landon Warner, "Ohio's Crusade for Reform, 1897–1917," Ph. D. diss., Harvard Univ., 1949, 250ff.
31. Hays, "History As Human Behavior."

Lutheran among immigrants. The native-American element in Democratic precincts is not so clearly defined, but the immigrant component was distinctively German, Bohemian and Irish Catholic, and German Lutheran. Economic issues, such as corporation control, seem to have been almost irrelevant in the face of a range of social and cultural differences involving nationality and religion, which centered primarily on prohibition and Sunday observance.

Evidence such as this suggests that the period 1874-92, far from being one of stalemate and barrenness in politics, as tradition would have it, involved significant cultural conflict. Consider, for example, the sharp rise in Democratic congressional strength in 1890, which is one of the most perplexing bits of voting behavior of the entire period. The rise had little to do with agrarian unrest because it took place, for the most part, east of the Mississippi and north of the Ohio. In at least three states cultural factors were dominant: in Iowa the adverse reaction to prohibition, and in Wisconsin and Illinois an even stronger reaction to the language restrictions of the Bennett and Edwards Acts. These factors, moreover, carried over into the twentieth century. Distinctions in Iowa between Insurgent and Old Guard voters were cultural, and the sharpest political shifts in the state's history, in 1916 and 1918, involved issues of prohibition and language.

Grass-roots voting behavior can also illuminate more fully the forces involved in reforms in municipal government. Liberal historians have long suggested that municipal reform came on a popular wave of discontent with a business-politician combination involving an exchange of favors to businessmen and graft to political leaders. Recent research has modified this view to the extent of emphasizing that lower socioeconomic groups, both immigrant voters and organized labor, opposed such innovations as the commission and city manager forms of government. The reform impulse, the argument now goes, came from the middle class. But the nature of the leadership, organized groups involved, and voting support in such issues suggest that the source of reform drives lay in the upper classes. The best evidence for this is in the case studies of the origin of city manager government carried out by the Committee on Public Administration under Leonard White at the University of

Chicago in the 1930s.[32] Voting data from commission government elections in Iowa, which was a major center of this movement, indicate that silk-stocking districts provided the heaviest support for reform, just as working-class wards furnished its greatest opposition. Through changes in governmental structure, the leading business and professional groups sought to secure greater control of urban public affairs. Reform involved not an attack on the urban business community, but a drive by businessmen, usually spearheaded by a chamber of commerce, to influence urban affairs more effectively.[33]

V

THE increasing emphasis on social analysis has affected not only the treatment of specific historical problems but broader conceptions of change in industrial society as well. It has focused attention particularly on the systematizing and organizing processes inherent in industrialism as the dynamic force in social change in modern life. The following is a brief elaboration of some implications of such an overall focus.

Science and technology shaped the politics of modern American society. This is not to say simply that the subject matter of public policy concerned industry, labor, and urbanization, but that science and technology imposed a social discipline which "invaded a constantly increasing portion of the community's activities . . . , disintegrated the institutional heritage," and influenced fundamentally the patterns of social relationships.[34] That structure, moreover, involved the systematization of human relationships into a fairly distinct hierarchy of thought and behavior, involving top, middle, and grass-roots levels. Each level of this hierarchy comprised a different degree of the geographical scope of life, the cosmopolitanization of culture, and the unification of political processes.

Political movements in modern industrial society can be distin-

32. Stone et al., *City Manager Government*; Mosher et al., *City Manager Government*; Fred G. Kerschner, "From Country Town to Industrial City," *Indiana Magazine of History* 55 (1949), 330.

33. James Weinstein, "Organized Business."

34. Clark Kerr et al., *Industrialism and Industrial Man* (Cambridge, Mass., 1960), 33–46.

guished in terms of the role which they played in this evolving structure. Many were involved in constructing systems of human activity in industry, labor, agriculture, government, or education and with perfecting the techniques of control which these systems require. A gradual rather than a sudden development, this process constituted an evolution from smaller to larger and larger systems, accompanied by a persistent upward flow of the location of decision making. One envisages a network of human relationships emerging from the demands of industry and technology, reaching out to encompass an ever-wider number of people and range of activities. Nationwide corporations drew many local firms into a single entity; social scientists perfected systems of personnel control in industry, government, and education; metropolitian centers drew small towns and rural communities into their economic, social, and cultural orbit.

At the base of the hierarchy of political action were forces standing apart from innovating tendencies, yet drawn into them. Metropolitan and cosmopolitan influences constantly threatened local life. Ethnic ties became weaker; rural life was reorganized around larger centers of school and church community; local elites declined in significance in the face of national elites with wider prestige; the standards of a wider professional life invaded the educational institutions responsive to local forces;[35] the small town became a satellite of the larger city; suburban areas were drawn into the larger metropolitan community; county officials accustomed to the selection of local welfare officials on a friends-and-neighbors basis were required by federal social security agencies to use professional standards.[36] The quality, activities, and political role of local life were drastically modified by the larger affairs which now engulfed it.

This framework helps to distinguish levels of political activity and to establish relationships among them, thereby placing in proper focus the inadequacy of top-level political history. In particular, it raises a whole series of problems of social analysis at the points where cosmopolitan and local forces met.[37] Who, for example, were the personal links between local society and the larger

35. Alvin Gouldner, "Cosmopolitans and Locals: Toward an Analysis of Latent Social Roles," *Administrative Science Quarterly* 2 (1957), 281–306; and (1958), 444–80.

36. "The Battle of Blue Earth County," in Harold Stein (ed.), *Public Administration and Policy Development* (New York, 1952), 89–105.

37. Robert K. Merton, "Patterns of Influence: Local and Cosmopolitan Influentials,"

world, and did those who provided these connections change over the years? What were the stages by which individuals and communities were drawn into the larger society? What types of communities resisted, and perhaps successfully, these influences? Illumination of problems such as these would prevent one from generalizing directly from one level of political life to the entire society, and, in turn, would deepen our understanding of the workings of the structure of politics as a whole.

Two phenomena illustrate these problems more concretely. One is the development of the county agent system in agriculture. This did not arise simply from the political or economic growth of agriculture, or from what has traditionally been labeled "Progressive reform." As Grant McConnell has shown, the impetus for the county agent movement came from railroads, mail-order houses, farm equipment manufacturers, and mortgage bankers, all of whom feared the loss of rural business, and from land-grant college agricultural experts who worked closely with business groups.[38] The county agent, in other words, served as a representative in a local community of outside forces, a contact man between local farmers and the wider scientific and economic influences of industrial society. His role is to be understood in terms of the way in which the larger industrial, cosmopolitan, and systematizing influences of modern society reached out to transform rural and small town life.

A second example is the impact of the First World War on the United States. The war speeded up greatly tendencies in political structure, and especially the systematization and nationwide organization of economic life. The war witnessed an upward shift of decision making so that many groups exercised less influence than formerly. Rail-shippers, for example, now confronted a railroad administration strikingly unreceptive to their demands, whereas in previous years they had found a spokesman in the Interstate Commerce Commission. The pressures of wartime patriotism silenced temporarily those who felt this type of frustration, but after the war they rebelled against these innovations of system.[39] Therein lies one

---

in Merton, *Social Theory and Social Structure* (Glencoe, Ill., 1957), 387–420; Arthur J. Vidich and Joseph Bensman, *Small Town in Mass Society* (New York, 1960).

38. Grant McConnell, *The Decline of Agrarian Democracy* (Berkeley, 1953), 19–35.
39. K. Austin Kerr, "Shipper Groups and the Transportation Act of 1920," M.A. the-

important key specifically to the decision against continued federal control of the railroads, and generally to the massive rebellion against Wilson and the Democratic party first evidenced in 1918 and reaching staggering proportions in 1920.

The character of the middle levels of political life frequently stemmed from the evolving relationships between the top levels of politics and the grass roots. On the one hand, those engaged in local activities organized in larger geographical units to exercise some control over vast private and public forces which they could not, as individuals, influence. Hence the rise of the trade association in business, labor, and agriculture, or the regional or national ethnic or religious group. On the other hand, as administrators executed policy on higher levels, they found that they had lost contact with the grass roots, and so encouraged the formation of the same intermediate organizations both for administrative convenience and political support. Thus, for example, the promotion of trade associations by the War Industries Board during the First World War, or of neighborhood clubs by the citywide welfare agency which had taken the place of personal charity provided by the ward leader.

One intriguing aspect of political evolution at the middle level concerns the changing nature of statewide decision making as a product of the tension between locally oriented tendencies in rural and small-town life on the one hand and consolidating tendencies of larger urban centers on the other. Faced with dominant and unfriendly small-town and rural state legislators, large cities turned increasingly to the federal government not only for financial aid but also for assistance in establishing political and administrative systems with a statewide focus which encompassed urban-metropolitan life. Effective state highway commissions, for example, responsive to urban views on highway development, were accepted by many state legislatures only as a necessary condition for receiving federal aid. Urban areas thereby used federal power to shape the character of state government. Rural areas, on the other hand, by constantly resisting urban-sponsored state programs, drastically limited positive state government and shaped it largely as an economic broker between federal agencies and the state's citizens. Historians have

sis, State Univ. of Iowa, 1960, and Kerr, *American Railroad Politics, 1914-1920* (Pittsburgh, 1968) for accounts of this process in one important area of wartime policy.

neglected the changing role of state government in modern industrial society, treating it in limited fashion as a miniature example of
reform or a bulwark of private enterprise. More correctly it is a product of the interplay between local life and urban systematizing and
cosmopolitan forces.

VI

THE foregoing examples illustrate the new ways of looking at the
years 1880–1920 which historians are increasingly emphasizing.
They are not meant to be exhaustive as theories of explanation but
to serve as instances of the growing stress on the analysis of social
patterns and processes. The liberal framework, more concerned
with the formal and the episodic, has become increasingly restrictive rather than conducive to further social analysis. It has prevented historians from giving full attention to the political role of
working people, the influence of ethnocultural factors in politics,
the changing characteristics of elites, the role of the business community in reform, the treatment of urban life as a system of social
organization, the source of antireform impulses, the conflict between local and cosmopolitan cultures, the growth of bureaucracy
and administration, the growth of education as a process of cultural
transmission and social mobility, the development of ideology and
its relationship to practice, and the examination of interregional
economic relationships. Most important, it has obscured significant
shifts in the location and techniques of decision making in a more
highly systematized society.

Instead of generating more careful examination of questions
such as these, the liberal conception of history brought about an almost complete abandonment of the analysis of social and political
structure. Advances in the emphasis on social, economic, and intellectual data have not produced overall syntheses of this material
with political history. Instead, authors of modern American history
texts compartmentalize topically distinct material with no attempt
to establish relationships of structure or process. Even in chapters
on more conventional political history, emphasis on material which
relates events to underlying structure has sharply declined. Thus,
information concerning the political source of the movement to

regulate railroads is usually limited to statements that the "public" or the "people" demanded a change. Finally, the increasing emphasis on the cultural and political homogeneity of American society has involved an almost complete neglect of the examination of the structure of political groups in favor of themes concerning common cultural characteristics. By their failure to stimulate deeper investigation into the nature of fundamental political relationships, traditional viewpoints have demonstrated their decline in usefulness.

If new departures in research such as I have outlined above continue, we are, I think, well on the way to some basic reorientations in approach not only in studies of specific problems but in overall conceptions of political life as well in the decades from 1880 to 1920. In the future, historians will be concerned less with the formal and the episodic and more with social analysis; they will borrow heavily from the social sciences for ideas concerning political patterns and processes; they will proceed through comparative study; and they will emphasize the political relationships which evolve in industrial society. It seems safe to predict, moreover, that future analysis will center on the relative roles of people at all levels of political life in decision making, within the context of a more highly organized and systematized social order. The groundwork for such an orientation has been established during the last decade and a half; its further progress during the next fifteen years, I am convinced, will be even more remarkable.

[3]

New Possibilities
for American Political History:
The Social Analysis of Political Life *

IN recent years American political history has undergone some severe challenges from within the profession. Many have cast aside
the traditional study of politics as too concerned with dramatic
events and formal institutions, too remote from human experience
and values, in favor of a more satisfying economic, intellectual, or
social history. But these lines of inquiry, although pursued vigorously, have failed to reorient the profession toward the very human
qualities of the past they professed to seek. Stressing the formal
relationships among ideas, intellectual history has created a past
world divorced from human circumstance and situation in which
ideas seem to sweep men on through the course of history. Influenced by the abstract quality of theory, economic history has become caught up in the impersonal description of aggregate economic forces. The study of American character has prompted social
history to focus on uniform social psychological patterns. Despite
advances in these fields, historians still await an approach which can
recapture human experience, thought, values, and practice in its
variety of situations and circumstances.

These emphases, moreover, have failed to provide an overall
context for examining historical change. Remaining separate and
compartmentalized, they have fractured history rather than synthe-
sized it. Economic, intellectual, and social history have moved far-

*This paper was delivered at the annual meeting of the American Historical Associa-
tion, Dec. 29, 1964, and was reprinted in Seymour Martin Lipset and Richard Hofstadter
(eds.), *Sociology and History* (New York 1968).

ther apart rather than closer together. Each maintains that its facet of human experience is more significant than that of the others, but none has brought forward a framework to bring diverse aspects of human life together and provide a substitute for the rejected conceptual unity of political history. Our textbooks have become separate chapters on economic, social, and intellectual life, sandwiched in between sections of a traditionally oriented political history, which remain more akin to separate catalogs of information than integral parts of a single social fabric. Academic log-rolling has predominated over conceptual synthesis, and the acquisition of monopoly over specialized pieces of information has prevailed over the intellectual risk of coping with their interrelationships.

The time is now ripe for a new consideration of political life as the major context of historical inquiry, and for its special potential both for focusing on the human quality of the past and integrating its diverse facets. For since political history is concerned with the conflicts among the varied goals and values which arise in society and with the distribution of power which is responsible for the choice of one goal over another, it emphasizes both the particular human situations from which those strivings arise and the larger arena in which the struggle for dominance takes place. It can bring into one context both the fundamental realities of inevitably limited human experience and the larger realm of social choice. But in order to play this role political history must differ radically from its earlier counterpart. It must broaden its conception of the nature of political life from formal institutions to the entire range of the clash of goals in society; it must think more in terms of patterns of human relationships than of isolated people and events abstracted from the fabric of society; and it must be willing to explore both new concepts and new methods of inquiry.

This development is now taking place. Approaches to political history far different from those used previously are under serious exploration.[1] This paper is an attempt both to articulate these developments more fully and to outline the possibilities which they entail for the revitalization of political life as the central focus of history.

1. For two convenient compilations of work in this vein see Thomas C. Cochran, *The Inner Revolution* (New York, 1964) and Edward N. Saveth, *American History and the Social Sciences* (Glencoe, Ill., 1964).

I

Limitations of Conventional Political History

TRADITIONAL political history has come under attack from a number of different sources. In 1948 Thomas C. Cochran criticized the "presidential synthesis," the practice of dividing political history into four-year intervals marked by presidential elections.[2] The ebb and flow of political impulses, he argued, was independent of these formal divisions. Fundamental shifts in political attitudes might well come between presidential elections and last longer than a four-year period, for they reflect changes in attitudes and impulses entirely unconnected in origin with the formal timing of election contests. Cochran's article stressed the distinction between the formal and the informal characteristics of politics, between those more observable and outward conditions of political life and the more underlying impulses for influence and power which arise out of the entire range of human endeavor. The political historian must go beneath the external manifestation and examine the roots of political life.

One example of the traditional political history which Cochran criticized is the tendency to describe the political parties in terms of their formal expressions of policy rather than of the great variety of groups of which they are composed. Parties of the post–Civil War era are known as high-tariff or low-tariff, sound-money or silver parties, depending upon their platform statements and campaign oratory. Few have gone beyond the high tariff–big business image of the Republican party of those years to investigate its internal composition, the characteristics of the delegates to conventions or state executive committees, the composition of its voting support, the voluntary groups associated with it, the different outlooks and voting patterns of different segments of its congressional delegations, the impact of the new Western states admitted in the late 1880s on the intraparty balance, or the patterns of forces within state Republican organizations.[3]

2. Thomas C. Cochran, "The Presidential Synthesis in American History," *American Historical Review* 53 (1948), 748–59.
3. A recent study, relying heavily on a formal approach to political history, is Stanley L. Jones, *The Presidential Election of 1896* (Madison, Wis., 1964).

For years historians and political scientists described the distinctions between legislative and executive branches of government, especially on the state and local level, in formal terms. The first makes laws; the second executes them. The city council creates policy; the city manager carries it out. But both executive and legislative branches in state and municipal government are the focal point of political forces; both make political decisions, and, in fact, represent different constituencies. The governor, elected at large, reflects the changing composition of the state's voters; as they become more urban, the governor tends to represent the views of the cities.[4] But the legislature, slower to change, represents the views of people in rural areas and small towns. In the city the council members reflect the views of the many and diverse segments of the community in their local and regional interests, while the executive represents the views of those business and professional groups with citywide interests and perspectives. These distinctions are not apparent through a reading of the formal governmental responsibilities of governors and legislators, but they become clear from an examination of the political impulses which play upon decision makers and to which those decision makers look for support.[5]

Movements with the same outward, formal characteristics may often involve vastly different political goals. Joseph Gusfield has recently outlined the variety of impulses in the drive for prohibition.[6] In its pre–Civil War phase the upper class used temperance to protect itself against the stirrings of the "lower orders" of society. In the post–Civil War era, on the other hand, prohibition involved a middle-class attempt to establish its particular values in the midst of the emphasis on material growth and the leadership of the new industrial elite. The movement which began in the 1890s, far more successful, stemmed from the rural drive to contain and control the growing cultural power of the cities which threatened older, rural ways of life. In all of these instances prohibition or temperance were instruments of social control, but the group which desired control and the group which was to be controlled, the problem to be solved

4. V.O. Key, *American State Politics* (New York, 1956), 76.
5. For a critique of older views of municipal government see Lawrence J.R. Herson, "The Lost World of Municipal Government," *American Political Science Review* 51 (1957), 330–45.
6. Joseph R. Gusfield, *Symbolic Crusade* (Urbana, Ill., 1963).

and the group which defined the problem and sought prohibition as the solution to it, all differed.

Political history, then, must go beneath the outward, formal characteristics of political life to investigate the more fundamental impulses of the drive for influence and dominance; these impulses determine the character of political action and should establish the framework of political analysis.

A second criticism of traditional political history has focused on the failure of historians adequately to analyze election returns.[7] Most elections are examined as outcomes of particular campaigns; consequently the margin of victory for one contest is given. But rarely are the results of that contest compared with past elections, and even more rarely are the results presented in such a way—percentage strength—that comparisons can be made. The important long-range historical fact about elections is not necessarily the outcome of any one contest but the degree to which they reveal shifts or continuities in political attitude. It is impossible to determine whether a single election deserves analysis without a series of data which indicate the degree of stability or change in voting over time. With such data one can discover that the early 1850s witnessed a revolution in political attitudes which persisted until 1893, that the election of 1883 rather than that of 1884 was the crucial year of Democratic gains; that the Democratic upswing in the early twentieth century was six years in the making and not just a product of the debates of 1909; that the Republican victory of 1918 was often far more crucial than that of 1920 in establishing the new Republican dominance of the twentieth century. Each of these examples concerns a shift or trend in voting which the traditional method of treating elections has failed to emphasize.

Historians have also neglected the disaggregate analysis of elections, the examination of the different patterns of voting by different groups of people which the overall returns do not reveal. How did different ethnic, religious, and racial groups or different socioeconomic classes vote? Were ethnocultural factors more powerful than socioeconomic ones in establishing voting patterns? An excel-

7. Lee Benson, "Research Problems in American Political Historiography," in Mirra Komarovsky (ed.), *Common Frontiers in the Social Sciences* (Glencoe, Ill., 1957), 113–83; *The Concept of Jacksonian Democracy* (Princeton, 1961).

lent example of this type of study is a recent article on German po-
litial attitudes in the election of 1860 which demonstrates that Iowa
Germans were strongly Democratic.[8] Only with an intensive examination of voting returns and an association of those returns with
demographic patterns of all kinds can the different political attitudes of different segments of the population be determined. The
overall returns often obscure marked shifts in voting behavior. Recently historians have begun to stress the significant Democratic urban gains in the election of 1928, despite the Hoover victory, but
only after the importance of this shift was emphasized by a political
scientist and popularized by a journalist-sociologist.[9] A similar phenomenon took place in 1948 when, in the face of the Truman victory, Dewey scored marked gains in the cities. Such trends as these,
which occurred in many elections and which the general returns obscure, await a disaggregate analysis to bring them to light.

Still a third criticism is that the heavy emphasis on the individual and the episodic has obscured the need for investigating the
larger structure and processes of political life. Political historians
have devoted considerable effort to examining prominent political
leaders and dramatic political events. Stimulated markedly by the
preservation of personal manuscripts, the study of individual politicians has gone on apace. This has focused political history on the
ideas, actions, and interrelationships of a few prominent leaders
and has diverted attention from the broader composition of political parties and the environment within which both party and leader
exist. Political biographies assume, with no rationale for defining
the problem, much less resolving it, a particular relationship between the individual and his "times." The impact of a president as
a political leader, however, cannot be determined unless one has
studied his party, his administrative agencies and his legislatures as
thoroughly as the president's personal affairs. Yet what biographer

8. George Daniels, "Immigrant Vote in the 1860 Election: The Case of Iowa," *Mid-
America* 44 (1962), 146–62. See also Arthur Gorenstein, "A Portrait of Ethnic Politics,"
Publication of the American Jewish Historical Society 50 (1961), 202–38; and Robert P.
Swierenga, "The Ethnic Leaders and the First Lincoln Election," *Civil War History* 11
(1965), 27–43.

9. Samuel J. Eldersveld, "Influence of Metropolitan Party Pluralities on Presidential
Elections," *American Political Science Review* 43 (1949), 1189–1206; Samuel Lubell, *The
Future of American Politics* (New York, 1952), 28–57.

has done this? James MacGregor Burns in his treatment of Franklin D. Roosevelt has moved most fully in this direction.[10]

By the same token, much of our political history is episodic, concerned more with the isolated event than the political context. Legislative history invariably focuses on the drama of the single legislative decision, rather than the network of political forces within which the decision was made. The exciting and colorful struggle over antitrust legislation in the early twentieth century obscured the contemporary patterns of economic politics and their relationship to public policy. Small businessmen, for example, against whom the Sherman Act had been most effectively used, sought to modify that act not by strengthening it but by circumventing it through legalized minimum price fixing. The dramatic strikes of the late nineteenth century, as Herbert Gutman has shown, obscured the close relationship between middle and lower classes in instances of industrial strife and the great difficulty, rather than the ease, with which employers disciplined their labor force.[11] The dramatic controversy over the Supreme Court in 1937 obscured the patterns of political struggle in the first four years of the New Deal which lay behind it, the forces sharpened by executive policies developed under such agencies as the NRA and the PWA, and the resulting contest over executive and legislative power.

This emphasis upon the individual and the episodic one might well describe by the phrase "abstracted empiricism," in the same way in which C. Wright Mills used it to describe similar tendencies in sociology.[12] For it conveys accurately the idea that historians have abstracted individuals and episodes from context, examined them apart from that context, and placed them back into the stream of history without regard to that context save for temporal sequence and topical similarity. But historical problems must be defined in terms of the relation of people and events to each other. How important is one episode, for example the election of 1896, in relation to other election episodes? How important is one individual in relation to the human context? How representative is an individual of a

10. James MacGregor Burns, *Roosevelt, the Lion and the Fox* (New York, 1956).
11. Herbert Gutman, "The Worker's Search for Power: Labor in the Gilded Age," in H. Wayne Morgan (ed.), *The Gilded Age* (Syracuse, 1963), 38–68.
12. C. Wright Mills, *The Sociological Imagination* (New York, 1959), 50–75.

broader group? How distinctive is this particular political drive—is it typical of a widespread impulse, or is it atypical? The context of political relationships whether in space or in time, rather than the frequency of appearance in the historical record or the sensationalism of the event, should determine the particular aspects of political history worthy of study.

The inadequacy of conventional political history is illustrated in even more striking fashion by omissions in the treatment of highly significant problems. The assumptions of political historians have guided them to certain topics and not to others. Now that assumptions about political behavior are changing and more evidence about political life is building up from sociology and political science as well as history, the nature of the problems considered worthy of investigation is changing. Conventional political history appears to have large and almost unexplainable gaps.

Consider, for example, the growth of bureaucracy and administration in the years since the mid-nineteenth century, the elaboration and expansion of systematization which is part of the evolution of the technical-scientific world.[13] Textbooks invariably fail to treat this extensive political change. They will consider it tangentially when discussing the growth of big business or of government. But they do not consider it as a general development: the increase in the size and scope of affairs which are subject to systematization and control; the changing techniques of control; the similarities in public and private bureaucracies in the need for long-range planning, in utilizing experts, in fashioning favorable public relations; the extension of these processes in the mid-twentieth century to our educational system.

An equally striking gap is the failure to consider changes in socioeconomic classes. Some treatment of this occurs for Early American history and for the agrarian South. For the most part, however, we know little about the evolution of the upper class in the nineteenth and twentieth centuries, its changing composition and character, the differential movement into it by religious and ethnic groups, its wider public role. The only scholarly historical treatment of this phenomenon is by a sociologist, E. Digby Baltzell, in his

13. Dwight Waldo, *The Administrative State* (New York, 1948); Barry Karl, *Executive Reorganization and Reform in the New Deal* (Cambridge, Mass., 1963).

book *Philadelphia Gentlemen*.[14] We speak blithely of the "middle class" in the nineteenth century, without even investigating its composition. We accept the image, for example, that the urban middle class of small businessmen was overwhelmingly native American, when it appears more likely that the majority were immigrants. Nor do we know much about working-class people and their political attitudes, save their role in organized labor and trade union activity. Cutting across all of these features of class analysis is the problem of social mobility, a process which we assume to have happened, but which we have not examined. Curiously, despite the dominance of liberal historiography, our framework of political analysis has failed to turn our research attention to these socioeconomic dimensions of political life.

An equally striking omission is the role of ethnocultural factors in politics. Recent texts have recognized these factors by incorporating some of Samuel Lubell's ideas into the treatment of the New Deal.[15] But the first full-length treatment of religion and voting in American history appeared only this year and was written by a sociologist, Seymour Lipset.[16] The very great significance of religion and nationality in differentiating the voting patterns of the nineteenth century is apparent to anyone who examines precinct voting returns. They also established a degree of continuity in voting distinctions which constitutes one of the most important conditions of American political structure. But the assumptions of our conventional political history have obscured rather than illumined these factors.

Still a fourth example is the conflict between rural and urban areas.[17] Because of the issue of reapportionment we are clearly aware of the contemporary significance of this problem. But we have failed to bring it into focus as an historical development. The city has changed our political values, established new contexts for political debate, affected the nature of intraparty struggles, and de-

14. E. Digby Baltzell, *Philadelphia Gentlemen* (Glencoe, Ill., 1958).
15. Lubell, *op. cit.*
16. Seymour Lipset, "Religion and Politics in the American Past and Present," in Robert Lee and Martin E. Marty (eds.), *Religion and Social Conflict* (New York, 1964).
17. See Gordon E. Baker, *Rural Versus Urban Political Power* (New York, 1955); Don S. Kirschner, *City and Country: Rural Responses to Urbanization in the 1920's* (Westport, Conn., 1970).

termined the balance of power within state legislatures. All of this should provide one of the major frameworks for the treatment of a whole range of historical phenomena, from ideologies and values through economic policy to the basic struggle for political power. And these conflicts go well back into the nineteenth century. But one can glimpse almost nothing of the entire problem in text books, save, perhaps, for the decade of the 1920s. Instead, the historian must turn to political science and sociology, in such works as *Small Town in Mass Society* by Arthur Vidich and Joseph Bensman,[18] to secure insight as to the impact of the wider, metropolitan, technological, scientific society upon an earlier small-town and rural America.

One could continue this list of omissions, but these examples establish the point. Conventional political history has been so preoccupied with the outward and formal, the episodic, the unique, and the individual that it has failed to draw attention to some of the most significant developments of our political past. The assumptions of that outlook have limited and narrowed our vision rather than illumined and expanded it. They have separated us from the very thing with which we should be most concerned: the determination of those broad patterns of continuity and change which arise out of the network of social relationships established in the course of history.

II
The Social Analysis of Political History

THESE concerns, it is apparent, do not involve an interest in new subject matter in political history, the addition of new facts to old, so much as the development of a new perspective and a new set of problems for investigation. For they stress the examination of human behavior itself, its ideology and its practice rather than its formal products, and of social patterns and social processes which arise from that behavior rather than the individual and episodic. Implicit in many of the new stirrings in American political history is the desire to understand the impulses and strivings which arise out

18. Arthur J. Vidich and Joseph Bensman, *Small Town in Mass Society* (New York, 1960).

of human circumstance and situation, the degree to which people hold these in common or in distinction, and the degree to which they persist or change. The emphasis is on human behavior and human relationships, and on the social patterns and social processes to which they give rise. The conceptual framework involved, therefore, can be described by the phrase "the *social analysis* of political history."

This approach requires, first of all, a broader conception of the nature of political life. In the past we have confined political history to political parties and their activities: party organization, the selection of candidates, electoral contests, executive appointments, and legislative action. But political life involves the origin, clash, and resolution of all value conflicts in society, whether expressed through political parties or not. The context of political analysis must range far beyond the political party to the broader environment of human relationships within which it functions and which it reflects. This environment is not merely the background to party action, but the context within which political groupings are defined and basic political impulses analyzed and placed in relationship to each other. Other systems of decision making, such as the administrative process or the give and take of nonpartisan interest-group action, each of equal importance to the political party as instruments of expressing political goals, function within the same context. The analysis of each rests upon the patterns of human relationships which grow out of economic, social, and ideological life; systems of decision making are the instruments whereby these values and goals are expressed.

The religious composition of voting patterns in the nineteenth century illustrates this problem.[19] Evangelical protestantism found expression in mid-century in the Republican party. The more ritualistic Catholic and Protestant faiths, in reaction, aligned themselves with the Democratic party. The wide clashes over prohibition and Sunday observance, over Sunday schools and revivals as legitimate techniques of instruction and conversion, over the individual soul or the historical institution as the focal point of religious activities— all these took place outside the realm of party politics. They can be

19. This analysis is based upon voting patterns in Iowa between 1887 and 1920.

observed within the context of denominational decision making in annual conferences and theological seminary policy, in competition between youth groups such as the Methodists and the Lutherans, in local battles over Sunday baseball games, or in disputation in the religious journals. But they are brought to bear in political party battles which focus all of these value conflicts into a contest for public policy and political leaders. The final expression of the conflict cannot be separated from all that lay behind it. The one is as legitimate and as essential a part of political history as the other.

Traditional distinctions between political history on the one hand and ideological, economic, social, and cultural history on the other are artificial. For political life deeply involves the clash of values, the drive for dominance, the resolution of differences in every realm of human affairs. The distribution of the power to secure and disseminate information and ideas; to govern relationships within economic trade groups; to organize and manage economic ventures; to control residential communities against change; to develop, influence, and use educational facilities; to establish the policies of religious institutions are in themselves political phenomena. All involve the expression of different goals and values in contexts which are public rather than personal and private; all involve the attempt to control the ideas and practices of other people so that one's own values can be realized more fully. Power and decision making, therefore, are not isolated segments of the social order which can be examined separately from ideological, economic, social, and cultural affairs, but permeate all realms of life. Our analytical perspective must be equally broad.

Within this context of political history, the social analyst must determine initially the nature of political structure, the groupings of ideas and practices into which the political order can be divided and from which attempts to influence the course of public affairs arise. What distinct political groupings exist among nationality, religious, and racial groups; among occupational and trade groups; among people of different socioeconomic levels; among different geographical sections; among areas of different degrees of urbanization; among people of different educational levels? Survey data secured through polls enable us to develop a fairly complete picture of different voting groups of the past three decades. But we have no such comprehensive view of the period before the 1930s. Our objective, however, should be the same as that of the survey specialists, to secure a broad picture of the significant groupings into which the political order can be divided. Our approach to this problem has been almost casual, as an appendage to the investigation of other matters. It must now be undertaken more thoroughly so that the total range of political groupings for any one time of history can become the context within which political events are understood.

Many current attempts to revise older views of political history consist of a more precise definition of political groups. Some seek to separate more clearly the distinctions among voters in popular elections;[20] others seek to define systematically the groupings among legislators in roll-call votes;[21] still others search for divisions among political leaders.[22] Some define more precisely the distinct divisions among bankers in the Jacksonian Era, or the divisions in the contest over the currency in the Greenback Era.[23] Such studies as these have advanced our knowledge of political groupings significantly. But they are only beginnings. Since most of them describe the patterns of groups which form around specific issues, they do not provide a view of the full range of groups in the political structure and the total pattern of the peculiar distribution of power. Yet it is in the direction which such studies as these have outlined that we must turn for a more satisfactory treatment of political structure.

An example of this approach is contained in Robert Wiebe's book on businessmen and reform in the Progressive Era.[24] Wiebe seeks to understand the struggle over banking policy and the formation of the Federal Reserve Act by sorting out the segments of the banking community and relating their conceptions of what policy should be to their position in the structure of the banking world. The Eastern banker, dominant in the banking community, wished a currency based upon federal and railroad bonds and a cen-

20. Benson, *Jacksonian Democracy.*

21. Joel Silbey, *The Shrine of Party; Congressional Voting Behavior, 1841–1852* (Pittsburgh, 1967).

22. See, for example, recent literature on the 1780s, such as Forrest MacDonald, *We, The People* (Chicago, 1958); Jackson Turner Main, *The Anti-Federalists* (Chapel Hill, 1961).

23. Robert Sharkey, *Money, Class and Party* (Baltimore, 1957).

24. Robert Wiebe, *Businessmen and Reform* (Cambridge, Mass., 1962), 62–65.

tralized banking system. The regional bankers, led by those in Chicago, sought an assets currency and a regionally based organization. But the country bankers wanted land-mortgage paper to be included as a base for issuing currency and an organization resting upon local clearing-houses. Each of these groups within the banking community lived in a different banking world and as a result formulated different ideas about public policy. The history of every legislative enactment should provide as complete a treatment of the structure of relevant political groupings.

From what particular segment of the political structure does a particular political impulse arise? This is one of the most fundamental questions in political analysis. Does it come from one socio-economic group or another, from one ethnocultural group or another, from leaders or from the grass roots, from one geographical section or another? The peculiarities of a political movement are rarely observable from the political ideology, whether it be federalism, states' rights, antitrust or socialism. They can be determined, however, from the way in which the people involved in that movement differ from others in the political structure. From what particular religious denominations or segments of denominations did antislavery impulses in the pre–Civil War years spring? Was there any connection between these particular groups and the particular segments from which the Republican party drew its initial strength? It is doubtful whether an extensive description of antislavery ideology can answer these questions. They can be dealt with, however, by tracing the peculiar geographical location of those segments of the Presbyterian or Methodist churches, for example, from which the demand for antislavery pronouncements came and by observing the peculiar sources of Republican party voting strength at the precinct level.

In defining the source of a political impulse, it is especially important to be able to determine not only that it came from a particular segment of the political structure, but that it did not come from other segments. The peculiarities of a phenomenon grow not only from its own characteristics, but more significantly from the ways in which it differs from other phenomena. Some attempts at the social analysis of political history have gone astray because they sought to associate distinctive political behavior with groups which themselves were not different from other groups. One must know, for example, not only who antislavery leaders were, but also how they differed from slavery apologists; not only who New England Mugwumps were, but how they differed from Republicans who did not bolt the party or from Democrats who were their new associates in 1884; not only who the Progressive Era reformers were, but how they differed from their political opponents.[25]

Fundamental to the social analysis of political history, therefore, is an understanding of the group character of politics, not simply in the sense of active, organized interest groups impinging directly on the legislative process, but in the sense of shared attitudes, ideas, situations, and goals which produce uniformities in political thought and practice. The dramatic episodes and personalities, the products of legislation and party conventions provide at best only a superficial context of political relationships. Political structure, instead, grows out of the persistent, ongoing, day-to-day relationships established among people in their work, their community life, their religion, recreation, and education, and out of the patterns of dominance and subordination which these activities generate. Historians have not devoted their energies extensively to the determination of political structure; yet political history cannot be understood even in its most elementary form without knowledge of the characteristics of that structure and the peculiar origins of political impulses within it.

The social analysis of political life requires an understanding of political process as well as political structure. How do the patterns of political forces change? With time new political groups emerge and others decline; groups formerly subordinate may become more influential. The context of ethnocultural politics in the late eighteenth and early nineteenth centuries which involved establishment and disestablishment gave way in the mid-nineteenth century to a context of evangelical protestantism and the reaction to it.[26]

25. For studies which fail to take this precaution, see George E. Mowry, *The California Progressives* (Berkeley and Los Angeles, 1951), 86–104, and Alfred D. Chandler, Jr., "The Origins of Progressive Leadership," in Elting Morrison et al. (eds.), *The Letters of Theodore Roosevelt* (Cambridge, Mass., 1951–54), vol. VIII, Appendix III, 1462–1464. Two studies which use a more satisfactory method are E. Daniel Potts, "The Progressive Profile in Iowa," *Mid-America* 47 (1965), 257–68; William T. Kerr, Jr., "The Progressives of Washington, 1910–12," *Pacific Northwest Quarterly* 55 (1964), 16–27.

26. Lipset, *op. cit.*

The old commercial-agrarian political leaders of the pre-1850 years gave way to the new industrial political elite which formed effective ties with the urban masses.[27] Economic groups, organized along trade lines, began in the late nineteenth century to establish a new, nonpartisan system of economic politics not known before. The socioeconomic background of urban political leaders in the early twentieth century shifted from working and lower middle class to upper middle class.[28]

One of the most useful devices for determining the timing of political change is the analysis of election data. By arranging party percentages of the total vote in a time series, one can observe the shifts and stabilities in popular voting sentiment over a long period of time.[29] An index of party strength in Congress, for example, indicates that since 1874 the greatest shift in political sentiment took place in 1894 (32 percentage points), the next greatest in 1890 (23 points), and the third greatest in 1932 (20 points). Since the two most drastic changes took place in off-presidential years and in elections which historians have hardly mentioned, such an approach indicates the extent to which the use of quantitative data can direct attention to changes not customarily observed. The election of 1896, for example, continued a voting pattern first established in 1894; to understand the vote in 1896, therefore, one must first understand the causes for the revolutionary change of 1894. Traditional evidence has obscured the fact that the dramatic election of 1896 was a contest of ideology and leadership; the voting realignment which lay behind it had already taken place.

The analysis of political history would be greatly enhanced if we knew precisely when major changes took place in different segments of the political structure. When, for example, did shifts occur in the occupational background of legislators? In the percentage of eligible voters which actually voted? In the balance of political power between rural and urban areas as revealed, for example, in the constituencies of state legislators? In the upward shift in the lo-

27. Ari Hoogenboom, "An Analysis of Civil Service Reformers," *The Historian* 23 (1960), 54–78.
28. Samuel P. Hays, "The Politics of Reform in Municipal Government in the Progressive Era," *Pacific Northwest Quarterly* 55 (1964), 157–69.
29. These conclusions are based upon an examination of the party affiliations of each member of Congress since 1874.

cation of decision making from smaller to larger units of government? In the relationships between lower- and middle-class groups from cooperation in the nineteenth century to hostility in the twentieth? In the balance of power within the Democratic party against the South in the twentieth century? Data about the changing backgrounds of those elected to city councils and school boards, for example, raise several questions. Why, at certain points in history, did city councilmen from the old patrician upper class give way to those of the newer entrepreneurial groups, and why in turn did these give way later to lower- and middle-class groups? Why, in the twentieth century, was this tendency reversed in some cities? Not all changes can be described in quantitative terms. But the observation of change is a major starting point for some of the most significant historical investigations.

Observation of the location of change is as important as observation of its timing. For change may not take place uniformly throughout a society. If it is greater in one geographical area than another, analysis is facilitated by the attempt to associate that particular change with characteristics peculiar to that area. The Populist movement took place in areas other than those where the Granger movement had been strong; it can be understood, then, through an analysis of the conditions peculiar to the trans-Missouri West and the South as distinct from the changing economy of the old Granger areas. The massive changes in electoral behavior in the 1890s took place primarily in the North and East. Over two-thirds of the congressional seats which changed hands between 1890 and 1898 came in areas north and east of the centers of agrarian unrest. To understand these changes, therefore, one must investigate the North and East rather than, as has been done, concentrate almost exclusively on the South and West. The rise of the Democratic party in the decade after 1904 was peculiarly located in a belt of states from Illinois to New Jersey: why? In the late 1840s, and early 1850s, the Republican party made particularly heavy inroads into former Democratic areas in a belt of counties beginning in southern New York and northern Pennsylvania and extending west in the same latitude. Why? Understanding of why change takes place, therefore, is greatly facilitated by pinpointing where it takes place.

Within a year computations for all county election data for President, governor, U.S. representative, and U.S. senator since 1824 will be readily available. From these data we can secure a complete picture of the timing and distribution of changes in election behavior throughout the entire United States over a period of 140 years. As a result, a host of problems for analysis will come to the fore. Not only will we be able to pinpoint precisely all changes over time and all peculiarities of distribution of those changes over space, we will also be able to distinguish between those changes of greater and of lesser magnitude. The effect of such a catalog of changes will be to bring into focus many problems for analysis which have heretofore escaped our attention. It will lead to studies providing a far more comprehensive picture of both political structure and political process and will stimulate the social analysis of an increasingly wider range of historical evidence.

III
Situational Analysis

THE social analysis of political history, the examination of both structure and process, focuses on the human situation. Human experience and action are not universal but limited, and from such limited rather than universal existence grow limited rather than universal patterns of thought and behavior. Each group has a particular "situation" in society, with a distinctive consciousness of the world, distinctive goals, values and behavior, all of which are understandable only in terms of that situation. Knowledge of the world is circumscribed by the extent of the world with which one comes into contact. The person whose consciousness is limited to a local community from which he does not move physically or psychologically has a limited and circumscribed set of values and behavior. Those whose contacts and experiences are geographically broad and varied have an altogether different, yet also limited, pattern of thought and action. The blue-collar workingman views the world differently from the white-collar clerk, the lower-income group differently from the upper, the Catholic from the Jew or the Protestant, the Italian immigrant from the Mexican, the New Englander from the Southerner—all because the circumstances in which they live are different, and the contexts in which their ideas and attitudes develop are peculiar to those circumstances.

The initial question to be asked of any historical problem is: What particular people, at what particular time, in what particular place thought and acted in what particular way? Every historical question is a question concerning human behavior; it should be referred back not to a general scheme or idea, but to people who are thinking and acting in a particular situation. Instead of intellectual history, there is the history of people who have ideas; instead of economic history the history of people who organize production or consume; instead of political history the history of those who seek influence to make their goals and values prevail. Historical analysis has a tendency to move to higher grounds of broad forces conceptualized in suprahuman terms, sweeping men on through time. Social analysis is a healthy antidote to this tendency, for it forces one to think in terms of the peculiarities of the human situation and to constantly modify the broader outlines of history in terms of the limitations of human consciousness and experience. Each historical question, then, is traced back to the human situation from which it arises and is understood in terms of that situation.

The failure to adopt such an approach has severely limited the analysis of those movements in American history variously called "reform," "progressive," or "liberal." These are presumed to have arisen from universal impulses of "progress," from the gradual realization in political life of the forces of reason, enlightenment, or good will. But such an approach does not facilitate more precise analysis. Only particular groups sought these changes, and examination of these groups demonstrates that their interest arose from their particular circumstances rather than from general conditions of "progressiveness." Why, for example, were some professional groups rather than others interested in changes in municipal government in the Progressive Era?[30] Why civil engineers rather than mechanical, electrical, or chemical? Why ministers from upper-class parishes rather than from parishes of other income levels?

30. These observations are based upon several studies under way at the Univ. of Pittsburgh of the role of professional groups in municipal reform in the city of Pittsburgh during the Progressive Era.

Why schoolteachers from the more well-to-do school districts rather than from the school system as a whole? Why particular groups of lawyers rather than others? Why doctors concerned with communicable disease rather than surgeons? Why architects who designed large structures, such as office buildings and churches, rather than those who designed residences? These particular groups of people became involved in municipal reform because of desires peculiar to the goals and values of the particular segment of the profession in which they worked.

The patrician liberals of the latter half of the nineteenth century have been described as an example of the "reform" movement. But the limited treatment of this group, already carried out by Ari Hoogenboom in his study of civil service reform and Geoffrey Blodgett in his treatment of the Mugwumps and the Democratic party in Massachusetts, indicates that patrician liberals can be understood only in terms of their particular situation.[31] The whole problem awaits a full-length treatment. It should take the form of a collective biography of several hundred members of the group and a complete picture of their historical situation: their competition for leadership with the new industrial entrepreneurs, the changes experienced in their residential communities as they underwent inmigration from other socioeconomic groups, the challenge to their intellectual world of literature and art by new ideas, their relationship to the new political leaders arising in the Republican party. The patrician liberals form a fairly coherent political movement; one must understand their political role not in terms of the sweep of reform in general but of their unique historical situation in particular.

Two different approaches are possible in situational analysis. The first starts with the results of behavior, with institutions, public policies, movements, ideas, or broad social changes and traces these back into the human situation from which these emerged so as to determine their roots in human behavior. What, for example, was distinctive about the particular people involved in a particular political party or faction, such as the Gold Democrats or the Anti-Masons, and how were they different from those involved in other

31. Hoogenboom, *op. cit.*; Geoffrey Blodgett, *The Gentle Reformers: Massachusetts Democrats in the Cleveland Era*, (Cambridge, Mass., 1966).

parties? How were Federalists different from anti-Federalists; Bull Moosers from regular Republicans? What particular groups were adversely affected by the "distribution revolution" at the turn of the twentieth century, and how did they, as a result, react? What precise groups were helped and what were hurt by the NRA codes; which ones wanted restrictions on the work day and which did not, which higher minimum wages and which lower? Who supported the prohibition movement, and who opposed it? Which particular groups in local, provincial America accepted cosmopolitan ideas and thereby changed their patterns of life, and which ones resisted these innovations? Who were involved in the social gospel emphasis or the antitrust movement in the Progressive Era? Who interpreted the post-1929 innovations in public affairs as socialism, and who did not? In each of these cases a product of human behavior, whether it be ideological, economic, or political, is traced back to its situational roots.

The direction of analysis can be reversed by starting with the human situation and determining the peculiar types of resulting conceptions, values, and action. In the pre–Civil War years did the economic leaders of the East behave differently from those in the newer, trans-Appalachian areas? Did Lutherans from the eighteenth-century migrations to Pennsylvania react differently to antislavery agitation from those in the nineteenth-century migrations to the Midwest? How did the value orientation in the sectarian college in New York and Michigan in the latter nineteenth-century differ from that in the new state universities? What were the peculiar views and objectives of small businessmen in the twentieth-century world of mammoth corporations? Did academics in small and relatively isolated colleges in the mid-twentieth century behave differently from those in large, cosmopolitan universities; those in New England institutions differently from those in the Midwest in the Progressive Era? Did the rural and small-town American view the world and behave differently from the city dweller? Was the economic outlook of New England in 1910 different from that of the Midwest, the South, the Mountain states, or the Far West? Did Negroes vote in distinctive patterns in the 1930s? What distinctive approach to public affairs was manifested by the Eastern European émigré who came to the United States after World War II?

It should be clear, once more, that I am not speaking about formally organized groups alone. Such groups may exist in the form of country clubs, trade associations, the Sons of Italy, labor unions, professional education organizations, or associations to protect civil liberties. But social groupings may be informal as well as formal, growing out of common circumstances and shared attitudes. To the social analyst these patterns of life are just as important as, perhaps even more important than formal groups. The latter are more easily observable, but they are not necessarily more significant; they serve as clues to patterns of group behavior rather than exhaustive descriptions of it. Social data which describe income levels, occupations, places of residence, religion, nationality, education, or race help to define continuing and persistent shared attitudes which are above and beyond the formal organizations themselves. The explicit assumption is simply that societies are not homogeneous but heterogeneous, and that the values and behavior of each subdivision are understandable in terms of the particular characteristics and experience, the particular situation of the people involved.

It should also be clear that in relating behavior to situation I am not referring to a "self-interest" type of thought and action which is so prevalent in the liberal analysis of history and popular thought. To argue that the ideas or actions of a group cannot be understood apart from their particular circumstances and conditions of life is not to argue that the group deliberately weighs each action in terms of calculable benefits. Each group inevitably relates broad questions of public affairs to its own particular experience; it is impossible for it to act otherwise. This is especially true of the "disinterested" person, so common on the "good" side of the traditionally defined liberal-conservative political struggle. For the "disinterested" person's definition of the public good is inevitably a limited one, understandable in terms of his own particular experience and his own particular conception of the good society which arises from that experience. That view may differ widely from the views of others. Groups act not from "self-interest" but from "limited perspectives," from conceptions of their society and themselves which are bounded by their own experience and therefore directly related to it.

Leaders of the conservation movement in the Progressive Era, for example, clearly did not act from "self-interest" in the usual sense of the term.[32] They did not self-consciously calculate benefits to themselves. Yet they most assuredly sought to define public policy in their own terms. The assumptions of science and technology bounded their world. This prompted them to define ultimate values in terms of efficiency, and "progress" as the degree to which the goals of efficiency were realized. It made them favor manipulative decision making by experts and made them suspicious of the give and take of a more pluralistic political system. It caused them to define democracy in terms of equality of benefits rather than equality of political power. Their world view was limited and circumscribed by the world within which that view was formed, and such a view, rather than bringing them more closely in touch with other segments of the political order, actually alienated them from it. They must be described, therefore, not as the instruments of universal impulses, but as particular people with particular experiences proposing particular policies. Their behavior involved not "self-interest" but "limited perspectives."

The rationale for a situational analysis of politics lies in a focus on man's conscious life, an attempt to understand human perspectives and human conceptions of the world and to relate political life to those particular perspectives. One of man's most basic motives is the search for clarity and understanding of the world around him, to be secure ideologically within that world, and to exercise influence over it. The mere drive for understanding is a political drive, because understanding is a prerequisite for control. But such an impulse for understanding does not take place within either a vacuum or a context of universal experience of reason, spirit, or good will. It occurs within particular environments, in situations peculiar to the experience of a particular group of men. And the particular perspective of particular people can be understood most fully in terms of the particular situation in which it develops and is played out. The context of such an approach is that of an active, creative, searching mind, formulated and working within the framework of an inevitably limited human experience.

32. Samuel P. Hays, *Conservation and the Gospel of Efficiency* (Cambridge, Mass., 1959), 1–4, 261–276.

IV
Evidence and Conceptualization

THE social analysis of American political history has been retarded by the historian's unimaginative preoccupation with traditional types of evidence and his consequent failure to conceptualize in working with that evidence. Historians are empiricists *par excellence* to a degree which distorts rather than clarifies the past. By feeling that they cannot "go beyond the evidence" they in fact permit the weight of historical evidence, without discrimination, to impose itself on their studies and to determine the categories of historical description. Evidence may well distort history, because that which is readily available may not be significant and that which is highly significant may be entirely unavailable or difficult to secure and organize in usable form. Too often historical studies are chosen simply because evidence is at hand and can be worked up into a coherent study within a relatively short period of time. Such studies may not be high in a scale of significance and frequently impose upon the author a difficult burden of demonstrating, often in a final chapter and often with considerable strain, their larger relevance.

Progress in any field of knowledge comes from constant interaction between conceptualization and evidence. The initial definition of a problem may well come through being impressed with the nature of particular evidence, but it might well also come through exposure to a concept derived from a more theoretical work, a contemporary study, or treatment of an entirely different geographical area. Such ideas might direct one's attention to facets of history and types of historical evidence never before encountered. Evidence may then modify the original concept considerably, but the concept has played a significant role in providing insight into a heretofore unobserved facet of the past. Too complete immersion in evidence may well dull the historical imagination so as to obscure other possible ways of looking at the past, and may require a complete shift from evidence into more abstract concepts in order to free one's imagination for a fresh set of observations. These concepts may prove to be false, but far more is gained by testing an hypothesis which may be either true or false than by accumulating evidence which does not provide significant historical understanding.

Several types of evidence have distorted the study of American political history. Each implicitly involves assumptions about the nature of society or social change which limit the historian's angle of vision or fix his attention upon particular facets of society and obscure others. More important for our purposes here, this evidence encourages a way of looking at history quite different from that involved in social analysis and in fact predisposes the historian to turn away from an examination of political structure, political process, and the human situation. It becomes, therefore, an impediment rather than an aid to research.

Much evidence is institutional evidence. It is the product of a particular institution such as a church, business, trade union, nationality group, government agency, professional society, college, university, or public welfare association. Whether in the form of published reports or newspapers and newsmagazines or more ephemeral descriptions of activities, this evidence is produced to establish the image which the institution feels desirable to maintain before its contemporary public. The limitations in its use by historians, however, lie in the fact that institutions and their participants are frequently not explicitly self-conscious about many of the social processes in which they are involved. The very factors in which a social analyst is most interested might also be unexpressed assumptions or privately discussed conditions which are not explicitly recorded in "external evidence." Some of these might be self-consciously discussed in "internal" evidence available in private manuscripts, but others might be observable only in indirect ways.

The history of education, for example, is intimately interwoven with changing political values and perspectives.[33] But this connection is not made clear so long as the history of education focuses primarily on the growth in numbers of students, teachers, and schools and in amount of financial support; the changing policies and practices of pedagogy; or the changing relationships between local, state, and federal educational administration. These problems occupy the attention of the historian primarily because they are the matters about which "external" evidence, readily available, is concerned. But education reveals far more about social structure and

33. An excellent approach to the history of education is Bernard Bailyn, *Education in the Forming of American Society* (Chapel Hill, 1960).

social change than this evidence would suggest. For it plays a significant role in vertical social mobility on the part of both students and teachers; in horizontal geographical mobility from local and restricted communities into more cosmopolitan and varied environments; in elaborating the administrative structure of modern systematization, its reliance upon trained experts, and its division of groups between the managers and the managed; and in either transmitting or modifying values and culture from one generation to the next.

These facets of the history of education concern social structures and processes of change which are rarely made explicit by those involved in education. Relevant evidence, therefore, is not directly available in those sources which institutions produce. Hence historians have rarely investigated them. Yet the sensitive analyst, either by a more acute attention to the indirect implications of formal institutional evidence, or by the discovery of new and more appropriate sources, can find material relevant to these problems. Consciousness of the significance of those questions, however, will arise only insofar as the student develops through his own imagination or through ideas from other disciplines concepts about social mobility, local-cosmopolitan relationships, or administration as a process of decision making.

Without such conceptual imagination, moreover, the connection between education and political life remains obscure. Once the conceptual framework is shifted to types of human relationships involved in education, then the connection becomes clear and the possibilities of exploring common types of relationships become sharper. The upward social mobility of both students and teachers is closely related to the changing political attitudes which social mobility produces. The systematization in the administrative process in education is an integral part of the entire process of systematization which pervades almost every realm of modern society.[34] The parochial or cosmopolitan character of educational institutions is a specific example of the same dimension in political life. The social analysis of political life in its broadest scope, therefore, requires a more imaginative set of concepts, freed from the limitations of institutional evidence.

34. Raymond E. Callahan, *Education and the Cult of Efficiency* (Chicago, 1962).

Ideological evidence has been as powerful a factor as institutional evidence in limiting our range of historical vision. Traditional political history has been severely narrowed by a preoccupation with evidence about the ideas expressed in party platforms, by candidates in campaign speeches, and by legislators in congressional debate. For the political historian works under a powerful impulse to organize this evidence into logical categories of ideas and then to assume that these categories can be applied directly to the nonideological world. If the political protagonists argued that the political world was divided primarily between the business community on the one hand and the mass of the people on the other, then this was so. Almost unconsciously the historian of ideas is tempted to transfer his conceptions about the structure of ideas to assertions about the structure of society. Such a process has drastically limited rather than expanded the possibilities of understanding society and social change by diverting attention from nonideological conceptual frameworks which relate more to what people did rather than what they said.

The "people versus the interests" framework of liberal historians, which has dominated the interpretation of the years since mid-nineteenth century, is a major case in point. It has obscured such plausible hypotheses that the Republican party was during the years from 1850 to 1893 a cultural entity rather than an instrument of big business, that the tariff was an understandable and natural product of working-class demands rather than an imposition upon them by employers, that the post–Civil War years were rich with grass-roots political conflict rather than decades of sterile shadow boxing in the spirit of nineteenth-century "me-tooism," that the major question concerning the elections of the 1890s is why the Republican party secured such enormous gains in 1894 and held the loyalty of these voters for over a decade and a half, that the "public" regulation of private business is most often a case of certain segments of private business seeking to use government to control other segments of private business, that reforms in municipal government came not from the lower and middle classes but from the dominant business and professional elements of the community.

The liberal ideological framework which has dominated the treatment of this period of political history has, like a "steel chain of ideas," bound our historical imagination to a limited set of problems. One of the major tasks of the social analysis of political history now is to break through this limited vision by means of looking at new types of evidence and delving into new conceptual alternatives. We need especially to understand the sharp difference between ideology and practice, between what people say they do and what they do. This is not to say that ideology is unimportant; it is, of course, a powerful factor in any historical situation. It is merely to say that the categories derived from ideological evidence are no safe guide to an understanding of political practice.

The personal record is a third type of evidence which is abundant to the point of being overwhelming and which by its very weight unconsciously distorts the writing of history. Biographies, memoirs, and personal manuscripts are one of the most widely used sources of political evidence. Yet these sources give rise to a conception of political history as a network of personal relationships among a few leaders and party politics as a process of interpersonal maneuvering. Such a focus precludes attention to the wider structure of political life or to political process. It draws attention away from such evidence as popular voting, legislative roll calls, or the data about hundreds of political leaders who left few manuscripts but about whom statistical information is available. In recent years the history profession has not considered political studies to be adequate unless they are based upon a wide coverage of personal manuscript sources. At the same time, however, it has not demanded equal use of these other types of evidence. The great concern with personal manuscripts has channeled interest into a narrow range of evidence and, consequently, into a narrow range of problems. It has created a weight of interest and preoccupation, a climate of opinion, which is relatively unreceptive to the social analysis of political history.

The impact of individuals upon larger events may well be great, but it cannot be demonstrated, nor can the precise interaction between individuals and larger affairs be determined, merely by observing the behavior of individuals or recounting their public actions or their reputations. For decision makers work within persistent patterns of social relationships which establish an environment of action not readily manipulable by individual decisions. Concentration upon personal manuscripts has almost precluded a concern for the reconstruction of these social patterns. This is not so much a product of explicit and deliberate choice in social theory but of almost accidental immersion in a particular type of evidence which by its own weight establishes the historian's assumptions concerning social theory and the limits of his vision. Preoccupation with any type of evidence can so dull the historical imagination. It can be overcome only if one is willing to conceptualize at some distance from the evidence, look at new and different types of data, and then select evidence to test particular hypotheses.

Perhaps the most significant and widespread type of evidence which limits the historical imagination is that represented by sensational events. The historian's attention is almost naturally drawn to those events which gave rise to dramatic newspaper coverage or which aroused some unusual degree of sensationalism. If they were in the headlines, they were in the minds of most people, it is argued; their prominence in the historical record indicates accurately their prominence in the consciousness of people in society as a whole. Such episodes provide a clue to the preoccupations of the "average man," who is the object of study in "social history," and therefore to the more fundamental processes of political life.

The sensational event, however, provides few such clues. Surely our picture of the history of workingmen in the latter part of the nineteenth century, as one historian has recently pointed out, has been distorted by concentration upon the sensational labor upheavals of the railroad strikes of 1877, the Haymarket riot, the Pullman strike, and the Homestead strike.[35] Far more significant features of that period of history are to be found in the less public, less sensational records, in reports of industrial commissions, in judicial proceedings, in local newspapers, and in the census returns. Without these the meaning of the event is impossible to determine. Moreover, preoccupation with event and episode produces a picture of relationships over time which are sequences of isolated incidents tied together purely by chronology rather than continuing patterns of human relationships. The sensational event provides few clues as to the nature of social structure or process, or the kinds of groups

35. Gutman, *op. cit.*

into which a society is divided, their interconnections, and their changes over time. The sensational event dictates a certain structure to history which is almost structureless, save the accidental juxtaposition of those events in a time sequence. Those who become immersed in event history, in fact, by the very weight of their preoccupation are prone to deny the existence of systematic human relationships and to distrust conceptualizations about social structure and social process.

The social analysis of political history requires a new formulation of the problems of political history, and this, in turn, requires that the historical imagination be freed from the limitations within which traditional evidence has confined it. Instead of being overcome by the weight of evidence, of merely organizing it into logical categories, one should define the elements of political structure and political process which are important to investigate and then search for evidence which has a bearing on those problems. This approach, in fact, will lead the political historian to vast amounts of evidence, abundantly available, which he has never tapped. For lying in unused archival sources there are innumerable records with which the social analyst can reconstruct political history in a sharply new and different way.

V

Quantitative Data

THE most promising current methodological innovation in the social analysis of political history is the use of quantitative data. These data are far more plentiful than we have been accustomed to think. In a host of scattered archives are masses of information about popular voting, legislative voting, demography, and thousands of political leaders who left no papers. This evidence is bulky and difficult to use because of the enormous task of compiling and presenting it in manageable form. But it is, nonetheless, of enormous value. Moreover, there is not only an increasing desire to use it but a growing ability to cope with it through new techniques of data compilation, storage, and retrieval.

One of the most important types of this evidence consists of popular election data, which constitute the only comprehensive information in documentary sources approximating a record of public opinion. Many of these data have been published in state manuals,[36] and often in the form of precinct as well as county returns, but many are also available in a variety of state reports, city directories, or city council minutes, and great quantities lie in state and local archives and newspapers. Recent investigations have made clear that a very high percentage of past election returns are extant in one form or another and that the task of making these available for use is only a matter of time, effort, and funds.[37]

Many other types of quantitative data are also available. Substantially complete legislative voting data at the federal and state levels have been published in the *Congressional Record* and its predecessor volumes and in state Senate and House Journals. Newspapers and city council proceedings contain the votes on issues in city councils. Vast amounts of demographic data concerning economic, religious, educational, and ethnic characteristics of counties and even wards are available in federal, state, and local censuses, in municipal and county archives, and in the compilations of private associations.[38] The microfilm publication of the federal manuscript population schedules, especially those from 1850 to 1880, presents untold opportunities for the political historian, for here is information concerning every individual in the United States, by name, where he lives (in cities even the precise street and house number), his age, his occupation, where he was born, where his mother and father were born, and in some years the value of his personal and real property. Several students have already used this material to determine patterns of social mobility; it can be used with equal value in describing the ethnocultural and socioeconomic composition of voting subdivisions.

The scattered but extensive information in county and municipal archives is formidable to use, but can provide far more insight

36. For a bibliography of state manuals see Charles Press and Oliver Williams, *State Manuals, Blue Books and Election Results* (Berkeley, 1962).

37. Walter Dean Burnham, "Pilot Study: Recovery of Historical Election Data" (mimeo), prepared for the Committee on Political Behavior, Social Science Research Council (1962). See also Walter Dean Burnham, "Sources of Historical Election Data: A Preliminary Bibliography," Bibliographic Series No. 10, Institute for Community Development and Services, Michigan State University (East Lansing, 1963).

38. A bibliography of state censuses is Henry J. Dubester, *State Censuses* (Government Printing Office, 1948).

into the dynamics of social change than we have had in the past. Economic records of taxes, real estate assessments, and value of personal property have been used in the study of Early American history. There is no reason, save that of time and cost, why the same kind of data should not be used far more extensively in investigating the nineteenth and twentieth centuries. An excellent example of the possibilities is the study by Sam Warner, Jr., of the process of suburbanization in Boston, *Streetcar Suburbs*.[39] Through the examination of 23,000 building permits issued for Roxbury, West Roxbury, and Dorchester, Massachusetts, between 1870 and 1900, Mr. Warner has presented the first precise picture of the process of urban outward migration and vertical mobility from blue- to white-collar occupations. His study is a model in the imaginative use of local quantitative records for the analysis of social processes.

Equally extensive is the source material concerning individual political leaders. Historians have only recently undertaken studies of groups of political leaders—as contrasted with individuals—in order to determine patterns in the origin and nature of political leadership. For the most part confined to national figures, these studies have relied heavily upon information drawn from existing biographical compilations or from personal manuscripts. They have, therefore, been limited in coverage. But information is available in great abundance about tens and hundreds of thousands of political leaders at the state and local level. City directories indicate the occupation and address of every adult inhabitant; they reveal changes in both occupation and residence within and between generations, and therefore demonstrate patterns of social mobility. Social registers provide ample information about upper-class groups to examine fully a facet of political life hardly investigated. Manuscript census returns, both federal and state, provide sources which permit an extensive analysis of political leadership for some years. Such sources make available an almost unbelievable amount of information about individual political leaders which permits types of collective-biography analyses hardly even imagined in the not too distant past.

From these types of evidence one can reconstruct the character-

---

39. Sam B. Warner, Jr., *Streetcar Suburbs* (Cambridge, Mass., 1962).

istics of communities at the grass-roots level. This can be done especially with ward and precinct data. For although counties are rarely homogeneous in either social or economic characteristics, many wards and precincts are relatively so. At this level one is able to isolate communities of German Catholics, of coal miners, of lumbermen, of the upper class, of Quakers, or of Scotch Highland Presbyterians, to name only a few. Since election data are available for these same ward and precinct units, the analysis of voting patterns can be made fairly precise. At the same time, the abundant personal data enable one to establish family ties and family relationships from one generation to the next. Patterns of social mobility, intermarriage, and occupational and educational changes can be observed within specific contexts so that the resulting generalizations are fairly exact.

Because such studies are possible, the increased use of quantitative data should give rise to a renewed interest in both local history and genealogy by professional historians. Mr. Warner has amply illustrated the possibilities that urban local history holds for the analysis of broad social change. The genealogical compilations in the Eastern states pertaining to families of the seventeenth and eighteenth centuries have provided an enormous amount of information for those who wish to undertake more detailed studies of Early American history. Similar genealogical collections for the trans-Appalachian region are badly needed. The more traditional political historian is well aware of his indebtedness to the editor of personal manuscripts of political leaders. Perhaps in the future we will have as kind a regard for the person who undertakes the equally thankless task of compiling basic data about local communities or painfully constructs family histories.

The major problem with which this material confronts historians is the task of making it usable, or reducing vast amounts of data to comparable quantitative units, and of presenting it in forms which facilitate analysis. Although perhaps 90 percent or more of all popular election data ever recorded is still available, little is collected in one place and even less is available in the form of percentages. Researchers have neither the time nor the facilities to bring the data together in proper form, and although studies of relatively small geographical areas over very short periods of time are feasible, larger ones covering more election units and defining longer trends, or comparative studies of different types of electorates, are now impossible to undertake. But the development of new technologies and the increasing interest in financing their use provide an opportunity for solving some of these problems. A project is now under way to do this for popular voting; if successful, as it appears it will be, the same approach can be applied to other data.

Some three years ago several historians and political scientists formally requested the Social Science Research Council to take up the project of collecting, computing, and making available historical popular election data. The council, in turn, asked W. Dean Burnham, who had compiled county returns for presidential elections in the nineteenth century, to survey the problem. This investigation, in the summer of 1962, revealed the vast extent of the available data, and the council then provided funds for Mr. Burnham to make a more extensive and precise determination of the sources of data. This he did during the 1963-64 academic year from his location at the Survey Research Center at the University of Michigan. The work moved so well that by the fall of 1963 attention turned to the actual collection and computation of data.

At the same time the Survey Research Center expressed an interest in popular election data. Established originally to collect survey data through interviewing and questionnaire techniques, the center began to collect documentary census data as well, and the extension into historical election data seemed to be a natural evolution of its concerns. This development tied in closely with the center's changing role in the academic world. In 1961 it helped to create the Consortium for Political Research. It invited academic institutions to join in annual financial support of the new institution and in turn receive political data which it would collect in its library, and to participate in summer training seminars at the University of Michigan. Originally established for the use of political scientists, the consortium could readily draw in those in other disciplines interested in political research.

In late 1963 these two developments began to converge. The transfer of data to Ann Arbor was tackled by historians themselves. In January 1964 the American Historical Association established the Ad Hoc Committee to Collect the Basic Quantitative Data of

American Political History. Within three months committees in forty-six states were photocopying materials in their own states to be sent to the consortium. The original project called for election returns since 1824 at the county level for the races of president, governor, and U.S. senator and representative, as well as other state-wide races in years when these elections were held. The project is now over 90 percent complete. The response from historians has been gratifying, for it reveals a considerable interest long felt to exist but now confirmed. Meanwhile, the consortium secured $144,000 from the National Science Foundation to process the data and to support a project director. It seems feasible, therefore, to anticipate that the county data now being collected will be computed, processed, stored, and available for research in about a year.

The success of the initial project has encouraged the AHA Committee to move on to other tasks. It now plans to collect data concerning county elections prior to 1824, primaries of all kinds, and state referenda. It will provide for the collection of minor civil division returns—ward, township, precinct—not on a comprehensive scale but where they are needed for specific research projects. It has under way discussions which will lead to the collection of the demographic data needed to interpret election returns—nationality, race, religion, production, employment, income, communications, education, transportation, and degree of urban or rural population. Steps are already being taken to bring together congressional roll-call votes, both those already tabulated in earlier projects and those not yet tabulated, and to make them available to researchers through modern data-processing techniques. An integral part of this project will involve more extensive and more readily accessible biographical information about legislators. It is hoped that legislative data for states can be developed as well, although on a more selective basis, in response to immediate research needs.

With this large amount of quantitative data available to us, we can be optimistic about the degree to which our knowledge of both political structure and political process will be advanced. At the same time, however, let us make no claims that the millennium is around the corner. Many items of needed quantitative data will not be available, and many facets of political life, highly important for social analysis, cannot be investigated through their use. Moreover, quantitative data will often lead to confusion rather than clarity simply because, like other data, they will be used to disprove more than to prove, to qualify and hedge, and to render conclusions which the methodological purists will disavow. Despite all this, the fact remains that the use of quantitative data constitutes at the present time one of the most promising opportunities for political historians, and the social analysis of political history, in which these data will be of considerable aid, is the area in which we can currently make the largest gains in our knowledge of the political past.

A further word of caution. As the collection of quantitative data increases and as support for and popularity of their use grow, we must approach them with discrimination. It is as fruitless to accept as important every piece of quantitative data as to accept every piece of nonquantitative data. Statistics can become as dead a weight, as distorting an influence as can the mass of personal manuscript evidence in our archives. No matter of what kind, evidence must be used selectively, and unless the criterion of selection, unless the conceptual framework which defines the problem is defensible, the evidence will not be selected with adequate discrimination. As it is not justifiable to write a biography because a man's papers are easily available, so it is not justifiable to devote resources and energy to the analysis of statistical data because funds are available and it is the thing to do. The basic element in any methodology is to make sure that it is relevant to the task at hand. Methodology should follow from rather than dictate the nature of the problem to be studied.

VI
Comparative Analysis

THE social analysis of political history facilitates and stimulates comparative study, the examination of apparently similar phenomena under different circumstances or of differences in the incidence of those phenomena. As a method of analysis comparative study sharpens distinctions which are otherwise not apparent. A more traditional and formal approach fails to identify such comparisons and contrasts because it does not give rise to analytical categories with respect to which distinctions and similarities can be observed. An emphasis on structure and process, however, focusing on patterns of human relationships, brings such common categories into sharp relief and permits comparative analysis.

The phenomenon of human migration illustrates these possibilities. For decades historians have studied both the westward movement and immigration from Europe, but rarely has anyone even suggested that these might fruitfully be analyzed comparatively. Even more rarely has anyone suggested that they both might be explored in relation to other migrations. For American history has witnessed four major types of human migration: from the East to the West, from Europe to America, from rural to urban America, and from the central city to the suburb. All of these have in common the element of physical movement of people, but all of them also involve social processes. Who migrated and why? What was the impact of migration on the community from which it came? What effect did the process of migration have upon the social organization of the migrants? To what degree did migration involve an attempt to preserve a past social organization, to create a new one, or to escape from confining social patterns? What kinds of new social organization did the migrants create in their new residence? Insight into any of these questions would be enhanced by observing the same process in different migration contexts.

A comparative study of migrations in terms of their impact on political structure and political process would shed considerable light upon our political history. The political complexion of many communities depends upon the political attitudes formed by migrants in their previous location. Yet, the nature of the migration produces different effects. The stability of party affiliation in many areas of the country in the nineteenth century grew out of the stability of ethnic and cultural attitudes transplanted and preserved in new areas; this, in turn, depended upon the ability of migrating groups to maintain their social and therefore political attitudes from erosion in a more rational-secular society. Some migrations, however, involved individuals rather than groups, a process of breaking away from traditional patterns and considerable vertical as well as horizontal mobility in which the individual went through a rapid transformation of his values, sought to achieve a higher class position, and developed different political attitudes. This might well have been the case with migration from rural America to cities and migration from the central city to the suburbs. These speculations suggest some of the possibilities of a comparative study of migration for political history.

A second possibility for comparative study lies in the political impact of depressions. The two most violent depression-caused political upheavals about which we know anything at all are those of 1893 and 1929.[40] Both have striking similarities. That of 1893 had a more dramatic and sudden impact, the voting shifts it produced being confined to the elections of 1893 and 1894. The 1929 depression, on the other hand, did not produce its full effect on the voting public in 1930 or even in 1932; its effect was spread over a period of a half-dozen years. Both were violent reactions to the party in power, the Democrats in 1893 and the Republicans in 1929. Both led to long-term shifts in voter preferences, toward the Republicans in the 1890s and the Democrats in the 1930s.

Each of these political changes went through a similar three-phased process. The Democratic gains of the 1930s involved initially a shift of ethnic voters in 1928 under the leadership of Al Smith. As a result of the Depression, however, a second phase took place, involving a shift of all voting groups toward the Democratic party and extending further the urban majorities which Smith established. By 1934 still a third stage developed in which lower-than-median income groups shifted even more strongly Democratic, and more-than-median income groups moved back toward their more Republican leanings. A similar sequence took place in the 1890s, but with different parties being the beneficiaries of the shifts in stages one and two. The Democrats in 1890 made major congressional and state gains. These seem to have arisen from the intense cultural conflict of the preceding decade which came from reaction against the political activities of evangelical protestantism in such forms as anti–foreign language and prohibition laws. In 1892 this shift was a major element in Cleveland's victory. When the 1893 depression inaugurated a second stage, a massive revolt against the party in power, it reversed rather than continued the political trend of four years earlier, producing a sharp break in the pattern rather than a cumulative

40. I am indebted to Paul Kleppner for the development of data concerning the 1894 and 1896 elections.

effect. The election of 1894 corresponded to the election of 1932 in that voters of all kinds shifted sharply toward the party out of power. And the election of 1896 corresponded to that of 1934 in that a marked polarization of voting took place, with a major segment of voters continuing to shift toward the dominant party, the Republicans, while another large segment reverted to its previous loyalties.

The political impact of other depressions is not clear because the effect of such crises as those of 1819, 1837, 1857, and 1873 on voting patterns is known only in the most general way. The shifts might have been less dramatic or might not have involved the juxtaposition of both ethnocultural and socioeconomic changes in close temporal proximity. Therefore, one cannot now define the kinds of comparative problems which would arise from such an approach to these earlier elections. But the similarities and differences in the depressions of 1893 and 1929 suggest what could be done.

Urban political structure might well be still a third possibility for comparative analysis. The political leadership of upper classes, for example, differed in different cities. In the nineteenth century Eastern-seaboard city, upper classes played a major role in political life. Although some aspects of this phenomenon have been studied, such as in Ari Hoogenboom's work on civil service reformers, its development as an extensive political movement has not. More important, the contrast between these cities and those west of the Alleghenies, such as Buffalo, Pittsburgh, Cleveland, and Cincinnati, has not been explored. Here the upper class was not deeply involved in either the Liberal Republican movement, civil service reform, or other manifestations of Eastern genteel reform. Here the upper class probably had shallower roots, weaker traditions of civil leadership, and fuller appreciation of the role of the new industrial labor force than was the case in the seaboard cities.

Reforms in the structure of municipal government around the turn of the twentieth century could also be better understood through comparative study. In all cities there appears to have been an upward shift in the location of decision making. For systematization and organization in industrial society gave rise to integration in political, economic, and ideological life.[41] Business and professional

41. Hays, "The Politics of Reform."

leaders who carried out these processes in their private affairs were in the forefront of the movement to systematize government and to shift decision making into the hands of fewer people with more expert technical advice. This entire movement reveals processes of social integration in the evolution of cities and especially in the evolution of political relationships. Did these occur in the same way in cities in different geographical locations, of different size, of different degrees of cultural homogeneity? What different forms did the drive for political integration take? Did political integration proceed in roughly the same degree in all cities? Comparative study of this kind should create far more insight into the larger processes of urban social organization.

One of the most significant larger comparative studies concerns the origins and nature of the different systems of decision making which have arisen in the course of American history. Three of these could come under study: the political parties which grew up in the late eighteenth century; the nonpartisan economic politics which developed in the late nineteenth century; and the systematized, administrative decision making which emerged at about the same time. Each of these is a distinct political system, each involving different processes by which decisions affecting large numbers of people are made. Each grew up to express political forces which other systems could not adequately express. Each involves different political clienteles, different environments for operation and different methods, and distinct conceptions of what a political system is and should be.

In *Political Parties in a New Nation*, William Chambers develops a scheme for analyzing the functions of political parties which could be applied to other political systems as well.[42] The political party must mobilize large numbers of voters for the election of national leaders; this new setting of national decision making greatly broadened the scope, the problems, and the tactics of political action. It required the development of a political ideology, for example, as the only way in which many diverse groups could be communicated with and focused on a single goal.

This method of decision making became a millstone around the

---

42. William N. Chambers, *Political Parties in a New Nation* (New York, 1963).

necks of those specialized economic groups in labor, industry, and agriculture who in the late nineteenth century wished to stress a particular legislative policy. Both their clientele and their objectives were more limited. They did not wish to be drawn into a political party in which many diverse groups vied for expression, in which their own goals would be watered down and their resources dissipated for political aims in which they had no direct interest. These groups, therefore, established political forces resting largely upon their economic organizations—trade unions, trade associations, farm cooperatives—which gave them economic bases from which to finance and organize political representation. Their clienteles were now disciplined through their economic organizations, rather than approached through ideology, and their tactics were attuned to legislative infighting rather than mass voter appeal.

The administrative process involved a still different clientele and a different method of decision making.[43] It arose from an attempt to coordinate and systematize, to bring together a great variety of factors for a single end. Those involved in it considered both the representative system of political parties and the log rolling of economic groups to be wasteful and ineffective, incapable of providing the required centralization of decision making. The administrative system, therefore, needed to develop no ideology or method of give-and-take compromise for its immediate functioning. It served to draw an ever-widening range of factors into a single orbit of influence and a single point of control, and to establish an orderly flow of influence between individuals in the hierarchy from the top down, on a person-to-person basis. Its tactics changed when it could not incorporate into its orbit of decision making factors it wished to control. Thus, it often bargained with labor on equal terms and fashioned ideology through the medium of public relations to influence public opinion. These processes, however, were viewed only as extensions of a tightly knit, centralized system of decision making into a larger arena.

Examples of questions which are susceptible of comparative analysis could be multiplied many times. They include such specific problems as the legislative behavior of moderate and conservative

43. Waldo, *op. cit.*

Republicans since the 1930s; the impact of new immigrant workers on the political life of rural raw-material-producing communities, communities along developing lines of transportation, or cities; the leadership of Whigs and Democrats in the 1840s; the voting patterns of Germans in Pennsylvania and Germans in Missouri in the years after 1850; the different political environment of the South and the West in the late nineteenth century. Or it could involve more general concerns such as the relationships between political ideology and political practice at different times, the interaction between grass-roots and national-level strata of political activity within the political parties, or the relationship between political elites and political masses. However specific or general, such comparative studies can be defined far more easily and thoroughly through the social analysis of politics. For political relationships are far more susceptible of comparison and contrast than are isolated episodes and events or formal characteristics. The social analysis of political history, therefore, brings into focus a host of comparative problems which under a more conventional treatment remain almost totally obscure.

VII
History and the Social Sciences

THE social analysis of political history involves a close relationship between history and the social sciences. Both concepts and methods developed in the social sciences are extremely useful to any historian who wishes to undertake political analysis within the guidelines proposed in this paper. Yet history is not a social science, and the relationship between the two should be one of mutual cooperation rather than fusion. The social analysis of historical change requires not only that the historian be willing to borrow from the social sciences, but that he be clear about what he should borrow and what he should not. For political history has suffered from too much influence by the social sciences in some respects, as well as from too little in other. The social sciences are cast in an entirely different framework from the study of history, and the two should approach each other with a willingness to cooperate when their interests dovetail and an acceptance of disagreement when their interests diverge.

By failing to utilize the social sciences, historians have been hampered in carrying out the very task which they presume to pursue. For the study of history is the attempt to reconstruct the process by which societies change over time. The emphasis is on society as a whole, not isolated segments of it, and broad changes over time, not episodes. The social sciences have developed more conceptual frameworks through which these problems can be approached than have historians. Examples of such works, in addition to those cited in previous pages, include Daniel Lerner, *The Passing of Traditional Society*; Dwight Waldo, *The Administrative State*; Gerhard Lenski, *The Religious Factor*; William Kornhauser, *The Politics of Mass Society*; Ferdinand Tönnies, *Community and Society*; Seymour Lipset, *Political Man*; Robert and Helen Lynd, *Middletown*; Robert Dahl, *Who Governs?*; Maurice Stein, *The Eclipse of Community*; and scores of others.[44] Studies of the process of modernization in the non-Western world, as some of these references indicate, can be especially useful for the development of concepts about both political structure and political process.

The historian can also benefit extensively from the healthy interest in quantitative data displayed in the social sciences. The historical record contains enormous amounts of quantitative data. Its use involves no esoteric or mysterious statistical methods, but only the simplest forms of quantification, the use of absolute and relative figures, the observation of changes in relative values over time, and simple correlations. These elementary devices one would hardly dare to glorify by the term statistics. Their use involves only a willingness to take the fullest advantage of quantitative data as a major type of historical evidence.

From the social sciences, then, we can secure both ideas and techniques as to how to undertake the systematic analysis of human situations and human relationships. We can become aware of the fact that political values and political actions are not fleeting and

44. Daniel Lerner, *The Passing of Traditional Society* (Glencoe, Ill., 1962); Dwight Waldo, *The Administrative State* (New York, 1948); Gerhard Lenski, *The Religious Factor* (New York, 1961); William Kornhauser, *The Politics of Mass Society* (Glencoe, Ill., 1959); Ferdinand Tönnies, *Community and Society* (East Lansing, Mich., 1957); Seymour Lipset, *Political Man* (New York, 1960); Robert and Helen Lynd, *Middletown* (New York, 1929); Robert Dahl, *Who Governs?* (New Haven, 1961); Maurice Stein, *The Eclipse of Community* (Princeton, 1960).

capricious, but patterned in both space and time. We can develop a sensitivity to the various ingredients of political systems, to the relationship between political leaders and political followings, the interaction between ethnocultural and socioeconomic political structures, the relationship between ideology and practice, the interaction between levels of political life within political parties, the roles of parties, nonpartisan economic politics and adminstration as different types of political systems, and the relationship between parochial and cosmopolitan political life. Historical scholarship in the United States has not generated, by itself, a sensitivity to these facets of social relationships despite the fact that history professes to be concerned with society and social change. Our major current task in history is to develop this sensitivity, and one of the most effective ways it can be done is through a judicious exposure to the social sciences.

Despite all this, however, history is not a social science, for the context within which it pursues social analysis is quite different from that of the social sciences. The social sciences seek to understand the present and history the past. The concepts of the former, therefore, are intended to analyze a relatively static society, while history must develop concepts to understand change over long periods of time. As economics, sociology, and political science drift farther away from their earlier historical interests, the role of history as the discipline focusing on change over time becomes sharper. As historians borrow from the social sciences, in fact, they often find common cause with those apparent minorities in the social sciences who seek to use their discipline to understand long-run change. Within a favorable climate, however, it is relatively easy to translate concepts used to analyze contemporary society into concepts which relate to change over time. The constant interest in the time dimension, therefore, makes it imperative that the historian borrow from rather than accept fully the framework of the social sciences.

The social sciences are interested not only in understanding the present, but also in prediction and control. Their spirit is reformist. They seek to determine the present so as to change the future. They are guided by normative concepts which involve such values as the most efficient use of resources, the involvement of more citizens in the political process as informed voters, the reduction of social tension, the promotion of social welfare or public health, or the creation of a different balance between population and resources. Their major framework of analysis often is not one of how society changes, but of how certain impediments to desirable change can be overcome. The public health specialist, for example, becomes interested in the social sciences because they might help to explain, and thus better to counteract, resistance to desirable public health measures. The political scientist seeks to understand how legislative decisions are made so that legislatures can function more in accordance with his conception of what is desirable. The economist seeks to understand the urban economy so as to counteract more effectively those forces which retard economic growth.

This normative spirit has influenced the study of American political history, which has long been closely associated with political economy and sociology. Studies by political economists of the tariff, labor, or trusts, of governmental regulation or governmental reform, and by social workers of immigration, poverty, and slums, serve as major historical source materials. In using them, historians have unconsciously accepted their implicit normative definition of political relationships. The tariff involves a political struggle between what is good for the public—the economist's conception of the most efficient allocation of resources—and the selfish "interests"—those who would compromise the ideal economy. The contest for municipal reform involved the public interest—the ideal government of the political scientist—in conflict with the selfish interests of the pressure group or machine. This transfer of a normative framework into a descriptive framework, the attempt to apply concepts derived from thinking about what ought to be to concepts about what was, has long restricted the imagination of the political historian. The social analysis of political history will not proceed fully unless it is set loose from this normative framework to conceptualize freely within the context of change over time alone.

Finally, history differs markedly from the social sciences in its approach to quantitative data and statistical method. For in the attempt to claim membership in the scientific world, the social scientist has become less sensitive to problems of social analysis which those techniques cannot reach. The historian is far more aware than is the social scientist that the significance of a problem does not depend upon its susceptibility to statistical treatment. Despite the vast advances that can be made by using quantitative data, many problems in political history cannot be reached in this way. It would be tragic if historians failed to take the fullest possible advantage of the new opportunities which quantitative data and their related technology make available to us. It would be equally tragic if political historians confined themselves to such problems alone. Historical investigation should be guided by the degree to which it enhances understanding of political structure and political process rather than by the techniques of utilizing evidence. The re-creation of the past involves the construction of a mosaic in which perhaps only 25 percent of the pieces are known. With the quantitative evidence now at our disposal we can add significantly to those available pieces, but it will raise the total to scarcely more than the 50 percent level. We must still interpolate, fill in the gaps by inference, and be willing to paint a total picture with insufficient pieces. This involves an attitude toward evidence which today is not received with open arms in the social sciences.

Political history offers a rich opportunity for the study of the past. Its concern for the variety of perspectives and values which contend for dominance inevitably draws it toward an understanding of different human situations which are limited by the finite scope of human pespective. At the same time it seeks to determine the patterns of relationships, of dominance and subordination which develop among these groups. Since every area of human life involves the desire of some to influence others and inequalities in the distribution of the ability to command that influence, the range of political life is as broad as the scope of society itself, rather than limited to particular institutions. Political history, thus conceived, can well restore itself as the major integrative context of history. But it cannot perform this function unless it undergoes profound changes. It must greatly broaden its perspective to encompass the full range of value conflicts throughout society; it must develop concepts concerning structure and process and focus more directly on patterns of human relationships; and it must be willing to use the vast store of available quantitative data. With these shifts in perspective, the future holds bright possibilities, indeed, for the study of American political history.

[4]

A Systematic Social History *

SOCIAL history has long been the most mysterious branch of the profession. While generating such new fields as intellectual, labor, cultural, and urban history, it remains a source of continual innovation. When other historical disciplines become sterile and unexciting, repeating old clichés and adding new facts to old concepts, social history remains attractive as a potential source of new answers and gives rise to a continual flow of creative ventures into new fields. Yet, at the same time, this indeterminate quality of social history renders it amorphous, undefined, and often incoherent and has obscured and retarded some of its most fruitful possibilities. For the proliferation of subject matter has held back development of conceptual framework. While giving rise to new content, social history has failed to develop its promise of bringing order into the subject matter of history as a whole.

Social history is concerned with large numbers of people and their interactions—the whole of society. To be grasped by the human mind, such broad phenomena require generalized descriptions of characteristics shared by many people. Unless social history is to be content simply with the episodic and the unique—in which case it cannot even be called *social* history—it must develop categories within which mass data (information about large numbers of inarticulate people and everyday events) can be organized and comprehended. Let us put the problem in a more extended fashion. History is the study of societies as they change over long periods of time. This focus is the context of our endeavors as historians; it lies at the root of the hunch that social history is fundamental. Social

*This essay first appeared in *American History: Retrospect and Prospect*, Edited by George Athan Billias and Gerald N. Grob. Copyright © 1971 by The Free Press, A Division of The Macmillan Company.

history, therefore, should generate concepts of social structure and social change which will enable us to organize the patterns of human relationships within past societies. Yet it has not done so. By this failure social history has fulfilled neither the promise of its own concerns nor the possibilities of its contribution to the ordering of history as a whole.

This essay will be devoted to problems of conceptualization and data development in social history. We will consider both future promise and present conditions, not the least of which is to clear away the limited vision of past assumptions. These assumptions influence our angle of vision, our views of society and social change, our selection of evidence, our entire range of forays into the past. In doing so they limit our imagination and hamper creative conceptualization. At the same time, alternative directions are emerging, to the extent that we can sort out the more from the less fruitful and can determine where the possibilities are greatest. The time is ripe for social history to struggle seriously with the conceptual needs of its discipline.

I

SOCIAL history of the United States has developed within three different contexts, each of which has stemmed from a particular historical circumstance and imposed a separate mark upon the discipline. The first consists of social history as a neglected body of information. The field arose originally within the context of an already highly developed discipline dominated by constitutional, political, and diplomatic history. Convinced that other aspects of the past should be explored, historians began to investigate a variety of topics under the general title of social history: labor, immigration, religion, ideas, cities, social reform, music and art, American Indians. These had little unity of content save that in some vague way they dealt with people. Some were lumped together; the phrases "social and economic" history or "social and intellectual" history arose to describe fields and courses. And specialized instruction developed in labor, immigration, urban, and intellectual history.[1]

1. The *History of American Life* series, edited by Arthur M. Schlesinger, Sr., and Dixon Ryan Fox (13 vols.) and published between 1927 and 1948, illustrates the range of content in early social history.

Social history, then, organized historical evidence that did not fit into previous topical categories; new bodies of information were split off from old. Human life, the assumption went, comprised distinct types of activities, each one considered by itself; as fields of inquiry became more complex, another type of human activity became a separate field of study. Historical inquiry became structured, therefore, in terms of distinct bodies of information. These "topical fields" of history constituted logical distinctions in the observable, manifest activities of man. The new fields of inquiry are still called social history, based upon the belief that a distinctive type of manifest activity justifies a separate category of history. One body of data—social life—takes its place alongside other bodies of data—economic, political, and diplomatic life.

But social history is more than distinctive content; it is, instead, a distinctive way of looking at many different kinds of content. Social history focuses on society, and society concerns the relationships among men. The key concept is relationships. Social history is concerned with human interaction, no matter what its manifest topical content, whether economic, political, religious, or intellectual. It seeks to clarify patterns in human relationships which emerge and change in the course of long-run social transformation. What characteristics do people hold in common or in distinction? What patterns of dominance and subordination, of hierarchies of value arise in any realm of life? What variations in attributes develop in beliefs, in values, in range of social contacts, in material level of living? The history of an individual personality is one thing. But social history assumes that when large numbers of people exist in relationship to each other, whether in city, region, or nation, in church, industry, school, or profession, patterns of common and distinct characteristics emerge. The task of social history is to describe and analyze these patterns.

In the twentieth century, for example, administrative systems have developed rapidly so as to constitute a major context of human life and relationships. Despite this, historians have not adopted them as a focal point of description and analysis. As a type of social organization, these systems cut across many facets of life. Historians sometimes describe single administrative systems within the separate categories of economic, religious, political, or educational history.[2] But dealt with in this way the patterns of human relationships implicit in administrative systems do not come into sharp focus; they are obscured amid the details of separate topical content. W. Lloyd Warner and associates have recently produced a more satisfactory framework for the consideration of administrative systems in the twentieth century which does cut across different cases in the economy, religion, government, and education.[3] The social historian could well take this pioneering effort in recent history to explore administrative systems as a major framework for the history of twentieth-century America.

One spin-off of social history—immigration history—has considerable promise for a broader treatment, but the potential has remained unrealized. For it has remained far too restricted to migration of Europeans to the United States. Geographical movement constitutes a focal point for the study of continuity and discontinuity in a wide variety of social institutions. To examine the process fully, however, requires that it be freed from the particular circumstances of time and place and linked with other instances of migration as a common context for investigation. Migrations from east to west within the United States, from abroad, from rural to urban areas, from the central city to the suburbs, are separate instances of a similar process. Each involves common problems for investigation. Who migrated; what happened to people in the process of migration; what happened to the communities of out-migration and those of in-migration? Social historians should consider migration as a single type of historical phenomenon which cuts across economic, political, intellectual, and religious categories of information and brings together historical data in a different framework.

We are speaking of categories of structure and change as the proper mode of organizing social history. These categories arise out of patterns of human interaction and the processes of change in those patterns. But they are invariably at odds with existing frameworks of organization because their criteria, types of structure and change, differ markedly from the criteria that have emerged in the

2. See, for example, Alfred D. Chandler, Jr., *Strategy and Structure: Chapters in the History of the Industrial Enterprise* (Cambridge, Mass., 1962).
3. W. Lloyd Warner, Darab B. Unwalla, and John H. Trimm, *Large-Scale Organizations*, vol. 1 of *The Emergent American Society* (New Haven, 1967).

past. The traditional emphasis on social history as a logically distinct body of data about separate human activities has imposed a framework upon the discipline which has determined its content and inhibited its growth as a systematic study of the patterns of long-run change in social structure. We labor under the weight of a past that casts an unimaginative shadow over the present.

Two current developments illustrate these limitations. One of the most recent spin-offs in social history is urban history, giving rise to new courses, textbooks, and monographs. For the most part, however, anything that happened in a city is considered as urban history. The activity-content, "within a city," determines the legitimacy of subject matter. Few studies have focused on the most important characteristics of cities—their patterns of social structure and changes in those patterns. Cities are cases of intensive human interaction; they display patterns of organization, both horizontal and vertical, which should guide the development of the field. Moreover, urban history conducted in this way provides an excellent opportunity for bringing into history as a whole a more systematic study of both structure and change. But for this to take place, the framework of thinking about urban history must change from categories of events happening within cities to patterns of urban social organization.

A second emerging field is political behavior. Interest in popular voting, legislative roll calls, and political leadership has given rise to quantitative studies in political history.[4] For the most part, however, these remain tied to the traditional concern for political events rather than structure; they focus on political decisions and the complex of factors which influenced those decisions rather than the persistent patterns of values held in common or in distinction.[5] They perpetuate the isolation of politics from the larger social order by stressing political events as distinct from other events. A structural approach brings them together, for underlying patterns of social relationships become political structure when considered from the point of view of inequalities in the distribution of power. By

4. Allan G. Bogue, "United States: The 'New' Political History," *Journal of Contemporary History* 3 (1968), 5–27.

5. Heinz Eulau, *The Behavioral Persuasion in Politics* (New York, 1963), argues for the use of new techniques to explore old problems in politics, that is, "the institutional political order."

describing more completely political attitudes and perceptions, actions, and behavior, we can recreate the structure of political relationships—a description that is impossible to generate if one remains concerned primarily with unique events. The most important contribution of quantitative political studies to history lies not in the explanation of political decisions but in the more complete description of the patterns of relationships among people who hold similar or different political values.

Social history has been influenced, secondly, by the climate of social reform from which it arose. Agrarian and urban social movements provided the background for its origin in the 1920s; the more intense climate of reform in the 1930s accelerated it. The impact of social movements upon social history was not minimal; in fact they exercised an overriding influence upon its perspective. Social movements operated within a "problem-policy" context. The rationale of each followed a similar sequence: the growth of urban-industrial society created "problems" which, in turn, "demanded" solutions. Some forces were in the forefront of reform, while others —"conservatives"—resisted them. Movements led to actions, usually state and federal legislation, and these laws, in turn, produced administrative agencies that tackled the problems with varying degrees of success. In such a framework the contemporary activist emphasized the social problem and how it had arisen, the "need" for change, the movement for change and the forces resisting it, the resulting action and its success or lack of success. Those who wrote from the context of administration worked within the same framework and perpetuated the same outlook. Their need to justify their actions only reinforced the basic context of description and analysis.

From this background of reform arose many of the new topical interests of the social historian. Working-class conditions and movements generated an interest in labor history and the history of socialism. Equally, the "immigration problem" generated interest in the study of immigration and the conflict of cultures within the nation; urban poverty and urban "problems," social welfare movements and the growth of municipal services; prohibition movements, an interest in the history of prohibition and temperance; the recurrent debate over Indian policy, the growing awareness of race in American life, and the persistence of religious conflict, a concern for "minority groups."

Social history absorbed the "problem-policy" perspective of social reform as well. This took place, in part, because many social historians were sympathetic to reform, but also because they relied heavily upon evidence generated by social movements. In so doing they were influenced deeply by the assumptions of those who developed and used that evidence in the first place; an angle of vision was transferred almost imperceptibly from one context to the other. Even those critical of the goals of reform absorbed its social perspective, differing from those sympathetic to reform only in their value judgments, not their basic context of description. The sequence of thought generated by reform movements in the Progressive Era, as a consequence, became incorporated into history as a basic framework: urban industrial society grew, created problems, gave rise to movements to solve those problems which in turn created opposition and produced legislation and eventually solutions. Few have questioned this basic framework of description; most have been absorbed in the task of detailing its specific phases. They have remained captives of the contemporary perspective of that segment of the past they wish to study.

Several emphases and omissions illustrate this limited perspective. In a problem-policy approach, for example, those people making up the "problem" are examined more closely than those involved in "reform." Labor, the immigrant, the black, the urban slum are studied, dissected, analyzed ad infinitum. The spate of studies emanating from the settlement houses and the Chicago school of sociology typify this approach. Each assumes that problems arise out of particular human circumstance and that variations in circumstance must be described to understand variations in problems. But reform and reformers are assumed to have arisen from more universal circumstances, from more generally agreed-on concepts of justice, democracy, rationality, "progress," or equality which need not be reduced to peculiarities of circumstance. Reformers who defined the investigations and wrote the reports of the Pittsburgh Survey, for example, detailed in extensive fashion the "problems"—working-class groups, communities, minority races, and nationalities—they wished to do something about. But they said almost nothing about reform itself, save to criticize its weakness, and the historian is now forced to go back and start from scratch if he wishes to describe the social bases of "reform" as well as of "problems."[6]

Emphasis on conditions reformers define as problems, moreover, omits important aspects of social change—for example, vertical mobility. Since reformers were concerned with the lack of mobility—poverty—as a problem, they rarely studied mobility, even at the level of upward movement out of poverty. Following the limited perspective of reformers, historians have equally failed to describe vertical mobility. One of the most fundamental processes in American history, therefore, remains relatively unexamined. The same distortion is happening now. The enormous current emphasis upon black poverty has produced a limited vision among "reform" writing, almost none of which describes the process of black vertical mobility in recent years. For a description of mobility is inconsistent with the perspective of a movement which seeks to marshal strength by emphasizing the lack of mobility. Since black vertical mobility after World War II will be represented by far fewer contemporary studies than black poverty, historians in the future will be tempted to adopt the same limited vision unless they can escape the perspective of the movement and examine the empirical data without preconception.[7]

The "problem-policy" bias of social history has even larger implications: for example, its impact upon the treatment of ideological evidence. Social movements invariably generate descriptions of both their present and their past as a means of mobilizing popular support. These descriptions usually reflect the particular bias of the

6. Paul Underwood Kellogg (ed.), *The Pittsburgh Survey* (New York, 1909–14). A similar perspective underlies the recent *Toward a Social Report*, issued by the U.S. Department of Health, Education, and Welfare (Washington, D.C., 1969).

7. Black mobility is indicated by the following national statistics of occupational distributions of "Negroes and other races":

	1940	1950	1960	1969
White-collar	5.9%	10.2%	16.0%	26.2%
Blue-collar	16.6%	23.4%	26.0%	32.4%
Unskilled	77.5%	66.3%	58.0%	41.4%

The data are found in the annual issues of the *Statistical Abstract of the United States* and the "Annual Average" reports in the U.S. Department of Labor, Bureau of Labor Statistics, *Employment and Earnings*.

social movement as to the nature of society and social change. Historians, in turn, frequently accept these descriptions with little question when they deal with the same events. Consider, for example, inequalities in the distribution of income and wealth. Social movements have tended to stress that "things are getting worse," which in turn implies that "things were better" in the past. Conceptions of an equalitarian past abound in Populist and Progressive literature; they were carried over into historical writings. Historians have accepted these descriptions with few attempts to determine their accuracy. But data since 1946 indicate that income distributions have changed only in the most minor degree over the past twenty-three years; less satisfactory but acceptable data indicate some but not substantial change since 1910 in income distributions; and wealth distribution data from the seventeenth, eighteenth, and nineteenth centuries indicate the persistent prevalence of striking inequalities in which urban commercial and industrial development only created greater inequalities than the inequalities of rural property ownership.[8]

I do not suggest that historians should ignore ideology, for explanations of past and present are powerful roots of human action. But historians have all too often taken such explanations as accurate descriptions of the past rather than ideas generated by a movement to establish its legitimacy. By being too closely tied to the ideological perspective of social reform, historians have accepted the assumptions of that perspective and failed to generate a larger view of social change. Since the task of recreating descriptions of social systems from social data is enormous, one is tempted to accept ideological formulations of what society is and has been like. Yet the desire for economy of time and energy is no excuse for becoming the captive of the ideology of a social movement. Above all, the so-

8. For twentieth-century data see Gabriel Kolko, *Wealth and Power in America* (New York, 1962), 9–29. For the eighteenth century see James Henretta, "Economic Development and Social Structure in Colonial Boston," *William and Mary Quarterly* 22 (1965), 75–92, and Barton Meyers, "The Distribution of Wealth in a Series of Massachusetts Towns in the Year 1771," seminar paper, Univ. of Pittsburgh, 1968. For the nineteenth century see Robert Doherty, *Society and Power: Five New England Towns, 1800–1860* (Amherst, Mass., 1977); Michael Holt, *Forging a Majority: The Formation of the Republican Party in Pittsburgh, 1848–1860* (New Haven, 1969), 320; J.E. Davidson, "God Speed the Plough: A View of Agricultural Society," seminar paper, Univ. of Pittsburgh, 1969.

cial historian should be able to distinguish in his perspective between ideology and practice, examine each separately, and relate the two as separate phenomena of social history.

Concentration upon the manifest expressions of social movements has diverted attention from the reconstruction of latent social change, that element of long-run change due not to the explicit organization of reform or formulation of an ideology but to the accumulation of choices made by millions of people in their daily lives. Migration and vertical mobility are examples. Organized social movements and written records of ideology are the most convenient sources for historical research; consequently they obscure the evidence required to recreate the patterns of human values and actions in social change. Absorption in the evidence and assumptions of problem-policy statements has diverted historians from the path of a systematic description of social structure and social change. They have examined pieces of society from the vantage point of those pieces rather than society as a whole. The reformist orientation of social history must be cast aside in favor of more objective conceptions of structure and change if social history is to fulfill its promise.

A concern for understanding the conscious life of man and his perceptions, ideas, and values constitutes a third source of social history. The phrase "social and intellectual history" is now a commonplace. This concern has taken many forms—the formal patterns of thought among the "major" thinkers; the ideas in popular culture as expressed in mass media; description of "myths" of the West, the Jacksonian "persuasion," the "machine in the garden."[9] That form which focuses on "patterns of culture" has often been described as "social and cultural history." This source of social history is its most elusive, its most unformed component. Confusion about how one deals with the conscious life of man in history is partly responsible for the confusion in what social history is all about. More important, powerful tendencies within the study of

9. Henry Nash Smith, *Virgin Land: The American West As Symbol and Myth* (Cambridge, Mass., 1950); John William Ward, *Andrew Jackson, Symbol for an Age* (New York, 1955); Marvin Meyers, *The Jacksonian Persuasion: Politics and Belief* (Stanford, 1957); Leo Marx, *The Machine in the Garden* (New York, 1964).

ideas and values have prevented the conscious life of man from being drawn effectively into the context of social history.

Concepts of structure and change, the central focus of social history, provide ways of looking at the conscious life of man as well as his external circumstances. Social history, as we have argued before, does not constitute the study of a separate body of facts—conscious experience and values—but a way of looking at those facts. Just as there are patterns and structures to religious institutions along a community-society continuum, so there are patterns and structures to the experiences and values of people within those institutions. The concern for pattern, distinctive experiences held in common; the arrangement of these patterns into contexts of dominance and subordination, of old and new, of local and cosmopolitan—all this lies at the root of a social history of man's conscious life. One task of social history is a systematic description and arrangement of these patterns.

The most crucial aspect of the social description of man's conscious life is the basis upon which categories are constructed. Empirical description of a wide variety of human characteristics has given rise to the concept of variation: that most properties of men, whether their economic condition, social involvements, attitudes, or values, vary in intensity along a scale. Attitudes toward organized labor today vary from one end of a scale to another; so did attitudes toward slavery in the nineteenth century.[10] Similar variation undoubtedly obtained in the past in conceptions of past, present, and future, in preferences for one's personal life, in religious outlook, in appropriate norms of behavior for one's self and others. Distributions, of course, display central tendencies, and this enables one to speak of the attitudes of Americans "as a whole," for example, differing from the British "as a whole," but the effectiveness and precision of both description and analysis depend upon the completeness of the intervals along the continuum.

Social historians, however, have described the conscious life of man in terms other than variation. For example, there is a powerful tendency to dichotomize. When historians abstract ideas from their

10. A spectrum of attitudes toward labor, using evidence available to the historian, has been developed with congressional roll-call votes in George M. Belknap, "A Method for Analyzing Legislative Behavior," *Midwest Journal of Political Science* 2 (1958), 377–402.

human origin and organize them in terms of their inherent logical meaning, they tend to establish mutually exclusive categories. Dichotomies are stimulated even further by the tendency to relate ideas to action, and to organize them on the basis of action. In political action we dichotomize in terms of conservatives and liberals, of laissez faire and positive government, of the New Freedom and the New Nationalism. These categories do not reflect the variation in human experience but the process by which activist organizers of ideas shape them into systems of explanation for political combat. These dichotomized descriptions of ideas are projected back into the larger stream of history, thereby distorting the description of the social order as a whole and diverting historians from the empirical description of variation in human experience.

The concern for national values and national character, another tendency in social history, has also retarded empirical description. For in such efforts as the "American civilization" approach, the emphasis upon national values has prompted aggregate description of ideas and values within a nation and turned attention away from more important disaggregate descriptions. Description of any system, be it nation, region, state, community, or city, if only on the aggregate level, limits statements to the central tendencies of that system, rather than the interaction among its subparts. Aggregate data about election returns—the percentage of the vote for president throughout the nation, for example—represent a primitive form of description which limits analysis sharply. But when variation of the vote for states, counties, and minor civil divisions is described, analysis can be pushed forward extensively by comparing and contrasting different intensities of the vote. Aggregate income data for the nation as a whole tell very little; far more important is the distribution of that income within the nation as a whole and as between geographical regions, races, and rural and urban areas. The same holds true for ideas and values. Aggregate description of ideas and values for an entire nation determines differences as between nations, but it fails to provide the elementary descriptive framework within which to analyze the dynamics of a given social order.

The weakest link in the historiography of national cultural values is the selection of evidence to describe aggregates. Since it is safe to assume that values are held in variation among people, only by a description of variation can one provide a satisfactory account of the entire range of values and their central tendencies. But cultural historians are not prone to be concerned with the construction of scales of variation. They pick out a variety of types of evidence—the rationale for selection usually remains unclear—and assume that in some way it adds up to a description of the whole.[11] Such an approach not only fails to provide a description of the scale of variation —thereby limiting drastically the quantity and quality of description —but precludes any possibility of determining the accuracy of the aggregate description. In such a case the historian falls back upon the mere assertion that in some way what a novelist, for example, writes reflects the values of the society as a whole, or that he "feels" that another particular type of evidence does, thereby creating a jungle of uncertainty.

An unsystematic description of patterns of conscious life can be readily rationalized: an appeal to intuitive judgment that this piece of evidence represents experience and thought throughout society, a lack of evidence often accompanied by a statement of the difficulties of developing evidence which does exist, a shift of argument to an attack upon environmentalism, an appeal to the uniqueness of each individual, and the distortions of describing common characteristics of conscious life. These are all diversions from the main task; they reflect the chaos of the failure to develop a more systematic description of human experience and perception. Until it can overcome these tendencies and order conscious life in history more effectively, social history cannot fulfill its promise.

II

SOCIAL history is concerned with structural changes in society over long periods of time. The crucial concept is *social structure,* those patterns of human interaction which relate some people and differentiate others, which reflect characteristics held by some in common and by others in distinction. The historian is uniquely concerned

11. A recent attempt which uses this method to describe large-scale social change is John Higham, "From Boundlessness to Consolidation: The Transformation of American Culture, 1848–1860," William L. Clements Library (Ann Arbor, 1969).

with *long-run social change*, change over not just two or three years but over decades and centuries. While other disciplines emphasize structure, only history focuses on large-scale changes in structure over long periods of time.

Traditionally preoccupied with narrative about events and individuals, with the episodic and the unique, historians have devoted insufficient attention to social structure. This has played a major role in retarding the growth of social history, for a description of social structure is the first and elementary task of social history. We must find ways of adding up the attributes of individuals into single descriptive statements about many people, of describing the religious values not of one leader but of many adherents, the characteristics of riots and rioters in not one but hundreds of cases. The groupings and subgroupings which these characteristics reveal must then be ordered in some meaningful relationship so as to bring out the structure, the broad interactions of dominance and subordination —for example, as between sectors of society. Such a reconstruction of the social order becomes the basic framework of thought for social history.

In its most elementary form the concept of structure rests upon the empirical fact of distinctive similarity. Some people have characteristics in common; they are Catholics, blacks, lower-middle-class, Republicans, or college students. They hold these characteristics in distinction from other people who are Protestant, white, upper-middle-class, Democrats, or educated at an eighth-grade level. Because people hold such characteristics in common we can speak of patterns of characteristics. These patterns range over the entire gamut of human properties. They include experience, thought, values, occupation, recreation, and organizational involvements and actions. Such patterns hold for the people of one nation, for one geographical section of a society, or for any nongeographical subgroup as opposed to another.

One might conceive of these patterns as purely horizontal, as constituting distinctively shared characteristics that involve no hierarchies of thought or value, of capacity to influence, of dominance or subordination. But vertical structures that do involve such hierarchies are far more prevalent than purely horizontal structures. Inequalities in the distribution of wealth and income, of education and ability, of knowledge and access to knowledge, of involvement in cosmopolitan institutions, of access to decision-making centers in formal administrative systems, of economic distance between geographical places—all these give rise to hierarchies of more and less which in turn constitute vertical patterns of social structure. We therefore often imply a vertical dimension when we speak of social structure, even though horizontal structures also exist, simply because it seems to be so widespread a characteristic of social institutions.

Empirical data reveal the pervasiveness of such distinctively shared characteristics in societies, past and present. Simply to recreate a faithful description of the past, therefore, requires that we think in terms of structure. However, one can emphasize a more pragmatic problem as well. If history is to be more than an account of a few isolated individuals, if we are to describe people and characteristics throughout society, we are forced to think in terms of distinctively shared characteristics. The human mind cannot comprehend and communicate to others information about very many discrete individuals. Systematic study in any discipline requires that masses of data be categorized to facilitate understanding and analysis. If we cannot do this, we abandon the opportunity to describe social phenomena.

Concepts of social structure must be flexible and imaginative. Much of the objection to the idea of structure lies in its association with a rigid view of groupings arising primarily from the means of production. But vertical structures are far more complex and varied. Cosmopolitan experience, for example, wide-ranging and mobile, with an awareness beyond immediate circumstances, occupies a higher level in the structure of human consciousness than does a parochial view, limited and narrow, confined to a constricted range of contacts.[12] Divisions between managers and managed today are more pervasive than those between capital and labor. The spectrum of white-collar workers, ranging all the way from clerk to corporate manager, constitutes a vertical structure within the hierarchy of dependent occupations which, in turn, parallels the hierarchy of educational levels and resulting skills created by modern educational

12. The now-classic description of local-cosmopolitan patterns is Robert K. Merton, "Patterns of Influence: Local and Cosmopolitan Influentials," in Merton, *Social Theory and Social Structure* (Glencoe, Ill., 1949), 387–420.

systems.[13] These examples emphasize the desirability of maintaining a flexible view as to the types of social structure prevalent in history.

Social structure can be recreated in a wide variety of contexts. Some studies have reconstructed community social systems. One might arrange the subparts of the community in terms of ethnicity and religion, occupation, income levels, degrees of involvement in voluntary associations, race, or levels of education. Others stress the distinction between old upper-class families and new, or between stable and migratory groups. One might reconstruct the social system of an entire state. A study of Massachusetts in the 1780s has placed every town in the state on a community-society scale consisting of degrees of involvement in the wider economic network and in the state's political institutions.[14] Or one might consider the nation as a social system, a perspective used in E. Digby Baltzell's description of the shift from a local to a national upper class in the latter part of the nineteenth century.[15]

An emphasis upon structure as the focal point of social history runs counter to the predispositions of many historians who prefer to stress homogeneous characteristics. They tend to consider inequalities in wealth or income, for example, as short-lived and temporary phenomena, arising out of a previous condition of substantial equality and giving way to subsequent recreation of equality. Both views are highly dubious. Historians, for example, have long believed that the inequalities of the Gilded Age grew out of previous equality. Recently, Douglas Miller has questioned this argument by demonstrating the prevalence of sharp inequalities in the years between 1830 and 1860. Yet even Miller is deeply affected by the ideology of equality when he argues that prior to the 1830s "inequalities of wealth were comparatively slight."[16] Available evidence indicates the prevalence of inequalities throughout American history. In Salem, Northampton, and Worcester, Massachusetts, for example,

13. C. Wright Mills, *White Collar* (New York, 1951) remains the best introduction to white-collar occupations.

14. Van Beck Hall, *Politics Without Parties; Massachusetts, 1780-1791* (Pittsburgh, 1972).

15. E. Digby Baltzell, *Philadelphia Gentlemen: The Making of a National Upper Class* (Glencoe, Ill., 1958).

16. Douglas T. Miller, *Jacksonian Aristocracy* (New York, 1967), ix.

Robert Doherty has found that in 1800 the top ten percent of the population owned 72 percent, 45 percent, and 50 percent of the wealth respectively.[17] Historians have been equally misled by assuming that the reforms of the New Deal and the prosperity of World War II generated substantial equality; they accepted too readily that view which was popularized by Frederick Lewis Allen's *The Big Change*.[18] For income distribution data demonstrate the remarkable persistence of inequality in the past quarter of a century.[19] The lesson of these errors is clear: historians must avoid the lure of an ideology of homogeneity if they are to describe reality.

One of the main current tasks of social history, then, is to reconstruct social structure in all of its settings: the community, the city, the region, the church, the political party, education, the business world, the trade union, the nation. Our failure to give sufficient attention to this problem is directly responsible for the major conceptual weakness of textbooks and other syntheses in American history. To rectify this by generating patterns of social structure constitutes the most important potential contribution of social history to the discipline as a whole.

And what of the event, the individual, and the unique? Although they cannot serve as a major context of description, they can constitute instances for the investigation of structure. Starting with an event such as ratification of the Constitution, issuance of the "Definite Platform" in the Lutheran Church in 1855, a prohibition referendum in the 1870s or 1880s, or acts of violence such as the railroad riots of 1877, one can determine the pattern of human involvement which lay behind it. The event serves as the opportunity for an exploration into structure rather than an end in itself. Or one can consider the event or individual as one instance of a class of events or individuals and examine antislavery leaders as a whole rather than just William Lloyd Garrison or Theodore Dwight Weld, or civil disorders as a whole in the nineteenth century rather than just the Homestead Strike or the anti-draft riots of 1863. The individual or the event takes on significance in systematic social history not in itself but in relation to social structure. They may be repre-

17. Doherty, "Comparative Study of Social Change," *loc. cit.*
18. Frederick Lewis Allen, *The Big Change* (New York, 1952).
19. Kolko, *Wealth and Power*, 14.

sentative, and therefore can "stand for" a larger group of people or class of events. Or, as in the case of war, depression, or revolution, they may have had a significant impact on social structure. These cannot be assumed, or arrived at through ideological claims to change, but must be demonstrated through evidence concerning representativeness and social patterns.

It is not sufficient to determine the characteristics of people or events in isolation. Even more important is their location in the larger pattern. From what particular segment of the social structure did a given event or episode arise? Did religious evangelicals come from the isolated, remote sectors of society, such as the frontier, or from the most cosmopolitan areas of the East?[20] Did they stem from the lower, middle, or upper segments of the social order? Did the movement for the popularization of education and science in the first half of the nineteenth century stem from the public in general, workingmen, the middle class, or the elite?[21] Did the colonization movement and the antislavery movement have distinctive sources within the social structure? From what particular source came the movement for Indian rights in the post–Civil war era? To omit the structural context of individual happenings is to greatly limit the quantity and quality of historical description.

For the task of generating systematic descriptions of social structure, historians can draw upon a considerable body of well-developed concepts, especially from sociology. Some are more useful than others; all require some modification to fit the context of history. The following, by no means exhaustive but merely illustrative, constitute frameworks I have found useful in ordering the structure of American urban-industrial society since the mid-nineteenth century.

The first consists of ethnocultural patterns which arise out of differences in ethnicity, religion, and race. These have been profound and pervasive in American history. At times we have recognized them as factors contributing to a given outcome or event, such as the American party in the 1850s or the Al Smith candidacy

20. Robert W. Doherty, *The Hicksite Separation* (New Brunswick, N.J., 1967).

21. Charles Bidwell, "The Moral Significance of the Common School," *History of Education Quarterly* 6 (1966), 50–91; Michael B. Katz, *The Irony of Early School Reform: Educational Innovation in Mid-Nineteenth Century Massachusetts* (Cambridge, Mass., 1968).

in 1928. But rarely have we developed them into a pattern of ongoing human relationships which constitutes a framework of historical development. Reconstruction of popular voting data in the nineteenth century has played a major role in generating thought about ethnocultural "factors" in terms of structure rather than event. It now appears that religion and ethnicity, for example, were far more responsible for party preferences in the last half of the nineteenth century than were economic or socioeconomic factors.[22] These voting data, in turn, have drawn attention to the value systems underlying partisan preferences and the accompanying ethnic and religious institutions. These, when considered in their own right, generate a picture of an ongoing pattern of perceptions and values which vary along a continuum. Voting data have generated this framework because they provide a measure of attitudes of a large portion of the social order—whether nation, state, county, or urban subcommunity. To a greater extent than data about single events, or ideological formulations or articulate spokesmen, voting data describe a wide spectrum of people. They enable us to generate a scale of attitudes and, in turn, a pattern of variation and a framework of structure.

Voting data create the possibility of going beyond manifest to underlying patterns of structure, of cutting across traditional ideological battles and formal denominational religious lines. Frequently, for example, Catholics and German Lutherans voted together because of their common traditionalistic and ritualistic value orientation and their common aversion to evangelical religion.[23] However, German and Norwegian Lutherans, many of the latter being pietists, were at different poles of the religious value spectrum. Evangelicals of all Protestant denominations tended to cluster together. These historical patterns remind one of a similar reorientation toward a description of religious values which Charles Glock and Rodney Stark have found for the mid-twentieth century, a "new denomina-

---

22. This view was first expressed forcefully by Lee Benson in *The Concept of Jacksonian Democracy: New York As a Test Case* (Princeton, 1961). See also Paul J. Kleppner, "Lincoln and the Immigrant Vote: A Case of Religious Polarization," *Mid-America* 48 (1966), 176–95, and Frederick Luebke, *Immigrants and Politics: The Germans of Nebraska, 1880-1900* (Lincoln, Neb., 1969).

23. Paul Kleppner, "The Political Realignment of the 1890's: A Behavioral Interpretation," unpub. ms., Northern Illinois Univ.

tionalism" which cuts across formal denominations and ranges religious values into patterns of traditionalism and modernism.[24]

American historians have long been under the influence of "progressive" and "liberal" thought which has discounted ethnocultural differences as the product of manipulation by dominant economic forces. Such conflicts are not fundamental, so the argument goes, but derivative, the product of dominant employers seeking to divide the working class and to divert attention from "real" economic issues. This tendency has more recently been reinforced by "status" historians who translate ethnic and religious conflicts into matters of self-conceptions of rank and status in society, and search into man's unconscious for a description of the forces at work.[25] Such a view betrays an economic determinism that considers economic factors as "hard," fundamental, and irreducible to other forces, but ethnic and religious conflicts as "soft," derivative, coming to the fore in prosperity when economic conflict supposedly diminishes, and explainable as derivative from more subconscious forces. But there is every reason to look upon ethnic and religious, as well as racial conflicts, as fundamental in themselves, inherent in man's basic predispositions, constituting a pattern of social structure as irreducible to other factors as those which arise from differences in occupation.

A second dimension of social structure arises out of variations in occupation, income, and living standards. Historians have neglected this almost to the same degree as ethnocultural structure. For most have viewed economic conflict as between the demands of the "public" or the "people" on the one hand and "private interests" on the other, or between the large business sectors of the economy on the one hand and labor and agriculture on the other. These approaches are not based upon concepts of socioeconomic structure and without this firm base are diverted easily into contexts of moral progress in the face of evil power or homogeneity emerging out of previous differences. Consequently, concepts of economic conflict have generated few attempts to re-create socioeconomic structure. Studies of

24. Charles Glock and Rodney Stark, *Religion and Society in Tension* (Chicago, 1965), 86–122.
25. Richard Hofstadter, "Fundamentalism and Status Politics on the Right," *Columbia University Forum* 8 (1965), 18–24.

trade union and agricultural protest, which have been abundant, are no substitutes for studies of socioeconomic structure.

A few have moved in a more adequate direction. Gabriel Kolko's book on *Wealth and Power in America* brought to the attention of historians statistical data on income distribution in the twentieth century, data that can be followed regularly in the publications of the U.S. Census Bureau.[26] Others—for example, Josephson and Miller for the nineteenth century and Bridenbaugh and Main for the eighteenth—have attempted to describe social classes.[27] Main's are the most systematic, but even these suffer from the incompleteness of the scales of variation. The most satisfactory efforts are studies of single communities in which the number of people and amount of data are sufficiently limited to permit a reconstruction of the patterns in the entire structure. These include Kenneth Lockridge's study of Dedham, Massachusetts, and Robert Doherty's forthcoming study of five New England towns and cities in the first half of the nineteenth century.[28] These could be expanded to encompass larger social units, such as a state, a region, or the nation. It is not the possibility of this which has hampered us, but the diversion of those interested in socioeconomic differences from problems of structure into episodes of economic and political conflict.

Still a third pattern of social structure consists of adminstrative systems and the relationship within them among individuals at different levels of those systems, with different degrees of education and skill and different capacities to manipulate knowledge and influence decisions. The evolution of administrative systems, both private and public, is one of the most profound developments of urban-industrial society since the mid-nineteenth century. The structure of human relationships which they involve should consti-

26. Kolko, *Wealth and Power.*
27. Matthew Josephson, *The Robber Barons* (New York, 1934); Douglas Miller, *Jacksonian Aristocracy*; Carl Bridenbaugh, *Cities in the Wilderness* (New York, 1938); Jackson Turner Main, *The Social Structure of Revolutionary America* (Princeton, 1965).
28. Robert Doherty, *Society and Power*; Kenneth Lockridge, *A New England Town, The First Hundred Years: Dedham, Massachusetts, 1636–1736* (New York, 1970); Lockridge, "Land, Population, and the Evolution of New England Society, 1639–1790," *Past and Present* 39 (1968), 62–80. See also James T. Lemon and Gary B. Nash, "The Distribution of Wealth in Eighteenth-Century America: A Century of Change in Chester County, Pennsylvania, 1693–1802," *Journal of Social History* 2 (1968), 1–24.

tute a central focus of history. The past century has witnessed a persistent development of administrative systems: an elaboration of their size and scope; extension of the realms of life they encompass; upward flow in the location of decision making; internal elaboration of their hierarchies and layers of skill, education, rank, and scope of authority and control; and separation of the top of the hierarchy from the bottom. At the same time, upper levels of administrative systems have come together in a common climate of thought and opinion, perception of the world, and sense of stake in the entire social order, while those at the lower end of the system have remained more fractured and less capable of manipulating the instruments of information and communication which constitute sources of influence within the system.

The general importance of administrative systems as a pattern of social structure is clear, but the stages and processes of their development are not. Those stages need to be elaborated by research. One dimension of the sequence might well be the stages of increasing scale of life touched by the system, scale in terms of wider geographical areas, such as from region to nation to international areas, or an increasing number of functions within the system, from sales to capital accumulation to planning and research and development. A second focal point of investigation is the effect of crises of war and depression on the growth of administrative systems. Do they accelerate the pace of system or do they change its direction? Still a third problem is the changing relationship between tendencies toward centralization and countertendencies toward decentralization; for example, in the cities between centralization focused on corporate systems, government, the central city, redevelopment, professionalization and higher education on the one hand and the decentralization of life in residential institutions—home, family, church, recreation, school, and suburbanization—on the other. For recent twentieth-century America, social scientists have studied many aspects of these problems, but it remains for the historian to be able to observe their growth and development over time.

A fourth type of structure, the community-society or local-cosmopolitan pattern of social relationships, is receiving more attention from historians. This pattern emphasizes the geographical range of human experience, thought, and action, a range that extends from a limited, parochial context on the one hand to a wide, cosmopolitan one on the other. The community-society spectrum has extensive applicability to history, since these differences occur in a wide range of human affairs. It includes the range of business activities from neighborhood to national or international markets; of religious values from separation from the world to deep involvement in it; of communications networks from those concerned with daily and personal life to impersonal media providing information about the wider world; of factors one wishes to control and therefore the method of decision making preferred, whether decentralized and local or centralized and national.

Many historical data can be understood through a community-society typology. William Benton found that the range of involvement in military activities during the Revolutionary War was related to Federalist or anti-Federalist attitudes.[29] Robert Doherty discovered that the range of social involvements paralleled the range of religious values.[30] Van Beck Hall has found that the intensity of involvement in the wider economic world in Massachusetts in the 1780s was consistent with formal political preferences.[31] Elsewhere I have elaborated a connection between the range of social involvements on the one hand and the choice of instruments of decision making—party, functional group, or corporate system—and their scope of competence, in the early twentieth century.[32] These studies indicate the applicability of the community-society framework to many areas of life in many periods of time.

The vertical dimension of each of these four contexts of social structure should be stressed. Empirical data reveal persistent inequalities in the distribution of income and wealth, education, skills and training, access to information and communication, degrees of involvement in the wider world, and range of perception and value orientation. These inequalities array themselves into pat-

29. William Benton, "Pennsylvania Revolutionary Officers and the Federal Constitution," *Pennsylvania History* 31 (1964), 419–35.
30. Robert W. Doherty, *The Hicksite Separation*; "Social Bases for the Presbyterian Schism of 1837–1838; The Philadelphia Case," *Journal of Social History* 2 (1968), 69–79.
31. Hall, *Politics Without Parties*.
32. Samuel P. Hays, "Political Parties and the Community-Society Continuum," in William Nisbet Chambers and Walter Dean Burnham (eds.), *The American Party Systems: Stages of Political Development* (New York, 1967), 152–81.

terns of dominance and subordination. Moreover, the process of vertical mobility, pervasive and continual in American history, has created not homogeneity of condition but a constant extension, elaboration, and re-creation of inequalities. Individuals move rapidly through the social structure, but the outlines of that structure, and especially its vertical dimension, persist. Some structures may well be homogeneous in some characteristics, and more so at one time than another; black urban social structure, for example, has become far more heterogeneous since World War II. One's approach to the elaboration of structure should be flexible. But available evidence indicates the overwhelming persistence throughout American history of a vertical organization of society in which variation in attributes generates patterned inequalities.

III

Social history is concerned not simply with structure but also with changes in structure. This is the special province of the discipline. Yet American historians have provided few concepts of long-run social change, few systematic patterns that can serve as frameworks for historical change. For the most part, they construct time sequences in terms of the temporal succession of isolated events, rather than patterns of change. The traditional context of thought is not the process of change between terminal points of a long period of time but a given event as following another given event. Consequently social historians have few available concepts concerning types of changes, patterns of change, or processes of change. Since social scientists have been relatively unconcerned about long-run social change, we cannot borrow concepts from them as readily as with social structure. We are relatively unprepared, therefore, to consider social change.

A useful context in which to elaborate both the limitations of event-sequence and the possibilities of pattern description is voting behavior. Traditionally, American historians describe one election as a distinct event and another as a still separate event. Few links between elections are made in terms of degrees of change from one to the next. College texts in American history, for example, rarely describe elections in a framework of change over time save in terms of gross reversal of party majority since the previous election. Rarely, in fact, are election results described even in terms of percentages of party strength—usually absolute majorities or the fact of victory or defeat are used—which alone permit comparison over space or time.

An event-sequence approach to elections assumes an unrealistic notion of the relationship between voting and human values. We have long focused on issues as the crucial aspect of elections. Questions for debate arise in the course of elections, and voters, in turn, consider the evidence and choose a candidate on the basis of issues. We speak of the outcome of the election of 1844 in terms of Texas; of 1890, the tariff issue; of 1920, the League of Nations. But voting is related to deeply rooted social values rather than to shifting "issues"; voters express by their choice a persistent conception of society, value preference, and negative reaction to parts of the social order. These values are not turned on or off every four years; they remain highly stable, and the vote is only one of a variety of their expressions. Just as the views of workingmen or the attitudes of prohibitionists persist over time, so do their preferences for political parties and candidates. The most obvious characteristic of voting patterns over long periods of time is the lack of change, so much so that some of the highest statistical correlations that can be obtained with historical social data involve the distribution of the popular vote in successive elections.[33]

Because of this underlying characteristic of voting, historians have been drawn to periods of voting realignments as a peculiar kind of change which calls for intensive analysis. Most voting changes involve only a shift of voters across the board from one party preference toward another in some slight degree. But some involve a reshuffling of preferences so that some voters shift strongly and others weakly, or some shift in one direction and others in the op-

33. The high level of these correlations is illustrated by the following matrix of inter-correlations of Illinois elections, 1888–1900, for the U.S. House of Representatives, based upon county data.

	1888	1890	1892	1894	1896	1898
1890	.851					
1892	.913	.877				
1894	.925	.889	.918			
1896	.930	.867	.801	.863		
1898	.942	.822	.853	.902	.950	
1900	.947	.824	.842	.885	.979	.968

posite. These types of changes involve new patterns of relationships among voters different from previous patterns. Such realignments took place in the early 1850s, the mid-1890s, and the early 1930s. They constitute a type of political change, usually over a period of several elections, sharply delineated from other types of change. Political historians are just beginning to classify types of changes in voting behavior, largely because data to develop descriptions of long-run social change have not previously been available. But some patterns are becoming clear. Frameworks for presidential history, for example, are sharply at variance with patterns of voting cycles. Categories of stability and change over time, as revealed by the election data, provide an altogether different context of temporal description.[34]

The lack of data by which to measure change over long periods of time is, of course, one of the major limitations in describing social change. Descriptions of internal structure over time are especially difficult to secure. Data for wealth and income distributions in recent years are excellent; with it we can describe long-run patterns of inequality in the twentieth century. For earlier years, however, income data are not available, and wealth data must be used. Yet, even though abundant evidence is available, little has been used to reconstruct distributions so as to observe change over time. Some efforts are now under way, limited mainly to selected communities. But until more extensive descriptions are completed we will not be able to describe one of the most crucial contexts of long-run change in American history.

Just as the description of the structural roots of events at one point of time is a major task of social history, so is a description of the structural roots of change. From what peculiar sources did change arise? It is not realistic to assume that social change occurs uniformly throughout all segments of society. For change arises within particular segments, is diffused through others, and is resisted by still others. A spirit of economic entrepreneurship developed differently in the South than in the North; where, within the social structure, was this spirit uniquely generated? Did innovation in agricultural practices come from farmers or from urbanites who

34. The first and still classic statement of this problem is by Lee Benson in Mirra Komarovsky (ed.), *Common Frontiers of the Social Sciences* (Glencoe, Ill., 1957), 113–83.

organized agricultural improvement societies? Where within the social order did the idea of Darwinian evolution arise, through what routes was it diffused, and from what segments came resistance? Did the movement for urban "reform" in the Progressive Era spring from the lower-, middle-, or upper-class groups?[35] Do urban riots in the mid-1960s arise from the poor or the upwardly mobile lower middle class?[36]

Societies display, in varying degrees, forces generating change and those resisting change. Are these located in the social structure in a random fashion, or are they persistently rooted in particular segments? American historians have long argued, for example, that business generally is conservative and resistant to change, and that forces making for change come from the lower levels of the economic order. Yet it seems more accurate to argue that private corporate business has been a powerful force for change in modern America, sweeping away old institutions and creating new, and that innovation generally has come distinctively from the upper levels of the social structure, where psychological mobility, science, technology, education, and administrative systems have found distinctive support. On the other hand, conservatism—resistance to change—more frequently has been located in the lower reaches of the social order, where familiar primary-group relationships provided protection against innovation from the outside, cosmopolitan world.

Relationships between events and patterns of change over time are similar to relationships at one point of time. The event is relevant insofar as it sheds light on the pattern, derived from concepts of long-run change, rather than because it is an event. The context of description is long-run change; the unit of description extends over a relatively long period of time, and each event is then evaluated in terms of its contribution to that pattern of change. Moreover, intervening events need not be described if they are not closely related to the process of change itself. One may discuss electoral change between any two terminal points, for example, without de-

35. Samuel P. Hays, "The Politics of Reform in Municipal Government in the Progressive Era," *Pacific Northwest Quarterly* 55 (1964), 157–69.

36. See, for example, the *Report of the National Advisory Commission on Civil Disorders* (New York, 1968), 172–78, for a summary of data concerning rioters as compared with other groups in a number of cities in 1967.

scribing intervening elections. The initial perspective, whether it be events or long-run change, establishes the context of description. If long-run change, then events are important only insofar as they shape or reflect the pattern and process of change.

For many years, for example, the Civil War was considered the major turning point in American history, in both political and economic development. This view is now called into question largely because the Civil War as an event is being placed within the descriptive context of long-run change. Measurement of economic growth in the nineteenth century has shifted the focus away from the war and toward the 1850s as the first decade of industrial development. The question now under debate is whether or not the war affected this growth by accelerating or retarding it. At most it apparently had little effect; in a few sectors of the economy, such as capital formation, it probably accelerated growth; in others, such as transportation, it exercised a retarding influence. The context of these arguments now differs sharply from that of the past, for the focus is long-run economic change, and the war is considered as only one of a number of events in that development.[37]

Voting data require the same shift in perspective. The realignment of the early 1850s produced patterns that persisted until the 1890s; seen from this perspective the war is not a terminal point in the description of voting changes. The war affected little the pattern of party preference; in fact, the realignment of the 1850s played a major role in shaping the subsequent conflict. These two shifts in the context of description, one economic and the other political, enable us to pose the crucial question: To what extent did the event—the war—alter the course of long-run social change? We can no longer assume that what happened during the war was crucial. We now juxtapose that event against the process of long-run change and determine the interaction between the two. Our perspective has shifted from a description in terms of event to one in terms of change over time.

Two types of long-run social change seem especially appropriate

---

37. The original article in this reorientation was Thomas C. Cochran, "Did the Civil War Retard Industrialization?," *Mississippi Valley Historical Review* 48 (1961), 197–210. A review of the ensuing literature can be found in Stanley L. Engerman, "The Economic Impact of the Civil War," in *Explorations in Entrepreneurial History*, 2nd Ser. (1966), 176–99.

for conceptualization and research. The first is mobility and the second systematization. Historians have dealt with mobility, both geographical and vertical, in only the most rudimentary fashion. The two cases of geographical mobility which have been given most attention, the westward movement and migration from abroad, have rarely been considered from the point of view of the general role of population movements in social change. Vertical mobility has been treated only in the most general, often ideological terms, and only in very recent years have historians attempted to describe it more precisely. Yet mobility has been one of the most pervasive processes of social change throughout American history. Americans have constantly been in motion, horizontally and vertically, and mobility has continually eroded old and created new social institutions in rapid sequence.

I have mentioned previously four types of geographic mobility: to the West, from abroad, from rural to urban areas, and from central to peripheral sections of cities. Common characteristics of these migrations serve as a guideline for developing a description of the migration process, its roots and its consequences. For example, who migrated and who did not? In the rural Northeast in the last half of the nineteenth century, who was attracted to the city and who remained behind? Among contemporary urban blacks, who chooses to move to the metropolitan periphery and who does not? Is migration a function of educational and occupational levels, of intelligence, of religious values? Does out-migration from rural community or city center drain the community of its capacity to innovate, to generate new enterprise, to respond creatively to adversity? To describe migration and its impact is not an impossible task. For twentieth-century rural migration to the cities, moreover, historians have a number of studies conducted by rural sociologists to draw upon. The least that can be said is that we have not tapped extensively the sources of available evidence.

Description of vertical mobility in American history is equally deficient, involving general statements as to the degree of "opportunity," about gross comparisons with Europe, of relative disparity or homogeneity of condition in the United States. Vertical mobility has constantly taken place in our past, but it generated inequality rather than equality. There took place a continual process of differentiation in levels of livelihood, of creation and re-creation of socio-economic differences between those who moved up, those who moved down, and those who remained stable. The overall structure of socioeconomic distinctions remained relatively similar over time, but the scale of the entire structure grew rapidly, and an equally rapid movement and differentiation took place within it. At the same time as the structure remained relatively similar, within it a constant movement of individuals took place.

This general description can be rendered more precise by sorting out different facets of vertical mobility. One involves changes to different levels of occupation, income, and standards of consumption; individuals can be traced through such changes either in their own lifetime or from fathers to sons. A second consists of movement from community to society networks, from more parochial environments of limited patterns of human interaction to more cosmopolitan contacts over wide geographical areas. The effect of war, of the recruitment of soldiers from traditional, stable settings and their involvement in a wider set of experiences, for example, played an important role in their process of vertical movement. Still a third involved upward shifts in roles in bureaucratic systems, including changes in occupation, the formal acquisition of skills, the climate of expertise and the manipulation of impersonal things, and the capacity to influence the system in which one worked.

A second approach to vertical mobility is its comparative description as between ethnic, religious, and racial groups. These represent value orientations and loyalties distinct from socioeconomic and community-society patterns but which in the course of modern American history were transformed by them. Within each ethno-cultural group some moved up and others did not, thereby generating separate and parallel vertical structures. Comparison and contrast of the process within each separate group provides considerable insight into vertical mobility as a whole. Does it develop more rapidly in one than another? Do particular religious, ethnic, and racial values stimulate or depress the desire to move upward? Do external environmental conditions accelerate or retard their movement into the larger society? At the same time there are vertical differences in the tendencies to cross ethnic, religious, or racial lines. Do these come at the lower or upper levels of vertical systems? Can we apply

Milton Gordon's concept of the eth-class, that vertical movement increases contacts across ethnocultural groups within given vertical levels rather than across vertical levels within given ethnocultural groups?[38]

A crucial dimension of mobility is psychological or ideological mobility, the process by which human consciousness becomes transformed from a limited and circumscribed context of experience to one of wider range in which personal knowledge is increasingly supplemented with impersonal information. Such expansion of human consciousness greatly increases the scope not only of information and ideas about the world, but of possibilities and choices open to the individual, and of types of acceptable behavior. In extreme cases such as the injection of radio into peasant communities, the impact of psychological mobility is dramatic.[39] But it obtains in less extreme cases as well and constitutes a significant dimension of mobility in American history. It played a major role in both horizontal and vertical mobility, for it constituted the changed state of mind closely bound up with a choice to move or to improve one's condition of life. Moreover, such a concept, focusing on human experience rather than on ideas abstracted from that experience, enables social historians to shift the description of conscious life from the logical content of formally expressed ideas to the context of human experience in given environments.

While mobility generated variety, choice, and physical movement, systematization drew people into increasingly more articulated networks of large-scale human interaction. Corporate system, the self-conscious dovetailing of individuals and things into single managerial contexts for predetermined ends, has become more highly elaborated since the mid-nineteenth century in private business, government, religion, and education.[40] But integrated networks of human interaction resulted also from individual decisions made by large numbers of people to prefer the benefits of system: the speed and flexibility of new highways, the variety and service of the supermarket over the corner grocery store, the improvements in education made possible by larger school systems with larger tax bases and more

38. Milton Gordon, *Assimilation in American Life* (New York, 1964), 51–54.
39. Daniel Lerner, *The Passing of Traditional Society* (Glencoe, Ill., 1958), 136–68.
40. Warner, *Large-Scale Organizations*.

varied technical resources. Through such forces as these, individuals have become more tightly involved in general networks of human activity, more integrated into large private and public systems.

During the late eighteenth and nineteenth centuries, for example, Americans became more deeply involved in the political system as voters. Although in the 1780s many held the legal right to vote, few did so; by the last third of the nineteenth century many did. Although this overall change is clear, its stages of development are not. In the early nineteenth century, party competition sharply increased voting turnout at the state level.[41] But not until several decades later did the same take place for presidential elections.[42] Studies under way that emphasize ethnicity and religion in establishing voting patterns in the last half of the century suggest that a persistent and stable party involvement might well have been a function of competing ethnic and religious involvements, that participation in the wider political system was a product of participation in smaller units of social life.[43] Moreover, voter turnout reached a peak in the late nineteenth century and declined to a lower level in the twentieth, reflecting perhaps the declining influence of smaller ethnocultural contexts of social organization.[44]

As workers, Americans became involved in more highly organized and disciplined work systems from the early nineteenth century to the present day. The shift from independent artisan work to the modern mass-production system came about over many decades, involving a persistent extension of discipline and control within the system. The early New England textile ventures, for example, created the discipline of scheduled work hours and artificial light. But this did not generate a full-blown industrial discipline; it constituted only the first stages in a steady elaboration. Even as the larger umbrella of managerial organization developed in the nineteenth century, the production system often remained at the small

41. See data in David Hackett Fischer, *The Revolution of American Conservatism* (New York, 1965), 188–90.

42. Richard P. McCormick, "New Perspectives on Jacksonian Politics," *American Historical Review* 65 (1960), 288–301; see a critique of McCormick in Charles Sellers, "The Equilibrium Cycle in Two-Party Politics," *Public Opinion Quarterly* 29 (1965), 16–38.

43. Paul Kleppner, *The Cross of Culture: A Social Analysis of Midwestern Politics, 1850–1900* (New York, 1970).

44. Walter Dean Burnham, "The Changing Shape of the American Political Universe," *American Political Science Review* 59 (1965), 7–28.

work-group level involving primary relationships—the glassblower with his helpers, the rolling-mill operator with his hired assistants. These constituted a series of small-group work situations organized by the skilled artisan, the relatively "autonomous" worker who enjoyed considerable freedom from day-to-day discipline from top management and therefore exercised considerable leverage in decisions made in the system.[45]

The closer articulation of labor into the larger industrial discipline accelerated rapidly in the late nineteenth and early twentieth centuries as the system became rationalized and top management through "scientific management" sought to destroy small-group loyalties within it. Americanization—the instruction of immigrant workmen in English—played an important role in this development. It eliminated the need for management to reach workmen through foremen who knew foreign languages, established direct communication, and facilitated control within the plant. The development of workmen's compensation insurance also accelerated rationalization.[46] It eliminated worker leverage against management through the courts in accident cases and gave rise to control systems within the plant to promote safety and reduce system costs. Workmen became more deeply involved in the large corporate system of work discipline as well as of benefits.

A third focal point for the study of systematization is its impact on community. The city was a source of centralization, of systematization, both within its immediate metropolitan area and in the larger region. These tendencies drastically affected smaller communities within the city and the region. Such communities stood at the threshold of either being drawn into the system or left out of it, of relative involvement or lack of involvement. What happened to such communities? The elaboration of a system of intercity hard-surfaced roads, the development of state and federal programs of grants-in-aid from larger to smaller centers of life, the shift from county-run poorhouses for the elderly to state and federal systems of old-age pensions, the consolidation of schools and the elabora-

---

45. Benson Soffer, "A Theory of Trade Union Development: The Role of the 'Autonomous' Workman," *Labor History* 1 (1960), 141–63.

46. Roy Lubove, "Workmen's Compensation and the Prerogatives of Voluntarism," *Labor History* 8 (1967), 254–79.

tion of school administration at the county, regional, and state level—all these developments involved the local community more deeply in wider systems, necessitated linkages with those larger systems, or produced protective ideologies and devices against those influences.[47] The urban subcommunity, which at one time played a significant role in urban government through ward representation and ward officials, declined in political creativeness as municipal government became more highly systematized with citywide elections and stronger executive branches.[48] Communities as well as individuals were deeply affected by systematization.

Finally, systematization can be viewed from the vantage point of those who elaborated it—the managers, the experts, the technical subordinates who continually sought to rationalize more fully, to reduce waste in time and motion. This took place over a long period of time; it continues in the mid-twentieth century. Its stages of development included changes in the training of engineers; the elaboration of school administration; the development of industrial psychology and personnel management; the growth of planning within the private corporation prior to its development in government; the evolution of the independent public corporation at federal, state, and local levels; the internal elaboration of corporate organization and control. From such sources of innovation there developed new systems of control, new sources of knowledge about affairs to be controlled, new attitudes toward the wider political order, and new cadres of technical experts. These elaborators of system were the agents of revolutionary change in modern America.[49]

IV

SOCIAL history, then, requires more satisfactory concepts; it also needs to improve methods of social description. Social history rests

47. An excellent case study of the role of the community in the wider society is Arthur J. Vidich and Joseph Bensman, *Small Town in Mass Society* (Princeton, 1958); a more general treatment is Roland Warren, *The Community in America* (Chicago, 1963).

48. Hays, "Political Parties and the Community-Society Continuum," *loc. cit.*, esp. 174–76.

49. Several studies detail various aspects of these changes: Raymond E. Callahan, *Education and the Cult of Efficiency* (Chicago, 1962); Loren Baritz, *The Servants of Power* (Middletown, Conn., 1960); John Kenneth Galbraith, *The New Industrial State* (Boston, 1967), 22–34.

upon social data. Large numbers of people cannot be described with evidence about a few events or individuals, but only with data about large numbers of people. To deal with such evidence, moreover, requires systematic methods of developing, ordering, and manipulating vast amounts of data. All this requires changes in the prevailing work habits of the profession. For those habits have in the past played a major role in prompting the historian to bypass the enormous amount of social data in the historical record. Social data, the excuse frequently is given, are too time-consuming to work up. It takes far less time, for example, to write urban history from the newspaper narrative than from the tax records. It is easier to describe the share of wealth owned by the top 10 percent of wealth holders rather than to construct a distribution for all wealth holders. But such an approach, often carried out under the guise of having examined "all relevant evidence," has limited sharply the range and variety of evidence used by historians and in turn the range and variety of historical description. If we are to engage in social description, there is no satisfactory substitute for the compilation of data about large numbers of people.

Basic to systematic social description is a reconstruction of the patterns of variation in human characteristics. Rarely are these characteristics uniform or sharply dichotomous. Empirical description reveals rather a more common pattern of variation from one extreme of intensity to another in such characteristics as voting preferences, wealth, attitudes and beliefs, or ideological mobility. This variation can be described for the characteristics of individuals or of categories of individuals such as counties, cities, religious denominations, or labor unions. We have already spoken of the tendency of historians to remain content with dichotomous descriptions, with twofold mutually exclusive categories of "either or." Such categories rarely are faithful historical descriptions of the range of human characteristics; more frequently they arise from the fact that they are easier to generate. It is more difficult to obtain and develop evidence that will describe the range of properties from one end of a scale of intensity to another. But it is not at all impossible, and today it constitutes one of the greatest opportunities for making substantial descriptive contributions to social history.

Quantitative data provide the most satisfactory evidence for the description of variation, for they enable one to assign a precise value of magnitude to a person or group of people in describing characteristics and to indicate the degree of similarity to or difference from others. A township cast 20 percent of its vote for the Republican party as contrasted with another which cast 80 percent. We know that the two townships differ and how much they differ; this is far more precise than the fact that one is Republican and the other Democratic. Moreover, every township in question can be ranged on a scale from one intensity of Republican vote to the other, thereby providing a picture of variation in the level of vote within the entire population. Or, to use another example, variation in economic condition, whether in terms of property ownership or income, can be described in far more precise terms for an entire population through quantitative rather than qualitative evidence. With the former we need not speak just of the rich and the poor, but can say precisely that the top 10 percent of property owners hold 55 percent of the property, that the bottom 50 percent of income earners earn 22 percent of the income. Without quantitative data one is tempted to believe that characteristics are uniform, or at the most dichotomous, descriptions which are more than likely incorrect. Quantitative data bring out the pattern of variation and make our descriptions more complete and more accurate.

Even without extensive quantitative data, however, a description of variation is still possible. Above we have been discussing "interval" data in which a value can be assigned to each unit and the precise interval relationship between units (65 percent as compared with 68 percent) can be described. But we can also speak of variation in less precise terms, of simply "more" or "less," using "ordinal" measurement, in which all we know is the *ranking* of units in terms of their properties. Without more precise information, for example, we might classify communities into degrees of evangelical religion—least, average, and most—in order to determine the differences among them in educational institutions or religious controversies in the 1830s and 1840s. In such a classification the historian uses a variety of incomplete quantitative and qualitative sources to determine, in his own judgment, the intensity of the characteristic. Description of variation in values and ideas in history depends far more on this ranking of qualitative evidence than the availability of a continuous series of interval data.

Descriptions of variation, either over space or time, generate definitions of historical problems. Variation immediately raises questions as to why it occurs. If there is a range of religious values from evangelical pietism on the one hand to liturgical traditionalism on the other, if there is variation over time in the exercise of church discipline, if it is found that doctors vary as to the degree of their involvement in municipal reform in the early twentieth century, if there is variation in views as to the appropriate unit of banking administration, why does this variation occur? Why the inequalities in the distribution of characteristics? To pursue such a question, a research design is then formulated to discover systematic variations that parallel those of the phenomenon under observation. If we find that a particular historical phenomenon—such as conceptions of America as an entity separate from England, attitudes toward the slavery question, voting preferences, the location and timing of slave revolts, or white attitudes toward blacks in the mid-twentieth century—varies in the same manner as do other phenomena, both "objective" and conscious, then we assume some sort of relationship.[50] Such observations do not constitute "explanations," but more complete description, description of systematic relationships, and thereby enhance the quality as well as the amount of ordered historical evidence.

One aspect of this method is the attempt to sort out the general from the particular. To what extent are phenomena such as upward mobility among Italians in the twentieth century or the old-middle-class background of Progressive party leaders in 1912 characteristics held in common with other similar groups (Poles, Jews, and blacks in the one case and Old Guard and Democratic leaders in the other) or characteristics held uniquely? To establish precise relationships one must first of all establish this distinction. Much historical research fails simply because the capacity to establish such

50. See, for example, Richard Merritt, *Symbols of American Community, 1735–1775* (New Haven, 1966); Marian D. de B. Kilson, "Towards Freedom: An Analysis of Slave Revolts in the United States," *Phylon* 25 (1964), 175–87; Louis Harris Poll, *Pittsburgh Post-Gazette*, Aug. 15, 1966.

distinctions is not built into research designs. As William Sewell has written recently, this simple design constituted one of Marc Bloch's major contributions; we could well return, with profit, to his methods.[51] The controversy over the nature of Progressive political leadership in the early twentieth century, for example, would not have occurred had research designs been conducted in this fashion. That controversy was simply a descriptive one. What were the characteristics of Progressive leaders? The Mowry-Chandler studies described such leaders by themselves and thereby were unable to distinguish the general—the characteristics of leaders from all political parties—from the particular—the characteristics of Progressive party leaders. Since their descriptions were faulty, their reasoning from those descriptions was incorrect; they explained the peculiar behavior of Progressive leaders in terms of characteristics not peculiar to them.[52]

Through the process of distinguishing the general from the particular comparative history takes on meaning. The tendency to limit comparative history to the comparison of entire societies, America and Europe for example, has in the past reduced its usefulness as a method. It should be extended to national settings, to sort out the general aspects of those phenomena from the particular, to distinguish similarities and differences. Migrations from rural Europe to the United States could be described far more precisely if they could be compared with migrations from the same origins in Europe to other continents besides North America and to other nations within Europe. The two studies of the development of the Jewish community between 1890 and 1914 in the Lower East Side of New York by Moses Rischin and of London by Lloyd Gartner are cases in point.[53] But they were carried out in separate projects, and

51. William H. Sewell, Jr., "Marc Bloch and the Logic of Comparative History," *History and Theory* 6 (1967), 208–18.

52. George E. Mowry, *The California Progressives* (Berkeley, Calif., 1951), 86–104; Alfred D. Chandler, Jr., "The Origins of Progressive Leadership," in Elting Morrison et al. (eds.), *The Letters of Theodore Roosevelt* (Cambridge, 1951–1954), VIII, Appendix III, 1462–64; E. Daniel Potts, "The Progressive Profile in Iowa," *Mid-America* 47 (1965), 257–68; William T. Kerr, Jr., "The Progressives of Washington, 1910–12," *Pacific Northwest Quarterly* 55 (1964), 16–27; Samuel P. Hays, "The Politics of Reform," *loc. cit.*

53. Moses Rischin, *The Promised City: New York's Jews, 1870–1914* (Cambridge, Mass., 1962); Lloyd P. Gartner, *The Jewish Immigrant in England, 1870–1914* (Detroit, 1960).

therefore the categories of description vary as between the two studies. Moreover, the comparative quality of their descriptions could be enhanced if set alongside studies of similar migrations of eastern European Jews to eastern European cities and to cities on other continents.

One example of effective comparative research design is Sigmund Diamond's description of the similarities and differences in the processes of colonization in French, British, and Spanish colonies in the New World. Diamond is interested in these colonial ventures as examples of social planning and its unintended consequences, especially the change from corporate venture to autonomous society. The quality of his description and analysis is enormously enhanced by the ability to distinguish the particular process of colonization in each instance from the process of colonization in general. Because his conclusions rest on a comparative base, they will be relevant to general propositions about social planning and its unintended consequences in many different times and places.[54]

Comparative history need not be confined to similar types of phenomena in different national settings. It is useful in sharpening research designs for studies within one country as well and for the entire range of historical phenomena. Any two geographical areas may be juxtaposed to examine their similarities and differences— regions, states, cities, rural areas, communities within a city. And the same can be done for any two nongeographical categories, such as political leaders of different parties, upper and lower socioeconomic groups, Reform or Orthodox Jews, local or cosmopolitan newspapers, those in favor of municipal reform and those opposed. Thus James Q. Wilson compared the political development of black communities in four different cities in the mid-twentieth century.[55] We may compare migration from rural to urban America with that from the central city to the suburbs, the development of small business in the nineteenth century when it was relatively autonomous with that of the twentieth century when it became more of a satellite to large corporate enterprises, the evolution of socioeconomic

54. Sigmund Diamond, "From Organization to Society: Virginia in the Seventeenth Century," *American Journal of Sociology* 63 (1958), 457–75.
55. James Q. Wilson, *Negro Politics: The Search for Leadership* (Glencoe, Ill., 1960), 21–47.

structure within the Italian and the black communities, or fringe political movements on the Right and the Left. Comparative research designs that sort out the particular from the general can be applied fruitfully to a wide range of phenomena; they constitute a crucial methodological device for sharpening the description of historical social phenomena.

Descriptions of conscious life—experience, perception, explanations, values—are the most unsatisfactory of all historical descriptions. They are also the most difficult to render systematic. Most involve aggregate characteristics rather than variations within a distribution. They describe the values or ideas of an entire society, an "age," a political party, or a region rather than a range of intensities along a scale, such as degrees of certainty as to the truth of the Biblical miracles, a range of attitudes toward the League of Nations, or preferences concerning slavery. Historians are prone to gather evidence from a variety of sources and to assume that in some general manner it adds up to an aggregate description. The representativeness of the data is rarely called into question, and procedures are rarely adopted for categorizing it in such a way as to establish variation.

Behind this state of affairs are difficulties encountered in securing systematic data to describe variation in values and perceptions. The current popularity of voting studies arises from the ready availability of voting data, of mobility and urban ecological studies from the manuscript census data. But how to describe conscious life systematically when the most visible historical record represents the limited, articulate sector of society which is not known to be representative? Unavailability of evidence is not the entire story, for extant evidence could yield far greater returns than it has. Qualitative evidence can often be used to generate systematic description; moreover, plausible inferences about conscious life can be made from a systematic description of "objective" conditions. We have taken up few of these opportunities.

I would suggest that we are on the threshold of a more adequate picture of the conscious life of the Jacksonian era, for example, as a result of the impact of systematic description. In the past we have assumed the existence of something called "Jacksonian Democracy," which should be described. Two recent attempts to reconstruct the conscious life of this "age" are Marvin Meyers' *The Jacksonian Persuasion* and John William Ward's *Andrew Jackson, Symbol for an Age*.[56] These are aggregate descriptions, intuitive and unsystematic in method. They use a variety of sources which reflect "popular" attitudes and values from which they reconstruct an aggregate description of human perception. Consequently the reader obtains the impression of a period of history dominated by a single overall perspective or set of assumptions, values, and explanations. No sense is conveyed of a range of intensities of values, beliefs, or perceptions, of a distribution for which the aggregate description is a central tendency. Consequently the description itself is limited to the assumed central tendency rather than the entire distribution, and there is no way of determining if the aggregate set of beliefs is actually a central tendency. In the absence of all this one is led to assume a condition of homogeneity of belief, an assumption that is highly dubious.

Several recent studies that reconstruct systematic variation in social structure in the nineteenth century suggest its implications for a similar description of conscious life. One involves differences between evangelical and conservative religious values. Timothy Smith has resurrected evangelical religion from the frontier and transferred it into the context of a growing optimistic, hopeful movement at the developing edge of social change.[57] Robert Doherty, in his studies of Presbyterians and Quakers, has added the distinction between religious traditionalism, the preservation of historic denominational ideas, forms, and practices, and evangelical Protestantism, which cut across denominational lines and emphasized hope and involvement in the wider, cosmopolitan world.[58] Analysis of the realignment of voting patterns which took place in the early 1850s and persisted to the early and mid-nineties confirms and elaborates this range of values. Traditionalists were more Democratic and evangelicals more Republican; almost every religious denomination can be ranged on a scale from the most traditional to the most evangelical by its members' voting choices. Thus, several

56. Marvin Meyers, *Jacksonian Persuasion*; John William Ward, *Andrew Jackson*.
57. Timothy L. Smith, *Revivalism and Social Reform in Mid-Nineteenth Century America* (New York, 1957).
58. Robert Doherty, *The Hicksite Separation*, and "Social Bases for the Presbyterian Schism," *loc. cit.*

different sources of evidence are making possible descriptions of a spectrum of religious behavior varying from one end of a scale to another which has a close relationship to a similar spectrum of political behavior. It is not confined to intuitive aggregate description, or dichotomies, but entails scales of variation.

A second set of studies concerns the social bases of phenomena usually associated with Jacksonian Democracy. One, for example, is the movement for public education. According to prevailing historical notions, this drive arose from a broadly popular, "democratic," or "public" demand for education, often from working-class movements. Yet studies by Charles Bidwell and Michael Katz indicate that it came from the upper middle levels of the social order.[59] It was associated with upward social mobility. Thus, it did not represent a broadly based movement toward equalitarianism. To the contrary; by creating and re-creating inequalities vertical mobility generated class differentiation. Those moving upward sought to distinguish themselves from those below them in occupation, income, and life style. The spirit of the drive was not to be similar to others, but to be different from them. The public-education movement in the Jacksonian era, therefore, played a role not in creating an aggregate, homogeneous set of values—"Jacksonian Democracy" —but in elaborating the inequalities and the distinct steps in a vertical scale of social structure.

What does all this have to do with conscious life, with experience, perception, explanations, values? We have been describing "objective" data more than conscious life. Yet it seems inconceivable that these "objective" data could not influence our views as to what people thought, believed, valued in the "Jacksonian Age." First, it makes clear the inadequacy of aggregate description and the necessity of scales of variation simply to describe conscious life adequately. It indicates, in other words, the necessity of establishing the social structure of human consciousness as basic to a satisfactory description of the Jacksonian era. Second, it establishes a strong case for inferring substantive descriptions of conscious life from "objective" data. Since religious traditionalists came into conflict with evangelicals on so many issues, for example, significant

59. Bidwell, "Moral Significance," *loc. cit.*; Katz, *Irony of Early School Reform.*

differences in perceptions, values, and experience certainly lay behind those conflicts. The objective data display the completeness and intensity of the range of behavior and suggest a similar completeness and intensity in the range of conscious life. We then can fit into this scale expressions of beliefs and values which admittedly are incomplete and represent only the articulate segments of the population. By establishing the range of the scale, the "objective" data set limits so that we know the portion of the entire society to which to attribute the particular conscious expression of opinion, rather than merely assume that it reflects the views of the whole. Moreover, once this precise location of opinion is established, we can then interpolate to the segments of the social order which are not articulate.

We can also examine conscious life directly by arranging expressions of opinion in systematic order through content analysis. The purpose of content analysis is to bring out patterns of thought, value, and perception which are not readily manifest. The historian usually arranges such evidence in terms of dichotomies, dichotomies often suggested by the manifest form of the evidence itself. But such evidence also contains subtleties of expression, admittedly more difficult to capture, which establish a wider range of variation in opinion. Content analysis seeks to find methods of establishing patterns among this variety of words, symbols, and reactions to events. Only the simplest and crudest such measurements have as yet been undertaken: for example, the description of the sense of being an American in the eighteenth century and the timing of that development by Richard Merritt, and the changing attitudes of farm journals toward business in the late nineteenth and early twentieth centuries by Louis Galambos.[60] Both of these studies describe aggregate views and are concerned with change over time rather than scale variation at one point in time. Gilbert Shapiro is developing a method for constructing a wider and more complex scale of content variation. Working with the *cahiers de doléances* of the French Revolution, Shapiro is attempting to describe their differences in content as between local, provincial, and national levels

---

60. Merritt, *Symbols of American Community*; Louis Galambos, "The Agrarian Image of the Large Corporation, 1879–1920: A Study in Social Accommodation," *Journal of Economic History* 28 (1968), 341–62.

and variations in them as between geographical areas and other social groups. Shapiro's method is far more flexible than those used by Merritt and Galambos, providing a far wider variety of categories of description.[61]

The possibilities of content analysis in revising categories of description can be seen in the meaning of tariff arguments in the late nineteenth century. Most descriptions of tariff ideology summarize the manifest logical content of tariff arguments, those for higher and those for lower rates and the arguments for each. The wide use of tariff ideology in party competition, however, indicates that it played a far more inclusive role than simply debate over a legislative proposal and involved more subtle and even symbolic meaning. One study has found, for example, that in the relatively good times of the late 1880s tariff arguments fused into general statements about positive government which interfered with private activities on the one hand, and negative government which respected personal liberties on the other. The wording and symbolism indicated that the tariff content of these arguments frequently conveyed meaning about cultural issues of prohibition and Sabbath observance. Democrats argued that Republicans sought to restrict personal liberty in both religious and economic life. During the depression of 1893 the context of the argument took on economic content, for example, as a means of job protection; in these years tariff ideology played a far different role than it had in the previous decade.[62]

The possibilities of content analysis seem to have been barely tapped. There is no reason why, for example, the range of religious values described earlier could not be established through the description of idea content as well as voting data. The success in establishing the latter should encourage the development of the former as a test-control procedure. Another possible type of scale provides a further illustration. A dichotomy of proslavery and antislavery views, appropriate for the rhetoric of the increasingly polarized political climate of the antebellum years, is not sufficient to describe variations in attitudes toward slavery. The range extends at least

---

61. John Markoff and Gilbert Shapiro, "Quantitative Studies of the French Revolution: A Concrete Analytic Code for the Cahiers de Doléances of 1789," unpub. ms., Univ. of Pittsburgh.

62. Paul Kleppner, *The Cross of Culture*, 147–57, 257–68.

from preservation of slavery where it was, to colonization, to limitation in the territories, to subordination of the free black in the North, to abolition, and to social integration. Although we are aware of the variety of views, we have not yet sought to construct a scale of variation so as to describe the poles and the intervening segments between them. When we do, we will have described the spectrum of slavery attitudes not as arguments but as dimensions of the structure of human consciousness.

Still a third major foray into the reconstruction of conscious life can be made for that period of the twentieth century after attitude surveys became available. These attitude surveys, in the form of public-opinion polls or survey research by sociologists, political scientists, marketing survey specialists, and others, constitute an abundant source of information for the study of the past. As these decades become a field of research by historians, such survey-generated data will constitute a major type of historical evidence. Indeed, historians might well become more involved in the description of the very recent past and generate survey data themselves by interviewing those who took part in activities they research or those involved in current affairs.

Survey data usually provide precisely the kind of disaggregate descriptions or ranges in variation in attitudes which the historian has far greater difficulty in reconstructing with presurvey evidence. As a result, the types of variations survey research describes can serve as models for working with earlier data. But they also provide raw material from which one can investigate more recent history. The more the historian is willing to deal with the present day the more he can construct his own survey categories, rather than rely on those constructed by social scientists, and thereby bring into the life of survey research the kind of historical dimension which is his peculiar contribution. Historians should be able to look to a time thirty, forty, or more years hence and ask the kinds of questions about the past other historians then will be asking. They can then formulate problems of social description in the contemporary world so as to provide current observation points for those aspects of long-run change. In this way the systematic description of conscious life for history would be enhanced significantly.

I am not speaking here simply of collaboration between history and the social sciences. For it seems obvious that the great majority of social scientists are not interested in long-run social change. I do not suggest, therefore, that historians become subordinate partners in the social science enterprise and merely provide the "background" to the contemporary investigations of social scientists. I speak of the historical enterprise per se, the reconstruction of social structures as they change over long periods of time, and the way in which the historian can generate descriptions in the contemporary world which are uniquely geared to that objective.

V

SOME will object that the preceding framework for social history is not history but sociology. If one defines history as a concern for the individual and the unique, this criticism is, of course, valid. But it is precisely this limited view which vitiates social history and renders it incapable of a systematic study of social change. In sociology, concerned with social structure, social historians can find much to bring system and order into a semi-anarchic field of study. Some sociological investigations are excellent examples of social history. *Middletown*, a contemporary study of Muncie in the early 1920s, has become an important historical monograph.[63] Baltzell's *Philadelphia Gentlemen* or Gusfield's *Symbolic Crusade* use historical materials within sociological frameworks.[64] To refuse to bring such studies as these into the orbit of the historical enterprise is to retain an arbitrary division between two disciplines where common problems call for common involvement.

At the same time, however, sociology lacks a framework of long-run social change. Involved first with social reform and then with a broader spirit of scientific instrumentalism, sociology in America has been concerned more with contemporary problems and short-run change. With this segment of sociology the historian can carry out few sustained common ventures. But others are concerned with long-run social change and with incorporating structural concepts

63. Robert S. and Helen M. Lynd, *Middletown* (New York, 1929).
64. E. Digby Baltzell, *Philadelphia Gentlemen: The Making of a National Upper Class* (Glencoe, Ill., 1958); Joseph R. Gusfield, *Symbolic Crusade: Status Politics and the American Temperance Movement* (Urbana, Ill., 1963).

into a framework of change over time. This brings sociology into the context of history and happily joins a concern for structure with one for long-run social change. The most fruitful opportunities for the development of social history lie in the close collaboration between that segment of social history interested in social structure and that of sociology interested in long-run social change. Some may prefer to speak of historical sociology; others of sociological history. Both refer to a common concern for large-scale structural changes in society over long periods of time.

A more serious objection to social history as social structure arises from the concern for the study of the conscious life of man. Many reject sociology as environmentalism, emphasizing the external circumstances of man's life rather than his experiences, his values, and his choices in the midst of indeterminate situations. Social structure seems to be associated with historical materialism, the onward sweep of institutions in which ideas and man's conscious life in general are derivative epiphenomena, reducible to external circumstance and squeezed dry by their own qualities. Lurking behind this view is the familiar image of Watsonian behaviorism, of stimulus-response psychology, of a theory of human development emphasizing "objective" circumstance as the primary causal force in human life.

This frame of reference for evaluating a structural approach to social history is far outdated; a dichotomy between environmentalism and conscious life does not exhaust the possibilities. It is, in fact, far more appropriate to reverse the image and examine the structure of human experience and conscious life not in terms of an environment pressing in upon man, but of man reaching out to comprehend his environmental circumstances. One of man's primary motives is the desire to understand his world so as to determine where he fits. Whether that understanding be simple or complex, supernatural or natural, based upon true or false data, it rests upon the drive for comprehension and explanation. Yet man can experience only a small portion of that world, and his understanding arises from his limited experience. The limits and peculiarities of man's thought and explanations, therefore, are directly related to the limits and peculiarities of his experience. One parallels the other.

Social history must describe the peculiar characteristics of both man's conscious life and his external circumstances. Whether or not one rests upon the other causally is of secondary importance. For through the description of distinctive characteristics of expressions of conscious experience, thought and values, and external circumstances, the distinctively shared characteristics of men in the past can be understood and developed into a pattern of structure. The major point at issue is not *whether* conscious life shall be described, but *how*—in terms of the unique and individual, or of shared characteristics. The latter, historians of ideas have failed to undertake, but it must be done if the history of man's perceptual world is to be incorporated successfully into social history.

The search for historical patterns of human relationships is now proceeding more thoroughly than in years past. It involves two facets: the generation of concepts and the development of data. Both are required; neither by itself is sufficient. Concepts without reference to concrete cases lead to irrelevant abstractions; data development without conceptual guides produces a mélange of unrelated and insignificant facts. But the constant interaction between concept and evidence, if guided by the search for structure in man's relationship with man, can produce a viable social history.

[5]

Social Structure
in the New Urban History *

I

THE major opportunity in urban history today lies in its capacity for formulating effective social theory, effective concepts as to how society is put together and how it changes. The city and its surrounding region are types of historical settings in which many facets of such matters can be dealt with in convenient and orderly fashion. Yet, although some notable progress has been made along these lines recently, there still remains a very strong predisposition in the historical profession toward a nonstructural approach. I have been particularly impressed with the way in which recent studies of geographical mobility and urban government have tended to turn thinking about cities toward concepts of individualization and homogeneity rather than toward patterns of variation and social structure. Here I want to deal with several aspects of these divergent tendencies: with some recent positive accomplishments toward a structural approach and with the nonstructural tendencies which mobility and governmental studies have generated.

American historians have perennially felt uneasy with the concept of social structure. For while it implies significant internal differentiation in human relationships, and inevitably of a vertical nature, the overwhelming predisposition has been to conceive of American society as homogeneous and undifferentiated. Concepts of this order abound in our historiography: "Jacksonian democracy" conveys the image of an undifferentiated, equalitarian economy

---

*Delivered as a paper at the Historical Urbanization in North America Conference, York University, Toronto, Jan. 24–26, 1973.

and politics; "equality of opportunity" indicates a society always becoming homogeneous even in the face of momentary deviations into inequality; the concept of "public interest" implies the existence of similar and equally shared values and goals among members of the body politic; and "cultural history" has arisen in more recent years to focus on the values and perspectives common to all in a society. All these reflect the constant tendency toward historical investigations which avoid structural considerations either by abstracting problems from structural contexts or assuming an undifferentiated society.

Urban history provides a significant opportunity to overcome some of these limitations in perspective. For the most part cities are societies which, because of their compactness and relatively defined limits, can be grasped, described, comprehended. The entire range of people within the social order of the city can be brought into the picture much more readily than for a larger social system. Moreover, because of the wide variety of evidence about urban people, differentiation within the city can be readily grasped. Traditional-type ecological studies provide an obvious opportunity for horizontal community description. But, with more work, evidence to bring out vertical differentiation is also feasible. For many years the community study, ranging upward in population size to include cities such as Muncie and Newburyport, has provided sociologists a focus for conceptualizing structure and change within a confined social order. There is no reason why historians should not take advantage of similar opportunities.

But I do not think that we are doing so sufficiently. Urban history has given rise to a great amount of research in recent years which has been relatively unrooted in structural concerns. As a result, although we know more and more about particular pieces of the city, we rarely are able to be very sensible about how these pieces fit together. It is convenient to fall back upon the old reform perspective: cities grew, gave rise to problems, and action was taken to solve those problems. The constant pressures for current "problem solving" tend to reinforce this perspective. Or it is equally inviting to describe a city, moving forward in growth and action, as an entity of common perceptions and values, relatively homogeneous, understandable primarily as an undifferentiated whole. Such vantage points, however, avoid confrontation with the differentiated and varied patterns of human perception and values in the city and lead us away from rather than toward an understanding of the city as a social system. We must bring our perspective back to a focus on the human content of urban life. There is a close connection between an appreciation of the varied human experience and circumstance of the city and a differentiated social theory about it.

As a working principle one might make the argument that no research design in urban history should be formulated without incorporating some elements of a structural context. For example, if we are concerned with values or perception, we must make some attempt to determine the precise human roots of those values and perceptions: how many people and what kinds of people as opposed to others who have different values and perception. Better still, we should encourage the development of structural studies per se, the construction of models of the urban social order as a whole. A description of the cognitive map of people who lived in Pittsburgh in 1880 would provide some sense of the variety of perceptual worlds then extant and enable the historian to fit into that map particular perceptual worlds. Without such a context it is impossible to know where the experience of any one group of people fits.

In the ensuing pages I wish to follow up this line of argument in more detail, first to give some examples of work which, in my view, does point toward a better structural sense of the city, and second, to examine some of the recent work in geographical mobility and urban government which has the opposite tendency. The purpose of all this is to try to sharpen the central task of urban history, the elaboration of social theory which spells out the structural location of social change.

II

RECENT urban research involves a number of examples which are structural in tone and spirit, such as the articles by Blumin and Katz in *Nineteenth Century Cities*,[1] but on the whole there have

1. Stuart Blumin, "Mobility and Change in Ante-Bellum Philadelphia," in Stephan Thernstrom and Richard Sennett (eds.), *Nineteenth-Century Cities: Essays in the New Urban History* (New Haven, 1969), 165–208; Michael B. Katz, "Social Structure in Hamilton, Ontario," *ibid.*, 209–44.

been few efforts to work out systematically the various types of differentiation within a given urban social order. Some work that has not been reported or published extensively is even more suggestive than that which has, and I would like to focus on these examples to indicate trends in research which seem to me to be most productive.

One has to do with vertical socioeconomic patterns, the pervasive distinctions which grow out of differences in occupation, income, and standards of living. The traditional reluctance of Americans and American historians to describe fully these patterns of the social order is still with us. In the past it has been striking that even "reformist" history of the Progressive and new Deal eras did not generate such studies. There is much about the "movements" of labor and agriculture which supports arguments about broad social forces contending in society, but there is mighty little which describes the socioeconomic system of given geographical areas. Urban history provides an opportunity to bring this dimension into American history. The work by Henretta and Kulikoff on Boston indicates what can be done with earlier materials.[2] Certainly when the massive projects undertaken by that quintumvirate of Blumin-Glasco-Griffin-Hirschberg-Katz are completed, we will know much more about all this.

One study by Robert Doherty, completed but not yet published, and reported on at the New Orleans meeting of the Organization of American Historians last year, provides an excellent model for dealing with socioeconomic patterns.[3] It encompasses five Massachusetts towns and cities, selected for their degree of involvement in or separation from the wider cosmopolitan-commercial world, over a fifty-year time span from 1800 to 1850. Doherty describes variation in socioeconomic patterns both with network circumstance—the more intense the external cosmopolitan-commercial involvement, the greater the internal inequality—and over time. Moreover, as a result he can locate a wide range of phenomena in each town and city within the socioeconomic order and do it comparatively, as among the five towns and cities. Such a model is basic. Certainly so-

2. James A. Henretta, "Economic Development and Social Structure in Colonial Boston," *William and Mary Quarterly*, 3rd Ser., 22 (1965), 75–92; Allan Kulikoff, "The Progress of Inequality in Revolutionary Boston," *ibid.*, 28 (1971), 375–412.

3. Robert Doherty, "Property Distribution in Jacksonian America," paper delivered at the meeting of the American Sociological Assoc., Denver, Aug. 1971.

cioeconomic differences in American society and in cities have been sufficiently demonstrated. But studies of individual cities or phenomena within individual cities rarely work out these elementary patterns of social differentiation and thus fail to describe the socioeconomic location of particular phenomena. It is not enough to describe the phenomena by themselves in a disengaged style. We should make sure that we know where they fit.

There is similar need for more highly developed description of urban ethnocultural patterns. The initial thrust in this direction has been in the field of voting analysis. Five major monographs have now elaborated ethnocultural factors in voting in a variety of settings, from urban to state to regional, from 1840 to 1900.[4] Only one of these, the study of Pittsburgh by Michael Holt, focuses exclusively on a city; it is supplemented for 1860 by the article by Paul Kleppner on religious differences in voting in Pittsburgh.[5] But this is only a beginning. A wide variety of patterns of ethnic, religious, and racial distinctions in urban life can be worked out in considerable detail for the city. Let me describe two such beginnings.

One is Larry Glasco's analysis of the 1855 New York State census data for Buffalo.[6] It yields some surprises. For example, of the native white ethnics, Yankees and Yorkers for the most part, only 2 percent were unskilled workers in a community where 70 percent of all occupations were unskilled. This is an even greater ethnic inequality in occupational distribution than most of us, I imagine, ever suspected. But on some other matters, especially life cycle, the topics that Glasco can deal with are unique. There is, for example, the ethnic difference in age at which young people left home for work, much earlier for Irish than native American, and much earlier still for Germans. While native Americans tended to stay in the

4. Ronald P. Formisano, *Mass Political Parties: Michigan, 1827-1861* (Princeton, 1971); Michael Holt, *Forging a Majority: the Formation of the Republican Party in Pittsburgh, 1848-1860* (New Haven, 1969); Frederick C. Luebke, *Immigrants and Politics: the Germans of Nebraska, 1880-1900* (Lincoln, Neb., 1969); Paul Kleppner, *The Cross of Culture: A Social Analysis of Midwestern Politics, 1850-1900* (New York, 1970); Richard J. Jensen, *The Winning of the Midwest: Social and Political Conflict, 1888-96* (Chicago, 1971).

5. Paul J. Kleppner, "Lincoln and the Immigrant Vote: A Case of Religious Polarization," *Mid-America* 48 (1966), 176-95.

6. Laurence Glasco, "Family Structures Compared: Irish, German and Native Born in Buffalo, New York," paper delivered at Conference on the Family, Clark Univ., Worcester, Mass., Spring 1972.

family as dependents longer, immigrant children worked outside the home earlier, as household servants or apprentices, later to become independent workers or housewives.

An even more elaborate description of ethnocultural patterns has been undertaken for Erie, Pennsylvania, in the twentieth century, 1900–1970, by William Garvey.[7] Garvey develops several measures that extend the description. Using a name identification index, supplemented by a telephone sample survey to corroborate it, Garvey extends the ethnic description down to the third, fourth, fifth, and successive generations, much better data than those provided by the census. In this way, for example, he describes precisely the declining Yankee portion of the population with each decade. He determines religious affiliation from a sample of obituary information about the church from which funeral services were conducted. Finally, he develops a vertical scale of all municipal occupations in the city for each decade, on the order of Henretta's for Boston, and describes the ethnic characteristics of each level. By this device he can show the decade-by-decade progress up the municipal job ladder by Italians, Poles, blacks, and other groups and can correlate that progress with data on occupational changes for the same groups in the sphere of private employment.

As structural studies of both ethnocultural and socioeconomic urban patterns proceed, they will intersect, hopefully, to establish a pattern of transformation from one to the other. It seems clear that within each ethnocultural group a parallel vertical order emerged so that each group developed its own socioeconomic order. Moreover, it also appears that ward political leadership for each group appeared at one level of class formation and citywide leadership at still another level. Moreover, this change seems to involve an important transition from attachments and loyalties across socioeconomic levels within ethnocultural groups to attachments and loyalties across ethnocultural groups within socioeconomic levels. These changes Garvey can show in Erie decade by decade because of the completeness of his measures of both differentiating factors. To describe that

7. William Garvey, "The Ethnic Factor in Erie Politics, 1900–1970," Ph.D. diss., Univ. of Pittsburgh, 1973; for a shorter version see William Garvey, "Ethnic Politics in Erie," *The Journal of Erie Studies* 1 (1972), 1–18.

intersection of two dimensions, it appears, is one of the most fundamental of all focal points for a successful urban study.

A third facet of urban structural research which could be pursued more vigorously is that pertaining to urban elites and upper classes. We have only the Philadelphia example by Baltzell as a well-known work.[8] But the upper levels of the social order require as much attention as do the middle and lower levels in order to develop a complete picture of social and political structure. It could be pursued in several ways; the examples here are drawn from work done by students at the University of Pittsburgh. One has worked out the elite and upper-class patterns for Wilkes-Barre, Pennsylvania, from 1850 to 1920.[9] In 1880, after the first spurt of economic development, the upper levels of economic, political, and social life were dominated by four kinship groups, with old residents selectively absorbing the more affluent newer residents into patterned ties of personal connections. Another is working out levels within the upper class of Pittsburgh, by comparing individuals in three different upper-class directories.[10] People in the various levels differed as to their institutional involvements, their marriage and kinship patterns, their "old" or "new" local status. Especially important is the differential progress of the more newly arrived up the levels, with more openness at the bottom than at the top of the upper class.

A more extensive analysis has been designed by John Ingham in a recently completed dissertation.[11] Taking as his population iron and steel leaders of the years 1850-1880, Ingham works out their patterns of origin back into the early nineteenth century, their internal relationships as between "core" and "peripheral" status within their own communities, and the role of their descendants down to the present day. This model is applied to six cities: Pittsburgh, Philadelphia, Bethlehem, Cleveland, Youngstown, and Wheeling. From

8. E. Digby Baltzell, *Philadelphia Gentlemen: the Making of a National Upper Class* (Glencoe, Ill., 1958).

9. Edward Davies, "Wilkes-Barre, 1870–1920: a Study in the Evolution of Urban Leadership During Industrialization," seminar paper, Univ. of Pittsburgh, 1972.

10. George Bedeian, "Social Stratification Within a Metropolitan Upper Class: Early Twentieth-Century Pittsburgh as a Case Study," seminar paper, Univ. of Pittsburgh, 1974.

11. Published later as John Ingham, *The Iron Barons: A Social Analysis of An American Urban Elite, 1874-1965* (Westport, Conn., 1978).

this vantage point Ingham is able to establish the internal structure of an important segment of the upper levels of the social order in given cities, and to do it comparatively. Urban historians will be especially interested in his sharp disagreement with Baltzell's notion of a transition from a local to a national upper class. Ingham argues that upper-class systems in these cities are rooted in circumstances specific to those cities and that national ties are derivative and secondary, grafted upon more basic independent urban social structures.

Finally, one might work out the implications of a communications theory of urban structure, sorting out more local and more cosmopolitan relationships, community and society within the city. A considerable amount of evidence about human involvements could be brought to bear on such theory. One such study deals with women's clubs.[12] It sought to range a number of clubs in the early twentieth century on a local-cosmopolitan continuum by examining the institutional involvements and connections of their members. Some clubs were found to be highly local, involving people of the same general area; women's auxiliaries of men's fraternal and veterans' organizations were of this type, and their activities were almost entirely social and derived from the affairs of the men's organizations. Others were more cosmopolitan, with members of higher levels of education, living in a wider geographical area, and more concerned with civic affairs and public issues at the citywide level. The most cosmopolitan of all, the Consumers' League and related groups, were even more highly educated and took part in public affairs at a state and national level.

Another study examined these processes in religion, utilizing a communications variation of a sect-church continuum.[13] Selecting churches which from their general ideological orientation seemed to be more sectarian or more churchlike, the author examined their styles of religious expression and their personal and institutional involvements. The sect groups displayed a far more intensive level of primary group relationships and limited wider involvements. The

---

12. Marguerite Renner, "A Study of Women's Participation in Voluntary Organizations," seminar paper, Univ. of Pittsburgh, 1972.

13. Jeffrey Geffen, "Evangelical Protestants in Pittsburgh: A Comparative Study of Five Church Memberships in 1897," seminar paper, Univ. of Pittsburgh, 1972.

more cosmopolitan groups had a more open and varied style of religious commitment, far wider personal ties, and a wider range of institutional church activities. While the human relationships of the sect were limited and local, those of the church were broader and more cosmopolitan. Such patterns as these are more difficult to get at than are those for which census data are more directly relevant, but they display a dimension to urban social structure which seems extremely important. It may well be that much of the city's social order cannot be understood outside a communications or local-cosmopolitan pattern of human relationships.

III

SUCH studies as these turn our attention in urban history in a structural direction. But other studies run in an opposite vein. Studies of mobility, popular in recent years, have, I feel, had this effect. While providing far more insight than previously offered about mobility, they have helped to reinforce an individualized conception of the social order in which form and pattern in human relationships is obscured by the random choices of individuals. The data on geographic mobility have been particularly impressive. Every such study has indicated a low level of persistence and a high level of movement. The Knights-Thernstrom article in the *Journal of Interdisciplinary History*[14] was a kind of capstone to this approach, for it detailed not only the percentage of leavers but the very high rate of movement in and out of Boston over and above absolute growth. Howard Chudacoff's recent book on Omaha, *Mobile Americans*,[15] adds to the overall general impression. His evidence overwhelmingly underlines the fact of movement, individual movement.

These data have had a profound influence on historical perspective. They tend to generate an impression of society as an accumulation of moving, restless individuals, for whom stability and pattern are submerged by constant change. This is the message of Chuda-

14. Stephan Thernstrom and Peter R. Knights, "Men in Motion: Some Data and Speculations about Urban Population Mobility in Nineteenth Century America," *Journal of Interdisciplinary History* 1 (1970), 1–35.
15. Howard P. Chudacoff, *Mobile Americans: Residential and Social Mobility in Omaha, 1880-1920* (New York, 1972).

coff's book, as well as of Peter Knights's *The Plain People of Boston*.[16] It is revealed in the Thernstrom and Knights article in which they display skepticism about the "island communities" described by Robert Wiebe in *The Search for Order*,[17] and it is generalized to an even wider context by Rowland Berthoff in *An Unsettled People*.[18] Following conclusions he came to in the study of the anthracite region of eastern Pennsylvania,[19] Berthoff is impressed with the formlessness, the lack of structure and pattern in the American social order.

This sense of pervasive movement has several wider influences on the historical imagination. Especially it has helped to generate the view that the early stages of industrialization and modernization constituted a massive "breakdown" of old institutions, creating thereby social "disorder," "disorganization," and "alienation."[20] A mobile society is contrasted with an assumed previously stable one, and the concept of a "breakdown" in a previous social order is described. We read more frequently these days of a "breakdown" in the family and the community in the first half of the nineteenth century accompanying the acceleration of modernization. And the data about high levels of geographical mobility have played an influential role in that view. Breakdown creates a wide variety of social problems, of rootless individuals who have difficulty in living in a formless society and who give rise to certain kinds of aberrant behavior. Many forms of human activity in the nineteenth century are readily incorporated into the context of reactions against this rootlessness and of the search for meaning and order in the midst of disorganization and disorder.

One of the most popular of these is the rise of associational activity, which is described as a result of the dislocations of social change. More traditional societies were well-ordered, with family and community providing a stable context within which individuals

16. Peter R. Knights, *The Plain People of Boston, 1830–1860: A Study in City Growth* (New York, 1971).

17. Robert H. Wiebe, *The Search for Order, 1877–1920* (New York, 1967).

18. Rowland Berthoff, *An Unsettled People: Social Order and Disorder in American History* (New York, 1971).

19. Rowland Berthoff, "The Social Order of the Anthracite Region, 1825–1902," *Pennsylvania Magazine of History and Biography* 38 (1965), 261–91.

20. For a recent statement of this view see Richard D. Brown, "Modernization and the Modern Personality in Early America, 1600–1865: A Sketch of a Synthesis," *Journal of Interdisciplinary History* 2 (1972), 222–23.

found personal meaning. But modernization destroyed all this, producing individuals dislocated from context. In the search for meaning they formed associations. The supposedly high number of associations in nineteenth-century America was a direct consequence of the high degree of mobility, individualism, and alienation brought about by the early stages of industrialization and urbanization.

Let us, however, put associational activity in a firm structural context. Where, for example, in the social order were associations located? Who were members, and what were their activities in the light of the structural location of those members? When associational activity is placed in such a context, as Walter Glazer has done for Cincinnati in the 1840s, an altogether different picture emerges.[21] Only a small portion of Cincinnati's residents were involved in associational activity, and they were drawn from the upper levels of the city's social order. By other and independent measures of political, social, and economic activity, they were the dominant elements of the community, and their role in associational activities was related far more to their desire and capacity to shape and influence the social order than a reflection of their search for an escape from alienation. Glazer's evidence about the establishment of the Cincinnati observatory is particularly instructive. Long considered as arising from a popular association involving mass subscription for financial support, the drive to build the observatory was, in fact, a result of a carefully planned effort on the part of the very top levels of Cincinnati society. Such examples as these suggest that Tocqueville generally was a bad observer and that historians who rely on him are standing on erroneous evidence.

Those who are concerned with form and pattern, with structure, as this example suggests, are more likely to speak not of the "breakdown" in society, but of social "transformation." At first glance this may seem to be a minor variation in choice of words, but in fact it conveys a fundamental difference. Those impressed with structure are inclined to view individual movement as a process of change from one pattern of life to another, of the emergence of a new set of social relationships out of another, of a shift in involve-

21. Walter S. Glazer, "Participation and Power: Voluntary Associations and the Functional Organization of Cincinnati in 1840," *Historical Methods Newsletter* 5 (1972), 151–68.

ments and characteristics in which one social order gives way to another. It is often curious that almost every period of history in the United States has generated a concern for the "breakdown" of social institutions, and often the same kind of "breakdown" at almost every succeeding stage of, for example, the family or the community. All of which implies that each decade involved a sudden shift from stability to disorganization in one critical period. Far more plausible is a framework of persistent change, gradual, over the years.

There is an intriguing twist which is emerging here. Those who think in terms of structure are beginning to argue that what heretofore has been described as "social disorganization" may not be a characteristic of society in general but of life cycle. It may well be, for example, that much of the simple phenomenon of geographical mobility which has impressed historians of the nineteenth century is a phenomenon of youth. Current census data bear this out overwhelmingly; migration rates decline from birth to age 17, rise rapidly to age 24, and then fall sharply to age 65, when they level off.[22] And it is not irrelevant that much of the written record about "social disorganization" has a strong element of the older generation writing about the younger, and doing so in the same way again and again with each new generation. It may well be that the concept of "social disorganization" as a long-run change concept represents a perspective of a particular stage of life cycle as much as objective social data.

Mobility has not been described or read accurately because it has not been rooted sufficiently in concepts of social structure. If one visualizes only people moving about as individuals, a conception of an atomized society results. And this is a false conception, for geographical movement takes place within structure and does not erode it. We should recognize that mobility and structure coexist and that our task is to examine the structural location of mobility processes. Consider, for example, the geographically defined community. Individuals can move in and out of that community and yet its character can remain the same.[23] Here is mobility and yet

22. For data for the most recent period, March 1970–March 1971, see U.S. Bureau of the Census, *Current Population Reports*, Ser. P-20, No. 235, "Mobility of the Population of the United States: March 1970 to March 1971," Government Printing Office, 1972.

23. A suggestive example of movement through structure is in the account of the Lon-

persistence, movement of individuals and persistence of pattern. In this case it is the persistence of location, of geography, of human institutions. The physical structures of houses and stores, of churches and recreational centers all involved commitments which changed only slowly. The physical community, of course, does change with time. Yet it is quite possible for movement in and out to take place and the pattern of community to persist. The high degree of geographical movement of workingmen in the nineteenth century, for example, should not give rise to a notion of a formless and floating population, but to one of movement through locations of residence and institutions of work and recreation. Our task is to find the intersection of movement and structure.

Another variant on this same theme is the relationship between mobility and kinship structures.[24] It is quite probable that physical movement took place within maintained kinship ties. Kinship ties influence the direction and destination of migration, the temporary residential locations in the area of destination, the pattern of temporary movement back and forth as between rural-area and urban occupation, periodic returns to place of origin to participate in occasional visiting and family reunions, and even return at death for burial. Kinship structures in a more cosmopolitan and mobile society, of course, differ from those in a more parochial and stable one. But they remain with considerable influence as a pattern of social relationships over long periods of time. In our urban society today we continue to discover nuclear families with strong and supporting but dispersed extended family ties. Contemporary evidence supports this notion of movement within kinship structures, and there is no reason to suppose that it operated with any less potency in the past.

IV

STRUCTURAL aspects of the city have also been called into question by those who focus on increasing size and scale as the central ele-

---

don Irish by Lynn H. Lees, "Patterns of Lower-Class Life: Irish Slum Communities in Nineteenth-Century London," in Thernstrom and Sennett, *op. cit.*, 359–85.

24. See, for suggestive examples, James S. Brown, Harry K. Schwarzweller, and Joseph J. Mangallan, "Kentucky Mountain Migration and the Stem-Family: An American Variation on a Theme by DePlay," *Rural Sociology* 28 (1963), 48–69; and Scott Greer, "Urbanism Reconsidered," *American Sociological Review* 21 (1956), 19–25.

ment of urbanization. Cities grew rapidly in the nineteenth century, expanding in geographical area and complexity, in territory, in numbers of people, in the level of economic activity, in the perceptual awareness of their inhabitants, in the intensity of human interaction, and in governmental functions and administration. The central theme of urbanization, therefore, is the process of growth from small to larger scale, and in the complexity of human relationships. Such a view appears in comprehensive form in Michael Frisch's book on Springfield, Massachusetts, Seymour Mandelbaum's book on Boss Tweed, and in a particular case in Roger Lane's study of Boston's police.[25] These works reflect concern with crucial facts in urbanization. The growth of governmental functions, and especially the rapid development of administrative activities connected with the physical growth, policing, and protection of the city is particularly impressive.

Underlying this concern for increasing scale and complexity is a rather traditional concept of the organic city, of the city "as a whole" which involves a particular notion of the relationship between the whole and the parts. For the most part it consists of a conception of a relatively homogeneous city moving forward in thought and action as an undifferentiated "system." There is far less concern for locating these innovations and changes within particular segments of the social order, and far more concern for rooting them in some general way in the entire city. The implication is that for purposes of understanding change the city moves forward as a relatively homogeneous collection of people. The phrase "public interest" is used frequently not only as an object of perception and debate, but as an organic causal force as well. Size and scale, complexity, and the "need for efficiency" become "objective" forces in their own right, moving the city as a whole inexorably forward. Growth brings its own imperative, and the only significant contending forces are the "public interest" and those who resist this imperative, "private interest."[26]

25. Michael H. Frisch, *Town Into City: Springfield, Massachusetts and the Meaning of Community, 1840–1880* (Cambridge, Mass., 1972); Seymour Mandelbaum, *Boss Tweed's New York* (New York, 1965); Roger Lane, *Policing the City: Boston, 1822–1885* (Cambridge, Mass., 1967).

26. A recent variant on this theme is Sam B. Warner, Jr., *The Private City: Philadelphia in Three Periods of Its Growth* (Philadelphia, 1968).

There is no question, of course, that these phenomena are crucial in urban development, as crucial as is horizontal and vertical mobility. The problem lies in the structural context within which they are conceptualized. Increasing size, scale, and complexity can be linked to a differentiated as well as a homogeneous social structure. The peculiarity lies in the fact that so many, perhaps most, who stress size and scale prefer a concept of homogeneity rather than of differentiation, and thereby steer clear of efforts to elaborate the parts of the city's internal order and to root particular facets of size and scale to particular facets of that internal order. As with mobility, the problem lies not in the phenomenon studied, but with the way in which that study can be carried out detached from empirically developed concepts of urban social structure. Let me elaborate on these relationships with respect to two phenomena, the increasing scale of perception of the city and the evolution of administrative systems.

In the transition from community to society, one of the important elements is the increasing scope and variety of human imagination and experience. Modernization enhances the geographical range of awareness, and the acceptance and toleration of the variety of alternatives within that awareness. The usual contrasts here are, of course, the peasant community and the city. But we have learned that this is a false contrast, because the continuum from parochial to cosmopolitan perspectives exists within the city itself. There are those whose range of perception is limited to a small physical area within the city, namely, a few city blocks, and whose personal contacts are equally limited. And there are those with a much broader range of perception, who have a view of the "entire city" in some crude sense. The dynamics of change within the city involve both forces making for a larger perspective in the minds of more people, and forces making for more limited perspectives. Perceptions of the city are not homogeneous but differentiated.

As the city grows in size and scale, what happens to the perception of the city by its inhabitants? Does it grow in scope and uniformity in close relationship to the "objective" data? I think not. The difficulty is, of course, that we have very few studies which bear even tangentially on this question. But logic, reasoning from contemporary evidence, and the implications of existing urban studies would call for a context of variation, of differentiated structure in human perception. It seems even most probable that the complexity which accompanies urban size and scale increases not only the vertical levels of occupations, but also the variety of perceptions of the city. This differentiated perception is implicit in the work of such people as Kevin Lynch and Anselm Strauss, and especially in the information about the city by its inhabitants gathered by Henry Schmandt.[27] Even studies of small communities indicate differentiated perceptual worlds; for larger cities the differentiation, the structure, is more extensive and complex. At any rate, the implication of all this is that we cannot assume a homogeneous perception of the city, but must link particular perceptions with particular kinds of people. Our inquiry should be: whose perception?

A similar set of questions should be raised concerning the growth of urban public functions. Do these arise from a general public impulse, or from some more limited sector of the city? Evidence is abundant concerning controversies over such matters: Is street paving a public or private function; should public services such as sewers or gas lighting in particular sections of the city be paid for by the city as a whole; should the school system be expanded in numbers, to high schools, and in "quality" of instruction; should urban redevelopment focus on substituting for slum housing such innovations as highways, public arenas and stadiums, and commercial and office buildings; should the sale of alcohol and the desecration of the Sabbath with amusements be prohibited? It is relatively easy to assume that public functions in some way reflect the general values of the entire city in some homogeneous fashion, the "public interest." But if we do assume this, we ignore the differences in values inherent in the choices in such matters. And the form and pattern in those values and choices brings us back to social structure.

Traditionally among American historians these problems have been dealt with in terms of the conflict between "public interest" and "private interest." The latter seems to involve considerations of social structure, while the former does not. As a result the entire question has been thought of in terms of a link between some particular private interest and a public function. If we say, the argument goes, that a particular public function is rooted in some particular segment of the social structure, then we argue that public functions are simply products of private interests. The conceptualization should be more sophisticated than that, for the crucial aspect of social structure here is not "private interest" in the traditional sense of the word, but a particular conception of the public interest rooted in a particular vantage point. Public debates on these matters are controversies over different conceptions of the public interest, and the historical question then becomes one of sorting out not public and private impulses, but the structural roots of different conceptions of the public interest, different conceptions of the city, what it is and where it ought to go.

From this vantage point there is a close connection between changes in perception of the city and changes in views as to appropriate public policy. If one's perception of the city is rooted in community, in a network of relatively primary-group relations within a relatively small geographical area, reinforced as might well be the case by ethnic, racial, or religious ties, then one might well affirm the importance of a decentralized administrative system and limited citywide functions. If one's perception of the city is rooted in activities which cut across geographical sectors of the city and link the various parts in a whole, then it seems logical to conceive of the city in a broader fashion. Such would be the view of a banker whose loans extend to the entire city, a central-city merchant who draws customers from far and wide, a medical specialist with an office in a downtown building or attached to a hospital, a professional whose clients were drawn from a wide area, a citizen who lived in one part of the city and worked in another, or a manufacturer whose factory was in one section of the city and whose employees lived in scattered residential communities.

A variety of contexts might well give rise to a larger conception of the city. It is not far-fetched to argue that such a perspective is rooted in particular kinds of experiences and social relationships rather than others—cosmopolitan rather than local—and that such relationships and perspectives in private affairs generate particular views about public affairs, that the competence of government should be citywide rather than parochial.[28] The linkage here is between particular conceptions of the city and particular policy preferences. And the structural implication is that those particular conceptions do not automatically, of "necessity" (as the phrase goes), spring out of size and scale, but are mediated through particular people, in particular circumstances, developing particular ideas about what the city is and where its government should be going.

Two illustrations might make the argument more concrete. Both are research attempts to root centralization in municipal decision making in Pittsburgh in 1911—the shift from ward to citywide council elections—in more integrative private affairs. One sought to differentiate bankers involved in such reform activities from those who were not; the other did the same with doctors. In both cases the hypothesis was that those involved in citywide affairs were more active in reform than those whose activities were more local. The banker study distinguished three types of banks—citywide in the city center, regional, and community—and sorted them out by size of assets and deposits as well as the geographical range of their clientele.[29] The community involvements of their directors, including municipal reform, were studied, and a close correlation between scope of banking and level of activity in reform was found. The doctor study distinguished between specialists with a citywide clientele and the general practitioner with a local-community clientele.[30] The two were distinguished in several ways, the most extensive being the physical distance between home and office. It was assumed that the general practitioner would be more likely to live and work in the same building, or closely located buildings, while the specialist would live and work at greater distances. The distance between home and work was then related to community involve-

---

28. This approach and its implication for political life are developed more fully in Samuel P. Hays, "Political Parties and the Community-Society Continuum, 1865–1929," in William N. Chambers and Walter Dean Burnham (eds.), *The American Party Systems: Stages of Political Development* (New York, 1967), 152–81.

29. Frank Lukaszewicz, "Regional and Central Boards of Directors of Pittsburgh Banks in 1912," seminar paper, Univ. of Pittsburgh, 1966.

30. Ross Messer, "The Medical Profession and Urban Reform in Pittsburgh, 1890–1920," seminar paper, Univ. of Pittsburgh, 1966.

ments including municipal reform, and a relationship was found between distance and level of involvement.

There is no need to interpret these data by a theory linking private interest with governmental function. This only confuses the issue. The point is that the distinctive private involvements of people give rise to distinctive concepts about what governmental activities should be. Public views and preferences, perceptions of the city and its future, are not divorced from private views and preferences. These may be as "disinterested" as one might wish to affirm, and yet the relationship still holds. Hence, the structural roots of both perceptions of the city and preferences for public policy.

V

IN the final analysis, a focus on structure rests upon a desire to emphasize human values and choices in history. So far this field has been left almost entirely to those concerned with dramatic events or personalities. But the drama of value and choice is a more widespread phenomenon, extending throughout the social order. The historian engaged in social description, and especially in using mass data for that purpose, becomes aware of the range of value orientations that are embedded in private affairs and that, in turn, have a major impact upon public affairs. Hence the increasingly close connection between social and political history. This range of values, in turn, greatly affects choices, not as decisions which change as the wind blows but as persistent preferences growing out of persistent value orientations. If one reduces value and choice to homogeneity, this variation is obscured, and the richness of the drama of human life is hidden amid bland uniformity.

Through the elaboration of patterns of social structure the drama of this variation in value and choice can be brought to the fore. For structural concepts are simply ways in which patterns of value and choice can be ranged in some horizontal and vertical order. Such patterns are not infinite, but relatively limited. They seem to be more extensive than a traditional Marxist view would have it, based upon the "objective" considerations of property ownership and the workplace, but they are not unlimited. Our task is to find some way of describing structure so that we are capable of intelligently comprehending a social order and the patterns of variation of choice and value within it. To hold in mental suspension the characteristics of over 200 million people is impossible, but to comprehend a relatively limited number of structural patterns is clearly feasible. To work out such patterns is one of the central tasks of urban history and constitutes the larger potential contribution of urban history to historical social theory.

III.

THE EMERGENCE OF

MODERN POLITICAL SOCIETY IN AMERICA

THE preceding essays outlined my approach to the study of history and described what I perceive to be the inadequacies of traditional frameworks for reconstructing patterns of American society and politics. The six selections in this section represent different ways in which a more effective structure might be designed.

The two on municipal reform and conservation reflect attempts to work from major political controversies and issues back to their social roots and to detect patterns in the forces and values thus revealed. These essays are typical of a wide range of issue-oriented case studies which have been undertaken by historians and which generate an increasing body of information about the behavior of forces mobilized by political controversy. A great deal of progress in the reconstruction of the patterns of both society and politics and their interrelationships has been achieved in this manner.

Two of the selections are attempts to develop patterns from the level of "political forces in society" directly—organizational patterns in "The New Organizational Society" and patterns of evolving values in "Modernizing Values in the History of the United States." Many of the ideas in these articles arose from examination of the roots of political controversy, such as ethnocultural bases of voting behavior, but many derive from the examination of structural patterns directly. These two essays represent specialized efforts at synthesis; they take a single phenomenon, such as network organization or value change, and formulate patterns within that particular context. One might carry out similar structural analyses with respect to a wide range of subjects such as work, recreation, family, religion, or voluntary associations, each one generating its own patterns.

The two remaining essays, one on political parties and the community-society continuum and one on the political structure of the city, are devoted to syntheses on an even larger scale. The first attempts to work out a pattern of wide scope, integrating forces of smaller and larger scale. The second illustrates the possibilities of synthesis through the medium of a geographically defined social system focusing on the varied values and impulses within a given area of space. The synthesis is applicable to a small community, a larger region, or an entire nation as a means of ordering patterns of society and politics.

Despite the different analytical vantage points, one can readily observe in each of these contexts similarities in the implied (and often explicit) social concepts and in the direction of thought. Four of the essays stress the evolving organizational patterns of American society, with a special concern for scale and network theory. One on modernizing values places emphasis on evolving values; in connection with it one might read the later essay on "History and Genealogy" in Section III, which carries out an analysis in a similar vein. The sixth essay, the community-society analysis of politics, deals with important elements of both organization and values. The articles thus represent both the earlier concern for patterns of organization within the social and political structure and the later interest in processes of change, with a focus on values. It may be worthwhile to follow the interplay of thought between the organizational context and the value context within which these essays evolved.

[6]

The Politics of Reform in Municipal Government in the Progressive Era*

IN order to achieve a more complete understanding of social change in the Progressive Era, historians must now undertake a deeper analysis of the practices of economic, political, and social groups. Political ideology alone is no longer satisfactory evidence to describe social patterns because generalizations based upon it, which tend to divide political groups into the moral and the immoral, the rational and the irrational, the efficient and the inefficient, do not square with political practice. Behind this contemporary rhetoric concerning the nature of reform lay patterns of political behavior which were at variance with it. Since an extensive gap separated ideology and practice, we can no longer take the former as an accurate description of the latter, but must reconstruct social behavior from other types of evidence.

Reform in urban government provides one of the most striking examples of this problem of analysis. The demand for change in municipal affairs, whether in terms of overall reform, such as the commission and city-manager plans, or of more piecemeal modifications, such as the development of citywide school boards, deeply involved reform ideology. Reformers loudly proclaimed a new structure of municipal government as more moral, more rational, and more efficient and, because it was so, self-evidently more desirable. But precisely because of this emphasis, there seemed to be no need to analyze the political forces behind change. Because the goals of reform were good, its causes were obvious; rather than being the product of particular people and particular ideas in particu-

---

*Reprinted from *Pacific Northwest Quarterly* 55 (1964).

lar situations, they were deeply imbedded in the universal impulses and truths of "progress." Consequently, historians have rarely tried to determine precisely who the municipal reformers were or what they did, but instead have relied on reform ideology as an accurate description of reform practice.

The reform ideology which became the basis of historical analysis is well known. It appears in classic form in Lincoln Steffens' *Shame of the Cities.* The urban political struggle of the Progressive Era, so the argument goes, involved a conflict between public impulses for "good government" against a corrupt alliance of "machine politicians" and "special interests."

During the rapid urbanization of the late nineteenth century, the latter had been free to aggrandize themselves, especially through franchise grants, at the expense of the public. Their power lay primarily in their ability to manipulate the political process, by bribery and corruption, for their own ends. Against such arrangements there gradually arose a public protest, a demand by the public for honest government, for officials who would act for the public rather than for themselves. To accomplish their goals, reformers sought basic modifications in the political system, both in the structure of government and in the manner of selecting public officials. These changes, successful in city after city, enabled the "public interest" to triumph.[1]

Recently, George Mowry, Alfred Chandler, Jr., and Richard Hofstadter have modified this analysis by emphasizing the fact that the impulse for reform did not come from the working class.[2] This might have been suspected from the rather strained efforts of National Municipal League writers in the "Era of Reform" to go out of their way to demonstrate working-class support for commission and city-manager governments.[3] We now know that they clutched at straws, and often erroneously, in order to prove to themselves as

1. See, for example, Clifford W. Patton, *Battle for Municipal Reform* (Washington, D.C., 1940), and Frank Mann Stewart, *A Half-Century of Municipal Reform* (Berkeley, 1950).

2. George E. Mowry, *The California Progressives* (Berkeley and Los Angeles, 1951), 86–104; Richard Hofstadter, *The Age of Reform* (New York, 1955), 131–269; Alfred D. Chandler, Jr., "The Origins of Progressive Leadership," in Elting Morrison et al. (eds.), *Letters of Theodore Roosevelt* (Cambridge, Mass., 1951–54), VIII, Appendix III, 1462–64.

3. Harry A. Toulmin, *The City Manager* (New York, 1915), 156–68; Clinton R. Woodruff, *City Government by Commission* (New York, 1911), 243–53.

well as to the public that municipal reform was a mass movement.

The Mowry-Chandler-Hofstadter writings have further modified older views by asserting that reform in general and municipal reform in particular sprang from a distinctively middle-class movement. This has now become the prevailing view. Its popularity is surprising not only because it is based upon faulty logic and extremely limited evidence, but also because it, too, emphasizes the analysis of ideology rather than practice and fails to contribute much to the understanding of who distinctively were involved in reform and why.

Ostensibly, the "middle-class" theory of reform is based upon a new type of behavioral evidence, the collective biography, in studies by Mowry of California Progressive party leaders, by Chandler of a nationwide group of that party's leading figures, and by Hofstadter of four professions—ministers, lawyers, teachers, editors. These studies demonstrate the middle-class nature of reform, but they fail to determine if reformers were distinctively middle-class, specifically if they differed from their opponents. One study of 300 political leaders in the state of Iowa, for example, discovered that Progressive-party, Old Guard, and Cummins Republicans were all substantially alike, the Progressives differing only in that they were slightly younger than the others and had less political experience.[4] If its opponents were also middle-class, then one cannot describe Progressive reform as a phenomenon whose special nature can be explained in terms of middle-class characteristics. One cannot explain the distinctive behavior of people in terms of characteristics which are not distinctive to them.

Hofstadter's evidence concerning professional men fails in yet another way to determine the peculiar characteristics of reformers, for he describes ministers, lawyers, teachers, and editors without determining who within these professions became reformers and who did not. Two analytical distinctions might be made. Ministers involved in municipal reform, it appears, came not from all segments of religion, but peculiarly from upper-class churches. They

---

4. Eli Daniel Potts, "The Progressive Profile in Iowa," *Mid-America* 47 (1965), 257–68. Another satisfactory comparative analysis is contained in William T. Kerr, Jr., "The Progressives of Washington, 1910–12," *Pacific Northwest Quarterly* 55 (1964), 16–27.

enjoyed the highest prestige and salaries in the religious community and had no reason to feel a loss of "status," as Hofstadter argues. Their role in reform arose from the class character of their religious organizations rather than from the mere fact of their occupation as ministers.[5] Professional men involved in reform (many of whom—engineers, architects, and doctors—Hofstadter did not examine at all) seem to have come especially from the more advanced segments of their professions, from those who sought to apply their specialized knowledge to a wider range of public affairs.[6] Their role in reform is related not to their attempt to defend earlier patterns of culture, but to the working out of the inner dynamics of professionalization in modern society.

The weakness of the "middle-class" theory of reform stems from the fact that it rests primarily upon ideological evidence, not on a thorough-going description of political practice. Although the studies of Mowry, Chandler, and Hofstadter ostensibly derive from behavioral evidence, they actually derive largely from the extensive expressions of middle-ground ideological position, of the reformers' own descriptions of their contemporary society, and of their expressed fears of both the lower and the upper classes, of the fright of being ground between the millstones of labor and capital.[7]

Such evidence, though it accurately portrays what people thought, does not accurately describe what they did. The great majority of Americans look upon themselves as "middle-class" and subscribe to a middle-ground ideology, even though in practice they belong to a great variety of distinct social classes. Such ideologies are not rationalizations or deliberate attempts to deceive. They are natural phenomena of human behavior. But the historian should be especially sensitive to their role so that he will not take evidence of political ideology as an accurate representation of political practice.

In the following account I will summarize evidence in both secondary and primary works concerning the political practices in which municipal reformers were involved. Such an analysis logically

5. Based upon a study of eleven ministers involved in municipal reform in Pittsburgh who represented exclusively the upper-class Presbyterian and Episcopal churches.

6. Based upon a study of professional men involved in municipal reform in Pittsburgh comprising 83 doctors, 12 architects, 25 educators, and 13 engineers.

7. See especially Mowry, *The California Progressives*.

can be broken down into three parts, each one corresponding to a step in the traditional argument. First, what was the source of reform? Did it lie in the general public rather than in particular groups? Was it middle-class, working-class, or perhaps of other composition? Second, what was the reform target of attack? Were reformers primarily interested in ousting the corrupt individual, the political or business leader who made private arrangements at the expense of the public, or were they interested in something else? Third, what political innovations did reformers bring about? Did they seek to expand popular participation in the governmental process?

There is now sufficient evidence to determine the validity of these specific elements of the more general argument. Some of it has been available for several decades; some has appeared more recently; some is presented here for the first time. All of it adds up to the conclusion that reform in municipal government involved a political development far different from what we have assumed in the past.

Available evidence indicates that the source of support for reform in municipal government did not come from the lower or middle classes, but from the upper class. The leading business groups in each city and professional men closely allied with them initiated and dominated municipal movements. Leonard White, in his study of the city manager published in 1927, wrote:

> The opposition to bad government usually comes to a head in the local chamber of commerce. Business men finally acquire the conviction that the growth of their city is being seriously impaired by the failures of city officials to perform their duties efficiently. Looking about for a remedy, they are captivated by the resemblance of the city-manager plan to their corporate form of business organization.[8]

In the 1930s White directed a number of studies of the origin of city-manager government. The resulting reports invariably begin with such statements as, "the Chamber of Commerce spearheaded the movement," or commission government in this city was a

8. Leonard White, *The City Manager* (Chicago, 1927), ix–x.

"businessmen's government."[9] Of thirty-two cases of city-manager government in Oklahoma examined by Jewell C. Phillips, twenty-nine were initiated either by chambers of commerce or by community committees dominated by businessmen.[10] More recently James Weinstein has presented almost irrefutable evidence that the business community, represented largely by chambers of commerce, was the overwhelming force behind both commission and city-manager movements.[11]

Dominant elements of the business community played a prominent role in another crucial aspect of municipal reform: the Municipal Research Bureau movement.[12] Especially in the larger cities, where they had less success in shaping the structure of government, reformers established centers to conduct research in municipal affairs as a springboard for influence.

The first such organization, the Bureau of Municipal Research of New York City, was founded in 1906; it was financed largely through the efforts of Andrew Carnegie and John D. Rockefeller. An investment banker provided the crucial support in Philadelphia, where a Bureau was founded in 1908. A group of wealthy Chicagoans in 1910 established the Bureau of Public Efficiency, a research agency. John H. Patterson of the National Cash Register Company, the leading figure in Dayton municipal reform, financed the Dayton Bureau, founded in 1912. And George Eastman was the driving force behind both the Bureau of Municipal Research and city-manager government in Rochester. In smaller cities data about city government were collected by interested individuals in a more informal way or by chambers of commerce, but in larger cities the task required special support, and prominent businessmen supplied it.

The character of municipal reform is demonstrated more pre-

---

9. Harold A. Stone et al., *City Manager Government in Nine Cities* (Chicago, 1940); Frederick C. Mosher et al., *City Manager Government in Seven Cities* (Chicago, 1940); Harold A. Stone et al., *City Manager Government in the United States* (Chicago, 1940). Cities covered by these studies include Austin, Tex.; Charlotte, N.C.; Dallas, Tex.; Dayton, Ohio; Fredericksburg, Va.; Jackson, Mich.; Janesville, Wis.; Kingsport, Tenn.; Lynchburg, Va.; Rochester, N.Y.; San Diego, Calif.

10. Jewell Cass Phillips, *Operation of the Council-Manager Plan of Government in Oklahoma Cities* (Philadelphia, 1935), 31–39.

11. James Weinstein, "Organized Business and the City Commission and Manager Movements," *Journal of Southern History* 28 (1962), 166–82.

12. Norman N. Gill, *Municipal Research Bureaus* (Washington, D.C., 1944).

cisely by a brief examination of the movements in Des Moines and Pittsburgh. The Des Moines Commercial Club inaugurated and carefully controlled the drive for the commission form of government.[13] In January 1906 the club held a so-called "mass meeting" of business and professional men to secure an enabling act from the state legislature. P.C. Kenyon, president of the club, selected a Committee of 300, composed principally of business and professional men, to draw up a specific proposal. After the legislature approved their plan, the same committee managed the campaign which persuaded the electorate to accept the commission form of government by a narrow margin in June 1907.

In this election the lower-income wards of the city opposed the change, the upper-income wards supported it strongly, and the middle-income wards were more evenly divided. In order to control the new government, the Committee of 300, now expanded to 530, sought to determine the nomination and election of the five new commissioners, and to this end they selected an avowedly businessman's slate. Their plans backfired when the voters swept into office a slate of anticommission candidates who now controlled the new commission government.

Proponents of the commission form of government in Des Moines spoke frequently in the name of "the people." But their more explicit statements emphasized their intent that the new plan be a "business system" of government, run by businessmen. The slate of candidates for commissioner endorsed by advocates of the plan was known as the "businessman's ticket." J.W. Hill, president of the committees of 300 and 530, bluntly declared: "The professional politician must be ousted and in his place capable business men chosen to conduct the affairs of the city." I.M. Earle, general counsel of the Bankers' Life Association and a prominent figure in the movement, put the point more precisely: "When the plan was adopted it was the intention to get businessmen to run it."

Although reformers used the ideology of popular government, they in no sense meant that all segments of society should be involved equally in municipal decision making. They meant that

13. This account of the movement for commission government in Des Moines is derived from items in the Des Moines *Register* during the years from 1905 through 1908.

their concept of the city's welfare would be best achieved if the business community controlled city government. As one businessman told a labor audience, the businessman's slate represented labor "better than you do yourself."

The composition of the municipal reform movement in Pittsburgh demonstrates its upper-class and professional as well as its business sources.[14] Here the two principal reform organizations were the Civic Club and the Voters' League. The 745 members of these two organizations came primarily from the upper class. Sixty-five percent appeared in upper-class directories which contained the names of only 2 percent of the city's families. Furthermore, many who were not listed in these directories lived in upper-class areas. These reformers, it should be stressed, comprised not an old but a new upper class. Few came from earlier industrial and mercantile families. Most of them had risen to social position from wealth created after 1870 in the iron, steel, electrical equipment, and other industries, and they lived in the newer rather than the older fashionable areas.

Almost half (48 percent) of the reformers were professional men: doctors, lawyers, ministers, directors of libraries and museums, engineers, architects, private and public school teachers, and college professors. Some of these belonged to the upper class as well, especially the lawyers, ministers, and private school teachers. But for the most part their interest in reform stemmed from the inherent dynamics of their professions rather than from their class connections. They came from the more advanced segments of their organizations, from those in the forefront of the acquisition and application of knowledge. They were not the older professional men, seeking to preserve the past against change; they were in the vanguard of professional life, actively seeking to apply expertise more widely to public affairs.

Pittsburgh reformers included a large segment of businessmen; 52 percent were bankers and corporation officials or their wives.

14. Biographical data constitute the main source of evidence for this study of Pittsburgh reform leaders. They were found in city directories, social registers, directories of corporate directors, biographical compilations, reports of boards of education, settlement houses, welfare organizations, and similar types of material. Especially valuable was the clipping file maintained at the Carnegie Library of Pittsburgh.

Among them were the presidents of fourteen large banks and officials of Westinghouse, Pittsburgh Plate Glass, U.S. Steel and its component parts (such as Carnegie Steel, American Bridge, and National Tube), Jones and Laughlin, lesser steel companies (such as Crucible, Pittsburgh, Superior, Lockhart, and H.K. Porter), the H.J. Heinz Company, and the Pittsburgh Coal Company, as well as officials of the Pennsylvania Railroad and the Pittsburgh and Lake Erie. These men were not small businessmen; they directed the most powerful banking and industrial organizations of the city. They represented not the old business community, but industries which had developed and grown primarily within the past fifty years and which had come to dominate the city's economic life.

These business, professional, and upper-class groups who dominated municipal reform movements were all involved in the rationalization and systematization of modern life; they wished a form of government which would be more consistent with the objectives inherent in those developments. The most important single feature of their perspective was the rapid expansion of the geographical scope of affairs which they wished to influence and manipulate, a scope which was no longer limited and narrow, no longer within the confines of pedestrian communities, but was now broad and citywide, covering the whole range of activities of the metropolitan area.

The migration of the upper class from central to outlying areas created a geographical distance between its residential communities and its economic institutions. To protect the latter required involvement both in local ward affairs and in the larger city government as well. Moreover, upper-class cultural institutions, such as museums, libraries, and symphony orchestras, required an active interest in the larger municipal context from which these institutions drew much of their clientele.

Professional groups, broadening the scope of affairs which they sought to study, measure, or manipulate, also sought to influence the public health, the educational system, or the physical arrangements of the entire city. Their concerns were limitless, not bounded by geography, but as expansive as the professional imagination. Finally, the new industrial community greatly broadened its perspective in governmental affairs because of its new recognition of the way in which factors throughout the city affected business growth. The increasing size and scope of industry, the greater stake in more varied and geographically dispersed facets of city life, the effect of floods on many business concerns, the need to promote traffic flows to and from work for both blue-collar and managerial employees—all contributed to this larger interest. The geographically larger private perspectives of upper-class, professional, and business groups gave rise to a geographically larger public perspective.

These reformers were dissatisfied with existing systems of municipal government. They did not oppose corruption per se—although there was plenty of that. They objected to the structure of government which enabled local and particularistic interests to dominate. Prior to the reforms of the Progressive Era, city government consisted primarily of confederations of local wards, each of which was represented on the city's legislative body. Each ward frequently had its own elementary schools and ward-elected school boards which administered them.

These particularistic interests were the focus of a decentralized political life. City councilmen were local leaders. They spoke for their local areas, the economic interests of their inhabitants, their residential concerns, their educational, recreational, and religious interests—i.e., for those aspects of community life which mattered most to those they represented. They rolled logs in the city council to provide streets, sewers, and other public works for their local areas. They defended the community's cultural practices, its distinctive languages or national customs, its liberal attitude toward liquor, and its saloons and dance halls which served as centers of community life. One observer described this process of representation in Seattle:

> The residents of the hill-tops and the suburbs may not fully appreciate the faithfulness of certain downtown ward councilmen to the interests of their constituents. . . . The people of a state would rise in arms against a senator or representative in Congress who deliberately misrepresented their wishes and imperilled their interests, though he might plead a higher regard for national good. Yet people in other

parts of the city seem to forget that under the old system the ward elected councilmen with the idea of procuring service of special benefit to that ward.[15]

In short, pre-reform officials spoke for their constituencies, inevitably their own wards which had elected them, rather than for other sections or groups of the city.

The ward system of government especially gave representation in city affairs to lower- and middle-class groups. Most elected ward officials were from these groups, and they, in turn, constituted the major opposition to reforms in municipal government. In Pittsburgh, for example, immediately prior to the changes in both the city council and the school board in 1911 in which citywide representation replaced ward representation, only 24 percent of the 387 members of those bodies represented the same managerial, professional, and banker occupations which dominated the membership of the Civic Club and the Voters' League. The great majority (67 percent) were small businessmen—grocers, saloonkeepers, liverystable proprietors, owners of small hotels, druggists—white-collar workers such as clerks and bookkeepers, and skilled and unskilled workmen.[16]

This decentralized system of urban growth and the institutions which arose from it reformers now opposed. Social, professional, and economic life had not only developed in the local wards in a small community context, but had also on a larger scale become highly integrated and organized, giving rise to a superstructure of social organization which lay far above that of ward life and which was sharply divorced from it in both personal contacts and perspective.

By the late nineteenth century, those involved in these larger institutions found that the decentralized system of political life limited their larger objectives. The movement for reform in municipal government, therefore, constituted an attempt by upper-class, advanced professional, and large-business groups to take formal political power from the previously dominant lower- and middle-class elements so that they might advance their own conceptions of

15. *Town Crier* (Seattle), Feb. 18, 1911, p. 13.
16. Information derived from same sources as cited in note 14.

desirable public policy. These two groups came from entirely different urban worlds, and the political system fashioned by one was no longer acceptable to the other.

Lower- and middle-class groups not only dominated the pre-reform governments but vigorously opposed reform. It is significant that none of the occupational groups among them, for example, small businessmen or white-collar workers, skilled or unskilled artisans, had important representation in reform organizations thus far examined. The case studies of city-manager government undertaken in the 1930s under the direction of Leonard White detailed in city after city the particular opposition of labor. In their analysis of Jackson, Michigan, the authors of these studies wrote:

> The *Square Deal*, oldest Labor paper in the state, has been consistently against manager government, perhaps largely because labor has felt that with a decentralized government elected on a ward basis it was more likely to have some voice and to receive its share of privileges.[17]

In Janesville, Wisconsin, the small shopkeepers and workingmen on the west and south sides, heavily Catholic and often Irish, opposed the commission plan in 1911 and in 1912 and the city-manager plan when adopted in 1923.[18] "In Dallas there is hardly a trace of class consciousness in the Marxian sense," one investigator declared, "yet in city elections the division has been to a great extent along class lines."[19] The commission and city-manager elections were no exceptions. To these authors it seemed a logical reaction, rather than an embarrassing fact that had to be swept away, that workingmen should have opposed municipal reform.[20]

In Des Moines working-class representatives, who in previous years might have been council members, were conspicuously absent from the "businessman's slate." Workingmen acceptable to reformers could not be found. A workingman's slate of candidates, therefore, appeared to challenge the reform slate. Organized labor,

17. Stone et al., *Nine Cities*, 212.
18. *Ibid.*, 3–13.
19. *Ibid.*, 329.
20. Stone et al., *City Manager Government*, 26, 237–41, for analysis of opposition to city-manager government.

and especially the mineworkers, took the lead; one of their number, Wesley Ash, a deputy sheriff and union member, made "an astonishing run" in the primary, coming in second among a field of more than twenty candidates.[21] In fact, the strength of anticommission candidates in the primary so alarmed reformers that they frantically sought to appease labor.

The day before the final election they modified their platform to pledge both an eight-hour day and an "American standard of wages." They attempted to persuade the voters that their slate consisted of men who represented labor because they had "begun at the bottom of the ladder and made a good climb toward success by their own unaided efforts."[22] But their tactics failed. In the election on March 30, 1908, voters swept into office the entire "opposition" slate. The business and professional community had succeeded in changing the form of government, but not in securing its control. A cartoon in the leading reform newspaper illustrated their disappointment; John Q. Public sat dejectedly and muttered, "Aw, What's the Use?"

The most visible opposition to reform and the most readily available target of reform attack was the so-called "machine," for through the "machine" many different ward communities as well as lower- and middle-income groups joined effectively to influence the central city government. Their private occupational and social life did not naturally involve these groups in larger citywide activities in the same way as the upper class was involved; hence they lacked access to privately organized economic and social power on which they could construct political power. The "machine" filled this organizational gap.

Yet it should never be forgotten that the social and economic institutions in the wards themselves provided the "machine's" sustaining support and gave it larger significance. When reformers attacked the "machine" as the most visible institutional element of the ward system, they attacked the entire ward form of political organization and the political power of lower- and middle-income groups which lay behind it.

Reformers often gave the impression that they opposed merely

21. Des Moines *Register and Leader*, Mar. 17, 1908.
22. *Ibid.*, Mar. 30, Mar. 28, 1908.

the corrupt politician and his "machine." But in a more fundamental way they looked upon the deficiencies of pre-reform political leaders in terms not of their personal shortcomings, but of the
limitations inherent in their occupational, institutional, and class
positions. In 1911 the Voters' League of Pittsburgh wrote in its
pamphlet analyzing the qualifications of candidates that "a man's
occupation ought to give a strong indication of his qualifications for
membership on a school board."[23] Certain occupations inherently
disqualified a man from serving:

> Employment as ordinary laborer and in the lowest class of mill work
> would naturally lead to the conclusion that such men did not have suf-
> ficient education or business training to act as school directors. . . .
> Objection might also be made to small shopkeepers, clerks, workmen
> at many trades, who by lack of educational advantages and business
> training, could not, no matter how honest, be expected to administer
> properly the affairs of an educational system, requiring special knowl-
> edge, and where millions are spent each year.

These, of course, were precisely the groups which did dominate
Pittsburgh government prior to reform. The League deplored the
fact that school boards contained only a small number of "men
prominent throughout the city in business life . . . in professional
occupations . . . holding positions as managers, secretaries, audi-
tors, superintendents and foremen" and exhorted these classes to
participate more actively as candidates for office.

Reformers, therefore, wished not simply to replace bad men
with good; they proposed to change the occupational and class origins of decision makers. Toward this end they sought innovations
in the formal machinery of government which would concentrate
political power by sharply centralizing the processes of decision
making rather than distribute it through more popular participation in public affairs. According to the liberal view of the Progressive Era, the major political innovations of reform involved the
equalization of political power through the primary, the direct election of public officials, and the initiative, referendum, and recall.

23. Voters' Civic League of Allegheny County, "Bulletin of the Voters' Civic League of
Allegheny County Concerning the Public School System of Pittsburgh," Feb. 14, 1911, 2–3.

These measures played a large role in the political ideology of the time and were frequently incorporated into new municipal charters. But they provided at best only an occasional and often incidental process of decision making. Far more important in continuous, sustained, day-to-day processes of government were those innovations which centralized decision making in the hands of fewer and fewer people.

The systematization of municipal government took place on both the executive and the legislative levels. The strong-mayor and city-manager types became the most widely used examples of the former. In the first decade of the twentieth century, the commission plan had considerable appeal, but its distribution of administrative responsibility among five people gave rise to a demand for a form with more centralized executive power; consequently, the city-manager or the commission-manager variant often replaced it.[24]

A far more pervasive and significant change, however, lay in the centralization of the system of representation, the shift from ward to citywide election of councils and school boards. Governing bodies so selected, reformers argued, would give less attention to local and particularistic matters and more to affairs of citywide scope. This shift, an invariable feature of both commission and city-manager plans, was often adopted by itself. In Pittsburgh, for example, the new charter of 1911 provided as the major innovation that a council of twenty-seven, each member elected from a separate ward, be replaced by a council of nine, each elected by the city as a whole.

Cities displayed wide variations in this innovation. Some regrouped wards into larger units but kept the principle of areas of representation smaller than the entire city. Some combined a majority of councilmen elected by wards with additional ones elected at large. All such innovations, however, constituted steps toward the centralization of the system of representation.

Liberal historians have not appreciated the extent to which

24. In the decade 1911 to 1920, 43 percent of the municipal charters adopted in 11 home-rule states involved the commission form and 35 percent the city-manager form; in the following decade the figures stood at 6 percent and 71 percent respectively. The adoption of city-manager charters reached a peak in the years 1918–1923 and declined sharply after 1933. See Leonard D. White, "The Future of Public Administration," *Public Management* 15 (1933), 12.

municipal reform in the Progressive Era involved a debate over the system of representation. The ward form of representation was universally condemned on the grounds that it gave too much influence to the separate units and not enough attention to the larger problems of the city. Harry A. Toulmin, whose book *The City Manager* was published by the National Municipal League, stated the case:

> The spirit of sectionalism had dominated the political life of every city. Ward pitted against ward, alderman against alderman, and legislation only effected by "log-rolling" extravagant measures into operation, mulcting the city, but gratifying the greed of constituents, has too long stung the conscience of decent citizenship. This constant treaty-making of factionalism has been no less than a curse. The city-manager plan proposes the commendable thing of abolishing wards. The plan is not unique in this for it has been common to many forms of commission government. . . .[25]

Such a system should be supplanted, the argument usually went, with citywide representation in which elected officials could consider the city "as a unit." "The new officers are elected," wrote Toulmin, "each to represent all the people. Their duties are so defined that they must administer the corporate business in its entirety, not as a hodge-podge of associated localities."

Behind the debate over the method of representation, however, lay a debate over who should be represented, over whose views of public policy should prevail. Many reform leaders often explicitly, if not implicitly, expressed fear that lower- and middle-income groups had too much influence in decision making. One Galveston leader, for example, complained about the movement for initiative, referendum, and recall:

> We have in our city a very large number of negroes employed on the docks; we also have a very large number of unskilled white laborers; this city also has more barrooms, according to its population, than any other city in Texas. Under these circumstances it would be extremely difficult to maintain a satisfactory city government where all ordi-

25. Toulmin, *The City Manager*, 42.

nances must be submitted back to the voters of the city for their ratification and approval.[26]

At the National Municipal League convention of 1907, Rear Admiral F.E. Chadwick (USN Ret.), a leader in the Newport, Rhode Island, movement for municipal reform, spoke to this question even more directly:

> Our present system has excluded in large degree the representation of those who have the city's well-being most at heart. It has brought, in municipalities . . . a government established by the least educated, the least interested class of citizens.
>
> It stands to reason that a man paying $5,000 taxes in a town is more interested in the well-being and development of his town than the man who pays no taxes. . . . It equally stands to reason that the man of the $5,000 tax should be assured a representation in the committee which lays the tax and spends the money which he contributes. . . . Shall we be truly democratic and give the property owner a fair show or shall we develop a tyranny of ignorance which shall crush him.[27]

Municipal reformers thus debated frequently the question of who should be represented as well as the question of what method of representation should be employed.

That these two questions were intimately connected was revealed in other reform proposals for representation, proposals which were rarely taken seriously. One suggestion was that a class system of representation be substituted for ward representation. For example, in 1908 one of the prominent candidates for commissioner in Des Moines proposed that the city council be composed of representatives of five classes: educational and ministerial organizations, manufacturers and jobbers, public utility corporations, retail merchants including liquor men, and the Des Moines Trades and Labor Assembly. Such a system would have greatly reduced the influence in the council of both middle- and lower-class groups. The proposal

26. Woodruff, *City Government*, 315. The Galveston commission plan did not contain provisions for the initiative, referendum, or recall, and Galveston commercial groups which had fathered the commission plan opposed movements to include them. In 1911 Governor Colquitt of Texas vetoed a charter bill for Texarkana because it contained such provisions; he maintained that they were "undemocratic" and unnecessary to the success of commission government. *Ibid.*, 314–15.

27. *Ibid.*, 207–8.

revealed the basic problem confronting business and professional leaders: how to reduce the influence in government of the majority of voters among middle- and lower-income groups.[28]

A growing imbalance between population and representation sharpened the desire of reformers to change from ward to citywide elections. Despite shifts in population within most cities, neither ward district lines nor the apportionment of city council and school board seats changed frequently. Consequently, older areas of the city, with wards that were small in geographical size and held declining populations (usually lower- and middle-class in composition), continued to be overrepresented, and newer upper-class areas, where population was growing, became increasingly underrepresented. This intensified the reformers' conviction that the structure of government must be changed to give them the voice they needed to make their views on public policy prevail.[29]

It is not insignificant that in some cities (by no means a majority) municipal reform came about outside of the urban electoral process. The original commission government in Galveston was appointed rather than elected. "The failure of previous attempts to secure an efficient city government through the local electorate made the business men of Galveston willing to put the conduct of the city's affairs in the hands of a commission dominated by state-appointed officials."[30] Only in 1903 did the courts force Galveston to elect the members of the commission, an innovation which one writer described as "an abandonment of the commission idea," and which led to the decline of the influence of the business community in the commission government.[31]

In 1911 Pittsburgh voters were not permitted to approve either the new city charter or the new school board plan, both of which provided for citywide representation; they were a result of state legislative enactment. The governor appointed the first members of the new city council, but thereafter they were elected. The judges

28. Des Moines *Register and Leader*, Jan. 15, 1908.

29. Voters' Civic League of Allegheny County, "Report of the Voters' League in the Redistricting of the Wards of the City of Pittsburgh" (Pittsburgh, n.d.).

30. Horace E. Deming, "The Government of American Cities," in Woodruff, *City Government*, 167.

31. *Ibid.*, 168.

of the court of common pleas, however, and not the voters, selected members of the new school board.

The composition of the new city council and new school board in Pittsburgh, both of which were inaugurated in 1911, revealed the degree to which the shift from ward to citywide representation produced a change in group representation.[32] Members of the upper class, the advanced professional men, and the large business groups dominated both. Of the fifteen members of the Pittsburgh Board of Education appointed in 1911 and the nine members of the new city council, none were small businessmen or white-collar workers. Each body contained only one person who could remotely be classified as a blue-collar worker; each of these men filled a position specifically but unofficially designed as reserved for a "representative of labor," and each was an official of the Amalgamated Association of Iron, Steel, and Tin Workers. Six of the nine members of the new city council were prominent businessmen, and all six were listed in upper-class directories. Two others were doctors closely associated with the upper class in both professional and social life. The fifteen members of the Board of Education included ten businessmen with citywide interests, one doctor associated with the upper class, and three women previously active in upper-class public welfare.

Lower- and middle-class elements felt that the new city governments did not represent them.[33] The studies carried out under the direction of Leonard White contain numerous expressions of the way in which the change in the structure of government produced not only a change in the geographical scope of representation, but also in the groups represented. "It is not the policies of the manager or the council they oppose," one researcher declared, "as much as the lack of representation for their economic level and social groups."[34] And another wrote:

32. Information derived from same sources as cited in note 14.

33. W.R. Hopkins, city manager of Cleveland, indicated the degree to which the new type of government was more responsive to the business community: "It is undoubtedly easier for a city manager to insist upon acting in accordance with the business interests of the city than it is for a mayor to do the same thing." Quoted in White, *The City Manager*, 13.

34. Stone et al., *Nine Cities*, 20.

There had been nothing unapproachable about the old ward aldermen. Every voter had a neighbor on the common council who was interested in serving him. The new councilmen, however, made an unfavorable impression on the less well-to-do voters. . . . Election at large made a change that, however desirable in other ways, left the voters in the poorer wards with a feeling that they had been deprived of their share of political importance.[35]

The success of the drive for centralization of administration and representation varied with the size of the city. In the smaller cities, business, professional, and elite groups could easily exercise a dominant influence. Their close ties readily enabled them to shape informal political power which they could transform into formal political power. After the mid-1890s the widespread organization of chambers of commerce provided a base for political action to reform municipal government, resulting in a host of small-city commission and city-manager innovations. In the larger, more heterogeneous cities, whose subcommunities were more dispersed, such communitywide action was extremely difficult. Few commission or city-manager proposals materialized here. Mayors became stronger, and steps were taken toward centralization of representation, but the ward system or some modified version usually persisted. Reformers in large cities often had to rest content with their Municipal Research Bureaus, through which they could exert political influence from outside the municipal government.

A central element in the analysis of municipal reform in the Progressive Era is governmental corruption. Should it be understood in moral or political terms? Was it a product of evil men or of particular sociopolitical circumstances? Reform historians have adopted the former view. Selfish and evil men arose to take advantage of a political arrangement whereby unsystematic government offered many opportunities for personal gain at public expense. The system thrived until the "better elements," "men of intelligence and civic responsibility," or "right-thinking people" ousted the culprits and fashioned a political force which produced decisions in the "public interest." In this scheme of things, corruption in public affairs grew out of individual personal failings and a defi-

35. *Ibid.*, 225.

cient governmental structure which could not hold those predispositions in check, rather than from the peculiar nature of social forces. The contestants involved were morally defined: evil men who must be driven from power, and good men who must be activated politically to secure control of municipal affairs.

Public corruption, however, involves political even more than moral considerations. It arises more out of the particular distribution of political power than of personal morality. For corruption is a device to exercise control and influence outside the legal channels of decision making when those channels are not readily responsive. Most generally, corruption stems from an inconsistency between control of the instruments of formal governmental power and the exercise of informal influence in the community. If powerful groups are denied access to formal power in legitimate ways, they seek access through procedures which the community considers illegitimate. Corrupt government, therefore, does not reflect the genius of evil men, but rather the lack of acceptable means for those who exercise power in the private community to wield the same influence in governmental affairs. It can be understood in the Progressive Era not simply by the preponderance of evil men over good, but by the peculiar nature of the distribution of political power.

The political corruption of the "Era of Reform" arose from the inaccessibility of municipal government to those who were rising in power and influence. Municipal government in the United States developed in the nineteenth century within a context of universal manhood suffrage which decentralized political control. Because all men, whatever their economic, social, or cultural conditions, could vote, leaders who reflected a wide variety of community interests and who represented the views of people of every circumstance arose to guide and direct municipal affairs. Since the majority of urban voters were workingmen or immigrants, the views of those groups carried great and often decisive weight in governmental affairs. Thus, as Herbert Gutman has shown, during strikes in the 1870s city officials were usually friendly to workingmen and refused to use police power to protect strikebreakers.[36]

---

36. Herbert Gutman, "An Iron Workers' Strike in the Ohio Valley, 1873–74," *Ohio Historical Quarterly* 68 (1959), 353–70; "Trouble on the Railroads, 1873–1874: Prelude to the 1877 Crisis," *Labor History* 2 (1961), 215–36.

Ward representation on city councils was an integral part of grass-roots influence, for it enabled diverse urban communities, invariably identified with particular geographical areas of the city, to express their views more clearly through councilmen peculiarly receptive to their concerns. There was a direct, reciprocal flow of power between wards and the center of city affairs in which voters felt a relatively close connection with public matters and city leaders gave special attention to their needs.

Within this political system the community's business leaders grew in influence and power as industrialism advanced, only to find that their economic position did not readily admit them to the formal machinery of government. Thus, during strikes, they had to rely on either their own private police, Pinkertons, or the state militia to enforce their use of strikebreakers. They frequently found that city officials did not accept their views of what was best for the city and what direction municipal policies should take. They had developed a common outlook, closely related to their economic activities, that the city's economic expansion should become the prime concern of municipal government, and yet they found that this view had to compete with even more influential views of public policy. They found that political tendencies which arose from universal manhood suffrage and ward representation were not always friendly to their political conceptions and goals and had produced a political system over which they had little control, despite the fact that their economic ventures were the core of the city's prosperity and the hope for future urban growth.

Under such circumstances, businessmen sought other methods of influencing municipal affairs. They did not restrict themselves to the channels of popular election and representation, but frequently applied direct influence—if not verbal persuasion, then bribery and corruption. Thereby arose the graft which Lincoln Steffens recounted in his *Shame of the Cities*. Utilities were only the largest of those business groups and individuals who requested special favors, and the franchises they sought were only the most sensational of the prizes, which included such items as favorable tax assessments and rates, the vacating of streets wanted for factory expansion, or permission to operate amid anti-liquor and other laws regulating personal behavior. The relationships between business and formal government became a maze of accommodations, a set of political arrangements which grew up because effective power had few legitimate means of accomplishing its ends.

Steffens and subsequent liberal historians, however, misread the significance of these arrangements, emphasizing their personal rather than their more fundamental institutional elements. To them corruption involved personal arrangements between powerful business leaders and powerful "machine" politicians. Just as they did not fully appreciate the significance of the search for political influence by the rising business community as a whole, so they did not see fully the role of the "ward politician." They stressed the argument that the political leader manipulated voters to his own personal ends, that he used constituents rather than reflected their views.

A different approach is now taking root, namely, that the urban political organization was an integral part of community life, expressing its needs and its goals. As Oscar Handlin has said, for example, the "machine" not only fulfilled specific wants, but provided one of the few avenues to success and public recognition available to the immigrant.[37] The political leader's arrangements with businessmen, therefore, were not simply personal agreements between conniving individuals; they were far-reaching accommodations between powerful sets of institutions in industrial America.

These accommodations, however, proved to be burdensome and unsatisfactory to the business community and to the upper third of socioeconomic groups in general. They were expensive; they were wasteful; they were uncertain. Toward the end of the nineteenth century, therefore, business and professional men sought more direct control over municipal government in order to exercise political influence more effectively. They realized their goals in the early twentieth century in the new commission and city-manager forms of government and in the shift from ward to citywide representation.

These innovations did not always accomplish the objectives that the business community desired because other forces could and of-

37. Oscar Handlin, *The Uprooted* (Boston, 1951), 209–17.

ten did adjust to the change in governmental structure and reestablish their influence. But businessmen hoped that reform would enable them to increase their political power, and most frequently it
did. In most cases the innovations which were introduced between
1901, when Galveston adopted a commission form of government,
and the Great Depression, and especially the city-manager form
which reached a height of popularity in the mid-1920s, served as
vehicles whereby business and professional leaders moved directly
into the inner circles of government, brought into one political system their own power and the formal machinery of government,
and dominated municipal affairs for two decades.

   Municipal reform in the early twentieth century involves a paradox: the ideology of an extension of political control and the practice of its concentration. While reformers maintained that their
movement rested on a wave of popular demands, called their gath-
erings of business and professional leaders "mass meetings," described their reforms as "part of a worldwide trend toward popular
government," and proclaimed an ideology of a popular upheaval
against a selfish few, they were in practice shaping the structure of
municipal government so that political power would no longer be
broadly distributed, but would in fact be more centralized in the
hands of a relatively small segment of the population. The paradox
became even sharper when new city charters included provisions for
the initiative, referendum, and recall. How does the historian cope
with this paradox? Does it represent deliberate deception or simply
political strategy? Or does it reflect a phenomenon which should be
understood rather than explained away?
   The expansion of popular involvement in decision making was
frequently a political tactic, not a political system to be established
permanently, but a device to secure immediate political victory.
The prohibitionist advocacy of the referendum, one of the most extensive sources of support for such a measure, came from the belief
that the referendum would provide the opportunity to outlaw liquor more rapidly. The Anti-Saloon League, therefore, urged local
option. But the League was not consistent. Towns which were wet,
when faced with a countywide local-option decision to outlaw liquor, demanded town or township local option to reinstate it. The

League objected to this as not the proper application of the referendum idea.

Again, "Progressive" reformers often espoused the direct primary when fighting for nominations for their candidates within the party, but once in control they often became cool to it because it might result in their own defeat. By the same token, many municipal reformers attached the initiative, referendum, and recall to municipal charters often as a device to appease voters who opposed the centralization of representation and executive authority. But, by requiring a high percentage of voters to sign petitions—often 25 to 30 percent—these innovations could be (and were) rendered relatively harmless.

More fundamentally, however, the distinction between ideology and practice in municipal reform arose from the different roles which each played. The ideology of democratization of decision making was negative rather than positive; it served as an instrument of attack against the existing political system rather than as a guide to alternative action. Those who wished to destroy the "machine" and to eliminate party competition in local government widely utilized the theory that these political instruments thwarted public impulses, and thereby shaped the tone of their attack.

But there is little evidence that the ideology represented a faith in a purely democratic system of decision making or that reformers actually wished, in practice, to substitute direct democracy as a continuing system of sustained decision making in place of the old. It was used to destroy the political institutions of the lower and middle classes and the political power which those institutions gave rise to, rather than to provide a clear-cut guide for alternative action.[38]

The guide to alternative action lay in the model of the business enterprise. In describing new conditions which they wished to create, reformers drew on the analogy of the "efficient business enterprise," criticizing current practices with the argument that "no

38. Clinton Rodgers Woodruff of the National Municipal League even argued that the initiative, referendum, and recall were rarely used. "Their value lies in their existence rather than in their use." Woodruff, *City Government*, 314. It seems apparent that the most widely used of these devices, the referendum, was popularized by legislative bodies when they could not agree or did not want to take responsibility for a decision and sought to pass that responsibility to the general public, rather than because of a faith in the wisdom of popular will.

business could conduct its affairs that way and remain in business,"
and calling upon business practices as the guides to improvement.
As one student remarked:

> The folklore of the business elite came by gradual transition to be the
> symbols of governmental reformers. Efficiency, system, orderliness,
> budgets, economy, saving, were all injected into the efforts of reform-
> ers who sought to remodel municipal government in terms of the
> great impersonality of corporate enterprise.[39]

Clinton Rodgers Woodruff of the National Municipal League explained that the commission form was "a simple, direct, businesslike
way of administering the business affairs of the city . . . an application to city administration of that type of business organization
which has been so common and so successful in the field of commerce and industry."[40] The centralization of decision making which
developed in the business corporation was now applied in municipal reform.

The model of the efficient business enterprise, then, rather than
the New England town meeting, provided the positive inspiration
for the municipal reformer. In giving concrete shape to this model
in the strong-mayor, commission, and city-manager plans, reformers engaged in the elaboration of the processes of rationalization
and systematization inherent in modern science and technology.
For in many areas of society, industrialization brought a gradual
shift upward in the location of decision making and the geographical extension of the scope of the area affected by decisions.

Experts in business, in government, and in the professions measured, studied, analyzed, and manipulated ever wider realms of
human life, and devices which they used to control such affairs constituted the most fundamental and far-reaching innovations in decision making in modern America, whether in formal government
or in the informal exercise of power in private life. Reformers in the
Progressive Era played a major role in shaping this new system.
While they expressed an ideology of restoring a previous order, they
in fact helped to bring forth a system drastically new.[41]

39. J.B. Shannon, "County Consolidation," *Annals of the American Academy of Political and Social Science* 207 (1940), 168.
40. Woodruff, *City Government*, 29–30.
41. Several recent studies emphasize various aspects of this movement. See, for exam-

The drama of reform lay in the competition for supremacy between two systems of decision making. One system, based upon ward representation and growing out of the practices and ideas of representative government, involved wide latitude for the expression of grass-roots impulses and their involvement in the political process. The other grew out of the rationalization of life which came with science and technology, in which decisions arose from expert analysis and flowed from fewer and smaller centers outward to the rest of society. Those who espoused the former looked with fear upon the loss of influence which the latter involved, and those who espoused the latter looked only with disdain upon the wastefulness and inefficiency of the former.

The Progressive Era witnessed rapid strides toward a more centralized system and a relative decline for a more decentralized system. This development constituted an accommodation of forces outside the business community to the political trends within business and professional life rather than vice versa. It involved a tendency for the decision-making processes inherent in science and technology to prevail over those inherent in representative government.

Reformers in the Progressive Era and liberal historians since then misread the nature of the movement to change municipal government because they concentrated upon dramatic and sensational episodes and ignored the analysis of more fundamental political structure, of the persistent relationships of influence and power which grew out of the community's social, ideological, economic, and cultural activities. The reconstruction of these patterns of human relationships and of the changes in them is the historian's most crucial task, for they constitute the central context of historical development. History consists not of erratic and spasmodic fluctuations, of a series of random thoughts and actions, but of patterns of activity and change in which people hold thoughts and actions in common and in which there are close connections between sequences of events. These contexts give rise to a structure of human

ple, Loren Baritz, *The Servants of Power* (Middletown, Conn., 1960); Raymond E. Callahan, *Education and the Cult of Efficiency* (Chicago, 1962); Samuel P. Hays, *Conservation and the Gospel of Efficiency* (Cambridge, Mass., 1959); Dwight Waldo, *The Administrative State* (New York, 1948), 3–61.

relationships which pervade all areas of life; for the political historian the most important of these is the structure of the distribution of power and influence.

The structure of political relationships, however, cannot be adequately understood if we concentrate on evidence concerning ideology rather than practice. For it is becoming increasingly clear that ideological evidence is no safe guide to the understanding of practice, that what people thought and said about their society is not necessarily an accurate representation of what they did. The current task of the historian of the Progressive Era is to stop taking the reformers' own description of political practice at its face value and to utilize a wide variety of new types of evidence to reconstruct political practice in its own terms. This is not to argue that ideology is either important or unimportant. It is merely to state that ideological evidence is not appropriate to the discovery of the nature of political practice.

Only by maintaining this clear distinction can the historian successfully investigate the structure of political life in the Progressive Era. And only then can he begin to cope with the most fundamental problem of all: the relationship between political ideology and political practice. For each of these facets of political life must be understood in its own terms, through its own historical record. Each involves a distinct set of historical phenomena. The relationship between them for the Progressive Era is not now clear; it has not been investigated. But it cannot be explored until the conceptual distinction is made clear and evidence tapped which is pertinent to each. Because the nature of political practice has so long been distorted by the use of ideological evidence, the most pressing task is its investigation through new types of evidence appropriate to it. The reconstruction of the movement for municipal reform can constitute a major step toward that goal.

[7]

Conservation and the Structure of American Politics: The Progressive Era*

THE conservation movement has long provided grist for the historian's mill as a prime example of "progressivism." "Progressivism," so the argument goes, consisted of a public reaction in the early twentieth century against the domination of public affairs by an alliance of greedy businessmen and selfish politicians. In many facets of public life, the coalition of politicians and businessmen had distorted public values, thwarted public impulses, and created an arena of politics that was removed from public control. The reaction against this state of affairs came on an equally broad variety of fronts: reforms in municipal government, federal regulation of private business, laws to improve the conditions of workingmen. Through such innovations the public exercised control over private business affairs, thereby assuring that they be conducted in the "public interest."

The exploitation of natural resources was a major example of the misdeeds of private enterprise. Lumbermen cut timber with no thought for the morrow; private power companies developed rivers for their own benefit; cattlemen on the public range drove out the honest homesteader; mining companies plundered the reserves of ore without thought of the long-run public interest. The movement to preserve natural resources, which came to be called the conservation movement, therefore, constituted a means of public control of undesirable private enterprise. A whole range of public actions—executive orders and congressional legislation—were the accomplishments of the movement: establishment of the national

*Reprinted from Allan G. Bogue, Thomas D. Phillips, and James E. Wright (eds.), *The West of the American People* (Itasca, Ill, 1970), by permission of Peacock Company.

forests and the U.S. Forest Service, development of the national park system, establishment of federal irrigation works, the public regulation of private hydroelectric power production, the retention of the public lands in public ownership, and their controlled development under the Department of the Interior. An equally wide range of colorful battles and personalities enlivened the movement: the dramatic executive orders of President Theodore Roosevelt in establishing a host of national forests before Congress could act to prevent it; the colorful battle between ex-U.S. Forester Gifford Pinchot and Secretary of the Interior Richard Ballinger; the quiet lease of oil lands to private companies which led to the celebrated Teapot Dome scandal of the 1920s.

This interpretation of the conservation movement has been transferred directly from the movement's ideology to the historical literature. It constituted the movement's self-conception, and liberal historians—those who interpret history as a long struggle between business and its opponents—have taken it over as an accurate description of the past. But the ideologies of social movements, geared to combat in the arena of public opinion and public action, cannot be taken so readily as an accurate description of the times. Those ideologies, though crucial elements of social movements, without which they cannot be understood, describe reality only through a limited angle of vision. History requires a broader perspective. Liberal historians, in fact, have become a captive of "progressive" ideology in their treatment of the "progressive" movement, and of conservation ideology in their treatment of the conservation movement. We must move beyond the ideological perspective of conservation before it can be understood.

Let us first shift from the logical content of the laws, the statements of public policy, the administrative decisions and the judicial interpretations, and the publicly debated ideas to the people in the movement. Let us root a drive for political change in the situation and circumstances of those who spearheaded change. For history is the story of people and not of policies or ideas abstracted from human beings and human circumstance. If this be done, the most striking characteristic of the conservation leaders was their commitment to the efficiency, the rationality, and the system of modern technological life. Despite their preachments against waste, they were not Malthusian prophets of doom and gloom, but were swayed by the vision of the possibilities of applying science to modern life and, in this instance, to the care and development of natural resources. They were highly optimistic about the future; they were committed to the physical development of the material base of American society; and they had found the key in science, technology, and efficiency. They spoke their faith in efficiency as a gospel heralding the new day for America.

The conservation movement, therefore, must be understood as a phase of the impulse in modern science and technology for precision, efficiency, order, and system. One must trace conservation leaders not to a mass public from which they hopefully sought political support, but to the scientific societies, the technical training, the evolving administrative systems, and the practice of efficient management which constituted the climate within which these leaders lived and from which they brought the spirit of efficiency to the field of resource management. From this background arose ideas about sustained-yield forest management, multiple-purpose river development, classification of lands and scientific land use, the wisdom of resource development within "preserved" park lands. From the same sources came ideas about how decisions should be made and who should make them, certainly not by means of inefficient log rolling in Congress, the give and take of competing political demands, but by the systematic adjustment of rival uses to create the most efficient development of water, land, and minerals. Scientists and technicians who knew what was best as measured by a standard of efficiency should prevail over politicians who thought primarily of the limited and selfish private interests among their constituents.

The forward thrust of the conservation movement was rooted not in the public at large, not in a mass base, but in a relatively small number of articulate public leaders. There is considerable evidence, for example, that an organized conservation movement was an utter failure in enrolling large numbers of members, despite the efforts of such leaders as Gifford Pinchot to do so. Time and again, in fact, those leaders sought the refuge of executive action, freed from the limitations of congressional influence or public opinion, realizing that their best bet lay in a sympathetic President rather than a relatively unsympathetic Congress or an indifferent public. From their political philosophy emerges not a faith in mass involvement in decision making, but a fear of it and the desire to insulate efficiency from political impulses in the wider society. "Democracy" and the "public" to them, in fact, referred far more to equality in the benefits of the economic and political system than to equality of involvement in making public decisions.

If the forward thrust of the conservation movement was the establishment of efficiency and system in the rational use of resources, what of the opposition? For many years that opposition has been described simply as "selfish" private enterprise. But this is far too simple a notion. It seems clear, for example, that segments of the large private corporate systems of business enterprise shared with conservationists their zeal for large-scale centralized efficient management. But it seems clear also that the opposition is best described as a wide range of particularistic resource users who preferred that use conform to their immediate concerns rather than to the demands of an overall system. Standing at the opposite pole of the political spectrum to the conservationists were irrigators and shippers on the inland waterways; homesteaders, sheepmen, and cattlemen; big-game hunters and park and recreation enthusiasts; landowners whose property would be inundated by reservoirs and landowners who sought protection from floods. Each of these resource users was concerned with a particular resource problem to which he sought a particular and separate solution. And he wished to influence that decision, rather than simply permit an efficiency expert in Washington to make it.

A striking example of the tension between competing users occurred on the public lands. For decades the public range had been fought over by cattlemen, sheepmen, and homesteaders. Now cattlemen sought to stabilize the range and balance the annual forage growth and the number of cattle, thereby preserving an adequate and continuous supply of feed. But this required controlled use to make sure that the range was not overstocked. In cooperation with resource planners in Washington, cattlemen worked out a system of range management which would guarantee a sustained yield of forage based upon control of the number of animals using it. But sheepmen, often migratory and moving across wide areas of range land, complained that this favored the resident cattleman who had staked out a prior-use claim to the land. Homesteaders also objected, since they wished to move into former grazing lands to carve out permanent homesteads. But that was not all. Game hunters felt entitled to their share as well; they wished large areas of the public lands to be reserved from other uses—sheep and cattle grazing and homesteading—and for their particular use. How to decide amid these competing users? Conservationists would do it by some precise calculus of maximum benefit determined by scientists and technicians. But to range users this would shift the location of decision making beyond their capacity to influence it. They preferred the more open process of legislative combat and log rolling so as to gain as large a share for their type of use as possible.

Controversy over the range indicates dramatically how inadequate the liberal interpretation of the conservation movement has been. It was the large cattle owners in the West, organized in state associations, who worked closely with range management experts—conservationists—to establish a system of controlled range land use. They had a sympathetic ear in the old Bureau of Forestry and its successor, the U.S. Forest Service; after working out the details of range management for lands within the national forests, they proposed a similar system to cover all the remaining public lands, then under the jurisdiction of the Department of the Interior. But the opposition was too great; when it was presented to Congress the plan received short shrift. The demands of competing users as expressed through elected representatives overcame the combination of cattlemen and conservationists. In this case it seems clear that the small property owner succeeded in blunting the thrust of systematization, efficiency, and centralization.

A similar tension between planners and users arose in the treatment of river development. The vision of multiple-purpose river development was highly attractive. For the most part the waters in the nation's rivers flowed to the sea unused by man. They were not harnessed for navigation, for hydroelectric power, for irrigation; moreover, uncontrolled they wreaked havoc in periodic floods across the country. But modern engineering could change all this. The construction of large works, dams, locks, floodwalls, and ditches would bring about the means to control the flow of rivers, store the water in months of heavy rainfall, and release it according to plan throughout the remainder of the year. From a wide variety of sources, from engineering societies and electric power companies, from the U.S. Army Corps of Engineers and irrigation developers in the West, from shippers in cities on the inland waterways to owners of riparian lands, came the demand that large-scale river development be undertaken. By the first decade of the twentieth century these demands had converged upon the federal government; they added up to one of the most influential political forces in federal resource policy.

But how to develop rivers? Here, again, resource planners were convinced that one overall viewpoint should dominate, that river development involved the reconciliation of competing uses by means of precise, expert calculations, that the river and its tributaries comprised one unit which should be subject to one system for maximum, efficient development. Competition in water use was a severe problem. Those most concerned with floods wished public works to be built so as to provide maximum benefit for them. The irrigator wished water to be released for his needs, the user of hydroelectric power for his, and the navigator for his. If any one use dominated, so the resource planner argued, the maximum use for all would be compromised; multiple use became the watchword, an overall plan of balanced use which added up to the maximum possible utilization, taking all needs into account. The concept of multiple-purpose river development, with its centralized direction and reconciliation of competing uses by experts, was increasingly thrust forward in the first decade of the twentieth century. Few of these proposals reached the conceptual perfection desired by the most ardent planners.

Multiple-purpose river development ran afoul of the same kinds of political forces as did scientific land management. Particular kinds of users sought to influence public policy in their direction. The first to succeed were those interested in irrigation who had secured a law as early as 1902, the Newlands Act, to provide federal funds for irrigation development in the West. Next were the shippers on the inland waterways of the Ohio and the Mississippi. Thwarted in the first decade of the century, they began to secure a more sympathetic hearing in Congress after 1910, and a

number of river development projects emphasizing navigation ensued. Those concerned with flood control on the lower Mississippi
secured their demands in 1917. But an overall program of river development, with elements of multiple-purpose planning, a measure pushed for years by Senator Newlands of Nevada, failed when
the Water Power Act of 1920 preempted the field for single-
purpose development.

These are some of the details of conflicts over conservation policy. How are we to understand them? Do they reflect simple issues
of public control of private enterprise, as liberal historians have argued? To this writer, the answer is clearly that they do not. In fact,
one must scrap entirely the framework, the mode of thinking, the
ideological categories of traditional liberal history and reassemble
the past in entirely new patterns of thought. It is customary in liberal historiography to focus heavily on the public nature of federal
regulation of private business. Their very assertion of the public
will, the public interest, stamped such measures as part of the
movement which ran counter to private enterprise. Yet there were
forces far more fundamental at work in American society than this.
To grasp them we must shift attention from conservation as simply
a public policy and see it as a significant element in the evolution of
the political structure of modern America. Behind the substance of
programs, of sustained-yield forestry, multiple-purpose river development and efficient land management, behind the drama of
events and decisions in Congress and the executive branch lay an
unfolding pattern of political relationships. We should be concerned not just with those events and decisions, not with the way in
which political forces generated a given result, but with the way in
which those events and decisions can provide an opportunity to establish the patterns of forces which constitute the larger system.

Looked at this way, conservation, with its interplay between the
centralizing tendencies of systematization and expertise on the one
hand and decentralization and localism on the other, provides considerable insight into the larger processes of centralization and decentralization of which it is typical. One can conceive of these forces
as poles of a continuum. On the one hand many aspects of human
endeavor were bound up with the daily routines of job, home, religion, recreation, and education which focus on interpersonal rela-

tionships within relatively small, local geographical areas. These contexts of experience involve personal interaction, personal communication, a sense of consciousness and experience limited by specific locality, the desire to remain separate from the larger forces of society, and preference for a political system which provides considerable autonomy and influence for geographically organized subgroups. On the other hand, modernization gives rise to larger patterns of human interaction, to ties extending over wide geographical areas, to corporate systems which integrate far-flung activities, to impersonal means of communication and impersonal forms of understanding, to the use of expertise and to centralization in the process of decision making.

The dominant trend was toward centralization. In the early twentieth century many were drawn to the manifest characteristics of this process—efficiency, expertise, order—and called it "progressivism." Looking back, the political historian emphasizes two major forms of this process, systematization and functional organization. Systematization refers to the dovetailing of human relationships into interdependent activities, into more tightly knit and often centrally directed patterns. In some cases this process took place in consciously directed ventures; corporate systems—both public and private—planned efforts to bring together many resources into one venture for preconceived ends. But system developed in other ways as well, especially out of the daily choices of millions of people who wished to participate in the conditions of life brought about by greater system which they considered beneficial: patronizing large-scale supermarkets rather than neighborhood grocery stores; subscribing to the metropolitan newspaper and listening to the large-city radio rather than using local media with their emphasis on life in the small community. But no matter from what source, efficiency, expertise, system infused the entire order.

Functional organizations constituted an equally important aspect of the reordering of human relationships in modern society. They grew out of the ever-increasing specialization of the occupational structure and the equally significant focus on the acquisition of specialized skills, especially white-collar technical and professional skills, as preparation for specialized occupations. These functional specializations cut many ways: farmers who produced different commodities, merchants who bought and sold different goods, manufacturers who produced different products, workers with different skills, professionals with different types of highly developed expertise. These specialized functions generated a vast network of new human relationships, of ties with others on the basis of common functions and common outlooks. A host of contacts developed which gave rise to organizations called trade associations, trade unions, and commodity organizations. As the network of their economic affairs extended to ever wider circles, so did their organizations and the conditions they sought to influence.

As a result of these new patterns of organization the location of decision making shifted steadily away from the smaller levels of human interaction to the larger networks of life. A wide variety of developments in the late nineteenth and early twentieth centuries display this tendency: the shift from ward to citywide representation in urban government and the concomitant increase in executive power; a similar upward shift from the rural township to the county and from the county to the state in matters of school and road administration; the growth of federal regulation, such as in railroad affairs, which increasingly overshadowed state regulation. At each level of governmental life the thrust toward an upward shift in affairs transformed decision-making institutions. These changes did not arise out of political theory or the inherent rightness of proper public policies or constitutional arrangements. They stemmed directly from the fact that those involved in the new corporate and functional systems of social organization, and thereby in an increasingly broad network of human relationships, sought formal governmental systems which were in scope and applicability as broad as the scope of affairs they wished to influence and control. The upward movement of the location of decision making in formal governmental institutions reflected directly the more general upward movement in the level of human affairs.

Not all segments of society participated to the same degree in this process of social change. Many segments, often most clearly identified as distinct geographical areas, were relatively uninvolved in the major thrust of change. Often they were reluctant participants, at times attracted by the benefits of modern development, ever hopeful of economic growth and prosperity, yet at the same time fearful of social change and of the potential dependence upon larger outside forces which they could not control. Thus, the more undeveloped sections of the nation, some in the rural areas of the East, but others consisting of entire sections of the nation such as the South and the West, reached out for the advantages of modern life but also resisted the external influences over their affairs which it entailed.

The forces of modernization and the resulting tension between centralizing and decentralizing tendencies occurred in a wide variety of contexts. Natural resource—conservation—policies constituted one of these. They involved both the extension of the new techniques of modernization—system, expertise, centralized direction, and manipulation—and the activation of opposing forces at the more decentralized level. Conservation leaders sought to advance the spirit of "rational" use in resource development; they stressed efficiency, planning, the application of precise, technical knowledge to national problems. An integral part of this outlook was the preferable system of decision making, consistent with the spirit of efficiency, a process by which the expert, not the elected representative, would make decisions in terms of the least wasteful dovetailing of all competing uses according to "objective," "rational" criteria. They sought to advance one system of making decisions, that inherent in the spirit of modern science and technology, for another, that inherent in the give and take among smaller contexts of life freely competing within the larger system.

Struggles over conservation policy brought into particularly sharp focus one aspect of this tension in the processes of decision making—the conflict between federal and state authority. From one point of view the "states' rights" protest from the West against federal resource policy was simply a matter of political theory, another version of the struggle over federalism. But behind the debate over constitutional theory lay the tension between the underdeveloped West and the developed East. The West, an economically dependent region, faced particularly severe limitations of climate and transportation on its economic growth. Desperately requiring external sources of capital, both private and public, it courted federal assistance in development. At the same time, however, it bitterly resisted the resulting controls, the federal involvements in adjusting competing resource uses, the insistence that loans for irrigation works be repaid on schedule and that the cost of land-use management be paid for by user fees. In these controversies the states took the part of resource users in the West; the federal government spoke for the conservationists. But all this was merely a variant on the general tension which recurred in many forms throughout American society between divergent tendencies toward centralization and decentralization.

Conservation political struggles bring into focus two competing political systems in twentieth-century America. On the one hand is the spirit of science and technology, of system and organization, of the specialization of management and the creation of a social structure separating those who make decisions from those who have decisions made about them. This tendency shifted the location of decision making continually upward so as to reduce drastically the range of impulses impinging upon the point of decision making and to guide that process by means of large, cosmopolitan considerations, technical expertise, and the objectives implicit in the wider networks of modern life. These forces tended toward a more closed system of decision making. On the other hand, however, were a host of political impulses, diffuse and often struggling against each other, often separate and conflicting, each striving for a larger share of influence within the political order. This welter of impulses sustained a more open political system, a wider range of alternatives open for choice, in which complex expert knowledge possessed by only a few did not dominate the process of decision making, and the satisfaction of more limited impulses remained a constantly live characteristic of the political order.

The history of the conservation movement in the Progressive Era, therefore, sheds light not so much on the content of public policy but on the political structure of systematization, one of the most far-reaching aspects of modern American history.

[8]

The New Organizational Society *

THE rhetoric and symbolism of the years from the last part of the nineteenth century until the Great Depression were filled with images of science and technology, efficiency and system, and "businesslike" alternatives and policy making by experts. There was such talk as "scientific social work," "human efficiency" and "human conservation" in national life, "scientific management" in business and government, "business methods" in home, church, and place of work, and the systematic application of knowledge to "reform." All this was often summed up by the notion of a "progressive" society moving forward under a new awareness of the world, a new method of shaping it, a new future to be brought into being.

From this evidence it is relatively easy to develop an image of a new culture, infused with the values of science and technology, which was relatively homogeneous throughout the social order and triumphant by the time of the Depression of 1929. But science and technology and all that came with them were not simply new cultural values. In an even more profound way they gave rise to new forms of social organization. They created new ways of ordering human relationships. They transformed the manner in which American society was put together.

The self-images of science and technology and the rationales by which they appealed for greater acceptance have often obscured their profound effect on human relationships. For while the agents of science and technology have professed to themselves and to the world at large that they were neutral instruments rather than goal makers, they, in fact, were deeply preoccupied with shaping and

*Written as an introduction to *Building the Organizational Society: Essays on Associational Activities in Modern America*, Edited by Jerry Israel. Copyright© 1972 by The Free Press, A Division of The Macmillan Company.

ordering the lives of other men. They claimed to speak for, to embody, the values of society as a whole. On the contrary, however, they represented particular, not universal, values, rooted in particular perspectives as contrasted with other perspectives. Their work was to spread those values. To be sure, that task involved the dissemination of a new ideology, but it also required new forms of social organization which alone could make those values prevail. As long as science and technology are considered to be simply a culture diffused throughout the entire "public," their social and political character will be obscured. Only when their particular value thrust is brought into sharp relief can they be understood as processes of social reorganization.

The significance of the articles in this book lies in their potential for making historians more sensitive to the way in which men gathered together to reorganize American society. I do not propose to deal with the articles as such, or even to summarize their contents. Instead, I hope to develop a general theoretical framework within which they have larger meaning, to outline some conceptual patterns which can be utilized to explore the process by which men built the new organizational society.

I

THAT facet of social organization shaped by science and technology which historians have most frequently observed is the large-scale corporation. For the most part, corporate growth is described in terms of the changing size and shares of property and assets and within the general theory of profit making. Far less attention has been given to the corporation as a system of human relationships. The traditional focus has obscured the fact that the private corporate case of social organization is merely one instance of a more general phenomenon, evident in the city, medical, welfare, and military systems, religion, and education, that displays common patterns. Recently Lloyd Warner and his associates have dealt with all this for the entire twentieth century in the first volume of their study of *The Emergent American Society*.[1] They describe the in-

---

1. Lloyd Warner, Darab B. Unwalla, and John H. Trimm, *Large-Scale Organizations*, vol. 1 of *The Emergent American Society* (New Haven, 1967).

creasing scale of all such organizations, the emerging managerial structure, the shift of resources toward the top level of the system, and specialization and segmentation.

These characteristics describe the outward manifestations of structure rather than the spirit which gave order and meaning to corporate organizations. Large-scale systems are ways in which empirical inquiry and the application of knowledge are organized; they institutionalize science and technology. Such systems define what is to be examined, that is, what are "problems"; mobilize vast resources, private and public, to conduct focused empirical inquiry; and plan long-range strategies for the social change they wish to effect. Reason, science, and technology are not inert processes by which men discover, communicate, and apply facts disinterestedly and without passion, but means by which, through systems, some men organize and control the lives of other men according to their particular conceptions as to what is preferable. Because they are pervaded by this spirit of inquiry into and control over the external environment, I prefer to call them "technical systems."[2]

Large-scale systems began their initial period of rapid growth in modern America at the same time as acceleration began in man's imagination about what could be understood empirically; there is an intimate connection between the advance of empirical inquiry and that of technical systems. The acquisition of technical knowledge through ever more refined methods, the development and coordination of specialists in limited areas of knowledge, the application of that knowledge through predetermined and precisely controlled courses of action based upon planning—all these flowed from the desire to manipulate the environment through the empirical understanding of its complexities. The technical system of the modern world is vastly different from the bureaucracies and organizations of earlier times. When knowledge, communications, and the implementation of objectives were far more personal and direct, the inner drive of organized human endeavor was far different. In the modern technical system, however, there is a dynamic, self-

2. For the concept of "technical systems" developed here and the ensuing analysis, I am indebted to the discussions in an undergraduate seminar, "The Evolution of Technical Systems in Modern America," held during the 1969–70 academic year at the Univ. of Pittsburgh.

generating and self-sustaining, which embodies the spirit of science, empirical inquiry, and planned environmental manipulation.

A large number of examples testify to the rapid expansion of empirical inquiry for social change: investigation of conditions of the urban poor by settlement house workers as the first stage of "scientific" social welfare;[3] investigation of markets through "market research," of the potential abilities of employees through psychological testing,[4] of the processes of internal business organization through scientific management, of future market potential to plan production ahead of time[5]—all of which became popular in the more "progressive" business enterpises; the rapid growth of medical inquiry as a result of the germ theory of disease and the expansion of the social dimension of medicine in the form of public health; the growth of city planning in which engineers and architects described the physical city—the spatial patterns of transportation and buildings—in order to revise those patterns according to their views of a "better" city;[6] the expansion of education, in both the number of people educated and the variety of subjects taught, giving rise to inquiry into the psychology of education to make the process more "effective"; the examination and manipulation of the economy in World War I and the generation of statistical information about production, distribution, resources, and manpower;[7] and the extension of social research in the 1920s in such forms as the National Bureau of Economic Research and the *Report on Social Trends* sponsored by Herbert Hoover.[8]

Technical systems developed several characteristics worth stressing. The first was the way in which they ordered highly specialized

---

3. See, for example, Paul Underwood Kellogg (ed.), *The Pittsburgh Survey* (New York, 1909–14), and *Hull House Maps and Papers* (New York, 1895), the best known of a wide variety of similar investigations.

4. Loren Baritz, *The Servants of Power* (Middletown, Conn., 1960).

5. John K. Galbraith, *The New Industrial State* (Boston, 1967), 11–34.

6. Roy Lubove, *Twentieth-Century Pittsburgh* (New York, 1969), provides the best example of the role of planning in the urban environment.

7. This is described in a subsequent essay in this book by Robert Cuff, "The Cooperative Impulse and War: The Origins of the Council of National Defense and Advisory Commission."

8. See the subsequent article here by David Eakins, "The Origins of Corporate Liberal Policy Research, 1916–1922: The Political-Economic Expert and the Decline of Public Debate," and Barry D. Karl, "Presidential Planning and Social Science Research: Mr. Hoover's Experts," in *Perspectives in American History* 3 (1969), 347–409.

individuals into a coordinated work force. A technical system consisted of a great number of experts in limited fields of knowledge and action. Increasingly, specializations were closely associated with the acquisition and application of empirical knowledge. The number of experts proliferated, and the fields of expertise of each grew narrower. The force behind all this was the imbalance between the ever-increasing empirical world to be known, on the one hand, and the finite capacity of men to know that world, on the other. The empirical thrust which accelerated in great force in the latter part of the nineteenth century had an infinite quality about it. There seemed to be no limit as to what could be known; men were driven by the faith that if more effort could be expended, more could be known, and therefore more could be controlled. Yet this drive involved men whose capacities to know were limited by the finite time of their lives, their memories, and their physical and mental energies. Since the dilemma of infinite knowledge and finite capacities seemed incapable of fundamental modification, specialization of time, energy, and memory continued apace, and technical systems organized this process of proliferation of specialized knowledge into vast institutions of coordinated human endeavor.

A second characteristic of technical systems was their thrust for control. The empirical environment was not simply to be understood; it was to be changed. Reason is a medium not only of inquiry or communication, but of power; the technical system which mobilized that reason was a highly instrumental or political institution. It thrived on its power to establish goals for change and to effect change. There is often a predisposition to look upon modern technical systems as merely an accumulation of skills and techniques and for those involved in them to have self-conceptions of valueless and powerless activity. But this is inaccuarate. The crucial aspect of technical systems for historical analysis is the dynamics by which they defined particular, rather than universal, goals, and by which they developed the power to implement them.

Those who led technical systems spoke of the need to understand and control variables; this was another way of describing their political role. From the mid-nineteenth century onward one can discern a secular trend in the number and range of variables which decision makers in technical systems considered crucial for them to control. The shift from a limited local market to a widespread price-and-market system, which came about with the transportation and communication revolution of the mid-nineteenth century, expressed the new circumstances. An increasing number of factors impinged upon the business enterprise which were important to control but which first had to be understood. A similar spirit pervaded technical systems in social welfare, public health, education, the military, and a host of fields. Behind the growth of these systems was an increasing awareness of the complex environments in which they operated and an increasing desire not simply to know about variables, but to control them. By the 1970s their leaders had come to speak of the necessity of changing the "total environment."

Still a third characteristic of technical systems was their constant expansion of scope and scale of inquiry and control, and the concomitant upward flow in decision making as the system grew larger. Expansion of scope and scale was both internal and external. First, the technical system grew by internal differentiation, the development of new functions, the proliferation of internal tasks. Second, it grew by absorption of external variables which could not be controlled if they remained external, but had to be brought into the system; to control the price of iron ore required a vertically integrated steel system. Third, the drive for economies of scale involved a constant attempt to reduce costs by increasing the output, whether it was steel or numbers of students in the educational system. It should be observed that the long-run tendencies in system organization did not lean naturally toward decentralization and smaller units of organization but, on the contrary, toward larger and larger units of control even though the day-to-day operations were carried on in diverse places.

As scale increased there was a constant tendency for the location of decision making to move upward. In city government a ward focus of political life, with ward-elected councilmen and other officials, gave way to a citywide focus involving councilmen elected at large and increased powers for the mayor. Township government in rural areas gave way to county government and regional administrative organization. As retail units became integrated into large-scale merchandising systems, such as department stores, supermarket chains, and gasoline firms, the context of decision making moved upward from the smaller unit to the upper levels of the larger system. Moreover, as decision making moved upward, the unit of representation or competence of the decision maker, whether a legislator or a system manager, grew larger, and the number of people to whom he responded did also. Thus, the possibilities of personal contact between the decision maker and those affected by his decision grew increasingly smaller, and the gap between the top and the bottom of the system widened.[9]

II

THE technical system was only one facet of the new organizational society; another was the growth of functional relationships. As specialization grew in the new industrial-technical world, so did relationships among specialists. This phenomenon first appeared in primary and secondary production, as those with similar occupations in agriculture and manufacturing joined together to advance their common concerns. It developed more extensively among professional and technical experts as their number grew in later years. All these joined in highly specialized associations. By the mid-twentieth century specialization had pervaded the world of leisure and recreation, as an increasing number of experts in particular avocations joined with others of like mind to pool their efforts for shared objectives. In a more subtle and far-reaching manner, specialized communications developed in the mass media audience, in which people with similar interests knew and kept in touch with their world by means of selected portions of newspapers, radio, magazines, and television. The development of specialized worlds of experience and perception and of contacts among specialists of all kinds became a fundamental mode of organization in modern America.

Economic organizations in agriculture, labor, distribution, and manufacturing constituted the first instance of the emergence of this more general type of phenomenon.[10] They grew rapidly after

9. This process for urban educational government is described in a subsequent essay by David Tyack, "City Schools: Centralization of Control at the Turn of the Century." See also Samuel P. Hays, "The Politics of Reform in Municipal Government in the Progressive Era," *Pacific Northwest Quarterly* 55 (1964), 157–69.

10. See Samuel P. Hays, "Organize or Perish," in *Response to Industrialism* (Chicago, 1957), 48–70, and Kenneth Boulding, *The Organizational Revolution* (New York, 1953).

1897. Prior to that time, persistent but ineffective efforts had been made to bring together those in similar occupations for joint action. From 1897 onward they were far more successful. Organized economic groups blossomed forth in great numbers, growing stronger and more effective with each decade. This constituted a veritable organizational revolution which generated not only specific organizations, but also a pattern of relationships and interaction among them which became the context of an increasing amount of economic and political competition.

Functional organization was not confined to economic groups; it developed equally in the professional world. Today we are accustomed to a wide range of professional organizations among white-collar specialists in government, industry, and education. Many of these, such as the various branches of the engineering profession, the educational associations, or the medical organizations, trace their origins back into the nineteenth century. But these individual roots confuse observation of the more general pattern of rapid growth and new life from the late nineteenth century onward. Professional organizations accelerated in membership, growth, and activities and came into a new and vibrant life at approximately the same time as did economic functional organizations. Both reflected the changing structure of American society under the impact of specialized skill and knowledge.

The functional organization which drew together specialists was far different from either geographic or corporate forms of social organization. Functional groups joined people carrying out similar specialized tasks. They can best be contrasted with geographic organizations, involving relationships among people living in the same geographical area, such as a local community. The political party is a geographical organization, geared to achieving success among all voters in a given geographical area, no matter what their economic, cultural, educational, or occupational differences. Functional groups cut across geographical lines, uniting those with similar functions in different areas, often organizing in increasingly broader contexts— from the city and the county to the state, the region, and the entire nation. While the community is inclusive, taking in everybody within given physical boundaries, the functional group is exclusive, including those of similar function and excluding others.

Functional organizations should also be contrasted with technical systems. The latter are integrative, drawing together many specialized individuals into a single order of direction and control. They, too, are extra-community in their range of involvements. But, contrasted with functional groups, they brought together different rather than similar specialists and arranged them not into a coordinate but into a dominant-subordinate system of relationships. The technical system rested on the effective hierarchical coordination of many different functions, different occupations, into a smoothly operating integrated whole. Functional organizations, on the other hand, joined relatively similar individuals and fostered relationships among equals in a common effort.

The spirit of the revolution in functional organization was collective action to control one's surrounding environment. For those in agriculture, labor, commerce, and industry, the growing price-and-market system, vast and extensive, complicated and mysterious, was far too remote and massive to be influenced by individuals. Before such forces one felt helpless. While one person could not affect the level of wages in Philadelphia or the price of wheat in Chicago, many, joined in common action, might. In almost every field, therefore, the possibility of common action to exercise control over the conditions that affected particular occupational situations arose spontaneously. In almost every case it involved a marked shift in the tactics of control from individual and generalized outburst and protest to a focused, often highly limited and highly technical approach to specific problems in the economic system. Control was meaningless if action was diffuse and general; but organized influence could be brought to bear on specific points in the larger system with some degree of effectiveness.

The changing attitudes of farm movements toward railroads illustrate the shift in focus. In the last third of the nineteenth century many farmers were caught up with a generalized ideological attack on the iniquitous railroads and the capitalists behind them; this shaped the analyses of their problems and their tactics. The Populist party, for example, advocated in 1892 that the entire transportation system be changed from private to public ownership. In the years after 1897 one heard little about "changing the system"; instead, a focus developed on more limited and more highly organized action. Farmers formed occupational or commodity groups to bring pressure to bear on specific railroad practices. Public regulatory commissions arose as instruments of such action, and lawyers highly expert in the intricacies of rates and rate making became the spokesmen of farmers. Far from being concerned with ideology and overall questions of public or private operation, they focused on "regulating" limited conditions which affected them as shippers.

A similar spirit of collective action to influence the surrounding environment through technical expertise infused the organizations of professionals—the educators, doctors, engineers, and architects. A transformation took place among these experts from a primary emphasis on maintaining the standards of admission to and conduct of their profession to the development of a vigorous effort to influence the particular environment which they as specialists knew. They were the new "empirical professionals," increasingly accustomed to gathering information about their specialized worlds according to the spirit of empirical inquiry, and to applying that knowledge. They became special pleaders for more public interest in and financial support for their particular specialized concerns. They reshaped old organizations and formed new ones to carry out these objectives. While some professional organizations sought to protect the past, the thrust of the times was toward joint action to shape the future.

The medical profession and its new interest in public health can be taken as an example.[11] Empirical inquiry in medicine advanced rapidly after the acceptance of the germ theory of disease. More important, the possibilities for control of disease advanced sharply. Through its public health component, the medical profession became action oriented, making increasing demands upon public agencies, most frequently at the city and state level, for more resources and more controls to further the objective of improved health. The fact that their efforts received widespread support, as well as widespread indifference and some hostility, should not obscure the dynamics of their political role. As specialists they had joined to per-

11. The subsequent essay by John Burnham, "Medical Specialists and Movements Toward Social Control in the Progressive Era: Three Examples," illustrates some of these developments. I have also drawn from an essay by Nora Faires, "Public Health as a Technical System," written for the previously mentioned undergraduate seminar on technical systems.

suade, to exhort, to change the lives and habits of people, and to mold the specialized environment which they had come to know as experts and in which they had a particular concern for change.

All this injected into the political system a new form of politics based upon functional organization. Changes in American society brought into being not only a new set of functional relationships, but also new political tactics, extra-party, more limited, more precise, and more based upon linking experts in limited fields to influence the larger system. Its roots lay in the new bases of social organization, and it was deeply involved with the changing possibilities for influence and control within the system. Just as the new technical systems represented a new form of decision making, and thereby of political action, so did the new system of organized functional group action.

The rise of functional organizations greatly enhanced the opportunities for political expression in the United States. At the time, and continuously throughout the twentieth century, these groups have been criticized as "pressure groups," constituting an illegitimate influence in the political system, distorting the general "public interest" in favor of more limited "private interest." They have been considered as inhibiting influences in the political order, restricting the legitimate demands of "democratic institutions." However, examination of the roots of functional groups and their relationship to previous political institutions—political parties—indicates that they in fact expanded rather than restricted opportunities for political expression.

The political party, the major instrument of political expression since the 1790s, an innovative and liberating development in its day, had by the 1890s become an inhibiting and restrictive influence in political life. It was incapable of expressing the political demands arising from the new functionally based organizations. Organized geographically, the party was concerned primarily with victory in particular geographical areas. Few such areas were homogeneous, and heterogeneity in a constituency meant that no one group could express its views clearly and forcefully. Instead, compromise was the order of the day as the interests of many groups had to be reconciled in order to secure a coalition with sufficient votes for victory. If one wished to support a specific objective and it alone, he could not do so through the party. Functional groups grew up almost naturally, imperceptibly, as an alternative form of political expression. They provided an opportunity for individuals to support limited objectives with considerable effectiveness when that was not possible under the party system. Functional forms of organization greatly expanded the opportunities for political expression.

III

THE new organizational society involved still a third dimension, the shaping of linkages between smaller and larger contexts of life, between local and cosmopolitan areas, between community and society.[12] Modernizing forces tend constantly to integrate the social order more closely. The years after the late nineteenth century contributed their share of these forces in the form of new methods of transportation and communication: the automobile, the telephone, the radio. These greatly modified the experience and values of many Americans, but—as we argued previously—such changes should not be considered to be homogeneous throughout the population. They arose in particular sectors and worked their influence on other sectors; they generated distinct locations of innovation and resistance to innovation. They fashioned a structure, a pattern within the society as a whole and a pattern of human relationships which was new and different. They played their own particular role in fashioning the new organizational society.

The railroad and the telegraph, the major transportation and communications innovations of the nineteenth century, provided important but limited means of establishing relationships among people. They were relatively inflexible as to the number of individuals or geographical areas which could be linked, or as to their timing of contacts. Innovations after 1897 sharply altered this. The automobile and the telephone did not greatly lower the cost of transportation, as had been the case with the railroad in the nine-

12. For the approach used here see Robert Wiebe, *The Search for Order, 1877–1920* (New York, 1967); Roland L. Warren, *The Community in America* (Chicago, 1963) 53–94; and Samuel P. Hays, "Political Parties and the Community-Society Continuum, 1865–1929," in William N. Chambers and Walter Dean Burnham (eds.), *The American Party Systems: Stages of Political Development* (New York, 1967), 152–81.

teenth century, but they greatly enhanced flexibility and permitted relationships to be established between people and institutions in a far more varied and rapid manner. From whatever sources or motive, those who wished to reach other people or institutions could now do so with far greater ease and in far less time than before; people were linked in new and closer relationships. More were drawn into the larger society both to participate in it and to be influenced by others.

In this process the initiative came from the larger, more cosmopolitan centers. By the linkages they established, they shaped the new organizational society and established continuing relationships between larger and smaller contexts of life. The process took two forms, penetration and involvement. The new forms of transportation and communication permitted the forces of modernization to reach into every nook and cranny of American life, to carry the ideals and values of a secular, technical, urban society to every segment of the social order. But the imperialistic and relentless character of that penetration was greatly facilitated by the openness of the society for involvement. The same innovations that facilitated penetration, the automobile and the telephone, for example, made millions of people in the more parochial segments of society aware of the wider world and aroused in them desires for involvement, for sharing the ways of life which those external forces stimulated. The process of change took both forms.

Cosmopolitan forces were organized and powerful; they drew Americans everywhere into the network of their influence. The search for more consumers by business, for more spectators by organized sports, for more of the ill to take advantage of health facilities by organized medicine, for more adherents to modern culture by radio and television—all this enticed people into a new cosmopolitan world. Penetration and involvement resulted not in splitting off areas and people into more isolated and decentralized segments of experience and thought, but in drawing them more tightly into the orbit of the larger organizing forces of modern life. Involvement in the benefits of the wider system carried with it a closer involvement with the structure of political power—the pattern of dominance and subordination—developing within that system. The evolution of linkage systems brought an increasing share of the nation's population into the political structure of modern America.

Automobile transportation provides a striking illustration of the process. Prior to the automobile, most roads were developed for slow-moving traffic between limited points. The design of roads took place, for the most part, within township and county contexts, and their construction and maintenance were influenced by the same setting. Automobile traffic gave rise to demands for hard-surfaced roads to link cities and to the design and maintenance of a highway system that would encompass a wider area, usually the entire state. State highway commissions replaced local road bodies as the major force in highway construction and planning. The innovation replaced one conception of a travel pattern with another, an administrative agency of smaller scope with one of larger scope, and a set of local forces with cosmopolitan ones. The new system enabled the wider society to penetrate more fully into the more parochial sectors of the nation and, in turn, drew them more relentlessly into that wider arena.

A cumulative sequence of reorganizations of life ensued, each one a characteristic feature of the new organizational society. In rural areas a focus on the neighborhood school and church gave way to one first on the village and then on the town. The high school in the village provided a major step in the reorganization of education from the rural neighborhood to a larger context. This took place in the first three decades of the century. Thirty years later, high school consolidation shifted the context to still larger units with larger tax bases, expanding considerably the range from which pupils were drawn, over which friendships were made, and within which athletic prestige was generated.[13] As the number of hard-surfaced roads increased and the speed of the automobile as well, the range of daily movement expanded to fifty miles or more and enlarged the scope of daily activities which larger systems could penetrate and in which individuals chose to become involved.

The reorganizing effect of larger units of life upon smaller spared almost no human activity. In each case it was clear that the old organizational society was parochial and limited, while the new

13. This process can be observed in Kenneth Kammeyer, "A Comparative Study of Decision Making in Rural Communities," *Rural Sociology* 27 (1962), 294–302, a study of 110 small communities which voted on school district reorganization.

was cosmopolitan, more varied, and of larger scope and scale. In a subsequent chapter Peter Karsten describes the conflict between the more cosmopolitan U.S. Army and the more locally oriented National Guard; the former sought to reduce the influence of the latter and to integrate it into its own purposes.[14] Robert Dobriner describes the tension between those "old residents" in newly suburbanizing areas and the invading newcomers from the cities who had vastly different values and perspectives and who, by their personal relationships, sought to transform the community's contacts with the wider world.[15] The classic study of Springdale by Vidich and Bensman describes the impact of the larger world of government, for example, on the community which both invites and fears what is "out there."[16]

These phenomena, it should be stressed, reflected a new organizational society arising out of an old. Older forms comprised smaller contexts of life, were rooted in family and community, and entailed a wide variety of primary linkages rather than more extensive segmental connections. They were especially rooted in the organizing ties of race, religion, and ethnicity, which held men together in networks of common loyalty and feeling. The organizational life which Booker T. Washington promoted among Southern blacks and which Robert Factor describes in a subsequent chapter was typical of the older organizational society.[17] But the cosmopolitan forces of modern life drew individuals out of these contexts slowly but surely into human relationships that were more varied, more extensive, and more segmental.

In later years one of the most dramatic focal points of this change came to be the college and university world. For college students were often in transit from more parochial to more cosmopolitan contexts, in process of having their genealogical as well as their personal lives transformed by the forces of the new organizational society. Their great-grandparents lived in the context of the small

14. Peter Karsten, "Armed Progressives: The Military Reorganizes for the American Century," in this volume.

15. Robert M. Dobriner, *Class in Suburbia* (Englewood Cliffs, N.J., 1963).

16. Arthur J. Vidich and Joseph Bensman, *Small Town in Mass Society* (Princeton, 1958).

17. Robert Factor, "Booker T. Washington and the Transformation of the Black Belt Negro: Disorganization and Social Change," in this volume.

town or rural community, or the network of urban primary-group relationships cemented by common ties of ethnicity, religion, and race. Their marriage partners came from similar cultural groups; they moved about little; they were relatively removed from larger cosmopolitan life and fearful of its strangeness and variety, and preferred to live within the limited context of community. With each generation the pattern changed: friendships and marriages across ethnic and religious lines; children living at greater distances from parents; more education; occupations which commanded more income; an expansion of horizons and contacts. For some the transition came in their own generation; their move to college was a move out into the world, from one context of social organization to another. They were increasingly caught up in the wider society, re-organized, as it were, in the things and people with which they were linked in every realm of life.[18]

The new organizational forms of technical systems and functional associations constituted the destination of many individuals involved in these social processes. But those more limited and often formal aspects of new organizational life should not obscure the larger and more informal processes of organization in society as a whole. These informal linkages which shifted men's relationships from one setting into another were just as significant elements of the new organizational society as were the more formal and institutional relationships in technical systems and functional associations. It is relatively easy for the historian to get caught up in the intricacies of specialization and expertise, efficiency and managerial controls in modern society, for these are easy to delineate and conceptualize. These should not obscure patterns of human relationship as a focus for study or the manifold ways in which those patterns were transformed under the impact of modernization. The cosmopolitanization of society, the shift toward greater scale and variety in human relationships and perspectives, was pervasive and profound; often it was more basic than, and certainly it was coordinate with, the more formal organizational changes.

18. See James A. Davis, "Locals and Cosmopolitans in American Graduate Schools," *International Journal of Comparative Sociology* 2 (1961), 212–23. The analysis here is also based upon four-generation genealogies written by students in classes at the Univ. of Pittsburgh.

IV

IN the foregoing discussion I have stressed three facets of the new organizational society—the evolution of technical systems, the development of functional associations, and the transition from local to cosmopolitan contexts. All these, it should be stressed, did not bring organization to society where no organization had before existed. On the contrary, they transformed patterns of social relationships, replacing old with new, modifying that which had previously existed. Through each of these contexts that transforming process can be seen, as the old gave way to the new, as human relationships of ethnicity, religion, and race, of the small community, of primary-group ties gave way to the secondary relationships of specialized, widely organized, cosmopolitan, technical society.[19]

It is worth stressing that this view of social change between the late 1890s and the Depression of 1929 differs from traditional accounts. While older views focus on the differences between private and public impulses, this stresses the similarities between them; while older views stress the difference between profit-making and non-profit-making activities, this emphasizes their similarities. New forms of social organization were all-pervasive, affecting business and government and profit-making enterprise and non-profit-making service institutions in medicine, education, and welfare. More important, while older views are based upon the orderly arrangement of evidence about ideologies into opposing categories and forms of political conflict, the view presented here is concerned with evidence about people in context, their environment, their relationships with others, their perceptions of the world, their values.

What did the different facets of the new organizational society, as distinct from the old, have in common? First was the geographical scale of life. Such institutions as government, schools, business firms, churches, and recreational facilities had been far smaller in size and scope than they were to be later, far closer to the individuals whom they affected and more conducive to some measure of personal knowledge, contact, and involvement. In the old society, sustained human contacts, those which established the daily rela-

19. Many of these themes are well stated in the classic article by Louis Wirth, "Urbanism as a Way of Life," *American Journal of Sociology* 44 (1938), 1–24.

tionships between man and man, were confined to relatively limited areas. Although contacts over long distances, even between immigrants in America and the home country, were possible, they were infrequent. The range of human consciousness was limited, confined by personal experience within the context of home, work, church, and neighborhood recreation; the information with which one shaped his conception of the world—the past, present, and future—came more from personal experience than impersonal media.[20]

Throughout the nineteenth as well as the twentieth century, modernization processes persistently drew men into relationships on a wider scale. In the years between 1897 and 1929 all this seems to have accelerated. Marketing, for example, underwent profound transformation, as smaller centers of distribution, such as the neighborhood grocer, were transformed under the impact of larger systems, such as the department store, the mail-order house, the chain store, and local outlets owned by manufacturers. The impact of the automobile on the transformation of rural life has already been described. The scale of urban government increased significantly as the focus shifted from ward communities to the city at large. Welfare activities became rationalized into systems of fund raising and systems of support, replacing gradually the more small-scale forms of ethnocultural orphanages and county poor-farms. Professionalization led to increasing contacts by experts in similar fields over wide geographical areas.

The new organizational society also increased enormously the range of options as to what one could think, be, and do.[21] Variety and choice replaced a limited number of vocational alternatives, of leisure-time activities, of manners of personal behavior, of what views one could legitimately hold, of products one could buy. As transportation and communication facilitated contact over wider

20. This distinction as to the types of information through which views of the world are shaped is developed by Robert Merton in his article on locals and cosmopolitans, "Patterns of Influence: Local and Cosmopolitan Influentials," in Merton, *Social Theory and Social Structure* (Glencoe, Ill., 1949), 387–420. A similar distinction for political information and action is made in Roger E. Kasperson, "Toward a Geography of Urban Politics: Chicago, A Case Study," *Economic Geography* 41 (1965), 95–107.

21. The concept of psychological mobility remains virtually unutilized for American history. Its most suggestive formulation still remains Daniel Lerner, "Modernizing Styles of Life: A Theory," in *The Passing of Traditional Society* (Glencoe, Ill., 1962), 443–75.

areas, they also facilitated contact with a greater variety of people and things within those areas. If one became tired of the old and customary, he could readily search out and become involved in the new, even though it were at great distance. Increased variety and mobility were measures of the degree to which people were freed from old constraints in order to establish new relationships, from old networks of human interaction to participate in new ones. The new organizational society involved new types of linkages between individuals which earlier would have been impossible.

These more varied linkages were far more segmental than in the past. The new organizational society related people not in their entire lives, but only in particular functions. The ties which one established in his occupation differed from those in his home-related institutions, such as school, church, and recreation. At work his contacts gravitated toward those in similar occupations and during leisure time toward those engaged in the same avocations. Easy access to transportation and communication enabled one to establish relationships with particular people at some distance and to reduce ties with his neighbors. Increased variety and mobility not only destroyed the old organizational networks, but also established the pattern of the new.

Finally, the new organizational society displayed a marked vertical order, a hierarchy of dominance and subordination, of more and less. Not that a vertical order had not existed before; on the contrary it had always been characteristic of American society. Organizational processes transformed one vertical order into another; the new organizational society constituted a new vertical society as well. Moreover, as in the old, the vertical layers of the new organizational society consisted of different levels of organization and integration, with those of smaller scope and scale toward the lower end and those of larger scope and scale toward the upper, with those in a more parochial setting toward the lower and those more cosmopolitan toward the upper. But the new scale and segmentation created hierarchies and articulation, intervening layers between top and bottom, far more extensive than before.

As technical expertise, specialization, and large-scale systems developed, a marked social distance obtained within the new patterns of organization. This could well be observed in the hierarchy of levels of educational achievement which began to emerge in the early twentieth century. While in 1890 the educational pyramid was primitive, with only 3.5 percent of the 17-year-old population having graduated from high school and only 3 percent of the 18- to 21-year-old population being enrolled in college, by 1950 the corresponding figures were 59 percent and 30 percent.[22] By mid-century a marked vertical order in educational achievement had emerged which manifested the vertical arrangements throughout the entire social order which the new organizational society had brought into being. While managerial and technical experts, members of functional associations, and those with cosmopolitan relationships were disproportionately located in the upper half of the social order, those without such characteristics were located in the lower half. The new organizational society was not only larger in scale and more varied in its segmental contacts, but also more highly articulated in its vertical dimension.

The social processes which we have described involve some of the most significant and most persistent aspects of change in nineteenth- and twentieth-century America. To be sure, there were earlier beginnings. The large-scale management of railroad systems starting as early as the 1850s was one of the first massive examples of the new order. Moreover, local and parochial social organization in the last third of the twentieth century frequently remains as a persistent and powerful force. These changes were long-run; they covered many decades and a time span beyond a single century. Yet between 1897 and 1929 they displayed especially significant force. As the articles in this volume demonstrate, for the historian these decades provide an excellent opportunity to examine in detail the emergence of the new organizational society.

22. U.S. Bureau of the Census, *Historical Statistics of the United States, Colonial Times to 1957* (Washington, D.C., 1960), 207, 210–11.

[9]

Modernizing Values in the History
of the United States*

AT first glance it might seem overly audacious to undertake an exploration of the implications of *Becoming Modern* for the history of the United States. After all, it has been argued that the United States emerged almost full-blown as a modern nation,[1] the first one, and that its subsequent history is merely an unfolding of those early tendencies. What more is there to say? Yet the authors of *Becoming Modern* suggest that the attempt may not be all that fruitless. The individual modernization processes they have studied in less developed nations, so they argue, are likely to have taken place in "more advanced industrial and postindustrial societies."[2] From their point of view, therefore, the attempt may be not far-fetched, but instructive; it may well extend insight into the process of "becoming modern."

Their suggestion is, however, only barely sketched out and is not applied particularly to the task of reconstructing the long-run development of American society through several hundred years. It is that possibility which I wish to explore here. Research into the history of the United States has increasingly turned to social analysis, with a focus on the systematic understanding of social structure and social change.[3] Thus far, little of that research has been ex-

---

*This review article of Alex Inkeles and David H. Smith, *Becoming Modern: Individual Change in Six Developing Countries* (Cambridge, Mass., 1974), appeared in *Peasant Studies Newsletter* 6:2 (1977).

1. See, for example, Seymour Martin Lipset, *The First New Nation* (New York, 1963), which sets this tone.

2. *Becoming Modern*, 311–12.

3. For a statement of this approach see Samuel P. Hays, "A Systematic Social History," in George Athan Billias and Gerald N. Grob (eds.), *American History: Retrospect and Prospect* (New York, 1971), 315–66.

tended from the many case studies to the larger context of understanding massive social transformations. I am intrigued with the
relevance of the themes of *Becoming Modern* for such a task. At
this juncture the relevance lies more in the usefulness of the questions asked and the definition of the problems to be explored than
in the fit of the conclusions. It may well be, however, that *Becoming Modern* has some important suggestions to offer historians as to
how they should go about inquiring into the American past.

At the outset it should be noted that while previous application
of modernization theory to American history has focused primarily
on political institutions, the possibilities here emphasize more the
emerging individual values.[4] By emphasizing "nation building" in
comparative analysis, one can readily conclude that the course of
American history since 1789 has been the unfolding of already
"modern" institutions. But by focusing on individual values one
has a keen sense of enormous internal variation within the "new
nation,"[5] a process of "becoming" modern still under way, with a
subsequent process of change and development over the ensuing
two centuries since the establishment of that new nation. While at
the level of formal-institution building, therefore, modernization
theory may have only limited implications for the American historian, confined primarily to a set of international comparisons, the
themes in *Becoming Modern* provide an opportunity to sort out the
various strands within the internal evolution of American society.

Let us explore a bit the implications of this internal variation in
values as a point of entry into American history. The authors state,
in their brief note about these possibilities, that "even the most
highly developed nations have more and less modern portions of
their populations, according to differences in exposure to modernizing experiences."[6] Is this not simply a commonsense observation
about the American past and about every decade of its development? To many it might not be, for there is a powerful assumption

4. The emphasis on institutions can be followed in Rogers Hollingsworth (ed.), *Nation
and State Building in America: Comparative Historical Perspectives* (Boston, 1971).

5. Van Beck Hall, *Politics Without Parties* (Pittsburgh, 1972), is an excellent example
of analysis which outlines variations within a range of units of observation. See esp. pp. 3–22
for a description of variation among 343 Massachusetts towns in the 1780s in a variety of social characteristics.

6. *Becoming Modern,* 312.

in the minds of the American people, one widely shared by historians, that one can understand this society in terms of relatively homogeneous values. It is sufficient to determine what is common to this culture, so the argument goes. The major comparative question is the distinction between American society and other societies rather than the distinctions or variations in values within the United States itself.[7] The power of that assumption of common values is intense; my own view is that it has served to obscure even more than to illuminate and has constituted a powerful impediment to the exploration of American historical social change. If nothing else, the assumption that there is a range of individual values in American history, somewhat along a traditional-modern continuum as developed in *Becoming Modern,* would require us to explore variations in the values of the American people more seriously than heretofore.

Consider the variations in "objective" characteristics, as contrasted with the expressions of values. Certainly there were, and still are, in the United States the more educated and the less educated, in terms of time spent in education.[8] Certainly there were the more literate and less literate, although the precise levels are difficult to determine if one wishes to define literacy in terms of the capacity to read and write effectively rather than merely to read and write one's name. Certainly there were the more urbanized and the less urbanized, those engaged in the more modern forms of agriculture, commerce, and manufacturing, and those in the more traditional forms,[9] those more involved in the world of mass media and/or technical information[10] and those less involved. All too often we

7. Daniel J. Boorstin, *The Genius of American Politics* (Chicago, 1953), contains a succinct statement of the central theme which Boorstin has outlined more extensively in other writings.

8. Differential involvement in various levels of the education system can be observed, in an aggregate fashion, in U.S. Bureau of the Census, *Historical Statistics of the United States, Colonial Times to 1957* (Washington, D.C., 1960), 207, 210–11, Ser. H 225, 233, and 322.

9. A disaggregation of industrial work along these lines is in Bruce Laurie, Theodore Hershberg, and George Alter, "Immigrants and Industry: The Philadelphia Experience, 1850–1880," *Journal of Social History* 9 (1975), 217–48.

10. See Robert K. Merton, "Patterns of Influence: Local and Cosmopolitan Influentials," in Merton, *Social Theory and Social Structure* (Glencoe, Ill., 1949), 387–420. A similar analysis, with a focus on styles of political party action, is Roger E. Kasperson, "Toward a Geography of Urban Politics: Chicago, A Case Study," *Economic Geography* 41 (1965), 95–107.

assume that these variations in involvement in a wide range of social changes are not vital in understanding American society, that they pale before homogeneity in values. Perhaps the most powerful impact of *Becoming Modern* on American historians would be to dispel that assumption and to explore the value of these wide variations in involvement in American institutions for understanding the processes of social change.

There is still another broad "frame of reference" implied in *Becoming Modern* which can make a special contribution to the analysis of American history. This is the focus on individual modernization "as one requiring a basic personal engagement between the individual and his milieu."[11] This engagement involves a process of "selective perception" of the environment and a set of personal choices arising from that perception. Social change, therefore, is related not to an institutional superstructure which shaped and molded the individual but to the individual's own differential reaction to the world external to him. Not all perceived the same way; not all reacted the same way.[12] Both the perceptual quality of the context and the focus on personal values constitute major perspectives which are rare rather than commonplace in American historical analysis. I believe that they deserve far greater emphasis and that *Becoming Modern* serves as a useful guide for exploring their relevance. To describe the variations in shared perceptions of the world and to sort out the variations in values which arise from those perceptions would sharpen the analysis of American history considerably.

The implications of this approach are intriguing, for it means that rather than focusing on the way in which individuals are shaped by their external institutions, it emphasizes the way in which individuals, by their differential perceptions and reactions to that external environment, in fact shape the patterns of the social order. The fact that some perceive the environment in one way and others in another means a constant process of sorting out in terms of individual values, some more modern and some less so, which, in turn,

11. *Becoming Modern*, 310.
12. For implications of this for studies of vertical mobility, see review by Samuel P. Hays of Stephan Thernstrom, *The Other Bostonians: Poverty and Progress in the American Metropolis, 1880-1970* (Cambridge, Mass., 1973) in *Journal of Social History* 9 (1975), 409-14.

adds up to a sorting out of shared patterns of value. I am not fully sure where this direction of thinking might lead in the analysis of American history, but I find that an emphasis on individual variation in values as modernization proceeds, arising from varying individual perceptions of the world and its possibilities for one's life and future, makes a highly creative focal point for historical inquiry.[13] It enables one to develop a more appropriate balance between the analysis of structure and the analysis of change.

I

THERE is one aspect of all this which is especially intriguing for the analysis of American history—the constant re-creation of traditionalism in American society through immigration. Most—though by no means all—migrants to the United States from abroad prior to 1924 came from peasant backgrounds. With them they brought their traditional patterns of life, and by doing so they injected into American society a set of values more traditional than those already here. There were migrants from both the more traditional and more modern sectors of Ireland, for example, from the peasant communities of western Ireland as well as from the towns and cities of eastern and southern Ireland, but the former greatly outnumbered the latter. Often their communities in America merely transplanted, for the first generation, the patterns of life of the homeland —the Gaelic tongue, the folk religion, the kinship relationships.[14] In some cases, such as with the Confessional German Lutherans, they came to the United States in order to preserve their traditional values against innovations within Europe.[15]

Thus it was that in many instances the newcomers in one set of ethnic and religious traditions met and observed second- and third-generation descendants of immigrants from the same traditions who

13. See a statement of the potential for this focus in Samuel P. Hays, "History and Genealogy: Patterns of Change and Prospects for Cooperation," *Prologue* 7 (1975), 39–43, 81–84, 187–91.

14. An excellent analysis of Irish subcultures is Victor A. Walsh, "Class, Culture and Nationalism: The Irish Catholics of Pittsburgh, 1870–1883," seminar paper, Univ. of Pittsburgh, 1976.

15. An older, but excellent, account is Carl Mauelshagen, *American Lutheranism Surrenders to Forces of Conservatism* (Athens, 1936). See also Ralph Dornfeld Owen, "The Old Lutherans Come," in *Concordia Historical Institute Quarterly* 20 (1947), 3–56.

had come earlier. Frequently they remarked on the vast deviation from those traditions which generations of experience in America had brought about. The free play for modernizing forces in the United States served as a climate for change which permitted inherited traditions to become sharply modified. German Lutheranism is an especially useful context in which to examine this process. Lutherans came during a period of over 200 years, bringing wave after wave of those of a more traditional faith, with each wave producing a confrontation between the old and new forms of Lutheranism in America. While one segment of this particular culture was propelled along the route of modernization, another segment pulled it back into traditional patterns.[16]

From this perspective one of the most significant, and yet underemphasized, types of analysis of American ethnic history is the focus on subcultural variation within each identifiable ethnocultural group, for each group was far from homogeneous. Each displayed variations between the more traditional and the more modern.[17] For some the initial migration consisted of people from a highly homogeneous peasant culture, but within the modernizing climate of America some individuals soon became caught up in more modern values and institutions, while others changed far more slowly. Thus, variation developed along a more traditional, more modern continuum. For others, like the Germans, immigration reinforced these traditional tendencies. In later years, others came from a different, highly modernized background and, in America, reinforced tendencies among their own ethnic group toward more rapid modernization. For example, there was a constant interplay among eastern European migrants between those with a more national outlook, the urbanized professionals and intellectuals, and those with a more parochial and peasant outlook.[18] It seems appropriate, from this line of inquiry, to call for a more intensive analysis of subcultural development within particular ethnocultural groups.

16. In addition to Mauelshagen, see specific German Lutheran histories of the church in the United States, such as C.V. Sheatsley, *Evangelical Lutheran Joint Synod of Ohio and Other States* (Columbus, Ohio, 1919) for the ebb and flow of traditional-modern tensions.

17. See Walsh, "Class, Culture and Nationalism," a good analysis of subcultural variations.

18. See, for example, Giles Edward Gobetz, "The Ethnic Ethics of Assimilation: Slovenian View," *Phylon* 27 (1966), 268–73.

By the same token, one might carry out such an analysis of sub-cultural variations within American society as a whole. Consider one indicator which is fairly pervasive—size of family. The decreasing number of children per family over the long run, save for such deviations as occurred just after World War II, has long been noted in the United States. This process might well be disaggregated along the line of traditional and modern values. There is some evidence, for example, that in the nineteenth century, families who descended from earlier British ancestors, and who resided in cities, were reducing the number of their children. But this modernizing tendency was offset by the constant reinforcement of larger family size by immigrants who brought with them more traditional peasant values about appropriate family size. As exposure to modernization brought about changing values for these groups, newer migrants from rural areas within the United States, and from Mexico, reinforced again the pattern of larger family size. But with time, these too were affected, and by the 1960s the size of black and Mexican families declined sharply, especially with each increasing level of education.[19] Through such ebb and flow as this one can visualize the interplay of the more traditional and the more modern values in American history.

A number of research problems might well illuminate these processes. In one study, for example, the differential impact of modernization was observed on four German Lutheran villages established by the same body of migrants to the state of Michigan in the nineteenth century.[20] They were subjected to varying degrees of modernizing influences, one lying in the path of suburbanization from a nearby city, one located on a commercial travel route to the lumber fields, and two remaining relatively isolated from urbanization. The contrast and comparison after a century or more brought out the differential impact of modernization and the emergence of subcultures out of a previously relatively homogeneous culture. The differential impact of modernizing America could be observed in this way on a wide range of immigrant groups, thereby sorting

19. For the impact of education on fertility see U.S. Bureau of the Census, "Fertility Variations by Ethnic Origin," *Current Population Reports,* Ser. P-20, No. 226 (1971), Table 4, 16–20.
20. See Howard G. Johnson, "The Franconian Colonies of Saginaw Valley, Michigan: A Study in Historical Geography," Ph.D. diss., Michigan State Univ., 1972.

out the range of values implied in *Becoming Modern* and filling in the details of variations in those values as a context for the analysis of American history.

The richness of analysis which is made possible by the richness of cultural variety in America and the differential impact of modernization upon it focuses on one problem not dealt with in *Becoming Modern,* the possibility of selective factors at work before exposure to such experiences as education and factory work. Two illustrations come to mind. One involves the development in the United States of German Methodism, a religious style little known in Germany, but which developed among some Germans in the United States shortly after they arrived in the mid-nineteenth century.[21] Methodism and the evangelical style which it involved were closely tied up with modernization. Affirming the capacity of human beings to work out their own fate, as opposed to a fate previously ordained by God, focusing on intense emotional experiences of regeneration which created life anew rather than on the faithful perpetuation of traditional customs and practices, evangelical Methodism was found more among the modernizing sectors of the social order than in the more traditional sectors.[22] And it was found among Germans, people whose religious style, both Lutheran and Catholic, had been highly ritualistic and liturgical, emphasizing faithful observance rather than the assertive self-will. What was peculiar about the Germans who accepted this set of religious values, namely, Methodism, so different from the more dominant German cultural milieu from which they came? Was it some experience in America? The distinctiveness of experience in America for this particular group of Germans might well have been the case, but it does not seem likely. On the other hand, perhaps some tendency in the German society from which they came predisposed this segment of Germans to accept Methodism in America. Such a line of inquiry seems to lead not to institutional experiences in the process of modernization but to more deeply rooted predispositions of value prior to that experience.

21. Carl Wittke, *William Nast* (Detroit, 1960).
22. See, for example, Robert W. Doherty, *The Hicksite Separation* (New Brunswick, N.J., 1967); "Social Bases for the Presbyterian Schism of 1835–1838: The Philadelphia Case," *Journal of Social History* 2 (1968), 69–79.

Consider another example, an examination of the family histories of two groups of single men, one Serb and the other Greek, who came to America in the years just before World War I.[23] The analysis included extensive interviews with those still living in the first generation, their children, and their grandchildren. Both groups entered America with similar peasant backgrounds, practicing the same Orthodox faith. Both entered the steel mills of Aliquippa, Pennsylvania, for work. Within a few years, however, their involvement in this modernizing milieu differed markedly. The Serbs remained in the mills as blue-collar workers, displayed little interest in their past culture, were relatively indifferent to marriage outside their ethnic culture or their church, and devoted considerable time and energy to leisure and relaxation. The Greeks left the mills rather quickly, became store proprietors, participated heavily in education and became professionals, displayed a strong sense of national origin, organizing classes in Greek for their children and emphasizing periodic visits to Greece, and maintained much closer supervision of their daughters and direction of their marriage partners. What accounts for the vast difference in values? Are variations between traditional and modern values involved in these cases? It would appear so, and the roots of the difference seem to lie much deeper in the past than simply the experience with modernizing institutions.[24]

II

WHILE the line of inquiry in *Becoming Modern* can encourage a focus on significant aspects of the role of immigrants in American society, it can also provide a more adequate context for examining the impact of modernization on American rural communities as well. Here, again, we face the problem of prevailing assumptions that American farmers were "modern" sufficiently early in the history of the country and that these values were shared so widely that there was little significant variation. They were homogeneous, the

23. Marcia Chamvitz, "The Persistence of Ethnic Identity in Two Nationality Groups in a Steel Mill Community," seminar paper, Univ. of Pittsburgh, 1976.

24. The same kind of question is posed by Stephan Thernstrom in *The Other Bostonians*, 250–61.

argument might run, in the characteristics most highlighted in *Becoming Modern*: informed citizen participation, a marked sense of personal efficacy, a high degree of independence and autonomy, and a high level of cognitive flexibility that made them ready for new ideas and experiences.[25]

We have reason to be skeptical about these assumptions of homogeneity in American rural values. It may well have been the case that few American subsistence farmers were like the European peasants in the nineteenth century or those of Asia today. But this is beside the point. The question is the variation of values within the United States, and the degree to which that variation can be rightly described by the framework used in *Becoming Modern*. We must once again infer values rather than cite direct evidence. But American agriculture was clearly more or less subsistence, depending upon the context.[26] Household industry remained or declined in accordance with the extent and pace of new modes of transportation, such as the canal and the railroad.[27] Rural areas near such lines went through marked declines in household industry, but those away from them did not, and subsistence farming persisted. The same variation occurred between different sections of the nation as the impact of transportation and communication proceeded selectively.[28]

Or consider the variations in the degree to which farmers took up scientific agriculture. For many years the centers of dissemination of such innovations were the agricultural societies, often of the more affluent farmers, many of them reflecting the more cosmopolitan influences of the towns in or around which they resided. Other farmers, on the other hand, were far slower to accept such innovations as the careful selection of seed corn; only over a period of several decades (perhaps one could put it at fifty years) did the advocates of such selection persuade the majority of corn farmers of the wisdom of modern scientific methods as opposed to more tradi-

25. *Becoming Modern*, 19–25 and 99–109, for a summary of the major characteristics of modern man.

26. Variations in commercial agriculture as between places can be traced in Hall, *Politics Without Parties*, esp. 17–19.

27. George Rogers Taylor, *The Transportation Revolution, 1815–1860* (New York, 1951).

28. For an analysis of the differential impact of communication see Allen Pred, *Urban Growth and the Circulation of Information: The United States System of Cities, 1790–1840* (Cambridge, Mass., 1973).

tional methods often based upon folklore. We can, of course, over-emphasize the extremes, but it seems entirely reasonable to assume that there were more modern and more traditional sectors of American agriculture and that the course of history was the constant innovative impact of the former upon the latter.

Several recent studies in American history have observed the marked difference in political behavior between rural communities more closely involved with external transportation and communication networks and those more removed from them. Van Beck Hall sorted out 343 towns in Massachusetts in the 1790s along such a continuum and demonstrated their marked differences in preference for candidates for office as well as in voting on substantive issues.[29] Donald Cole found a similar distribution with respect to Whig-Jacksonian voting in 1832 in New Hampshire.[30] And several studies of the politics of banking in the nineteenth century sort out bank and anti-bank attitudes in terms of degrees of involvement with or separation from the larger commercial network.[31] These studies make abundantly clear the wisdom of assuming a marked variation among rural people in political attitudes, depending upon variation in degree of involvement in more modern economic networks. We can justifiably assume an underlying variation in shared personal values associated with this and explore it further along the lines of suggestions implicit in *Becoming Modern.*

Because of the high degree of commercial farming in the rural United States, however, it seems likely that the process of value change toward modernization took place in a distinctive fashion and depended as much on experiences within the rural community as on experiences after migration in a more urban context. We might visualize several aspects of this. It is apparent that although regions varied as to the degree of their commercial or subsistence farming, there was considerable mixture of both kinds of activities in the same general area, and it was difficult for a particular type of farming to remain wholly isolated for a long time. Thus, although there were more modern and less modern farming areas, there were

---

29. Hall, *Politics Without Parties.*

30. Donald B. Cole, "The Presidential Election of 1832 in New Hampshire," *Historical New Hampshire* 21 (1966), 33–50.

31. William Shade, *Banks or No Banks: The Money Issue in Western Politics, 1832–1865* (Detroit, 1972).

also more modern and less modern segments of particular areas. It seems likely that there was considerable transmission of the individual values inherent in modernization within the rural community itself, as between its more modern and its less modern sectors. We might well examine American farmers with a sensitivity to the precise problem posed in *Becoming Modern,* the relative impact of childhood experiences and adult experiences. In the context of the United States, it might well be that the former were more important than the latter.

Moreover, the stage process of movement from farm to small town to larger town to city, a facet of migration from rural to urban America often observed but rarely analyzed precisely, might well be a major factor in the process of value change. Perhaps we could visualize this as a communications process. We might well apply the context of Daniel Lerner's *Passing of Traditional Society,* which emphasized the key role of the communications process prior to the use of mass media.[32] Communications often came by word of mouth, in which the information passed over short distances initially from rural areas to nearby towns, and then, once in the town milieu, passed from smaller town to larger town, then from larger town to city. As one became more exposed to the wider communications network, one's horizons broadened, the possibilities of choice became extended, and the direction of value change became more pronounced.

Finally, we can explore directly the proposition emphasized in *Becoming Modern* that experiences in the more modern formal institutions played the heaviest role in value change. It has long been pointed out in American rural sociology that one factor in migration was an enhanced level of schooling. For some this was acquired in the rural area of origin; for others it came after moving initially to a small town. Little analysis of the value changes implicit in education has been made by American historians; instead they have been preoccupied with the description of the expansion of the educational system, its "improvement," its growth, and in more recent work, the purposes of social control on the part of those who organized the system. But here we should focus more on the value

32. Daniel Lerner, *The Passing of Traditional Society* (Glencoe, Ill., 1962), 43–75.

changes in the students themselves as they made choices either to participate or not in the system, to choose one or another of the options available to them. Instructive in this regard is the recent work of John Bodnar, who discovered that first-generation immigrants from abroad in the steel industry often urged their sons not to pursue education as a route to "betterment," but to remain in the safe, steady, secure job of the steel mills. Work and education might well have worked in different directions in value change.[33]

Some scholars have recently focused on the impact of the experience of factory work, the major emphasis of *Becoming Modern*; an example is the analysis by Herbert Gutman of immigrants in American history.[34] It has been argued that blacks underwent considerable adjustment in the shift from Southern rural occupations to Northern industrial jobs. Thus far, however, it does not appear that this argument has been precisely worked out. The conclusions of *Becoming Modern* would reinforce the emphasis upon the formative influence of the factory work experience. But it also seems probable that attitudes and values were shaped considerably prior to the factory experience in earlier years. Hence our belief that an analysis of the American scene might well emphasize the early childhood influences and the experiences in the rural and small-town community to a greater extent than in *Becoming Modern*.

III

LET us now shift the mode of analysis of the propositions in *Becoming Modern* to emphasize the impact of change on crucial sectors of human life such as religion, education, and family. This is a most auspicious time to do so, because these three fields of American history are just beginning to be influenced by social analysis, and the frameworks so far developed could readily be sharpened by a focus on the changes in values dealt with in *Becoming Modern*.[35] It is worth exploring here the directions in which such inquiry might

33. See John Bodnar, "Immigration and Modernization: The Case of Slavic Peasants In Industrial America," *Journal of Social History* 10 (1976), 44–71.

34. Herbert G. Gutman, "Work, Culture, and Society in Industrializing America, 1815–1919," *American Historical Review* 78 (1973), 531–588.

35. See the *Journal of Family History*, the first issue of which appeared in 1976.

proceed. As a convenient handle we will use at times the Lerner term, psychological mobility, as a surrogate for a wider range of characteristics of "modern man" outlined by Inkeles and Smith.

In all three realms, one can sort out the more traditional and the more modern values, the ways in which the modernizing climate of the United States worked so as to draw some people in each of the three institutions into its influence, while others held back to more traditional ways. Customarily historians have focused on the institutional growth of religion and education, denominational separation and merger, for example, in the first case and increasing size and complexity of the educational system in the second. The recent interest in the history of the family has a heavily demographic flavor, resting on such readily quantifiable variables as family size and customary varieties of patterns, such as nuclear and extended. Although in a few cases the analysis has gone beyond that level to explore the impact of modernizing values on the family, this remains a rather primitive stage of development in family history. In each case, therefore, of religion, education and family, one might with considerable profit redirect the course of historical inquiry to the long-run value-differentiating impact of the experience of modernizing influences within the United States.

The reinterpretation of evangelical Protestantism in the nineteenth century constitutes a new departure in the analysis of religion which can be brought readily into this context. Formerly, evangelical Protestantism in the first half of the nineteenth century had been interpreted through the eyes of twentieth-century fundamentalism. Since the latter was found to be located primarily in the more rural, the less modern, and the less educated sectors of American society, the nineteenth-century movement was thought to have had the same social roots. Thus, it was described as a frontier, backwoods movement, important primarily for its role in enhancing a sense of human contact and belonging in an otherwise drab and dreary existence.[36] More recent studies of Protestant evangelical religion, however, have had a sharply different emphasis; it was a heavily urban movement, associated not with the lower segments of

36. Whitney R. Cross, *The Burned-Over District: The Social and Intellectual History of Enthusiastic Religion in Western New York, 1880–1850* (Ithaca, 1950).

the social order, but with the upwardly mobile, more educated, and more cosmopolitan sectors.[37] Such evidence requires a major reorientation in thinking about the significance of the nineteenth-century version of this religious movement.

Evangelical Protestantism arose out of a prevailing religion which emphasized the practice of traditional values, faithful participation in the rituals associated with birth, baptism, marriage, and death, faithful attendance at religious services, and faithful acceptance of the beliefs associated with the historic church, such as the Westminster Creed and the Augsburg Confession. Religious practice involved the perpetuation of the historic traditions of the church, whether it be Presbyterianism, Lutheranism, or Quakerism. Increasingly, however, this religious style was found to be confining. Since it frequently required the outward expression of custom, such as in dress and speech, it tended to cut one off from others and to inhibit the establishment of relationships with people of other custom and expression. It placed an emphasis on the transmission of culture by word of mouth, through personal contact, and by means of formal institutions in a world which was increasingly using the printed word to learn, inquire, and communicate. And it carried with it a sense of fate, such as the Calvinist doctrine of predestination, in a world where it seemed that the human will could accomplish great ends.

The newer evangelical style, to many, seemed to be more appropriate to the changing society. Through the revival and an emphasis on inner personal transformation, it served to emphasize the individual's personal capacity to become something different from what had been fated for him and to modify the larger world. It gave a heightened sense of personal efficacy, mediated through a sense of freedom and independence from the confines of historic religious practice. It was no wonder that evangelical religion in these decades of the 1830s, 1840s, and 1850s was associated with advances in education and the growth in popular science. It was the more traditional sectors of religion that held back and emphasized an education that would inculcate traditional values rather than

37. See earlier works cited by Robert Doherty; also Paul Johnson, "A Shopkeeper's Millennium: Society and Revivals in Rochester, New York, 1815–1837," Ph.D. diss., Univ. of California at Los Angeles, 1975.

one which would propel one out into the wider world. As one individual said, it was not necessary to learn how to read and write to be a pious man. The theological focus of the new style was "arminianism," the assertion that one could, through an act of will, control one's fate and destiny. No wonder that the religious traditionalist looked upon all this with horror, as stimulating a completely unpredictable direction of values, as undermining the safe, the tried, and true ways of the past.

The extension of evangelical Protestantism in these decades of the nineteenth century, then, appears to be one of the important episodes in the extension of those modernizing values described in *Becoming Modern.* That role is underscored by the social analysis of differences between traditional and evangelical sectors of congregations in individual churches and is now being explored successfully by one researcher who has found an association between geographical areas which modernize economically in the nineteenth century and those which experience rapid growth in evangelical Protestantism.[38] There are even major differences in political-party affiliation, with the rise of evangelical Protestantism constituting the major element in the transformation of the Whig electorate of the 1840s into the Republican electorate of the 1850s, and the Democratic party giving particular representation to more traditional sectors of Protestantism.[39] The dividing line between traditional and modern in religion, it should be emphasized, cuts across the Catholic-Protestant divisions usually emphasized and points up the more important analytical concern for developments in religious values rather than denominational histories.

It should not be thought that evangelical Protestantism continued with the same social roots or continued to exercise a similar modernizing influence in later years. In fact, its role changed quite sharply. The advent of Darwin's theory of evolution and the growth of American cities created new situations which sharply split evangelical Protestantism into two sectors, which have been called

38. Doctoral diss. in progress, Univ. of Pittsburgh, by Linda Pritchard, on the social roots of evangelical religion in the 19th century.

39. See Paul Kleppner, *The Cross of Culture: A Social Analysis of Midwestern Politics, 1850-1900* (New York, 1970); Michael Holt, *Forging a Majority: The Formation of the Republican Party in Pittsburgh, 1848-1860* (New Haven, 1969); Ronald P. Formisano, *Mass Political Parties: Michigan, 1827-1861* (Princeton, 1971).

the "soft" and the "hard" sides of that movement. The first involved a continuation of the initial social roots in the more educated, the more upwardly mobile, the more cosmopolitan sectors, which accepted the challenges to theology represented by Darwinism and the "higher criticism" of Biblical scholarship and sought to make Protestantism directly responsive to changing urban society. The second, however, involved the transformation of the impulse into one peculiarly rooted in rural areas and people of lower socioeconomic and lower educational levels, highly suspicious of modern science, and affirming the greater importance of individual salvation over that of social amelioration. Far from affirming the capacity of the individual to modify the world through an act of will, evangelical Protestantism now disavowed personal efficacy in the wider world and affirmed the superior importance of dependence upon divine authority.

In such a context it is not at all surprising that new terminology should arise to describe the new departures. The transformed version of evangelical Protestantism was called "fundamentalism," and the reformulation of the initial impulse was called "modernism." The terminology is instructive. While the term "fundamentalism" did not immediately convey "tradition," it in fact espoused a "return" to the past or, to put it more correctly, to the past which it imagined to have existed. It involved, as it were, a creation of a new traditionalism, a twist in the analysis of *Becoming Modern* which may be one of the conceptual modifications required to apply the theory in a more modernized society. The term "modernism" is more instructive, for in fact it is in the history of American religion that the term "modern" has been used most explicitly as a self-description of an American social movement. Political movements used the term "progressive," which had a somewhat different and more extensive meaning. But the religious movement was more precisely called "modernism."

These modernizing tendencies continued into the mid-twentieth century as the larger "modern" world influenced other then-more-traditional religions. Especially dramatic were developments in the Catholic Church in the United States after World War II as a host of changing values in the wider world affected Catholics who were, themselves, becoming more involved in the values of that more cosmopolitan wider world.[40] Again, it is instructive that the process of change was described frequently as the "church in the modern world," while the defenders of the older traditions, for example the Latin Mass, were described as Catholic Traditionalists. But the Catholics were not alone in this phase of the impact of modernization on American religion. The German-origin Missouri Synod Lutherans also experienced considerable internal strife over modernizing influences. Historically, the Missouri Synod had remained the most traditional of all German Lutheran branches and the least influenced by modernizing tendencies. But this isolation was rudely disrupted by events in the post–World War II world, in which the full array of traditional and modern styles of religion were joined in sharp confrontation.

For over a century and a quarter, therefore, it appears that the values of modernism as elaborated in *Becoming Modern* played upon traditional religions in the United States. The expressions of this impact varied from time to time, but the interplay of traditional and modern values constitutes the most useful conceptual framework through which to understand the long-run pattern of social change which it involved.

IV

VALUE changes implicit in modernization can be observed in education as well as in religion. In this case the substantive work is less well developed, but the outlines are plausible. The role of education in enhancing modern values seems clear enough, yet because of the relatively high level of education in the United States at an early date, it might well be argued that in this realm the United States was "modern" throughout its history. Once again we are suspicious of such a notion. For the history of education in the United States is not the unfolding of homogeneous educational values. It is rather the steady involvement of more and more people in more and more education, so as to produce continual differentiation

40. Details of these innovations can be followed in the *National Catholic Reporter* (1964-).

between those more involved and those less involved in the educational process. The results are heterogeneity rather than homogeneity in the values created and modified by education and a constant distinction between those less affected by modern influences and those more affected.

Formal education continually extended the horizons of experience and exposed the individual to new ideas and new phenomena beyond those encountered previously. The experience of variety and options increased as one moved from primary to secondary and from secondary to higher education. Primary education was far more closely associated with community institutions and reflected the tendencies displayed at the level of primary-group relationships for transmitting values from the past. As one went to secondary and then to higher education, the educational setting became more divorced from the community and more influenced by the wider, more cosmopolitan, world. Higher education was, to a marked degree, isolated from that wider world and served as a setting within which modernizing forces had far freer rein.[41]

It should be emphasized that a perspective such as this rarely enters into the treatment of the history of education in the United States. It has been confined heavily to its external characteristics, the change in the number and proportion of young people in primary, secondary, and higher education in the aggregate, an increase in the number of teachers and the number and size of schools, changes in curriculum, the formal philosophies of education, the changing patterns of teacher education and recruitment. In more recent years it has been recognized, however, that changes in values and perspectives, in outlooks on life, in fundamental human preferences take place in the process of becoming educated. The emphasis given to changes in value in *Becoming Modern* reinforces the vast importance of examining the history of American education from this vantage point.

One of the more important tasks on this score is to examine the differential involvement of children in the educational system. Information about this is just emerging, and one of the most precise

---

41. See Philip E. Jacob, *Changing Values in College: An Exploratory Study of the Impact of College Teaching* (New York, 1957).

measurements is a study of nineteenth-century Pittsburgh elementary and public secondary enrollment.[42] For the former, there was little distinction between the participation rates by different ethnic groups, whether from abroad or native Americans. Irish boys and girls tended to be more involved proportionately than Germans and only slightly higher than native Americans. Immigrant children born abroad had slightly lower rates than immigrant children born in the United States. At the level of secondary education the differences were more marked. First, only 5 percent of those who entered high school graduated; 90 percent left after only one or two years, moving into low-level white-collar jobs. The public high schools were used heavily by the parents of lower-middle-class and skilled-worker occupations, and the students upon leaving school tended to move onto the next rung of the white-collar ladder. Distinctions such as these are still very poorly worked out, but it is only with such data that one can begin to speculate in an informed manner about the differential involvement of Americans in the value changes which took place within the context of education.

Despite the limitations from few available studies, we might make some plausible observations in the spirit of the value changes emphasized in *Becoming Modern.* The association of the primary school with the transfer of tradition can be observed in the parochial schools of the nineteenth century, in which primary education was guided and developed by religious institutions as an extension of those processes of cultural continuity at work in the home and the church. Lutheran and Catholic schools were the most widespread. However, among these parochial schools, those which persisted longest and with greatest effectiveness were in rural areas, which were more isolated from modernizing influences. The more secular schools, though rooted in community institutions, were more open to influence from the wider, cosmopolitan world and were therefore more important sources of cultural change. Even in this case, however, differences between rural and urban elementary schools seem plausible. Although nonsectarian, the rural elementary school remained far more defensive of "community ways" and

42. Carolyn S. Schumacher, "School Attendance in Nineteenth-Century Pittsburgh," Ph.D. diss., Univ. of Pittsburgh, 1976.

emphasized the transmission of the tried and true ways of the past to future generations, while the urban elementary school was more active as a transmitter of change.

With time two major changes took place in primary schools. First, some communities, usually those of higher levels of occupation and income and with wider and more cosmopolitan perspectives, began to make new demands upon the educational system. It should prepare all students in the community for life in the wider world, to perform effectively as citizens as well as workers, and to be more in tune with more cosmopolitan ways. Second, primary education began to be more formalized, more divorced from the daily life of the community, more organized and directed by professional teachers and school administrators. The initial expression of this was the scheduling of the school year to conform to the needs of the educational system rather than to those of the community. The greater autonomy of the school system provided greater opportunity for influences or values external to the community to be brought to bear in the experience of the child.

High school education extended the experience of young people much further and brought them further out into the larger world. This effect came slowly but persistently. By 1900 only 6.4 percent of the population over 17 years of age were high school graduates; by 1930 it reached 29 percent and by 1970 over 80 percent. Value changes wrought by secondary education, therefore, are more properly a twentieth-century phenomenon. Public high schools were initially urban developments; usually there was, at the start, only one in each city, often called Central High School. Students came from many different neighborhoods, coming into contact with other students whom they had not known before and bringing into their experience new ideas and new modes of behavior. The rural experience was similar, as the high school was located in a centralized place, a town, which was often removed from and foreign to the experience of country young people, a place where school children came into contact with different people in both the school and the community.[43]

An important agent for widening the horizons of young peo-

43. See Kenneth Kammeyer, "A Comparative Study of Decision Making in Rural Communities," *Rural Sociology* 27 (1962), 294–302.

ple, for stimulating involvement in the wider and more varied world, was the schoolteacher. Often primary school teachers came from the community in which the school was located, but secondary school teachers more frequently had had experience beyond the community in some academy or college and at times were people who came from outside the community.[44] In the community they constituted an agent of the outside world; citizens were half intrigued by that wider world and half fearful of its consequences for their young people and their social values.[45] The books which the teacher brought into the community, as well as the experiences, served often to inspire young people to even higher levels of education, to attend normal schools, and themselves to become lawyers, teachers, or doctors. In this way young people were enticed into the wider, more cosmopolitan, more secular world of more modern values.

Higher education provided a still more favorable setting for change, because it involved the temporary shift in residence of large numbers of young people out of their home communities into a climate in which variety and innovation had a greater opportunity for display, acceptance, and development. Here, again, we should remember that in 1930 only 12 percent of the population 18–21 years of age was enrolled in college; by 1950 it was 30 percent and by 1975 over 50 percent. The full impact of higher education on changing values is a product of the post–World War II years.

In the case of higher education, we have a more direct record of value changes because they have been studied intensively by social psychologists. Several facts have been observed. First, students who enroll in small colleges varied enormously in their value orientation, from being very traditional (in mid-twentieth-century American society terms) and authoritarian in their values, to being very nonauthoritarian. Colleges of a particular cluster of values tended to attract students of similar values. However, no matter what the character of the college, the impact of education was quite similar. In all there was a shift in values toward increased autonomy of per-

---

44. This conclusion comes from observation of the distinctive places of origin, as compared with other residents, of schoolteachers in selected communities, data from the 19th-century manuscript censuses.

45. Arthur J. Vidich and Joseph Bensman, *Small Town in Mass Society* (Princeton, 1958), 202–27.

son, greater self-awareness of emotion and impulses and increased readiness to express them, and a stronger interest in the arts and humanities. And third, the large university served as a center more conducive to value change than the small college or the specialized training school.

The college had not always been this way. In the nineteenth century it had been heavily involved in the transfer of traditional values at a time when it served primarily to train young people in the doctrines and traditions of particular religious sects so that they could become religious and lay leaders in that sect. But such institutions became increasingly secular, changed in accordance with changes in the wider world, and became instruments of value change themselves. Courses of instruction changed from the heavily classical, theological, and philosophical toward empirical inquiry into science, society, and personality. Even newer sectarian colleges, established in the late nineteenth century for religious purposes, became transformed with time from "Bible colleges" to "liberal arts" colleges, in a series of sequential stages which reflected the persistent impact of the external forces of modernization on curriculum and student life.[46]

The educational system, therefore, provided an instrument for modernizing forces to work their way out and a context in which the historian can observe this process concretely. Formal education was a setting for and an instrument of value change. The direction of change was toward a focus on the individual and his choices, an increasingly wide range of possibilities as to what one could think, be, and do, what kind of behavior was legitimate, which kinds of marriage partners were acceptable, and what views about the world one could legitimately express. Such changes were appalling to those not involved with them, thereby sorting out those less affected by and those more affected by modernizing values. It may well be argued, in fact, that as the educational system has become extended in time, and as an increasing portion of society has become involved in it, the variations in value change have become more highly articulated and finely graded within the entire society. It may well be that the impact of modernizing values on American

46. Ernest William Moore, "An Historical Study of Higher Education and the Church of the Nazarene, 1900–1965," Ph.D. diss., Univ. of Texas, 1965.

society is felt more severely, in terms of resulting social tensions, in the mid-twentieth century than ever before.

V

THE impact of modernization upon the family was closely intertwined with the changes we have observed in religion and education. Within the range of family patterns in the United States there were variations between the old and the new, between those caught up in change and those far less involved or resisting it. As with religion and education, innovations in family life involved major changes in values and especially in patterns of autonomy and dependence. It reflected the process of psychological mobility; the long-run change in family values in America has been toward greater options for individuals within it, options as to what is legitimate to think, be, and do.

This process can be examined with reference to three major facets of family life: relationships between husband and wife, the greater freedom and autonomy of women, and the relationships between parents and children.[47] In all three realms, a shift took place over the years from segregated roles within the family, in which patterns of domination and subordination persisted between husband and wife on the one hand and parents and children on the other, to a pattern of joint family roles, in which relationships were more equal and individuals more autonomous. These changes involved the process of increasing options with a focus on changing internal roles within the family under the impact of modernization. We can describe them as constituting a shift from an authoritarian to a democratic family.

The traditional family involved separate roles in work and play; few activities were carried on jointly. Even in preindustrial America, where women held a significant and vital economic role within the household, producing necessities for all members of the family, roles were segregated. As men transferred their work from the rural household context to the separated factory and office context, these

47. The following discussion is derived heavily from Herbert J. Gans, *The Urban Villagers* (Glencoe, Ill., 1962), and Jack E. Weller, *Yesterday's People: Life in Contemporary Appalachia* (Lexington, Ky., 1965).

roles became even more segregated. The husband earned the family income, and the wife managed the household and raised the children. Recreational activities were carried out separately. Men spent their nonworking hours at the saloon or, in middle-class society, joined with other males in the fraternal societies to socialize, play cards, and imbibe, or they formed all-male organizations of veterans of various wars such as the Grand Army of the Republic or the American Legion. Such all-male recreation groups had women's "auxiliaries," but these had carefully segregated roles and activities. In the church women had their segregated organizations, foreign and home missionary societies, where their leisure time often was spent.

In the twentieth century much of this began to change as many family activities came more under the joint supervision of both parents. There was an increase in planning family activities together, especially those related to recreation, vacations, the management of the house and property, and bringing up children—activities beyond the realm of earning a livelihood through work. Weekend recreation activity often took place together, as a family, and it became customary for fathers to play with their children in leisure hours. Vacations were often family vacations, and parents planned jointly the educational experiences, both formal and informal, which they wished to provide for their children. The fraternal society declined in popularity, and the country club, more family-oriented with activities for all members of the family, became more widespread. All this was evident also in the migration from the central city to the suburbs, which, we have stressed, focused far more than before on the family as a unit, with provision of internal space within the house, open family space without, and family-related community institutions which would enable the family jointly to realize ambitions for each of its members. This process of privatization of family life through suburbanization was closely related to the development of internal joint family relationships.

Closely related to all this, but even more pervasive in its consequences, was the long-run change in the status of women within the family. This involved cycles of change, with the change being more noticeable in some periods than in others. Yet it was steady and persistent. Gradually more women were involved in autonomous roles in more and more areas of life. One of the most obvious aspects of this was the shift in the role of women from preoccupation with household and child-raising duties to activities outside the home as the availability of household appliances and the decline in family size reduced the time and energy required for these former activities. All this was reflected by involvement of women in higher education, first in women's colleges and then in coeducational institutions, the rise of women's clubs in the late nineteenth century, the securing of the right to vote in elections by 1920, and, most crucial, the increasing involvement of married women in gainful employment in the mid-twentieth century.

The declining role of children in the lives of women can be observed in a variety of ways. First, women began to have their last child earlier in life; this, combined with greater longevity, meant that while in the mid-nineteenth century it was common for children under 21 to be living at home when the mother was 60–65 years of age and most frequently when one parent had already died, by the mid-twentieth century parents could frequently expect to have some 25 years of later life in which there were no direct child-rearing activities, and choices could be made to carry out other activities. This inevitably led to planning for new roles for those years. At the same time, after World War II young women increasingly began to postpone marriage and the birth of the first child. The planning of children came to be confined, as time passed, to a relatively small span of years in the life of mothers, perhaps during the ages 25–35 and even more precisely 27–32. These tendencies were still under way by 1977. All this meant that a much larger portion of the life of women, both in early and later years, was being freed from child-raising activities, inevitably leading to choices of roles other than child rearing and homemaking for a major portion of one's life.

We should observe two other indicators, the decline in the number of children and the increasing employment outside the home by married women. The decline in the number of children proceeded steadily throughout the nineteenth and twentieth centuries, modified only by a rise after World War II until 1957, when a downward trend continued; by 1977 it was below the level of the 1930s. This was closely connected with higher levels of education. Most recently, for such newly arrived urban groups as blacks and

Mexicans, family size steadily declined with increased levels of schooling. By 1977 the value changes involved had come to pervade almost every identifiable ethnocultural group in American society.[48]

Entry of married women to formal employment also proceeded apace and was closely connected with declining family size. For many years most employed women were either young unmarried women or older widows; few married women worked outside the home. In 1890, for example, only 4.5 percent of married women did so. This gradually increased. By 1940 it had reached 16.7 percent, by 1957 29.6 percent, by 1961 34.0 percent, and by 1970 well over 40 percent. The entry of married women into the work force greatly altered its female component from being overwhelmingly made up of unmarried women in 1890 (86 percent) to being dominated by married women in 1957 (54 percent). Over the years it became more and more acceptable for married women to work outside the home and to earn income, a change which greatly altered the autonomy and independence of women both within and without the family.

Changing relationships between parents and children comprised a third way in which the democratic family began to succeed the authoritarian family. We can speak of three stages in these relationships. The first was the *adult-centered* family, one which was run by adults and for adults, with little room for a stage in life focused on the child or child development. The child was treated primarily as a dependent for only a short time and was then expected to begin to behave like a little adult, with adult values and preferences being adopted at an early age. Parental authority, especially the authority of the father, was pervasive and strict.

Modernization modified this pattern significantly and increased the emphasis on child development. The period of "childhood" became longer and developed into a stage of child and adolescent growth and change. More attention was given by the parents to this process of development, and parents began to consider the allocation of family resources—time and income—to it. The relationship of parents to children became *child-centered* as the family's energies and preoccupation with children and their growth began to

48. See "Fertility Variations by Ethnic Origin," *supra,* note 19.

loom larger and larger in terms of total family activities. The family focus on occupation and income earning and the need to look upon young people as earners of income supplemental to that of the father declined as family income rose and the family devoted more effort and energy not only to its own receation and leisure time but also to family experiences and the growth of the child.

A variety of factors already touched upon were involved in all this. Parents began to limit the number of children, for they knew that their ability to invest time and energy in child growth and development was directly related to numbers. In the child-centered family, play with children was emphasized, and facilities for play were desired in residential choices. Education was stressed, so that the child could develop the skills to make his way in the world. All this required that the parents sacrifice adult pleasures and preoccupations to give the child what he wanted and demanded. The move to the suburbs came from this motivation; it provided a "better" setting for raising children. Child-centered institutions, such as Little League baseball and children's sections of public libraries, as well as country club facilities and schools, became vital family preoccupations.

Still a third stage is discernible, a shift from the *child-centered* to the *adult-directed* family which stressed even more strongly a comprehensive approach to child development. Major family resources were devoted to the child as a creative person whose potential abilities should be discovered, fostered, and developed. The child was not thought of so much as a person who could learn occupational skills but as one with potential creative abilities which should be developed so as to make life pleasant and enjoyable, fulfilling, and personally rewarding. There was an increased emphasis on informal aspects of development and growth outside the school system, on music lessons, crafts and skills, and hobbies. The role of parents came to be not just one of preparing the child to cope with the larger world by acquiring skills necessary for an occupation but of developing the child's full capacities.

These changes in the relationship of parents to children led increasingly to greater autonomy for the child within the family. There was an emphasis on a greater role for children in family decisions, in developing more freedom for the child's personal desires and activities within the household. One of the goals in moving to the suburbs was to enable each child, if possible, to have a separate room for his own privacy, possessions, and activities. Another was to secure more opportunities for the child to find positive support from others with similar interests and from institutions which could facilitate leisure time and developmental activities. Often this autonomy led to rebellion by the child against the authority of parents, but this rebellion was only one phase of the more general trend toward greater autonomy for the child within the family.

All these changes within the family comprised both an overall change throughout the social order and a differential change within it. It came first in one sector of society, was generalized through other sectors, and met stubborn resistance from still others. The source of innovation lay in the upper levels of the social order, with the upper middle class generating change most intensively, while those in the lower levels of society were more conservative in family values. As the 1970s proceeded, it appeared that the spectrum of family values was perhaps more extensive and its various segments more equally represented in American society than ever before. Conflicts among competing versions of proper and acceptable family relationships became more intense. Modernization had produced an elaborate spectrum of values throughout the social and political order.

To many readers it may well appear that the foregoing takes the implications of *Becoming Modern* far beyond legitimate argument. To others it may seem to be so commonplace as to be trivial. Yet, despite the fact that social analysis has begun to pervade the study of American history in massive ways in recent years, little of it has led to a systematic treatment of persistent and cumulative value changes which have come with industrialization, urbanization, and bureaucratization. There are patterns to these changes in values which provide some order and system to historical concepts, and it appears that the focus in *Becoming Modern* provides a framework for their analysis. That framework may not focus so precisely on the role of the workplace as it has in the nations examined by the authors. But it provides a more generalized system of analysis which brings sharply into focus the differential impact of widespread social change—modernization—on the values of the American people.

[10]

Political Parties and the
Community-Society Continuum*

I

$\mathbf{A}$MERICAN political historians are badly in need of conceptual frameworks through which they can formulate problems for research and develop contexts of understanding. Existing conceptual categories are, for the most part, traditional and conventional; as such, moreover, they are sterile. They have not given rise to the imaginative formulation of new problems, nor have they proved capable of responding creatively to new types of evidence or new ideas suggested by those working in other disciplines. It is time that we gave serious attention to this problem, for today it constitutes the major roadblock to advance in the study of the American political past. The repeated conventions of traditional views have become a steel chain of ideas which restrict rather than liberate, which confine rather than release the historical imagination. This is especially true for the period from the Civil War to the Great Depression, the period from about 1865 to about 1929, on which this chapter will focus.

Two general considerations should underlie the formulation of these conceptual frameworks. First, they should be oriented toward *structure* rather than *event*.[1] They should focus on patterns of hu-

*From *The American Party Systems: Stages of Political Development,* edited by William N. Chambers and Walter D. Burnham. Copyright © 1967 by Oxford University Press, Inc. Reprinted by permission.

1. The concept of political structure is dealt with more fully in Samuel P. Hays, "The Social Analysis of American Political History, 1880–1920," *Political Science Quarterly* 80 (1965), 373–94; and in "New Possibilities for American Political History: The Social Analysis of Political Life," Inter-University Consortium for Political Research (Ann Arbor, 1964), reprinted in Seymour Martin Lipset and Richard Hofstadter (eds.), *Sociology and History* (New York, 1968).

man relationships in the political system rather than on the succession of outcomes of political decisions. History is concerned with descriptions and analyses of societies as they change over time—that is, with social structure and social process. Political history is concerned with the struggle for dominance among people with varied political goals within that context of structure and change. The broad patterns of political relationships cannot be pieced together from a multitude of conceptually separate and distinct events, but must arise from a context which is structural in form.

Second, a satisfactory framework should encompass a wider range of systems of decision making than the political party itself. Functional and corporate systems coexist with but differ sharply from parties in urban-industrial America. The geographical representation inherent in the party system, for example, differs markedly from the functional representation inherent in the interplay of interest groups. Moreover, changes in one system of decision making may well be related to changes in another. Here I shall be concerned especially with the impact of functional and corporate systems upon political parties in the process of industrialization.

There is a special need to develop a framework which will link top-level national policies and grass-roots political behavior. Much of the criticism of past writing focuses on the overemphasis on national events, a perspective which has guided the preservation of records, the development of data, and the formulation of general ideas. Critics have urged, therefore, that attention must be shifted toward the grass roots. The analysis of popular voting behavior has stimulated this trend of thought, but a primary focus on the grass roots would be as one-sided as one on national events. Moreover, historians have erroneously assumed a uniform perspective in local and national political history, emphasizing that either national history is local and state history writ large, or local and state history is national history writ small. But political life at one level is of an entirely different order from that at another. They are linked not by logical similarity but by human interaction. A framework is needed which will account for different levels of political behavior and the interaction between them.

This essay suggests that a community-society dimension provides such a framework.[2] This dimension consists of a continuum of types of human relationships and therefore of identifiable group differences ranging from personal, community, face-to-face contacts on the one hand, to impersonal, mass relationships in the wider society on the other. It involves distinctions in the geographical scope and thereby the quality of human relationships; hence "community" and "society" as traditional terms. One conceives of community as human participation in networks of primary, interpersonal relationships within a limited geographical context. At this level there is concern with the intimate and the personal, movement within a limited range of social contacts, and preoccupation with affairs arising from daily personal life. Knowledge is acquired and action carried out through personal experience and personal relationships. Society, on the other hand, involves secondary contacts over wide geographical areas, considerable geographical mobility, and a high degree of ideological mobility with much variety and choice of what one can do, think, and be. It also involves the development of human relationships on the basis of similar functions, the establishment of organizational structures to coordinate activities beyond the confines of community, and the development of techniques to influence public affairs over broad geographical areas.

One can discover a community-society continuum in pre-urban-industrial society, such as William Benton describes for Pennsylvania army officers whose attitudes toward the federal Constitution of 1789 were closely related to whether they served inside or outside the state during the Revolution.[3] Yet the modernizing forces of science and technology gave rise to cosmopolitan tendencies in the late nineteenth century which were far more dynamic and extensive than those which existed in earlier periods of our history. The inno-

2. The most important early statement of this view is Ferdinand Tönnies, *Community and Society,* trans. and ed. by Charles P. Loomis (East Lansing, 1957). The view has been extended by American sociologists—e.g., Robert Merton, "Patterns of Influence: Local and Cosmopolitan Influentials," in Merton, *Social Theory and Social Structure* (Glencoe, Ill., 1949), 387–420. I make no pretense of applying these concepts in their original meaning, but only wish to acknowledge them as sources of inspiration. The most immediately relevant statement of the social theory underlying the argument in this paper is in Roland L. Warren, *The Community in America* (Chicago, 1963).

3. William Benton, "Pennsylvania Revolutionary Officers and the Federal Constitution," *Pennsylvania History* 31 (1964), 419–35.

vating sector of urban-industrial society was highly mobile, both ideologically and geographically; it involved the rapid elaboration of impersonal rather than personal relationships; it gave rise to modern bureaucratic organizations, with their emphasis on technical knowledge and professional expertise. Innovation constituted a world apart from local communities; the cultural values of cosmopolitan life, which grew rapidly in the cities, differed sharply from those in more traditional sectors of society.

Several elements of this social structure are of special relevance for political history. One concerns *social institutions,* those ongoing relationships among people of similar circumstance. These can be ranged on a continuum from the family institutions of residence, school, church, and recreation to those which bring together people of similar skills or economic functions, such as manufacturers, political scientists, or ministers, over broad geographical areas. Different positions on this continuum give rise to different political perspectives, values, and relationships. These differences are reflected in such matters as the relative absence of evidence about ethnocultural politics in nationally oriented literature and its abundance in locally oriented literature; the relative inability of the cosmopolitan reformer, whether a Bull Moose Republican or a "reform" Democrat, to communicate with working-class voters; and the conflict between the state highway commission and local county or township road officials.

A second aspect of the continuum concerns distinctions in *social perception.* One of the most important avenues for investigating political life is the distinctive way in which people in different circumstances perceive their political world. What is their conception of the range of political values, of their past, of their current situation and the causes of it, of the kind of society which should be created in the future? A community-society framework provides an excellent setting for the examination of political perception. For the range of human consciousness can be subdivided in terms of its geographical scope and variety, whether limited to a community of one's personal relationships or extended to the larger world of impersonal media, whether tolerating a limited or an extended variety of ideas and possibilities of human thought and action. Although historians cannot recapture attitudes through survey data as students of contemporary events can, they can often reconstruct through documentary data the perceptual worlds of different segments of the political structure.

Still a third feature concerns the *mechanisms of decision making.* At one end of the continuum local communities have preferred a political system with units consistent with their local community institutions. Urban communities battled for the ward system of city council representation, small-town bankers argued for a Federal Reserve structure which rested on local clearinghouses rather than central or regional units, townships fought against state highway and county educational authorities to retain local control. Those involved in institutions organized over large geographical areas sought systems of decision making the scope of which would be equally broad. Corporations involved in nationwide economic activities sought to shift public regulation from the state to the national level, professionals and executives of large-scale economic enterprises to shift city council representation from the ward to the city at large, and statewide groups to expand the administrative apparatus of the state as opposed to the local community. Preference as to the location of the level of decision making, therefore, was directly related to the scope and location of the activities which one wished to influence.

It should be emphasized that I am not speaking about a rural-urban continuum. In the past many have assumed that the community-society dimension was consistent with a rural-urban distinction, but it is not. Within the city, for example, both communities with locally oriented institutions and more cosmopolitan groups with geographically broad and often impersonal relationships exist face to face. Suburbs contain communities not only of a wide variety of class levels, but also of different degrees of involvement in local or cosmopolitan life. Rural areas may often be populated by cosmopolitans who prefer to live in the suburbs or city dwellers vacationing in summer homes or recreational havens. In his classic article on local and cosmopolitan influentials, Robert Merton emphasized that both groups live within the same urban geographical context but in different social worlds.[4] The types of

4. Merton, "Patterns of Influence."

human relationships stressed here, therefore, are independent of their physical location in city or country.

The community-society dimension is a useful framework for sorting out values, perceptions, and mechanisms in many fields of history. As mentioned above, William Benton has used it to distinguish Federalist and anti-Federalist attitudes of Revolutionary army officers. It is involved in the church-sect distinction in religion and in Robert Doherty's distinctions between those on opposite sides of religious controversies involving Presbyterianism and Quakerism in the first half of the nineteenth century.[5] It has helped to sort out proponents and opponents of municipal reform in the early twentieth century.[6] It can provide meaningful distinctions between segments of the educational world, whether students or faculty.[7] It facilitates investigation into the vertical as well as the horizontal dimension of human organization, in which larger units of institutions, perceptions, and actions are not merely smaller units writ large, but units of a different quality. It is an especially useful framework for the investigation of a period of history in which forces of industrialization and urbanization created a more highly systematized and organized society with varying degrees of involvement by different segments of the social order.

II

THE community-society structure of American life has been reflected in the structure of the political party. The party relied for victory on voters who formed their political values within the parochial context of community, yet it mobilized those voters for wider action by means of regional and national ideologies. At the same time, elected political leaders, while retaining close community ties, became involved in cosmopolitan political forces relatively di-

5. Robert W. Doherty, "Religion and Society: The Hicksite Separation of 1827," *American Quarterly* 17 (1965), 63–80, "Religion and Society: The Presbyterian Schism of 1837–1838," mimeo; "The Growth of Orthodoxy," *Quaker History* 54 (1965), 24–34.

6. Samuel P. Hays, "The Politics of Reform in Municipal Government in the Progressive Era," *Pacific Northwest Quarterly* 55 (1964), 157–69.

7. James A. Davis, "Locals and Cosmopolitans in American Graduate Schools," *International Journal of Comparative Sociology* 2 (1961), 212–23; Alvin W. Gouldner, "Cosmopolitans and Locals: Toward an Analysis of Latent Social Roles," Pts. I and II, *Administrative Science Quarterly* 2 (1957–1958), 282–306, 444–80.

vorced from community. Their political situation often thereby became paradoxical, for the party encompassed both local and cosmopolitan levels of thought and action.

Political parties, in contrast with other systems of decision making, were uniquely capable of expressing community impulses. Since the party's roots lay in geographically organized wards and precincts, in which it had to contend for majority support, it reflected closely the characteristics of community life. The party's leaders were closely akin to the community's leaders. If the community sustained a leadership of its more affluent families, so did the party; if it gathered around such local functionaries as the real estate developer, the saloonkeeper, or the grocer, so did the party. Moreover, the party's position on substantive demands reflected the community's values. If the community supported striking coal miners or opposed prohibition, so did the party. Often the community's indifference or the diversity of its impulses gave rise to initiative at other levels of political structure, but the party rarely could ignore clearcut community demands.

Despite all this, however, historians have usually reconstructed political parties from the top down, rather than from the bottom up. While arguing that political leaders invariably manipulated grass-roots political forces, they have failed to examine the data—popular voting and local leadership—which might lead to a different view. They have argued, for example, that the Republican party won in 1896 because it bribed or threatened workingmen to vote against Bryan, and that the urban "machine" controlled unsophisticated and ignorant immigrant voters contrary to their own wishes. Both contentions rest on slim evidence. They fail to take into account the shared patterns of values and the social organization of the local community as a fundamental and persistent force in political life, or the long-term durability of the alignments in question. A major task of American political history is to reconstruct the community roots of political parties.

Analysis of popular voting, for example, reveals the vast importance of community ethnocultural factors in electoral behavior. Liberal historians, stressing the political battles over the public regulation of private business, have argued that railroad, trust, tariff, and banking controversies shaped party followings in the Populist-

Progressive Era. Ethnocultural issues, such as Sunday observance and prohibition, they consider to be "red herrings," emotional rather than "real" issues, often concocted or played up by politicians to divert attention from the "more fundamental" controversies over public regulation of private business.[8] But ethnocultural issues were far more important to voters than were tariffs, trusts, and railroads. They touched lives directly and moved people deeply. The experience of voters was not related to national and cosmopolitan political perspectives but to day-to-day community life.

Several examples illustrate this rooting of voting patterns in community rather than in society. Party divisions after the Civil War grew out of the impact of evangelical Protestantism on the political world of the late 1840s and the early 1850s.[9] In the form of prohibition, nativism, and antislavery, that movement produced both a sharp realignment of voting behavior and a cultural unity for the Republican party.[10] The Democratic party, in turn, combined Catholics and German Lutherans and nonevangelical Protestant native-born Americans in a common hostility to evangelical imperialism and the negative reference groups espousing it. This alignment persisted with little change until the depression of 1893, with variations. In the late 1880s, for example, nativist groups secured laws in Illinois and Wisconsin which prohibited instruction in a foreign language in primary and secondary schools, public or private. Immigrant groups who were normally Republican joined immigrants who were already Democratic to provide the first Democratic victories in those states since the Civil War, most notably bringing victory to John P. Altgeld as governor of Illinois in 1892.

The years from 1893 to 1896 witnessed the first major voting realignment in American politics since the 1850s.[11] This realignment

8. See, e.g., Harold U. Faulkner, *Politics, Reform and Expansion, 1890-1900* (New York, 1959), 115–16. Hofstadter's "status" theory is based upon the argument that ethnocultural issues were less real, more derivative, less rational than economic issues. See his recent concise statement of this argument in his "Fundamentalism and Status Politics on the Right," *Columbia University Forum* 8 (1965), 18–24.

9. A general survey of ethnocultural factors in politics is Seymour Martin Lipset, "Religion and Politics in the American Past and Present," in Robert Lee and Martin E. Marty (eds.), *Religion and Social Conflict* (New York, 1964), 69–126.

10. Clifford S. Griffin, *Their Brothers' Keepers* (New Brunswick, N.J., 1960), 219–41.

11. See Duncan MacRae, Jr., and James Meldrum, "Critical Elections in Illinois, 1888–1958," *American Political Science Review* 54 (1960), 669–83. Further supporting data for the conclusions in the text were developed for the five East Central states during the summer

seems to have been a product of the depression of 1893 and of the shifting attractiveness of parties and candidates to ethnocultural groups. Many voters turned Republican in the elections of 1893 and 1894 and remained so in 1896. At the same time, moreover, William Jennings Bryan, as a political spokesman for evangelical Protestants, drew numbers of Protestant Republican voters into the Democratic party, while William McKinley established strong new roots among many urban-industrial immigrant and labor voters. The Republican party in the early twentieth century was very sensitive to these voters—see, for example, Theodore Roosevelt's appointment of Oscar Straus as Secretary of Commerce, or the Republican party's move in Congress to bottle up a proposal for a literacy test for immigrants. The Northern Democratic party, on the other hand, often served as a vehicle for Prohibition as well as anti-immigration sentiment, a position not unrelated to the party's electoral gains in the state and national contests of 1908, 1910, and 1912.

World War I and its aftermath brought about a massive shift of voters toward the Republican party.[12] The vast number of state legislative races in which the Democrats did not field candidates in 1918 and 1920 indicates the depth of the revolt. The proposed League of Nations was only partially responsible. Beginning as early as 1918, the shift arose from the adverse effect of the war on the personal lives of millions of Americans: resentment against sugar and flour rationing; price ceilings on agricultural products; the policies of the national Railroad Administration, the Fuel Administration, and other wartime agencies; the official and popular treatment of Germans, Scandinavians, and other immigrants; the Eighteenth Amendment; prohibition, as a Democratic measure; the disappointment of ethnic groups with the peace. In the elections of 1920 these personal resentments, focused on Woodrow Wilson, produced an astounding Republican majority.

An equally impressive shift in voting patterns took place in the late 1920s and early 1930s. Emphasizing ethnocultural issues, Al

---

seminar for historians at the Inter-University Consortium for Political Research, Ann Arbor, Mich., in 1965, but has not as yet been published.

12. This interpretation is based upon two state studies: one of Iowa, John T. Schou, "The Decline of the Democratic Party in Iowa, 1916–1920," M.A. thesis, Univ. of Iowa, 1960; and one of Pennsylvania, Joseph Makarewicz, "The Impact of World War I on Pennsylvania Politics With Emphasis on the Election of 1920," Ph.D. diss., Univ. of Pittsburgh, 1972.

Smith of New York forged a Democratic majority in the twelve largest cities in 1928.[13] Even more important, ethnocultural community voting patterns gave way to socioeconomic divisions, as workingmen increasingly voted Democratic—a change V.O. Key, Jr., noticed in New England industrial towns in the first decade of the twentieth century.[14] The votes for Eugene V. Debs in 1912 and Robert M. La Follette in 1924 both seem to be intimately tied in with this development.[15] From the midst of previously dominant ethnocultural concerns now emerged impulses arising from the technological organization of modern industrial society. Crystallizing these tendencies, the Depression and the early New Deal policies brought them into full force.

These examples relate voting behavior to the underlying patterns of local community attitudes. Those attitudes did not arise from broad cosmopolitan considerations, but from the patterns of value at the local, personal level. Larger national and cosmopolitan forces played a role when they touched directly the lives of voters in their community setting, as they did so dramatically in crises associated with war and depression; and these forces often only crystallized or exacerbated differences in value orientation which were already imbedded in social structure. One cannot deal long with election returns without delving more deeply into the dynamics of community life and its social structure out of which political thought and action arose.

Political parties involve far more than local community life. They form hierarchies of organization from the precinct to the national level, and they involve national leadership, national strate-

13. Samuel J. Eldersveld, "Influence of Metropolitan Party Pluralities on Presidential Elections," *American Political Science Review* 43 (1949), 1189–1206; Samuel Lubell, *The Future of American Politics* (New York, 1952), 28–57; J. Joseph Huthmacher, *Massachusetts People and Politics* (Cambridge, Mass., 1959).

14. V.O. Key, Jr., "Secular Realignment and the Party System," *Journal of Politics* 20 (1959), 198–210.

15. On this point I am indebted to Bruce Stave for the development of relevant data for Pittsburgh. The Franklin D. Roosevelt vote in 1932 was correlated with the Smith vote in 1928 at a level of .72, with the La Follette vote in 1924 at a level of .84 (but with the 1924 Davis vote at −.37), and with the Debs vote of 1912 at a level of .75 (but with the 1912 Theodore Roosevelt vote at −.34). The Democratic strength of 1932, therefore, seems to be positively related to the Debs, La Follette, and Smith votes, but negatively related to the Theodore Roosevelt and Davis vote in the city of Pittsburgh.

gies, and national ideologies. There is no more crucial aspect of this for the historian than political ideology, for ideologies are frequently instruments of mass communication which mobilize local impulses for national, cosmopolitan objectives. The party activist, such as the partisan newspaper editor, was not just an organizer of machinery but an organizer of ideas; he had the task of defining a common ground within the party and a ground of distinction from other parties. Through ideology he developed party cohesion by explaining to voters how, though often diverse, they were really alike, and how they were similar in their differences from voters of other parties. To do this he called upon ideas relatively divorced from community concerns and more relevant to the cosmopolitan world. Historians have assumed that national political ideologies represented beliefs which were homogeneous throughout all levels of the political structure. But, in fact, they arose more from cosmopolitan than from local segments of the party structure, reflected leadership strategy more than grass-roots values, and linked together the several levels of party activity. For the decades from 1890 to 1920, for example, highly visible national policies such as tariff and trusts provide an incorrect view of voter preferences. Those preferences rested primarily on ethnocultural attitudes which rarely appeared in national debate. This may seem to constitute inconsistent evidence about political behavior, but such inconsistency exists only if one assumes that local and national political perspectives *should* be consistent. The point is that they were not; different levels of political life gave rise to different concerns. The party mobilized voters on the community level by stressing ethnocultural issues which sustained local party loyalties and party differences, and at the same time emphasized altogether different issues, such as tariff and trusts, on the national level of debate. It may well be, in fact, that the stress on national ideology functioned primarily to obscure ethnic and religious differences which, if given free expression, might have hampered effective national party action.

Examination of the tariff as a substantive issue has confused historians. Tracing ideological tariff differences back into legislative votes and grass-roots impulses, they have failed to find clear, continuous distinctions—there were high-tariff Democrats and low-tariff Republicans—and have concluded that the tariff controversy was an "unreal" issue. Consequently, they deemphasize the issue and those periods of history, such as the 1880s, in which tariff debates ran high within and between parties. We can make more progress if we examine the tariff as an ideology. To both parties it constituted a process of self-identification and self-explanation. Whether or not congressmen voted consistently with that distinction in committee, and whether or not political economists believe that the distinction was substantive, are not important. Tariff arguments were ideological instruments of voter mobilization and party combat. The question arises, for example, as to whether the tariff or the money question was the major issue in the election of 1896, but the question itself is irrelevant. The important struggle during that campaign was not over two sides of an issue, but over whether or not one issue or the other should be the primary focus of attention. Party leaders contended over alternative explanations for the depression of 1893 and the ensuing economic crisis, and Bryan and McKinley each sought to persuade voters that he had the correct explanation for the cause of the depression as well as the most effective cure. Each tried to mobilize voters around explanatory ideological positions with which those voters could identify. In the end, McKinley's explanation in terms of the tariff made sense to discontented urban-industrial workingmen. His election was a victory not only for a particular group of voters but also for a particular explanation of events.

A recent study of party loyalty in the United States Senate during the period 1909-15 sheds some light on the distinction between grass-roots impulses and ideology.[16] One of the authors' major aims was to measure party cohesion. They discovered that tariff votes brought forth a high degree of party unity for both Democrats and Republicans; but much lower rates obtained for immigration and prohibition roll calls, which indicated a sharp intraparty division on these issues. I would suggest that the low cohesion on questions of immigration and prohibition reflected grass-roots voter preferences. Republicans who had inherited urban, immigrant, wet support in the political turnover of the 1890s, and who continued to be

16. Jerome M. Clubb and Howard W. Allen, "Party Loyalty in the United States Senate in the Taft and Wilson Years," mimeo, Inter-University Consortium for Political Research (Ann Arbor, 1965).

sensitive to the anti-prohibition views of these voters, disagreed sharply with dry Republicans. Democrats, on the other hand, came from both the immigrant wet cities of the North and the dry, native-American South and West. High cohesion on the tariff issue represented not common constituency views, but party ideology. One can readily discover Northern Republican support for lower tariffs, especially in committee, and Southern Democratic votes for higher rates. But on final votes, considerable regularity obtained because of the tariff's role in ideological cohesion for the parties.

Political leadership provides a useful means of examining the different levels of party activity within the community-society dimension. National leaders have predominated in party studies; state leaders have been much less examined; local leaders have gone almost unnoticed. We have assumed that local leadership either can be ignored or can be understood from knowledge about national leaders. The result is frustrating for a proper treatment of political structure, for leadership differs markedly at different levels of the hierarchy of political life. We must examine not only the levels separately, but also the interaction between them.

Investigations of "Progressive" leaders during the early years of the twentieth century suggest the possibilities. By investigating 100 individuals in each of three groups of Iowa Republican leaders— Progressive, Cumminsite, and Old Guard—E. D. Potts established that all three were similar in socioeconomic and ethnocultural backgrounds; they differed only in age and previous political experience.[17] William T. Kerr discovered a similar pattern in the state of Washington.[18] At the state level, therefore, it appears that the "Progressives" differed little from the typical Republican leaders. On the other hand David J. Carey examined 100 ward and precinct officials and candidates for local office in the Cummins and Old Guard factions in Burlington, Iowa, an especially heated center of Republican intraparty controversy.[19] These leaders differed in cultural and

17. E. Daniel Potts, "The Progressive Profile in Iowa," *Mid-America* 45 (1965), 257–68.

18. William T. Kerr, Jr., "The Progressives of Washington, 1910–12," *Pacific Northwest Quarterly* 55 (1964), 16–27.

19. David James Carey, "Republican Factionalism in Burlington, Iowa, 1906–1908," M.A. thesis, Univ. of Iowa, 1960.

occupational characteristics; but, contrary to the findings of earlier studies by Chandler and Mowry, the Progressives came more from blue-collar occupations and newer immigrant, non-Protestant groups than did the Old Guard. More important, however, Carey found that the sharpest differences involved not personal background characteristics, but institutional affiliations. Old Guard leaders were connected with banking, lumbering, and railroad groups, "Progressives" with commercial and mercantile interests.

These studies emphasize the vast importance of examining political leadership at all levels of political life, from the grass-roots to the national, from the local to the cosmopolitan, before any safe generalizations can be drawn about a political movement. We need not expect that party leaders at each level would be of the same personal background or institutional involvement. In fact, it would be surprising if this were the case. It would be more reasonable to expect an interaction of different types of people at different positions in the hierarchy, rather than a similarity at all levels. These are distinctions between different degrees of involvement in community and society.

Local leadership was deeply rooted in the local community. To take one example, urban political leaders—councilmen, school board members, justices of the peace, constables—had characteristics that closely resembled those of the ward communities from which they were elected. Liberal historians have completely missed this feature of urban political life. They have examined urban politics largely in terms of the efforts of enlightened people to throw off the influence of the political "machine." They have reduced the conflict almost to a simple notion of a struggle between honest and dishonest men. They have ignored grass-roots political leadership, for they have felt that party leaders manipulated the vote and that community political impulses were not indigenous but the product of external influences. Yet ward political leaders, even prior to the era of municipal reform, were a direct product of ward community life. They can be understood as community leaders, not in the sense of the kind of leadership the liberal analyst would like to have seen, but of the kind which the community in fact produced. In Pittsburgh, for example, the personal socioeconomic position of councilmen varied directly with the socioeconomic composition of the wards they represented.[20] Working-class wards most frequently elected workingmen, labor leaders, or men who provided the focal point of community contacts, such as saloonkeepers or grocers. Middle-class wards elected small businessmen such as grocers, druggists, undertakers, community real estate dealers, bankers, and contractors. Upper-class wards elected central-city bankers, lawyers, doctors, manufacturers. The leadership of such men, identified with their urban subcommunities, rested on community confidence. They spoke for their communities, rolled logs for them in the city council, and represented their economic and cultural interests.

As councilmen came to represent broader geographical areas, they became divorced from local community life and more involved in cosmopolitan urban impulses which were extracommunity in scope. Council candidates who ran in citywide rather than ward elections—this municipal reform was widespread in the Progressive Era—required citywide, rather than local prominence, and such recognition came only with involvement in extracommunity activities and institutions. The small storekeeper and clerk gave way as the typical city councilman to the prominent lawyer, the large-scale merchant, or the businessman with wide interests. Such men as these came to dominate the reformed city councils and the city school boards.[21]

Leaders at different levels of the community-society party dimension had correspondingly different perspectives. The scope of consciousness of the ward community leader was parochial and limited. When he thought of schools he thought of the ward school, the employment of teachers from the local community, and the use of the school building for community social activities. When he thought of justice, he thought of ways in which community residents could be helped through petty scrapes with the law. But the leader at the cosmopolitan end of the scale thought in terms of the city as a whole, of the need for smooth citywide traffic flows, of general problems of health and sanitation, of education as a system of training which should conform to professional standards. By the

20. Based upon an examination of Pittsburgh city councilmen from 1860 to 1911.
21. Hays, "The Politics of Reform."

very nature of his position in the social structure, his consciousness, his contacts, and his knowledge were far more extensive in geographical scope than the ward community.

III

CHANGES wrought by science and technology in modern America have had an enormous impact on the political party and its traditional local foundations. These changes fashioned not merely new subject matter for political controversy and new demographic roots for voting, but also new types of human relationships which in turn led to new systems of decision making. Arising at a level in the community-society continuum far above the grass roots, they shifted initiative upward in the expression of political impulses and were responsible for a decline in community involvement in the party. Preference for these systems of decision making, moreover, led to hostility toward political parties. Examination of these new systems provides, through comparative study, more insight into the community-society dimension as it pertains to political parties. It also brings into focus important changes in parties themselves as they adjusted to the new competition from rival decision-making institutions.

Urban, industrial society involved a fundamental reordering of human relationships which permeated not only economic and social life but political life as well. This reordering went through two stages. First, the revolution in transportation and in the acquisition and transmission of empirical knowledge destroyed the separateness and parochialism of economic, social, and ideological life in the grass-roots community. It brought about a more mobile society. Second, it gave rise to new forms of social organization at levels above that of the community, involving human relationships over broad geographical areas and often in impersonal rather than face-to-face contacts. Locally established relationships remained. But superimposed upon them now were large relationships called forth by the new accessibility of things, of people, and of ideas which the technological revolution and the expansion of empirical inquiry had fashioned.

This greatly expanded scope of human relationships established new contexts of control. It increased manyfold the factors which one had to take into account if he wished to influence the course of events. Now it became increasingly difficult even to understand the situation which one wanted to influence; confining one's knowledge to the personal communication of man to man no longer sufficed. The vast world of complex circumstances intruded into decision making and required new perceptions of the scope and complexity of the political arena and new devices for gathering information upon which decisions could be based. It also gave rise to new political mechanisms, to new means of control commensurate with the new scope of things to be controlled. It called forth devices for influencing selected types of human relationships over wide geographical areas rather than a majority of the voters in a limited community. It gave rise to functional interest groups and systems of corporate decision making. The local community remained as the basic element of the political party, but it no longer sufficed as the focal point for organizing new political impulses which arose beyond the local community.

Functionally organized economic groups in business, labor, and agriculture developed rapidly in the late nineteenth and early twentieth centuries to influence the wider price-and-market system. They drew together into separate instruments of action not a majority of those living in a limited geographical area, but those who performed similar economic functions over wide geographical areas. Such groups constituted supra-community organizations with roots in only specialized segments of local communities. People found that as individuals they could not influence the price-and-market system, but as groups they could—either directly, or indirectly through the instruments of government.

These groups sought to influence the political parties (for example, influencing planks in their platforms) and their legislative and administrative decisions as well. Many historians have tended to look upon such groups as influences outside the legitimate political system rather than as a set of forces in their own right. Yet they constituted a system of decision making which paralleled the political party but which differed in its structural roots. Functional interest groups rejected parties as appropriate instruments of political action. Since the party was geographically based, it rarely could speak with a clear-cut, single-interest voice; only rarely, and then at the smallest level of organization, did it rest on a homogeneous constituency. More often it faced conflicting and contending elements within it which had to be compromised for effective action. If one were concerned with a particular political goal, he found himself supporting other political goals in which he was far less interested, simply to secure sufficiently broad support for his own proposal. Since his aims were compromised, diluted, or sidetracked, he rarely felt that his view secured sufficient political expression.

In the latter part of the nineteenth century and the early twentieth century, labor and agriculture became disillusioned with their close connection with parties. Their inability to speak clearly through parties led them to establish other methods of political action based more clearly on function. Trade unions, through the Federation of Organized Trades and Labor Unions and later the American Federation of Labor, as well as through city and state organizations, adopted the policy of supporting and opposing legislators irrespective of party and solely in terms of their commitment to labor legislation. Farm organizations, such as the National Farmers Union, admonished their members to disavow partisan politics but at the same time not to give up political rights—in other words, to change political tactics. Commodity trade groups, frequently based on cooperative economic functions, became the major source of farm political power and political action. These functional groups were nonpartisan political organizations which sought to disentangle themselves from a geographical system of representation they found to be ineffective.

Heavy emphasis upon the relationship of functional groups to legislative and administrative decisions has obscured their characteristics as a political structure independent in origin from the formal institutions of government. The private interplay among functional groups was basic to and more fundamental than their public interplay. The injection of public agencies into the process often came as a result of the failure of groups to enter into or accept privately settled accommodations. Such measures as antitrust laws, or railroad, banking, and agricultural legislation in the years from the 1880s on to the Great Depression of 1929, were not so much attempts by the general public to restrict private business in the "public interest" as devices of some segments of private business to restrict other segments when their objectives could not be reached through private accommodation. The results of such legislation should be interpreted as governmental cooperation with private groups in the development and maintenance of a political structure and a decision-making system. The process can be observed in detail in the movement for railroad regulation.[22] Behind federal regulation lay the gradual organization of shippers and railroads, as well as railroad labor unions, as functional groups to protect their interests as consumers or producers of transportation service. Shippers, engaged in regional economic competition, complained that rate patterns gave cost advantages to other shippers. Bargaining between different groups of shippers went on through the medium of the railroad; mediators and arbitrators were called in. At the turn of the century both shippers and railroads became dissatisfied with this process and sought to shift it to a federal agency; hence Congress strengthened the law in the Hepburn Act of 1906. Federal regulation was only a new technique to resolve an old kind of conflict. It came not out of the nebulous blue of public demands, but from political bargaining between shipper and shipper which had been developing over the years.

Liberal historians have long been reluctant to take this development seriously. They have considered functional groups to be undesirable intrusions into a more desirable system of decision making represented by the rational voter choosing between candidates for public office. They have looked upon such groups as limiting, confining, and distorting a more legitimate political process, thereby reducing the opportunity for political expression. But, considered in terms of the social relationships in which they were rooted, functional groups expanded the opportunities for political expression by providing alternatives for the transmission of political impulses which the party could not clearly express. The party's need to appeal to diverse groups within given geographical areas, while giving single-minded expression to none, was a limiting and confining method of political expression to those who wished to give more concentrated support to specialized objectives.

22. K. Austin Kerr, *American Railroad Politics, 1914-1920,* (Pittsburgh, 1968).

The systematization of human relationships in large-scale, centralized corporate activity, whether private or public, constitutes still another process of decision making which affected political parties adversely. While the party rested upon geography, and the interest group upon function, the corporate system rested upon the integration of different functional groups, often located in different geographical areas, into single systems of activity and under centralized control. Beginning with the latter part of the nineteenth century, this process of decision making grew steadily in private economic affairs and in education, religion, and government; indeed, hardly a realm of life remained untouched. The corporate form of organization was primarily a political or decision-making system. The specialization of functions which divorced the entrepreneur from the capitalist gave rise to a separate group of decision makers within the corporate system and to a sharp differentiation between those who exercised control and those who were controlled —in short, between the managers and the managed. The integrative tendencies of the corporate system differed sharply from the system of functional-interest interaction which emphasized the give and take of bargaining among equals, and from the political party which stressed national mobilization of grass-roots political values. In the corporate system the initiative came from the top down, not from the bottom up or the middle out; and control flowed only in one direction. The relationships between center and periphery were administrative, and were designed to translate central decisions into peripheral action rather than to translate peripheral impulses into central action.

Systematization was closely related to professionalization, and especially to the growth of the empirical professions. The scope of interest of the professional concerned with such matters as education, health, welfare, and public works was increasingly universal rather than parochial, increasingly cosmopolitan rather than local. He valued ideological mobility rather than confined perspectives. Moreover, since his scope of vision tended to expand, he sought larger units of action, larger corporate systems of operation, through which he could apply his knowledge. The public health expert sought to reach and influence an increasing number of people; the educational leader wished to generalize his standards of education to all. Such professionals were influential in shaping the character of reform movements from the late nineteenth century onward. They found corporate systems of decision making to their liking, and they approved them not only because of their scope of coverage, but because of their coercive potential. The professional sought to carry standards of life generated by a few to the population at large. His task was to persuade the yet unconvinced, rather than simply to express the values dominant in the general public.

This upward flow in the location of decision making in private affairs gave rise to a similar upward flow in public affairs. The movement to reform municipal government after 1890, for example, was primarily an effort to centralize the location of decision making.[23] Prior to municipal reform, representation in city councils had been decentralized in a system of ward representation; council action, therefore, constituted a process of bargaining between locally oriented spokesmen. Mayors, often dominated by the councils, were weak. After 1890, however, reformers demanded more centralized decision making. They promoted the strong-mayor, then the commission, and finally the city-manager form of executive authority; and they urged that ward representation be abolished in favor of centralized, citywide representation. By 1929 the transition had had a profound effect. It produced a shift in political initiative upward from the urban subcommunities to forces of citywide scope.

The same upward shift in decision making took place between township and county on the one hand and the state on the other. The focal points of this transition were schools and roads. For several decades after 1890 state functions expanded rapidly, producing growth in appropriations and debts, in programs and administrative personnel.[24] Schools and roads constituted the major items of state expenditures. In each case the upward movement of decision making involved a shift in control over these affairs from local units

23. Hays, "The Politics of Reform."
24. Morton G. Keller, "The Economic Policy Making of the States Since the Civil War," paper delivered at the meeting of the Mississippi Valley Historical Association, Omaha, Neb., April 1963.

of government to higher units. While the local units wanted local control in order to retain farm-to-market roads or local schools insulated from the wider, cosmopolitan world, the state units wanted statewide, hard-surfaced road systems, and more modern standards of school curricula and administration. In each case professionals with cosmopolitan rather than local perspectives were extremely influential in shifting the scope of interest and level of decision making. The state highway commission supplanted the township trustee in road affairs, and the state superintendent of public instruction became an increasingly influential figure.

A similar upward shift in decision making took place between the state and federal governments. The most dramatic aspect of this process was the change in regulatory legislation. It is often argued that federal regulation of private business developed in an atmosphere of laissez-faire; actually, federal regulation more often merely shifted the location of regulation from state to federal levels in accordance with the expansion of the scope of economic activity itself from state and regional to national dimensions. State regulation of transportation, for example, was traditional in the United States; the perfection of the Interstate Commerce Commission only shifted this regulation upward. Many state pure food and drug laws were in force in the late nineteenth century; the federal law of 1906 nationalized regulation. In each case nationally organized businesses with markets and other interests beyond the confines of a single state actively promoted national regulation. They preferred a system of control consistent in scope with their scope of operations; they preferred to deal with one regulatory agency which had a uniform national policy rather than with many state agencies which had diverse policies. They preferred to narrow and limit the number of political forces with which they had to cope.

Initiative in these upward shifts in decision making and initiative in the formation of corporate systems of activity did not come from the grass roots or from the middle layers of political structure which were represented by functional interest groups. It came, instead, from the top. It came from those who had the scope of perspective to define possibilities in large ways, from the professionals, the businessmen, usually from upper-income rather than from lower-income groups, from those whose institutional involvements were already geographically broad.[25] This initiative, moreover, involved a process of influence and domination over centers of initiative of smaller scope; if desirable activity was now to be defined in terms of large areas and large numbers of people considered from a single vantage point, one could not accept more parochial definitions. Cosmopolitan life must overcome local life. The development of citywide representation and the city-manager system coerced and restricted centers of initiative in the urban ward communities. The growth of state highway commissions vastly reduced the influence of township and county officials. Far-flung corporate activities produced policies at variance with those of local communities. such as the use of injunctions in labor disputes instead of jury trials, which had usually reflected local rather than corporate views. National regulatory policies inevitably reduced the scope of jurisdiction of state regulatory agencies.

The domestic politics of World War I played a significant role in sharpening the conflict between cosmopolitan and local forces within the context of a system of corporate decision making. For example, during the war the federal government assumed management of the nation's railroads through the United States Railroad Administration.[26] The USRA developed policies geared to objectives which were national in scope. Its officials thought in terms of a single, most efficient transportation system, and they sought to persuade everyone involved in the entire process, from corporate executives to divisional traffic managers to local merchants, to dovetail their practices in that overall system. In fact, they forced them to do so. But each of these groups—local buyers and sellers of coal, for example—saw their problems from their own local point of view. They wished not to conform to a national system but to their own plan to maximize their business. They looked upon the USRA as coercive and authoritarian, as a usurper of executive power, and they demanded that the railroads be returned to private management

25. Hays, "The Politics of Reform"; Joan S. Miller, "The Politics of Municipal Reform in Chicago During the Progressive Era: The Municipal Voters' League as a Test Case, 1896–1920," M.A. thesis, Roosevelt Univ., 1966.
26. Kerr, *American Railroad Politics*.

and that the power of the Interstate Commerce Commission, suspended for the war, be restored. This they secured in the Transportation Act of 1920.

The growth of systematized decision making created a new structure of political relationships quite different from those in other systems. The relationship was clearly hierarchical, with a vast gap between those at the top and those at the grass roots in scope of perspective, in source of initiative, in ability to reach levels of decision making. A continuum of relationships developed which can be differentiated in terms of geographical scope of movement, perception, and influence. A continuous tension arose between those at different points of the community-society continuum, a tension which was a major element of political conflict. The systematization of modern life, in short, created a structure of relationships in which cosmopolitan elements, corporately organized, looked upon local life—including traditional political party life—as parochial, narrow, and unenlightened. Local communities, on the other hand, considered cosmopolitan influences and their bureaucracies to be imperialistic, dictatorial, and destructive of established values.

IV

THE development of systems of decision making at levels of political organization above the local community had significant repercussions on community political life and on political parties. The growth of functional and corporate systems not only created new processes of decision making alongside the old, but also inevitably involved the reduction of local political influence in favor of influence at a higher level of organization. The vitality of the roots upon which parties rested diminished drastically. The party itself was subjected to attack; it was forced to adjust to influences from new levels of political initiative. For their part, local community impulses became increasingly traditionalist and conservative. Innovation in the political order in urban-industrial America came from cosmopolitan rather than local sources, through administrative action and empirical inquiry which entered the social order not through community but through society. The local community, on the other hand, feeling threatened by these innovations, adopted a posture of defending and perpetuating those patterns of life and custom familiar to and sustaining it. It became tradition-oriented, seeking to preserve the past; in the midst of rapid social change, it took on a protective stance. The political party, resting uniquely on a geographical base and reflecting geographically organized community forces, was an especially appropriate vehicle of conservatism.

The transformation of evangelical Protestantism from an innovating to a protective political impulse illustrates this process. When evangelical religion swept through American Protestantism in the first half of the nineteenth century it was innovating, hopeful, progressive, positive about scientific inquiry, anxious to be involved in the larger world. It won out over more conservative religious tendencies. This stance provided much of the spirit and drive which the early Republican party possessed. By the early twentieth century, however, this same religious impulse faced a new industrial, urban, and scientific environment, one which was marked by the emergence of Catholics and Jews and the increasing popularity of secular thought. In the face of these changes, evangelical Protestantism became protective. It feared ideological mobility, the unpredictable ventures of the secular mind, the changing religious culture, the growing cities. Rooted in rural areas of the country, it launched a drive to protect its cultural heritage against erosion. From the 1890s on it concentrated on such efforts as prohibition, Sunday observance, anti-evolution laws, and the preservation of rural political power in state legislatures. The rural political party became the special instrument of this protective stance.

Community impulses in the city equally sought to maintain the past, but their efforts were less successful. For here cosmopolitan impulses were more powerful and better organized. Ward political forces could do little but fight a rearguard action against the innovating forces of cosmopolitanism. The attempt to retain the ward school quickly collapsed before the drive for the citywide school board. The feeble fight against urban city council reapportionment stands in dramatic contrast to the successful rural opposition to state legislative reapportionment of over more than half a century. Cities had the same conditions of unequal representation as did the states. As peripheral sections of the city grew, central sections grew less rapidly and then declined. For a short while the central city was overrepresented and the periphery underrepresented, but this did not last long. Almost every municipal reform movement in the early twentieth century involved the effort to shift representation toward areas of population growth. Where the movement did not reduce the power of older sections of the city through citywide representation, it did so by reapportioning council seats. The change came about so swiftly and often so quietly amid the claims and counterclaims of corruption that historians have not noticed it. It reveals that traditionalist forces were overcome in the city far more readily than in the countryside through the destruction of their crucial base of political action—geographical representation.

Community political impulses not only became more conservative; they also declined. Initiative now moved upward to extra-community forces. As a consequence grass-roots areas felt a loss of involvement in decision making and became more alienated from the wider political community. Those functions of the local political leader which consisted of conveying impulses from the community to the larger centers declined; and communities, in turn, felt that they had a decreasing influence on those more distant centers. As city-manager plans and citywide systems of representation arose, ward communities felt that decisions which affected them were made elsewhere and that they no longer had personal intermediaries through whom they could reach the centers of decision making.[27] In rural areas considerable influence was still retained over schools, but even here the township official increasingly lost authority to the county superintendent; moreover, his jurisdiction over roads gave way to the state highway commission. The transformation was driven home dramatically to the rural community when, because of the commission's power of eminent domain, roads were constructed through rather than around farms. Urban communities would experience the same powerlessness in later years when redevelopment authorities used a similar power of eminent domain to replace older patterns of physical community organization with new.

As the local political leader's function as a community representative declined, he was replaced by representatives of larger func-

27. For expressions of this view see Harold A. Stone et al., *City Manager Government in Nine Cities* (Chicago, 1940), 20, 225, *et passim*.

tional and corporate decision-making systems. These appeared in the community not as spokesmen for the community but as agents of extra-community forces. They served primarily to transmit decisions made elsewhere to the community, to secure information useful for decision making elsewhere, and to cushion the impact and enhance the acceptability of decisions made elsewhere. Firemen and policemen no longer were stationed in the communities where they lived, nor did they represent community organizations, but were assigned to their stations by citywide commissioners and boards. Community welfare councils were established to cushion the impact of the shift from the personal attention given by the ward leader to the more impersonal contact with the public welfare agency. The parent-teacher association replaced the ward school board as the representative of community interests, but it functioned more as an aid to the principal, the agent of the larger school system, than as a dominant and independent influence in the formation of school policy. Many functions formerly carried out by ward leaders who were closely interwoven with the party system were now taken up by others who were more closely connected with functional and corporate systems of decision making. Some indigenous community influences persisted. In some cities, for example, the ward judicial system, with its local justices of the peace and constables, remained as a community institution. Yet such indigenous leadership in the corporate city was rare. Community autonomy persisted and developed most fully in the suburban political jurisdictions, which vigorously defended their legal separateness precisely to retain a sense of influence and power over affairs which affected them. Within the city precinct and ward leaders remained, but with sharply changed functions. Although in some precincts they retained many of their older functions, in most they were reduced to petty affairs of party organization and to mobilizing votes on election day. The functions of the local party leader declined sharply as the focal point of social and political organization shifted to a higher level.

The emergence of new systems of decision making give rise to a widespread attack on the political party itself. From national to local levels the political party was considered to be dominated by the corrupt "machine," which rendered it unreliable as an instrument of public action. Demands for direct election of senators; for primary rather than convention nominations; for initiative, referendum, and recall; and for other devices to reduce the influence of the party in the selection of candidates persisted throughout the Progressive Era. In fact, when reformers could not agree on substantive issues, they could agree on procedural political reforms. Political reform was touted as a means whereby political power would be shifted from the "interests" to the "people," and mass involvement in decision making would be restored. In reality, however, the movement for political reform was an attack on the entire party system as it had developed in the nineteenth century, a rejection of community involvement in decision making, and a demand that public decisions be made through mechanisms other than the political party. It stemmed from fear of rather than faith in community political impulses.

This attack on the political party came not from the grass roots but from people involved in institutions at higher, extra-community levels of social organization. Very frequently they were themselves involved in newer forms of decision making. In Pittsburgh, for example, they came from the upper levels of society, from the highest echelons of the corporate world, and from the advanced segments of professional life.[28] In Chicago the Municipal Voters' League was composed of men from the city's dominant social and economic groups.[29] In Seattle and Des Moines the drive was spearheaded by the chambers of commerce. The characteristics of the candidates whom these reform groups backed, as contrasted with those whom they opposed, indicated that they preferred as decision makers those from their own levels of institutional organization and from occupational groups associated with corporate business and professional life. Those who sought political reform, therefore, were far more involved in a cosmopolitan than a local world, far more receptive to the political processes inherent in the corporate rather than the party system of decision making.

By the same token, the reform image of an appropriate decision-making system also arose from the cosmopolitan world. The reform-

28. Hays, "The Politics of Reform."
29. Miller, "The Politics of Municipal Reform."

er's model was the business corporation, not the political party.[30] The political party was too open to a variety of compromising and debilitating influences. It had to respond to the multitude of impulses arising from the community electorate; it had to compromise in making legislative decisions to secure majority support; it had to reward friends and defeat enemies on a party basis. In the business corporation, on the other hand, decisions could be made on the basis of efficient, systematic analysis, from a single vantage point, in which the overriding objective was the "common good." Increasingly through the years those involved in cosmopolitan life sought to divorce decisions from the electorate, in order to enhance the efficiency and system which they felt would implement their goals.

The attack on the party system and on its community roots frequently came only indirectly. Most emphasis was placed upon the corruption of political leaders and the capacity of the "machine" to command loyalty and influence votes. Most reformers, therefore, looked upon their activities as attempts to purify rather than to change drastically the system of decision making. But, in fact, they sought to make fundamental changes, for to them the shortcoming of the party system was its constant susceptibility to influence from the grass-roots community. Reformers frequently made explicit their objection to the community choice of workingmen, clerks, petty shopkeepers, and saloonkeepers as local political leaders. They often argued, in fact, that ward leaders could not make acceptable political decisions precisely because they were too close to their constituents. The political reform movement in the Progressive Era sought not to extend community involvement in political decision making, but to restrict it in accord with the requirements of new methods of decision making.

Faced with the rise of new systems of this kind and the atrophy of the community roots of its impulses, the political party in the twentieth century experienced a series of adjustments. As the location of decision making in the entire political system shifted upward, so did initiative within the party. No longer did community impulses of the ward and township play such a significant role.

30. Hays, "The Politics of Reform."

Now the party assumed a wider geographical perspective; and, in turn, forces organized on an extra-community level assumed a greater influence within it. This larger context of party activity produced at least two significant changes. First, the party increasingly selected decision makers who represented not geographical but functional areas of society, such as segments of the economic, ethnic, and religious communities. Second, these decision makers increasingly came, not from all socioeconomic levels, depending upon their community of origins, but from a particular segment of the socioeconomic system, the upper-middle class. In both of these changes the party made an adjustment to the new patterns of social organization with which it now was forced to compete. These changes were most dramatic in the cities. No matter what new forms of government emerged there, the geographical base from which decision makers were chosen through the party expanded sharply, and the number of people and variety of institutions which each decision maker represented expanded as sharply. Drastically reduced in size, city councils could provide representation to few distinct geographical communities. In this circumstance councilmen were often elected at large; but even when ward representation was retained areas of representation increased sharply in size. Decision makers now had to appeal to a broad range of the electorate. Party leaders, in selecting nominees for office, recognized this change in the structure of representation. They wished to select candidates who would appeal to the largest number of voters. What would be the criteria? To some extent they retained an area distribution, making sure that candidates came from different sections of the city. More important, however, they sought to grant representation to all the major functional groups of the city.

The process of "balancing the ticket" among economic and ethnocultural groups could be observed in the earliest departures from the ward system. Often suggestions arose for functional representation along economic lines: for councilmen chosen, for example, from manufacturers, bankers, professionals, labor, and merchants. At times only political defeat gave rise to an effective "balance." In Des Moines, for example, the first slate of candidates for the new city commission was drawn entirely from the business community, though balanced among its various sectors. No one identified with labor was nominated. The result was a disastrous defeat for the "businessmen's slate." Cities in Iowa that followed Des Moines in the drive for the commission form of government—Des Moines was a pioneer in this innovation—profited from its mistakes and "balanced" their tickets with workingmen's representatives. In Pittsburgh the new city council, reorganized in 1911 by replacing ward with citywide representation, included a labor spokesman; the position he held was referred to in the newspapers as "reserved for labor." The choice of the functional groups to be represented remained a major party choice; but the shift from geographical to functional representation was widespread.

The change in the character of working-class representation in city councils was significant. Formerly these representatives had often been unskilled or skilled workingmen, many of whom had no official position in a trade union. Although trade union officials were frequently members of city councils, many working-class councilmen were not union leaders. Moreover, people of other occupations —store clerks, bartenders, and small shopkeepers—often represented working-class wards. Now, however, as the initiative for selecting candidates moved upward to higher levels of social organization, the top-echelon trade union official became the functional representative of working-class people. The labor representative chosen for the Pittsburgh city council in 1911 was the immediate past president of the Amalgamated Association of Iron, Steel and Tin Workers, the largest organized labor group in the city's major industry. In other words, spokesmen for labor as an organized functional group replaced working-class community leaders as decision makers when the party made the adjustment to new systems of social organization.

The occupational characteristics of city councilmen as a whole shifted sharply upward in the community-society continuum. Councilmen now were lawyers and doctors with city contacts far wider than the local community, and bankers and businessmen of far more extensive activities than the community store. There were others, of course, but the center of gravity of the occupational structure of city councilmen clearly shifted from the lower and lower-middle class to the upper-middle class. While few of the council members during the days of ward representation in Pittsburgh, for example, were listed in the *Blue Book* (the city's social directory), an increasing number were so listed after citywide representation replaced ward representation. The change was most striking in school government, where the shift to citywide representation was more rapid and more complete. A study of school boards throughout the nation by George S. Counts in the 1920s indicated that their members came overwhelmingly from the upper occupational and professional groups.[31]

Political parties were equally sensitive to religious and ethnic functional groups. They maintained religious and ethnic balance on city councils, the particular balance depending upon the community's ethnocultural composition. The gradual involvement of "newer" ethnic groups came about as the party felt it necessary to recognize these segments of the community. But just as candidates who represented labor as a functional group were drawn from the top echelons of working-class organizational and social levels, so were the candidates who represented ethnic groups. The first Negro members of the Pittsburgh city council came from the Negro upper class—professionals and businessmen—a class level which gave rise to an outlook approaching that of the upper-middle-class segment of the white community.

The upward shift in decision making brought about an upward shift in the characteristics of decision makers in the community-society dimension, and a related upward shift in their socioeconomic class level. One observes a gradual exclusion of local community leaders from the decision-making process which, in turn, involved a gradual exclusion of direct representatives of lower socioeconomic groups. Decision makers, increasingly drawn from the upper-middle class, admitted other functional groups to the decision-making process only as they developed spokesmen of a similar community-society and socioeconomic position. A functional system of representation in a cosmopolitan upper-middle-class context had replaced a geographical system of representation which had involved leaders from all segments of the community-society and socioeconomic structure.

31. George S. Counts, *The Social Composition of Boards of Education: A Study in the Social Control of Public Education* (Chicago, 1927).

V

POLITICAL parties function within given environmental contexts. Both the goals which they seek and their techniques of action are closely related to the social circumstances within which they work. The most pervasive characteristics of that environment, moreover, are structural, those patterns of social organization which interconnect the shared experiences, perceptions, values, and actions of different groups of people. Just as the entire social order is a system of human relationships, so is the political party. Its various facets, whether they be popular voting, social and political perception, ideologies, leadership, or the interaction between levels of political activity, can be understood adequately only if each is located within a precise segment of the social and political structure. Our major current task in historical political research is to describe political structure and the changes therein over a period of time. We must root political parties in that structure.

A community-society dimension is a useful conceptual framework in this task. It brings out more sharply than other frameworks the changing human relationships within the party in the context of the changing human relationships in the larger social order. It enables one to examine the upper levels of political life, the grass roots, and their interrelationships within a single context. It stimulates examination of a large variety of political phenomena such as voting behavior, ideology, leadership, and the vertical dimension of the political order as closely interrelated facets of political life. It provides an opportunity, within a single system of thought, to examine differences in the geographical scope of human perception, of human relationships, and of systems of decision making in the political world. It provides a basis for fruitful investigation and examination of modern American political development.

[11]

The Changing Political Structure of the City in Industrial America*

THE rapid development of urban history in the past few years has witnessed far greater progress in the expansion of subject matter than of conceptual framework. Most urban history has been written as a narrative with a minimum of deliberately fashioned concept. As a result, the "reform" framework, inherent in the contemporary self-image of the city from year to year in the twentieth century, has become unconsciously transferred into the historical imagination to establish the prevailing pattern of writing about the city. Its sequence is simple: cities grew, they gave rise to problems, and reform forces arose to cope with those problems. The classic political contest in urban history is the struggle between those who would solve the difficulties of the city and their opponents.

The persistence of the "reform" context is surprising in view of the vast fund of information and ideas readily available for other approaches, which gives rise to concepts about patterns of human relationships in the city on a broader and less overtly normative basis. From one point of view, these concepts enable us to place the contemporary conceptions of the city's problems in context—namely, as the particular definition of problems from the particular vantage point or "image" of the city of particular groups of people. We can examine the special roots and perspectives of "reform" movements. From another point of view, they enable us to examine the entire range of human life within the city, the variety of people,

*This paper was presented at the Conference of the Australian–New Zealand American Studies Association, LaTrobe University, Melbourne, August 1970; it is reprinted here from the *Journal of Urban History* 1 (Nov. 1974), © 1974 Sage Publications, Inc.

the patterns they generate, and the relationships they establish among themselves, irrespective of our own normative concerns about the city. The conceptual possibilities for reconstructing the historical dimension of the city are readily available.

The "reform" context is even more unsatisfactory because it constitutes a rejection of the city, a constant unwillingness to consider the city in its own right and a constant search, through history, for something which to each writer the city instead should be. We must develop an approach which accepts the city as it is—its heterogeneity of ethnicity, religion, and race; its inequalities and the process by which vertical mobility constantly transforms one pattern of inequality into another; its tension between parochial and cosmopolitan life; its administrative and technical systems which order people into those who manage and those who are managed. This enormous variety of human life on the part of thousands and millions of people we must appreciate and comprehend in its own right—for what it was, not for what it failed to be—and order into patterns so as to enhance that appreciation and comprehension.

The following essay constitutes a conceptual framework which I have found useful in comprehending the evolution of the city since the mid-nineteenth century.[1] It has been influenced heavily by works in geography and sociology. Yet by the practitioners of those arts it would be considered primitive and elementary. Here I attempt to translate simple concepts from the relatively static framework of the social sciences into a historical context so as to stress change over time. In its broadest outline, urban development is considered a constant tension between forces making for decentralization and forces making for centralization in human relationships and institutions, between centrifugal and centripetal tendencies, between social differentiation and social integration. The city holds in balance in one historical context those attempts to separate from the wider world to establish smaller contexts of life in home, church, education, and recreation, and those attempts to discipline and link the productive and occupational activities of man into more

1. Two general works which have contributed much to this formulation are Roland Warren, *The Community in America* (Chicago, 1963), esp. 53–94, and Scott Greer, *The Emerging City* (Glencoe, Ill., 1962), esp. 29–66.

highly organized systems. The city is an excellent context in which to examine the evolution of these tensions in modern industrial society.[2]

I

DURING the last half of the nineteenth century, the physical limits of cities expanded constantly. In some cases, people moved outward from the center to the periphery to establish new residential communities.[3] In others, new migrants settled in areas adjacent to but distinct from the city's older districts. These trends brought about a greater dispersion of urban population, a more varied and decentralized life, and the development of subcommunities. The latter were not similar; each had distinct ethnic, cultural, occupation, and class characteristics. The physical growth of cities, then, involved social differentiation; new subcommunities created more varied cultures, and cities became more heterogeneous. This had a profound impact on the patterns of human relationships in the city so that by the end of the century it was far more decentralized than it had been seventy years before.

Prior to industrialization, cities had been relatively small, compact, and integrated. They were "pedestrian communities" in that the location of activities was determined by the time it took to walk between them, between residence and occupation, church and school, store and recreation facilities. The community tended to be a face-to-face community, in which human relationships were established by personal contact over limited areas. These relationships were close. Individuals could not live free from the view of others, from their approval or disapproval. In such a social situation, those who became dominant in economic, social, and religious life established and maintained acceptable patterns for the entire community. Differences in values which might lead to differences in public demands were not readily revealed in political affairs.

2. Many of the original data upon which this article rests are drawn from studies of the city of Pittsburgh, most of them seminar papers and dissertations produced by graduate students in the History Department at the University of Pittsburgh. It is understood that Pittsburgh may or may not be typical, and that comparative studies might modify the framework.

3. The now classic study of outward urban movement is Sam B. Warner, Jr., *Streetcar Suburbs* (Cambridge, Mass., 1962), esp. 1–66 and 153–66.

Two characteristics of these relatively integrated communities stood out. One was the physical intermixture of different social groups. Although the earlier cities were relatively homogeneous ethnically and religiously, they were heterogeneous in class terms, exhibiting distinct gradations from lower to upper.[4] Different classes had long existed in the American city. But their geographical separation was not as sharp as it became in the late nineteenth century. Factory owners often built their residences next to their factories and within sight of workingmen's homes. Laborers often lived in the back alleys in blocks where the more well-to-do lived on the main street. Clear-cut expression of the particular values of a social group requires geographical separateness and distinctiveness. Since in the pedestrian community distinct social classes did not live in distinct geographical areas but were intermixed, the clarity of their political impulses was limited.

Urban political leadership reflected the integrated community. City councils were usually elected in a town meeting to represent the city as a whole. Invariably, they were composed of men dominant in the community's social and economic life—bankers, commission merchants, lawyers.[5] Rarely were those in the lower three-quarters of the vertical social order selected. In later years, when councilmen were chosen by wards, working-class wards frequently elected workingmen. Election at large gave an opportunity for those dominant in the social and economic life of the community to be dominant in its formal political life as well. This, it should be emphasized again, was not due to the lack of social differentiation. There is ample evidence to demonstrate inequalities in wealth, and there is no reason to believe that these inequalities did not lead to differences in political outlook. But the lack of geographical distinctiveness of social differentiation reduced the capacity of the middle and lower classes to develop and express effectively their political views.

4. James Henretta, "Economic Development and Social Structure in Colonial Boston," *William and Mary Quarterly* 22 (1965), 75–92, provides one example of the description of the distribution of an urban socioeconomic variable. For similar descriptions I am indebted to Robert Doherty for data about several Massachusetts towns between 1800 and 1850 and to Walter Glazer for data about Cincinnati in the nineteenth century.

5. The Pittsburgh city council, for example, shifted from citywide to ward representation in 1834. An examination of most of the pre-1833 members revealed a predominance of representation from upper levels of the social order.

This pedestrian community of the early nineteenth century changed radically by 1900. The drive toward social differentiation had proceeded apace; it found expression in a variety of urban sub-communities, each with a distinct geographical identity, residential life, cultural pattern, and representation in city government. Many of these subcommunities grew out of migration from abroad. Irish and German migration brought into almost every city newcomers who divided along both national and religious lines. German Catholics, Lutherans, and Jews settled in different areas of the city and established separate churches, schools, and social organizations. Later southern and eastern Europeans added to the variety. By seeking to live in close proximity to those of similar nativity and religion, they created distinctive ethno-religious subcultures.

Subcommunities also arose from upward social mobility, which became transformed into geographical movement from the city's center to its periphery.[6] As the economy grew, opportunities at all occupational levels expanded. People moved upward in occupation and income; the drive toward social differentiation became intense. The upwardly mobile desired to establish new ways of life, to separate from their older environments and to live in a different community, where cultural patterns were similar to their new aspirations. They sought more space for play in the form of larger yards, wished their daughters to meet more acceptable future husbands, or wanted to associate in their nonwork hours with people of their own patterns of living. Outward urban migration arose from the desire to establish new residential subcommunities with church, school, and recreational facilities in areas distinct from older sub-communities. The desire for social differentiation could be realized only through geographical differentiation.

Cheap urban transportation, the trolley and the automobile, made this process possible. Horse-drawn vehicles on rails were in operation as early as the 1850s. In the 1880s cable-cars powered by

---

6. The first large-scale work on historical vertical mobility in the United States was Stephan Thernstrom, *Poverty and Progress* (Cambridge, Mass., 1964). Thernstrom's work is limited to a description of mobility upward from blue-collar to white-collar occupations. See also his later work, *The Other Bostonians* (Cambridge, Mass., 1973) and Herbert Gutman, "Class, Status and Community Power in Nineteenth-Century American Industrial Cities— Patterson, New Jersey: A Case Study," in Frederic Cople Jaher (ed.), *The Age of Industrialism in America: Essays in Social Structure and Cultural Values* (New York, 1968), 263–87.

central steam plants were experimented with but soon gave way to the electric trolley. At first trolley lines radiated out from the central city to only a few areas, but by the end of the century the electric trolley had opened up almost all the surrounding territory save that which defied penetration because of natural barriers. These innovations were as profound an element of the transportation revolution as were the steamboats and the steam railroads. They generated an extensive movement of population and restructured the urban social order.

The simplest expression of this change lay in the increasing distance between place of residence and place of work. Whereas formerly one had to live within walking distance of work, now he or she could live much farther away. Professionals and businesspeople who worked in the central city established residential communities elsewhere. Factory owners no longer lived beside their factories. Lawyers whose work required that they be near the centralized public records and legal institutions of the city and county courts lived out in newer and economically more substantial communities. Doctors, if they were specialists such as surgeons, lived in one place and carried on their practice in another.

This distance between work and residence created more distinct geographical specialization of activities in the city. Residential communities served the family; they included home, church, school, and recreation facilities, including residential play areas—yard space —as well as country clubs and golf courses. Communities became distinctive in terms of nationality, religions, and class patterns of residential life. While residential institutions could be decentralized, work institutions could not. The individual could readily move where he lived but not where he worked. His place of work, in fact, depended upon centralizing rather than decentralizing forces, those bound up with the organization of economic life into larger systems of production, merchandising, and banking. While the desire for social differentiation enticed people into a centrifugal movement of residential dispersion, their occupations involved them in centripetal and integrative forces. During the last half of the nineteenth century, decentralizing tendencies were the dominant of the two.

The heightened geographical mobility created by the trolley

greatly complicated the process of conserving residential communities. Each desired to maintain its distinctive patterns of residential life. This was extremely difficult to do, because mobility and stability were incompatible. One could not easily prevent other people of different classes, nationalities, races, or religions from moving into his community. Freedom to buy and sell property might quickly undermine established patterns. To protect themselves, communities experimented with a variety of techniques. That these were rarely successful testifies to the high degree of motion in the modern city. Upper-class communities experienced especially observable difficulties in self-maintenance.[7] During the latter half of the nineteenth century, new upper-class residential areas arose in which the wealthy, old and new, sought to disassociate themselves from the institutions and people of the older city. But, unable to control land transactions, these communities rarely lasted more than one or two generations. Real estate promoters converted their estates into smaller lots for middle- and lower-income families.

Decentralization of residential life created decentralization of related economic institutions. Community growth rapidly dispersed property ownership as larger holdings, usually in the form of estates owned by the well-to-do, were divided into smaller lots. One property owner frequently was replaced by several hundred, each one of whom now had a tangible stake in community life and demanded a voice in community affairs. Since the apportionment of city council seats to various wards frequently depended upon the number of property taxpayers in the ward, expansion of property ownership directly affected municipal government. Diffusion of property ownership diffused political impulses.

New subcommunities gave rise to new consumer-oriented stores designed to fill immediate personal and family needs. Grocery, drug, confectioner, milk, eating, and liquor stores each served a market within walking distance. Many were family-owned stores; almost all had a vital interest in the area's property conditions and its general growth and development. Ethnic communities gave rise to stores, which provided the particular food, dress, and other goods distinc-

7. Several studies of Pittsburgh upper-class communities illustrate this instability: Renee Reitman, "The Elite Community in Shadyside, 1880–1920," and Thomas J. Kelso, "Allegheny Elites: 1850–1907," seminar papers, Univ. of Pittsburgh, 1964.

tive to the nationality of the residents. Consumer-oriented small businesses expanded especially rapidly in urban immigrant settlements. The immigrant storekeeper became the backbone of the urban small-business community.

The physical development of the community generated economic enterprises which facilitated that growth—in banking, real estate, contracting, and transportation. These firms were often confined in their activities to a particular region of the city, were identified with it, and had a stake in its physical growth. They catered to a wider community than did the small retailer, to a larger subsection of the city than the neighborhood best called the urban region. Real estate firms arose to change large estates owned by single individuals into innumerable small lots owned by many; banks grew up to finance these real estate transactions and the building and development that followed; contractors built the new structures, streets, and sidewalks. These men identified closely with their regions; they became recognized as leaders by the people of the region.

Urban physical expansion provided opportunities for new entrepreneurs; regional developers were very different from those who had been concerned with growth in the older section of the city.[8] Many were immigrant leaders who, while profiting from development, provided essential services for community growth and became influential community spokesmen. New real estate development provided opportunities for new entrepreneurs in the new banks, trolley lines, real estate agencies, and construction firms. The boards of directors of community banks, for example, contained far more men of recent immigrant origin and Catholics and Jews than did the older, central-city banks. The more successful immigrant businessmen often combined real estate development and rental property with banking service. They worked closely with ethnic political leaders in their projects; both rested ultimately for their influence and their leadership upon the development of urban subcommunities.

Differentiation and decentralization in social and economic life

8. Relevant data for Pittsburgh are in Mary Young, "The Pittsburgh Chamber of Commerce and the Allied Boards of Trade in 1910," and Frank Lukaszewicz, "Regional and Central Boards of Directors of Pittsburgh Banks in 1912," seminar papers, Univ. of Pittsburgh, 1966.

gave rise to a decentralized political system. Increasingly the ward became the focus of politics.[9] Each community demanded separate representation so that its particular needs would be dealt with. Even prior to 1850, a ward system had begun to replace citywide representation; elected by wards, councilmen now represented their communities in the council's deliberations. School government often developed in a similar manner. Each ward had its own elementary school, often a focal point for community social affairs, administered by a ward-elected school board. Ward-oriented political life took precedence over a citywide political life. Through it, the varied urban subcommunities could express their distinctive viewpoints on public affairs.

Ward representation changed the kinds of men chosen as councilmen. Whereas earlier the great majority were from upper occupational and socioeconomic classes, by the end of the century they were from the middle and lower levels. Outward migration and geographical differentiation greatly reduced the number of upper-class and increased the number of middle- and lower-class wards. Each ward tended to select as representatives people who were like the majority of its inhabitants; the character of representation changed, as did that of the communities represented. At the same time, economic leaders of the new, decentralized communities began to play a larger role as councilmen. Identified with the real estate and business concerns of the community, they established personal ties with large numbers of residents in their business affairs. Economic and social leadership became translated into political leadership. By 1900, the typical ward-elected city councilman was a small businessman—retailer, director of a funeral home, real estate promoter and contractor, director of a community bank—a clerk, a skilled artisan, or an unskilled laborer. Professional and large business classes were greatly outnumbered.

The major concern of urban government lay with the city's physical development.[10] The overwhelming number of demands

9. This conclusion is based upon an examination of all Pittsburgh city councilmen since the establishment of the ward system in 1834, school board members at decade intervals between 1860 and 1910 for Pittsburgh, and city council members, selected at various intervals, of Cincinnati, Columbus, and Cleveland, Ohio. See also John Dankosky, "Pittsburgh City Government, 1816–1850," seminar paper, Univ. of Pittsburgh, 1971.

10. These observations are based primarily upon an examination of the proceedings of

made upon city council and of city ordinances pertained to the approval of subdivisions, of streets and drainage systems, of lighting and transportation. City taxes came from property owners, and city expenditures went for services to development; major council controversies came over taxation and expenditure. Considerable disagreement arose, also, over the question of private or public enterprise. Should private services be permitted without restriction, or should they be licensed and regulated? Should property owners pay for the development of adjacent streets, or should they be paid for through a general system of taxation and municipal expenditure? Whatever the answers to these questions, city government in the last half of the nineteenth century came to be a major instrument of physical growth and community development.

Because the city council consisted of representatives of different geographical areas, controversies over taxing and expenditure for urban development became controversies between different areas of the city. This process developed in the same way as it did in the state with conflicts between different counties, or in the nation between sections. Each urban community wished assistance for development; each wanted a gas light on this or that corner. Decisions were often made by "log rolling," in which one councilman voted for the proposals of others in exchange for their vote for his own. These controversies frequently sorted themselves out into disagreements between the city's older and newer sections. The older feared the newer. They often argued that the geographical expansion of the city was neither necessary nor desirable. Their taxes would be used to finance development in expanding areas in which they had no direct interest. They stood aghast at the willingness of the city council to incur indebtedness to finance new development. The older city usually was in the minority, for urban expansion and ward representation brought into government a large number of councilmen who reflected the views of the newly developing communities and who outvoted their opponents.

The use of city funds in community development, and the award of franchises to provide services such as transportation created opportunities for corruption. But this should not obscure the

---

the Pittsburgh City Council between 1850 and 1910. See also Seymour Mandelbaum, *Boss Tweed's New York* (New York, 1965), for the preoccupation with physical development.

more important phenomenon of decentralized urban growth. Many controversies over physical development were, in fact, phrased in terms of the issue of corruption. The most sensational case involved the New York City "Tweed ring." That controversy was fundamentally one between old and new New York City, a belief on the part of lower Manhattan that New York did not need to expand physically, and a demand on the part of those preoccupied with development further up the island that it did.[11] The city government threw in its lot with expansion and development and increased municipal indebtedness to help carry it out. Tweed's downfall was triggered by revelations of corruption in this venture, but the underlying opposition came from disagreement with the substance of his policies.

II

WHILE decentralization characterized urban development in the nineteenth century, by 1900 integration, although in evidence even earlier, was emerging as a dominant force.[12] Decentralization continued, but it became overlaid with new patterns of social organization which drew people together into closer-knit groups. As the density of population increased, the intensity of claim and counterclaim in decision making also increased. A new political order arose to limit the variety of such claims, to channel them into fewer centers of decision making, and to integrate more activities into a relatively small number of systems of human relationships. While the older city witnessed a process of dispersion, the new involved centralization.

Integrative tendencies in urbanization grew out of the transition from locality patterns of human relationships, which emphasized interaction among people living in the same geographical areas, to functional and administrative forms of organization, which emphasized interaction among people of particular functions, no matter where they lived, and among people playing different roles

11. Some elements of this conflict are described in Mandelbaum, *ibid.*, esp. 59–71.
12. A discussion of urban integration, as a process of organizing space, is in John Friedmann, "Cities in Social Transformation," *Comparative Studies in Society and History* 4 (1961), 86–103.

in the vertical hierarchy of organized administrative systems.[13] While the locality group was inclusive, encompassing all those living in a given geographical area, functional and administrative groups were exclusive, involving only those who had a common functional interest or were within a given administrative system. Whereas in former decades the locality context had been crucial in the effective expression of political impulses, new forms of social and political organization were more divorced from location in particular segments of the city. These new forms of organization rested on patterns of human relationships which cut across community and constituted a superstructure of contacts above and beyond it.[14]

Behind these new patterns of human relationships lay the growth of organizational technologies. Whereas production technologies, those which substituted machines for manual labor, dominated in the last half of the nineteenth century, organizational technologies came to the fore after 1875, which dramatically increased the speed and flexibility of human contacts. The telephone replaced the messenger boy, permitting contact and control—integration—in ways which had not been possible before. Organizational technologies gave rise to more precise coordination of human interaction so as to dovetail efforts efficiently. They made possible the new, more systematized, more coordinated patterns of human interaction.

The most visible expression of urban integration was the newly reorganized central city.[15] Formerly a mixture of residences, professional offices, factories, and public buildings, the central city declined as a residential and factory area with the advent of rapid transit, which stimulated movement out of the city's core to the periphery. In their place came new activities which emphasized the central city as the location of organization which reached out to gather in the entire urban area. The large office building was the

13. See Scott Greer, *The Emerging City,* 37–40.
14. A more extensive elaboration of the community-society continuum, especially as it affects political life, is in Samuel P. Hays, "Political Parties and the Community-Society Continuum," in William N. Chambers and Walter Dean Burnham, *The American Party Systems: Stages of Political Development* (New York, 1967), 152–81.
15. A description of the change in Pittsburgh is in Howard V. Storch, Jr., "Changing Functions of the Center-City, Pittsburgh, 1850–1912," seminar paper, Univ. of Pittsburgh, 1965.

most dramatic physical expression of this change. Within a few decades, these buildings replaced homes, churches, schools, the whole range of residentially related activities, in the city's center. Although innovation in structural steel and the elevator made this possible, the growth of rapid interpersonal communication reflects more precisely the state of organizational integration which lay behind it. The telephone first became a popular means of communication in the center city.

These changes can be charted also in the shifting location of private corporate management activities. In the nineteenth century, when management and coordination were relatively small compared with production, the former were carried out in the same building as the factory. As management functions grew, their physical location became more of a problem. At times, the mansions of factory owners, located near the factories, became a convenient location as the owners moved to upper-class communities. It came to be more convenient to locate near related institutions such as banks and advertising agencies, whose expertise was frequently called upon. The central office building located in the center of the city was the answer. Many of these were built either by industries for their management or by the estates of deceased entrepreneurs and then rented to the firm. In any case, the growing importance of coordination, internal and external, gave rise to a series of moves which led to the concentration of activities in the central city.

Here there grew rapidly a host of other centralizing institutions: large-scale retail establishments drawing customers from the entire city; specialized professionals, such as doctors, architects, and engineers who had a citywide clientele; lawyers whose work required that they be near legal records and the courts; banks whose financial networks fanned out to link transactions throughout the city and the region; public administrative agencies in recreation, planning, health, and welfare. The larger organizational life of the city focused on the center because here a host of interrelated activities associated with coordinating human relationships took place. The reorganization of the central city was not merely a matter of physical change, but of more intense human interaction at a level high on the vertical scale of social organization.

These integrative activities found organizational as well as locational expressions, the most important of which were the chambers of commerce representing the city's most powerful businessmen. There were several types of such bodies, distinguishable in terms of the geographical extent of their activities and clientele on the one hand, and their role in the scale of human contacts on the other. The neighborhood boards of trade represented small, consumer-oriented businesses in the relatively small communities; the regional chambers of commerce drew in banks, real estate firms, merchants, and professionals whose activities were larger than the neighborhood but smaller than the entire city; citywide chambers of commerce, composed of manufacturers, downtown merchants, central-city bankers, and managers of central-city property, represented the largest integrative tendencies of the city. These citywide chambers of commerce, rather than the smaller bodies, came to play an increasingly important role in municipal affairs. They constituted a crucial political force in the years from 1897 to 1929.[16]

The rapid rise of the empirical professions such as public health and education greatly accelerated urban integration.[17] The public-health doctor was one of the most politically active professionals. The germ theory of disease not only enhanced understanding of the causes of diseases but also made abundantly clear what needed to be controlled in order to prevent them. Moreover, public-health innovations could be brought about more effectively through one citywide context than many community ones. The dynamics of school politics was similar. Professional educators urged a host of innovations, such as longer school terms, more training for teachers, better facilities and equipment, teacher pensions, and new methods of capturing the interest of the pupil. But how to bring about change? Many school boards were conservative. The answer was to shift the

---

16. This scale has been worked out for Pittsburgh in Young, "The Pittsburgh Chamber of Commerce," and Lukaszewicz, "Regional and Central Boards of Directors." See also a similar attempt in Edward J. Davies II, "Wilkes-Barre, 1870–1920: A Study in the Evolution of Urban Leadership During Industrialization," seminar paper, Univ. of Pittsburgh, 1972.

17. This discussion is based largely upon studies of the internal structure of several professional groups in Pittsburgh, including William H. Issel, "The Pittsburgh Teaching Profession and Its Politics, 1900–1912"; Tom Henry, "The Pittsburgh Architect—1910—and Municipal Improvement"; and Ross Messer, "The Medical Profession in Pittsburgh, 1890–1910," seminar papers, Univ. of Pittsburgh, 1964.

context of school decisions from the many local-ward school boards to a central body where a more citywide perspective could be fostered and to which professionals would have direct access.

Two other professional groups, civil engineers and architects, were more concerned with urban physical organization. Civil engineers became the technical experts behind large public works such as water reservoirs, sanitary sewage systems, bridges, and paved streets. Since such matters affected the city at large, plans to facilitate them required a perspective far more extensive than that of the urban small community. And the same was true of that segment of architects who became interested in city planning. Often concerned with central-city office buildings, they became enamored of the possibilities of large-scale changes in the city and especially the center. This included the rearrangement of streets and buildings, the development of open spaces and parks, the extension of landscaping and beautification at the city center and elsewhere. Like the engineers, their citywide perspective prompted them to seek large- rather than small-scale physical changes.

These professional concerns were universal rather than particularist. The problems they dealt with cut across parochial community lines. The public-health expert faced tuberculosis and typhoid fever not simply in Ward 6, but in the entire city; the school professional wished to educate more rather than fewer children and for longer periods of time. The civil engineer and the architect sought to rearrange diverse and far-flung sections of the city according to more universal standards of efficiency and design. Professionals were not content merely to learn more; they wished to use their knowledge to change society. The new empirical professions were not inert, but highly political. They became infused with a missionary spirit to reduce disease, to lengthen human life, to enhance the quantity and quality of education, and to redesign the physical city.

Only a few, however, shared the professional expert's values, his vision, and the urgency of his concern. He constantly had to educate others, to search for political allies, and to overcome resistance from opponents. Since he sought to influence a wide range of people and affairs, he chose mechanisms of decision making and action which were equally broad in scope. At the municipal level, he constructed public health departments, relatively independent of community political impulses and of the city councils which reflected those impulses, so that he could operate freely from his own professional guidelines. He supported increased executive authority in the mayor in order to protect himself from popular forces. The new empirical professions played a major role in the integration of the twentieth-century city.

The urban upper class constituted still a third force in urban integration. In its residential institutions, the urban upper class was separatist; it sought to establish homes, churches, schools, and clubs apart from other classes, and increasingly beyond the city's boundaries.[18] In this, the upper class was no different in its localistic impulses than were other classes, thereby contributing to the decentralization and fragmentation of the city. But economic concerns required that it move in the opposite direction as well and stimulate integration. The occupations of the upper class were often in the central city, the corporate systems in which it worked were headquartered there, and the property it owned often was either there physically or represented by investment in corporations based there. The urban upper class faced two ways at once; decentralist in residential institution, it was integrative in its economic and occupational life. While it sought to separate itself from the city in one way, in another it was propelled back into the center of urban affairs.

The recent history of the upper class added a special integrative factor in the early twentieth century. Many of the upper class had grown up in the center city. Faced with an infusion of new people, a rise in property values and taxes, and the deterioration of their residential environment, they only recently had moved out. But many retained a strong nostalgia for the old area and could not avoid an interest in what happened there. The relocation of churches revealed this ambivalence.[19] Congregations invariably sold downtown

18. The most important study of the urban upper class in recent America is E. Digby Baltzell, *Philadelphia Gentlemen* (Glencoe, Ill., 1958). For some major revisions of Baltzell's argument see John N. Ingham, *The Iron Barons: A Social Analysis of an American Urban Elite, 1874-1965* (Westport, Conn., 1978). See also Davies, "Wilkes-Barre, 1870-1920" and Burton W. Folsom II, "The Social Order of the Anthracite Region: Scranton's Economic Elite, 1850-1880," seminar paper, Univ. of Pittsburgh, 1974.

19. The development of this process among Presbyterians in Pittsburgh is traced by Thomas Callister in "The Reaction of the Presbytery of Pittsburgh to the New Immigrants," seminar paper, Univ. of Pittsburgh, 1963.

churches for a healthy profit because of the rapid rise in land values. With the proceeds, they could build a new church in the suburbs and have funds left over. Many members, and usually those from long residence in the former location, wished these resources to be used for social welfare programs in the community where the church had been. Adding to this nostalgia was the fact that the location of the places of residence and of work of the upper class required that they pass through lower-class areas on their way between home and work, making the conditions there particularly visible to them. Such experiences as these added to the concern for welfare among the working class to limit its "disruptive" and "disintegrative" tendencies. Upward mobility reduced interclass communication drastically, but the peculiar experiences of the upper class in the early twentieth-century city gave rise to a desire on the part of some to reestablish some semblance of contact.

The urban upper class became involved in a host of social welfare programs: prohibition, control of prostitution, language instruction for immigrants, religious evangelism, public baths, playgrounds, better housing, restriction of child labor, and improvement of the working conditions of women.[20] The most visible and dramatic example of upper-class welfare was the settlement house.[21] Located in the midst of lower-class neighborhoods, the settlement house provided educational and social services for lower-income groups. Boards of directors and financing came from the upper class, who lived in outlying residential areas. They also provided the volunteer workers for settlement house activities. In this fashion, the settlement house constituted an instrument of interclass communica-

20. The "upper-level" character of social reform is indicated by a recent study of settlement house leaders, Allen F. Davis, *Spearheads for Reform* (New York, 1967). Davis does not carry out a thorough examination of such leaders but, occasionally, describes qualitatively their origins in the upper levels of the social order. He indicates a very high level of education—more than 80 percent had earned a bachelor's degree or equivalent at a time when only 5 percent of the population age 18–21 was enrolled in all institutions of higher education. Some of the most useful newspaper sources of evidence about social welfare reform in the Progressive Era are the upper-class society newspapers, often far more valuable than the general circulation media.

21. Davis, *Spearheads for Reform*, is the most complete treatment of the settlement house to date; he does not treat it, however, as an aspect of interclass communication. The approach here rests upon the examination of several settlement houses in Pittsburgh. See also Elizabeth Metzger, "A Study of Social Settlement Workers in Pittsburgh, 1893 to 1927," seminar paper, Univ. of Pittsburgh, 1973.

tion. The "gatekeeper" between the two classes was the settlement house director who lived and communicated within two different worlds, the world of the lower-class immigrant and the world of the affluent.

In these relationships between social classes in different sections of the city, women played an important role. Active in social welfare reforms, the members of women's organizations were drawn heavily from the upper classes, who had the leisure time to give to civic affairs. "Society" clubs served as headquarters for many civic reform groups; "society" newspapers provided one of the most extensive sources of information about welfare reform; "society" women often propelled their husbands into reform activities.[22] While men became involved in urban integration through the economic system and professional life, women did so through intuitive sympathy for other women and children, their common religion and ethnicity, and their nostalgia for their childhood communities. Much of the interclass communication which lay behind this aspect of urban integration came through special lines of interaction generated by upper-class women.

Forces making for integration in economic, professional, and social life came together in a drive for integration and centralization in decision making.[23] Reformers arose to modify the formal structure of municipal and school government and decision making in welfare and charitable activities. They were most disturbed about the ward system of city and school affairs which gave considerable influence to the decentralizing tendencies of urban communities. This, they felt, hindered a focus on a more comprehensive view of the city—the "public interest" they called it—in order to deal with its problems. As each urban group sought to implement integrative objectives, it became dissatisfied with ward government and supported more highly centralized methods of decision making.

One innovation was to increase the power of the mayor—for example, that he propose a budget which the council then might modify, rather than vice versa. Another was the commission form

22. See, for example, the pages of the *Pittsburgh Index* and the *Pittsburgh Bulletin*, 1890 and following.
23. A larger statement of this view is in Samuel P. Hays, "The Politics of Reform in Municipal Government in the Progressive Era," *Pacific Northwest Quarterly* 55 (1965), 157–69.

of government. A third was the city-manager system, in which an "expert" was hired to administer the city's affairs. Almost all such plans proposed a centralization of representation, a modification or abolition of ward representation in favor of citywide representation. The most successful attempt to centralize decision making came in school government. By the 1920s, almost every city in the nation had eliminated the ward in favor of the citywide school board. At times these were elected at large, but often they were appointed— for example, by judges of the municipal courts. Control in the school system shifted from the community to the city at large.

These drives for centralization of decision making came primarily from the upper levels of the social order.[24] The "good government" organizations were composed of people from upper occupational groups; the candidates they preferred for public office were from the same levels.[25] Entirely missing from the reform movement were the typical ward leaders of the previous era—the small storekeeper, the white-collar clerk, the skilled artisan. Instead, it was dominated by the central-city businessman, the advanced professional, and the upper social classes. Chambers of commerce often took the lead in reform activities; allied with them were a variety of voters leagues and civic organizations which brought in professionals and upper-class women. Their success in centralizing decision making shifted sharply up the occupational social levels from which decision makers were drawn. Now the vast majority of council and school board members were from the upper-middle and upper classes. The greatest change came in school boards. By 1924, such boards across the country were dominated by business and professional leaders.[26] A virtual revolution had taken place, reflecting the

24. For Chicago see Joan S. Miller, "The Politics of Municipal Reform in Chicago during the Progressive Era: The Municipal Voters' League as a Test Case, 1896–1920," M.A. thesis, Roosevelt Univ., 1966. For Philadelphia see Bonnie R. Fox, "The Philadelphia Progressives: A Test of the Hofstadter-Hays Thesis," *Pennsylvania History* 34 (1967), 372–94, and David Amidon, "The Philadelphia Bureau of Municipal Research, 1908–1920," paper presented to the Pennsylvania Historical Association, spring meeting, 1965.

25. Distinctions between reform-approved and reform-opposed candidates in Chicago are developed by Miller, "The Politics of Municipal Reform in Chicago," 31–36. Reformers preferred candidates of upper occupational and educational levels and Protestant native Americans; they tended to reject those at lower levels, Catholics, and immigrants.

26. George S. Counts, *The Social Composition of Boards of Education: A Study in the Social Control of Public Education* (Chicago, 1927).

triumph of centralizing over decentralizing forces in municipal and school affairs.

These changes in urban government marked the reentrance into political life of members of the upper class after several decades of relative absence. Dominating urban politics in the early pedestrian community, these groups had retired from municipal government as the city expanded, as ward government generated lower- and middle-class leadership, and as they were unable to exercise control in a city of varied and decentralized communities.[27] Their old methods of influence, via day-to-day contacts in the pedestrian community, no longer sufficed. By the early twentieth century, however, they had learned new methods of integrative control from their experience with corporate systems.[28] They became increasingly adept at communications technologies and the role of the professional expert in fashioning a stable and manipulable social order. Wishing to apply these techniques to public affairs and the model of the corporation to city government, they reentered public life through reform organizations. They were not expressing just personal values; they were reshaping the political order according to the inner dynamic of the changing economic and social order. They constituted the counter-thrust toward integration within the decentralizing society of the late nineteenth century.

Tendencies toward urban integration took place at a level far above the local community. They created networks of extra-community relationships. In the face of this new social order, the local community lost much of its autonomy and its salience. Whereas in the nineteenth century it was the dominant focus of urban life, in the twentieth century it became far less viable as more of the articulate sector of the city became involved in the development of functional groups and corporate systems. Although the

27. Matthew Holden, "Ethnic Accommodation in a Historical Case," *Comparative Studies of Society and History* 8 (1966), 168–80. Using Cleveland data on city councilmen, Holden stresses the attractiveness of corporate business activities rather than the relocation of the upper-class community as the major factor in the departure of upper-class individuals from city government.

28. The literature on the inner dynamics of systematization is extremely weak. Some suggestions as to the process are in John K. Galbraith, *The New Industrial State* (Boston, 1967), 11–34, and Dwight Waldo, *The Administrative State* (New York, 1948), 3–61.

urban community remained as a focal point of primary-group relationships for many people,[29] its significance and importance for the wider community declined as it became transformed from a creative urban force into an object of action generated elsewhere. Political institutions at the ward level declined; political involvement diminished; ward institutions became local representatives of wider systems. As innovation developed apace at the upper levels of the social order, community institutions at the lower levels atrophied and declined.

III

BY 1929, these integrative tendencies had run their first course of development. During the next four decades, a new phase appeared in which both decentralizing and centralizing tendencies appeared with new vigor and a forceful interplay. The automobile and the telephone gave rise to greater mobility and flexibility in human contacts, generating a new phase of outward movement. Systematization also moved on apace, creating ever larger units of administrative action which restrained the growth of autonomous units and integrated them into more universal perspectives and more centrally directed strategies. Interaction between centripetal and centrifugal forces remained the major context of urban history.

The twentieth-century city served as a giant social escalator, involving a constant flow of individuals upward through levels of occupation, income, and standards of living and outward to newer residential areas. Children and grandchildren of post-1880 southern and eastern European immigrants moved upward rapidly after the Great Depression.[30] Whites and blacks from the rural United States moved onto and up the same escalator.[31] As occupations and income rose, so did the distance of residence from the center city; one study of the 1960 census detailed this process for blacks, for whom the dynamics of upward mobility were similar to those for whites.[32] Upward mobility accelerated rapidly after the early 1950s

29. The outstanding recent study of this phenomenon is Herbert J. Gans, *The Urban Villagers* (New York, 1962).
30. See Samuel Lubell, *The Future of American Politics* (New York, 1951), 61–85.
31. For data on black vertical mobility, see table, p. 140n.
32. Leo F. Schnore, "Social Class Segregation Among Nonwhites in Metropolitan Cen-

as the mid-twentieth-century income revolution proceeded. National median family income in current dollars rose from less than $1,500 in 1939 to $3,390 in 1950, $5,620 in 1960, and $8,632 in 1968.[33]

Technological innovations in transportation and communication —the automobile and the telephone—made possible this outward movement. By its speed and flexibility, the automobile increased the range of short-term movement between home and work or between home and shopping areas. Now one could live five, ten, or fifteen miles from work and commute. Until the early twentieth century the telephone had linked business firms almost exclusively. It soon spread to households, permitting those living in widely scattered areas to establish intensive patterns of interaction and facilitating outward movement.

These innovations generated an outward thrust of business as well, the development of manufacturing, research centers, and storage and warehouse facilities on the periphery rather than in the center of the city. The gasoline motor truck and paved streets permitted close physical contact between such businesses and their markets, their suppliers, and their administrative headquarters. The telephone permitted a constant flow of communication and enabled the firm's headquarters to exercise supervision and control over elements physically decentralized. Decentralization in the location of industry should not be taken to involve autonomy of decision making, for such firms were integral parts of a larger system. Technology facilitated both physical decentralization and administrative control; the first depended upon the second.

This phase of suburbanization had several characteristics different from that of the nineteenth century. First, the outward spread of industry gave rise to an occupationally more varied set of suburbs; those who worked in suburban industries—blue-collar, white-collar, and professional—chose to live relatively close to them. Sub-

---

ters," *Demography* 2 (1965), 126–33. A convenient compilation of data describing black upward mobility is U.S. Bureau of the Census, "Social and Economic Conditions of Negroes in the United States," *Current Population Reports*, Ser. P-23, No. 24 (Washington, D.C., 1967).

33. Income trends can be followed most completely in U.S. Bureau of the Census, *Current Population Reports*, Ser. P-60, or in annual compilations by the same agency, the *Statistical Abstract of the United States*.

urban areas did not contain middle- and upper-class groups alone, but a wide variety of classes. Second, the mere size of the suburban scene provided a far larger number of communities and of choices of residence. Since these choices were made in terms of the class level of the community with which one wished to associate, the range of suburban communities reflected a more varied and precisely defined spectrum of classes than in previous years. Third, the vast size of the suburban spectrum gave rise to lateral movement within it, increasingly becoming more important relative to the center-periphery patterns which previously dominated. A structure arose within the periphery distinguishing those who lived and worked in the same suburb, those who lived in one suburb and worked in another, and those who lived in the suburb and worked in the central city.

These outward movements took place across rather than within city legal boundaries. Because the outlying areas wished to be included in the city's services, nineteenth-century urban boundary expansion met little opposition. Much outward population flow took place within the city's legal limits. By 1930, many cities were ringed with independent towns, boroughs, and townships, each with autonomous legal power derived from the authority not of the city but of the state. Many suburbanites had moved beyond the city's borders precisely to be in a community which had such political independence. In the city, residential communities had little power to maintain their stability; they were always threatened by forces which sought to change the patterns of land use and thereby to undermine its physical base. Outside the city, in a separate corporate town or township, such control could be exercised. Here it was possible to require that house lots be of a minimum size and houses of a minimum value.[34]

Suburban political units reflected a desire to separate one's community from the larger urban world. Nineteenth-century decentralization, within the city, did not lead to permanent political subunits. In fact, the urban community had little staying power in the face of integrative forces. Twentieth-century decentralization took place across the city's borders and enjoyed political jurisdic-

34. The recent politics of suburban areas is dealt with in Robert C. Wood, *Suburbia, Its People and Their Politics* (Boston, 1958).

tions separate from the city and capable of maintaining autonomous political and legal as well as social existence. Twentieth-century decentralization had far greater staying power than did that of the nineteenth.

The process of urban integration also continued. As the city grew, so did the range of people, activities, and land use which large urban systems sought to influence. One form of this impulse was the drive for metropolitan government, to extend the city's boundaries outward to encompass growing suburban areas, often to make the city's boundaries synonymous with the county's. The drive for metropolitan government extended the former drive for centralization of city government; once the latter movement had succeeded, it began to advocate a larger metropolitan system. Such a movement developed in almost every city, some as early as the late 1920s, but succeeded only rarely.[35]

More successful was the growth of specialized public functions which extended beyond the city's boundaries. Suburbanites demanded effective transportation to their work in the city; they supported metropolitan transit authorities to develop systems of public transit which went far beyond the city's borders. Because of their wider jurisdiction, county governments usually created such authorities. Similar agencies developed for countywide trash disposal and garbage collection, sanitary sewers, water systems, and health departments. These innovations gave rise to governmental institutions as wide in scope as the metropolitan area itself, and an almost imperceptible shift in decision-making power from suburban units to the larger authority.

Metropolitan authorities were corporations established for specific purposes with general powers to achieve them. Like similar state and federal corporations, they were free from traditional restraints by council and mayor. Still further removed from the city's active political impulses than were the mayor or council elected-at-large, they could carry out their task in terms of technical standards of professional expertise at the upper levels of the political order rather than have to respond to the constant suggestions and objections of open political debate. Innovations in government in the

35. An account of one case is Edward Sofen, *The Miami Metropolitan Experiment* (Bloomington, Ind., 1963).

years between 1897 and 1929 narrowed the actors in the decision-making process and the range of alternatives and debate; the authorities continued this process. Once given a grant of power, it became difficult to render the authority accountable to any other governmental body.

The urban redevelopment authority—the prime example—was not only divorced from other government bodies but also had the power of eminent domain. It arose to change urban patterns of land use, most frequently in the central city. What land uses should prevail? Invariably redevelopment involved a shift from buildings of lower value and tax return to those of higher. This meant the substitution of large-scale for small-scale enterprise, a perspective consistent with integrative objectives and congenial to those involved in large-scale private enterprise rather than those at the middle and lower levels of the social order. With the power of eminent domain, the authority could force property owners to sell. In this way, the expansion of the property stake in urban affairs, which came with the decentralization of ownership in the nineteenth century, was reversed. Land used by many small property holders was transferred to a relatively few large ones through the process of urban renewal.[36]

Professional and technical experts continued to extend their manipulative ventures as the drive toward more universal contexts of action grew. So also did the gap between these and impulses of smaller scale. Public-health leaders pushed such measures as fluoridation and air pollution control. Mental-health programs expanded rapidly. The drive for education continued unabated, with emphasis on better facilities, more intensive instruction, influence over preschool and home environment, and junior colleges. In such programs as these, the practice of control from the top by experts grew apace. School boards, already under such a system of decision making, concentrated on utilizing it more extensively. Public-health experts were less fortunate. The fluoridation issue became especially critical. Left to community popular vote, fluoridation was rejected more often than accepted. By the 1960s, therefore, public-health leaders sought to bypass the urban general suffrage, argued

36. An account of the role of redevelopment, seen from a critical view, is Martin Anderson, *The Federal Bulldozer* (Cambridge, Mass., 1964).

that public-health matters were not fit subjects for democratic control, and sought legislation to impose fluoridation on the entire state.[37]

Preference for top-level decision making on the part of professional experts was reflected in several political tactics. One was the creation of neighborhood groups, such as parent-teacher associations and neighborhood welfare councils, which served both to convey information about potential sources of discontent to central agencies and to implement general citywide policies. Their power, however, was confined to suggestion rather than decision. Another was the heightened interest in a systematic understanding of opposition to administrative proposals, not as a means to modify objectives, but so as to implement them more effectively. They began to study the sociology of public health, of education, of mental health. They were, of course, far more interested in the sociology of those whom they confronted than of their own values and professional social systems. They simply wished a more complete understanding of their political opposition so that they could better implement their goals.

Reaction against integrative tendencies in the city took several new forms and led to new types of balance between centrifugal and centripetal forces. As centralization rose in the pre-1929 years, the community declined as a viable political force. In the depression years of the 1930s, however, a reverse trend set in momentarily. Some smaller cities abolished the city-manager system; Cleveland, unique among the larger cities in adopting the plan, rejected it in the late 1920s. Other cities returned to the ward system of representation in the 1930s, and a noticeable increase took place in representation from working-class areas. In many instances, even with citywide elections, city councils contained more representatives of workingmen, but invariably these were prominent union officials

37. For the relationship between political structure and the success or failure of drives for fluoridation see Robert L. Crain and Donald B. Rosenthal, "Structure and Value in Local Political Systems: The Case of Fluoridation Decisions," *Journal of Politics* 28 (1966), 169–95. The authors argue that proponents of fluoridation come more from the upper levels of the socioeconomic order than do the opponents, and that the movement has a better chance of success in an urban government of centralized decision-making authority in which the executive is insulated from external "irregular" pressures. The strategies of fluoridation proponents, their successes and failures, and data on referenda can be followed most completely in antifluoridation literature such as *National Fluoridation News* (1954–).

who represented not geographical communities but functional organizations.[38]

Not until the political activation of urban blacks, when community became expressed through race, did community resistance against integrative tendencies revive significantly. The process was sharpened by urban redevelopment, which physically destroyed urban communities, most frequently black residential areas, in sections with the lowest property values. "Urban renewal" is "Negro removal" was the cry. This threat to the black community came at a time of rising black income, education, and awareness. Moreover, concentration of blacks in limited areas of the city gave a clear spatial and community form to the expression of black political aims. In the midst of a city and school government dominated by whites, blacks frequently demanded that a ward plan of representation and government supersede citywide forms, which provided minority groups little chance to express their demands effectively.

Those involved in smaller-scale economic, social, and political affairs and at the middle and lower segments of the political order found themselves cast in a defensive rather than a creative role. Initiative as to the formulation of goals for urban policy had shifted to institutions far above them. Because it foused on community change, urban redevelopment helped to reactivate these community impulses and met increasing opposition from them.[39] A variety of spokesmen arose to voice objections: homeowners, storekeepers, real estate firms, often the same types of people who once had represented the wards in city councils and school boards. Often they succeeded in changing a project, sometimes by postponing it but at other times by preventing its development. To the authorities, these were major irritants; following modern views of "conflict management," they sought to overcome resistance but not always with success.

Confrontation between officials who represented dominant po-

38. Some indication of these trends can be observed in Harold A. Stone et al., *City Manager Government in Nine Cities* (Chicago, 1940); Frederick C. Mosher et al., *City Manager Government in Seven Cities* (Chicago, 1940); Harold A. Stone et al., *City Manager Government in the United States* (Chicago, 1940). These provide case studies of a variety of cities and carry many aspects of city-manager government, including the problem of representation, down through the 1930s.

39. The opposition can be traced in Anderson, *The Federal Bulldozer*.

litical institutions and those who reflected community impulses revealed the institutional strength of the former and the weakness of the latter. Officials had a myriad of institutions into which they could retreat for strength. They could parry opposition by seeking more information, by reconsidering, by shifting to a different administrative channel. The institutional routines through which they could counter-thrust, hide, escape, or protect themselves, stall and wear down opponents, seemed almost endless. Community representatives were far more exposed. Their constituencies were institutionally weak, with few information resources to provide support and backing, and few agencies to constitute a legitimate source of waiting, parrying, and regrouping. The weakness of community impulses was reflected in the weakness of institutions into which community leaders could retreat and return with new political strength.[40]

Forces from outside the community arose to aid the reconstruction of its institutions. Social workers and federal antipoverty program employees urged residents of poor communities to organize and exercise political power, to make demands upon city government for help in improving their neighborhoods. These efforts to reenergize people at the lower levels of the politcal order were only sporadically successful. The apathy of residents, often highly mobile, uninvolved in their neighborhood, let alone the city, was difficult to overcome. Most frequently these efforts at community building aroused only a small segment—one or two percent—of the inhabitants, and served to speed them up the escalator and out into the wider urban society. Their major impact was to demonstrate that the disengagement of the bottom third from the larger political order was a permanent fact of life in modern American society.[41]

The community's weakness within the city stood in stark contrast to its strength outside the city. The independent legal status of the suburban community gave it an enormous capacity for strength

40. Lewis M. Killian, "Community Structure and the Role of the Negro Leader-Agent," *Sociological Inquiry* 35 (1965), 69–79, describes these differences for the Negro confrontation with the established political system.

41. See, for example, Frank Reissman, "The Myth of Saul Alinsky," *Dissent* (July-August 1967), 469–78. The classic description of the new urban poor is Michael Harrington, *The Other America: Poverty in the United States* (New York, 1962).

and persistence in the face of integrative urban impulses. It enabled them to ward off intrusions of influence from the city, such as lower-income or black migrants. They could frustrate efforts at metropolitan government, either by organizing suburban units into an opposition bloc or by influencing state legislatures to stipulate electoral provisions which loaded the vote on metropolitan government in their favor. The power of the state could also be used to reduce suburban autonomy, as in school district reorganization, carried out through state legislative and administrative agencies. Against such integrative pressures from either city or state, however, the suburban communities could throw a considerable and continual counter-force. Their capacity for resistance was far greater than was that of the urban community.

Within the city, the upper third of the social order, often similar in socioeconomic composition to persons from the most influential suburbs, exercised far more influence than did the lower or middle third. But the form of their political involvement shifted from geographical or area organization to functional organization. Increasingly, the active elements of the city came to be organized not by locality or community, but by specialized interests or functions, some in terms of occupation, trade associations, trade unions, or professional organizations; some in terms of specialized institutions such as libraries, art galleries, colleges, and schools; still others in terms of religion or ethnicity. Active elements in each of these functional groups were not the urban masses, but those in the upper occupational and organizational levels. The setting of urban politics came to be the interplay among functional groups in the upper levels of the political order, producing a pluralist political system, but distinctively within the top segments of vertical organization.[42]

Membership in city councils and school boards reflected functional politics. Officials elected citywide were nominated by parties or, if in a nonpartisan election, by a nonpartisan group. In each case, the nominating body usually sought to "represent" all segments of the city; these "segments" in turn were thought of in functional terms. Positions were "reserved" for labor, for each of the major re-

42. The classic statement of the "pluralist" conception of community decision making is Robert Dahl, *Who Governs* (New Haven, 1961). The limitations of the pluralist view lie in its failure to locate pluralism in the upper levels of the political order.

ligious or nationality groups, for blacks, for merchants, bankers, or manufacturers. These functional representatives came from the top levels of vertical organization. The upward shift in the scale of representation and functional representation seemed to go hand in hand. Spokesmen for working-class people were no longer skilled or unskilled workmen, as in the earlier city, but top union officials who came from managerial levels of society. Ethnic and religious groups came to be represented by the very highest vertical levels of the different ethnic and religious class systems. Black members of city councils and school boards were professionals and businessmen from the upper levels of the black community.[43]

Functional-group politics created a new context of active urban political life limited to the upper levels of the political order, and a new balance of urban forces in which centrifugal tendencies came to be the functional groups at that level. No longer did the centralization-decentralization balance encompass the entire social order as it had in the late nineteenth and twentieth centuries. Now it was confined, for the most part, to the active, articulate segments of the upper levels. Those seeking to integrate urban affairs more fully sought support, placated the opposition, and developed a firm political base largely within this context. Save for an occasional instance of an election, the active urban political order was limited to the upper levels of the vertical scale of society, and the middle and lower levels either remained apathetic and aloof or were cast in a negative or veto role.

As American cities moved into the last half of the twentieth century, their patterns of human relationships were very different from those of the mid-nineteenth century. A structure of human contacts, growing out of the greater speed and scale of communications and the expanded range of human thought, awareness, and action, had developed that was far broader in scope than the structure of a century before. The community of primary human relationships remained, but its influence in the entire political order had declined sharply. Above and beyond it, a network of func-

43. Drawn from data on Pittsburgh city councilmen, set against a study of the Pittsburgh black upper class by Marjorie J. Allen, "The Negro Upper Class in Pittsburgh, 1910–1964," seminar paper, Univ. of Pittsburgh, 1964.

tional and corporate institutions had developed which now consti-tuted the context of active political life. Innovation in the political order came from this level, the "public consciousness" generated by mass communication media was largely confined to it, and the interplay of day-to-day political differences took place within it. Over a century or more of development, the entire urban political order had expanded greatly, had rearranged itself, and had under-gone a sharp change in the location of political interaction and deci-sion making. From a previous balance which had tipped the scales of the city's active political impulses toward decentralization, they had shifted strongly toward centralization and upward in the verti-cal social and political order.

IV.
THE SETTING AND
RESOURCES FOR HISTORICAL INQUIRY

R<small>ECENT</small> developments in historical social inquiry, reflected in the previous essays, have required new materials for research, as well as training in new skills and have generated new courses in the history curriculum. The following five essays discuss several aspects of these trends.

The themes touched upon here include the substance of the research, teaching resources and curricula, the institutional arrangements whereby these can be fostered, and the value of social history in encouraging the study of history. During the period when these essays were written, I was chairman of the Department of History at the University of Pittsburgh for thirteen years; member of the Social Science Research Council for five years; program chairman for the annual meeting of the Mississippi Valley Historical Association in 1963; and participant in the historical data project of the Inter-University Consortium for Political Research. These activities led me to take part in various conference and professional meetings, to give lectures at several colleges and universities, and to continue my writing, all in an effort, in part, to promote the allocation of institutional time and resources to historical social inquiry.

Some of these essays describe innovations which can be carried out by academic institutions themselves as they foster the search for new historical understanding; others discuss the responsibilities and problems of specialized archival agencies as they seek to preserve the public records of municipal, state, and federal governments or of churches, universities, and associations. Professional organizations at all levels—national, regional, and state—could well develop activities more supportive of historical social research.

Because of the content of social history, and especially because of its focus on human life at the "grass roots" in all of its ramifications, support from national institutions, while extremely important, has limited potential. The National Archives of the Church of Jesus Christ of Latter-Day Saints, for example, is providing major assistance by making its records more usable to the scholar and the general public. But the greatest opportunities are at the local level, where time and energy can be devoted to the particular possibilities of community activities. From this conviction came my efforts to build resources for social research at the University of Pittsburgh, such as the Archives of Industrial Society and the Pittsburgh Historical Data Archives. I have suggested in several of the articles that colleges, and especially community colleges, should undertake these responsibilities. A number of such active enterprises throughout the nation have grown steadily in recent years, and major efforts to encourage their further spread have been undertaken by the Newberry Library in Chicago.

We must once again emphasize the importance of cooperation between academic historians and those engaged in community historical activities, such as family history. A steadily increasing interest in genealogy, in particular, stimulated local energies in this direction in the 1950s and 1960s, long before the bicentennial celebrations of 1976. That event gave rise to the publication of a number of community histories and to a considerable effort aimed at gathering reminiscences and carrying out oral history interviewing in order to increase the range of grass-roots historical materials. The article "History and Genealogy" is a plea for cooperation of this kind, for assistance from the historical profession in gathering and preserving local history materials and writing family genealogies as a critical facet of "grass-roots" history.

[12]

Archival Sources for American Political History *

Historians are beginning to exploit a vast quantity of source material for American political history heretofore hardly tapped. Archival materials for political history have traditionally been primarily the personal manuscripts of political leaders; in these the private and public, state and federal depositories abound. But lying almost unnoticed and relatively unused in county, state, and other archives are masses of information about popular voting, legislative voting, and demography—and about thousands of political leaders who left no papers. This evidence is more quantitative, more bulky, and more difficult to use because of the enormous task of compiling and presenting it in manageable form. There is a growing awareness of its vast importance, a growing desire to use it in research, and a growing ability to cope with it through new techniques of data computation, storage, and retrieval. It is on this type of archival source for research in American political history that I wish to dwell here.

Interest in these sources reflects dissatisfaction with the outward and formal, with the individual and episodic in political history and an interest in the social analysis of political life. The setting of political history concerns the distribution of power among the various distinct groupings—socioeconomic, ethnocultural, sectional, managerial and managed, local or cosmopolitan—which develop in society. One main task of the historian is to reconstruct a picture of these groupings and their changing interrelationships. But much of

*This paper was read at the joint meeting of the Society of American Archivists and the Mississippi Valley Historical Association in Cleveland, Ohio on Apr. 30, 1964. It is reprinted from *The American Archivist* 28 (1965) by permission of The Society of American Archivists.

the traditional emphasis on the outcome of single elections, on the campaign debates, on congressional proceedings, on the relations among party leaders, and on Supreme Court decisions fails to get at these basic patterns of political life and the impulses that spring from them. Such evidence deals with the results rather than the well-springs of political thought and action, and it fails especially to give a full account of the variety of political impulses vying for expression and the particular inequality in political power that develops.

This interest in the social analysis of political history is revealed in a number of recently published works. But it appears also in the research activities of students, at both the M.A. and doctoral levels, at several institutions where faculty members have been especially interested in such an approach. Some of these researches stress the analysis of popular voting and the association of demographic characteristics with differences in voting patterns over space and time. Others involve the systematic analysis of legislative voting patterns at both the federal and state levels and the association of differences with either the personal characteristics of legislators or the group characteristics of their constituencies. Still others are concerned with collective biography of political leaders—national, state, or local—to determine the characteristics of factions within parties, of different political movements, or of political leadership in general. Still further studies utilize material about nonpartisan economic and social groups interested in political issues to determine the patterns of forces involved in legislative battles.

The most significant aspect of these studies is that they are focused primarily on human behavior, on the way in which people think and act in specific historical circumstances. More important for our purposes here, they are based upon evidence that describes human behavior. Much of the traditional analysis of politics is derived from statements produced by people and institutions—statements intended to establish the particular picture of what these people and institutions are doing that they feel will elicit the most public support. Such evidence describes fairly accurately what people wish to think about themselves and their society, but it does not describe what they do. It especially obscures those elements of social structure that it is not considered wise to describe in detail. For example, ideological evidence would establish American society as overwhelmingly "middle class," primarily because most Americans wish to think of themselves in these terms. But evidence about what people do, their occupations, their income, their patterns of consumption, their residential locations, their activities, yields a picture of many different social classes. While ideological evidence obscures these groupings, behavioral evidence makes them clear. The need for such behavioral evidence, sufficiently extensive to describe large groups of people, has generated the interest in relevant archival sources and in the technological innovations to cope with them.

Research in this vein has advanced more fully in the field of early American history. Here statistical evidence about large numbers of people individually and collectively is available, and yet not in the abundance that overwhelms the student of the more recent past. Studies published or under way include those of colonial assemblies in the eighteenth century, the Massachusetts General Court in the seventeenth century, conventions called to ratify the Constitution of 1787, and voting in eighteenth-century Massachusetts and Virginia. The social analysis of political life in early America has been greatly facilitated by the rapid microfilming of newspapers and state and local records, by the early publications by historians and genealogists of family records and vital statistics, and by the activities of the Institute of Early American History and the *William and Mary Quarterly*, both of which have been peculiarly receptive to this approach.

But there is no reason why a similar interest and a similar approach cannot develop for other parts of the country and for later periods of time, and this is now happening. Vast quantities of similar evidence are available for a similar analysis of society in the South, the Midwest, the Mountain states, and the Far West. Local historical societies have not been so active in making this evidence usable as have societies in the original thirteen states, but there is no reason why the evidence could not be gathered, given sufficient time and resources. It may well be that such an interest will come primarily through the detailed examination of the nineteenth- and twentieth-century growth of industrialization in, and its impact on, specific communities, both rural and urban. The cost of accumulating the necessary data is greater, but new technologies hold out the possibility—at least for some data—of coping with the problem.

There is no reason, therefore, why the analysis of political life in the rest of the country cannot be as intensive as that now under way for early America.

Two implications of considerable significance emerge from this new concern. First, it implies a renewed interest in local history. Patterns of political structure and political process inevitably develop in a local setting; the struggle for control and power is carried out within the context of community institutions where the concerns of people concentrate. The politics of industrial society can be studied, for example, through the intensive examination of mining communities, or of city suburbs. Local history has already received a considerable impetus from the growing interest in urban history. Local historians and academic scholars have often been at odds because of their very different concerns, the former being considered "antiquarians" by academicians, and the latter too remote from reality by local historians. The analysis of political structure and political change in local contexts, however, offers the opportunity for the two groups to come together in a common effort. Information about local industry, religious groups, political parties, working and middle classes, nationalities, upper classes, and patterns of land ownership is of vital interest to the social analyst, and the records developed and kept by local historical societies are indispensable to his work.

The social analysis of politics also implies a crucial interest by the historian in genealogy. The shift from individual to collective biography in political studies requires information about enormous numbers of people. It requires that we know as much as possible about every individual who held office, who ran for office, or who occupied a position in party organization at every level. It requires that we know about the individual's ancestry as well as his descendants. It requires that we have extensive family histories of those whom we are studying. The vast collections of birth, marriage, death, and family records that genealogists have brought forth or inspired in the past—such as the Massachusetts town records or the microfilm records of the federal manuscript census returns—are invaluable to the social analyst. The relative lack of such research aids for areas outside the original thirteen states hampers his research.

Large collections of genealogical data are badly needed. There is no reason, therefore, why the academic historian should not support wholeheartedly the work of the genealogist. He should, in fact, insist on more complete family records than we have had in the past.

An enormous amount of evidence, useful for social analysis, lies ready to be tapped. A most important source is popular election data, which constitute the only comprehensive type of documentary information that approximates a record of public opinion. Much information on popular voting appears in state manuals, known by such titles as "red books" or "blue books"; these include returns for presidential and gubernatorial and often for other statewide contests, for Congress, and for the state legislature. In a number of states—for example, Connecticut, Pennsylvania, Ohio, Michigan, and Iowa—the returns are given for minor civil divisions, such as towns in New England or townships elsewhere and for wards and precincts in cities. Publication of election data in this fashion began usually in the 1860s and in many cases has continued until the present day. It is especially valuable if it includes minor civil divisions, which are usually small enough to encompass homogeneous population groupings of class, national origin, race, or religion. All such material, readily available, entails no special task of compilation; its use awaits only the application of modern methods of compilation, storage, and retrieval.

More effort is required to collect other election data found in scattered and often not yet known sources. State returns, especially before the 1860s, are frequently found in state house and senate journals. City returns, broken down by wards, are at times available in city directories. Some state returns exist in the midst of compilations of federal census returns brought together at the direction of state legislatures. Many returns are available in newspapers, although how many is not yet fully known. Newspapers will have to be relied upon especially for the years before the 1860s and for returns from minor civil divisions in a number of states. The microfilming of newspapers, already highly developed, is invaluable for any project to recover election data because it makes this diffuse source readily available. Suffice it to say that all these sources give promise that a formidable amount of election data can ultimately be recovered.

Manuscript election returns present a more difficult problem and one calling for more immediate attention. The material, available in both state and county archives, is abundant; yet the pressures of insufficient storage space, which frequently prompt local county officials to consider past records of little worth, threaten its destruction. One case in point will suffice. Indiana precinct voting returns have not been published, yet much is available in archives. In Harrison County, Indiana, for example, there are still extant the original voting returns, the tally sheets, and the complete poll lists for each precinct for each election since 1817, the year after Indiana became a state. These records are in good condition and are kept in orderly fashion. In the next county to the east, Floyd County, however, a new courthouse has been constructed recently. Although it contains ample storage space for present purposes in its basement vault, records were not transferred from the old to the new building but were sold to a scrap dealer or destroyed. Floyd County thus has no election returns of any consequence earlier than 1940. Although the problem of space for county records is real and acknowledged, it also seems clear that, if officials could be made sufficiently aware of the increasing interest in these records within the historical profession, means to preserve them would be found.

Substantially complete legislative voting data at the federal and state levels, for the most part published in the *Congressional Record* and in state senate and house journals, are more readily available. As is the case with published popular election data, the frontiers of research here lie in the use of modern technology for compilation, storage, and retrieval—methods that will enable the researcher to discover, in masses of data, patterns of voting not apparent on casual examination and to determine relationships between the votes of legislators and the characteristics of their constituencies. This approach has already been used to some extent with Congress but to a far less extent with state legislatures. Similar data for city councils are more elusive. Some information has been published in municipal reports of various kinds; far more lies in newspapers and municipal manuscript sources. Historians, moreover, have almost completely ignored the possibilities of analyzing city council voting patterns and of relating them to constituency differences; these now offer some of the most exciting unexplored frontiers in the systematic study of local history.

Both legislative and popular voting data require for their analysis a vast amount of related demographic data, of information about the economic, religious, educational, and ethnic characteristics of the ward or county whose voting patterns are under study or of the constituency the votes of whose legislators are being examined. Two broad sources of information exist for these purposes. The first is the census data, federal, state, and local, which have often been published but which exist in greater detail in unpublished form. The microfilm publication of the manuscript population schedules for the federal censuses, especially those from 1850 to 1880, has made it possible for historians to examine county, township, city, and ward demography far more precisely than in the past. But manuscript materials of state censuses have hardly been touched, and the precise data available in them as a whole are hardly known. Even less is known about the availability of urban demographic data such as those taken regularly for school purposes or those compiled by private economic, religious, or ethnic groups.

Equally important in its overall implications, but still more scattered and more difficult to gather, is the vast amount of information available in county and municipal archives. These are primarily, though not exclusively, economic records—of taxes, real estate assessments, and similar matters pertaining to property holdings and economic conditions. Such records have already been used in the study of early American history, and only the difficulty of making their analysis manageable impedes a similar approach to the nineteenth and twentieth centuries. An excellent example of this possibility for modern urban history is the study by Sam Warner, Jr., of the process of suburbanization in Boston, *Streetcar Suburbs*. Through the examination of 23,000 building permits issued for Roxbury, West Roxbury, and Dorchester between 1870 and 1900, Mr. Warner has been able to present the first precise picture of the process of urban outward migration and the rise from blue- to white-collar occupations. His study is a model in the imaginative use of local economic records for the illumination of social processes. As the vast importance of local economic records becomes clearer, the task of preservation becomes more acute. As the social analysis of history proceeds, the historian will be more dependent than ever upon the farsighted archivist who can foster the preservation of demographic records.

Equally extensive is the source material, waiting to be tapped, concerning individual political leaders. Historians have only recently undertaken studies of groups of political leaders—as contrasted with individuals—in order to determine patterns in the origin and nature of political leadership. For the most part confined to national leaders, these studies have relied heavily upon information drawn from existing biographical compilations or from personal manuscripts. They have, therefore, been limited in coverage. But information is available in great abundance about tens and hundreds of thousands of political leaders at the state and local level. City directories show the occupation and address of every adult inhabitant; they reveal changes in both occupation and residence within and between generations and therefore demonstrate patterns of social mobility. Social registers provide ample information about upper-class groups to permit the full examination of a facet of political life hardly tapped. Manuscript census returns, both federal and state, provide a wealth of information about individuals which, at least for the years 1850–80, currently permits an extensive analysis of political leadership. And local economic records provide even more data for individuals. Such sources make available an almost unbelievable amount of information about individual political leaders that permits types of collective biographical analyses hardly even imagined in the not too distant past. Although such data often require considerable work in compilation before they can be used, much can be explored efficiently and quickly even now.

In using this material the major problem confronting historians is the task of collection and classification, of reducing vast amounts of data to comparable quantitative units and of presenting them in forms that facilitate analysis. For example, although 90 percent or more of all popular election data ever recorded is still available, little has been collected in one place and almost none is available in the form of percentages. Enormous amounts of time and effort are therefore required to make such data usable, and researchers, whether graduate students or faculty members, do not have the time or the facilities to undertake the task. Studies of relatively small geographical areas over very short periods of time are feasible, but larger studies covering more election units and defining longer trends, or comparative studies of different types of electorates, are now impossible to undertake. The development of new technologies, however, provides the opportunity to solve some of these problems through modern methods of computing, storing, and retrieving data. A project is now under way to do this for popular voting; if this is successful, as it apparently will be, the way will lie open for the application of these techniques to other data, thereby enhancing enormously the opportunities for the social analysis of political history.

Some three years ago a number of historians and political scientists formally requested the Social Science Research Council to take up the project of collecting, computing, and making available past popular election data. Responding to this request, the council appointed W. Dean Burnham, compiler of county returns for presidential elections of the nineteenth century, to survey the problem. This Mr. Burnham did in the summer of 1962. His report drew the conclusion that a vast quantity of such data was still extant, some published, some in manuscript sources in state archives and in county and city record offices, and some in newspapers. From the standpoint of the physical availability of material the project was feasible. After receiving this report, the council provided funds for Mr. Burnham to make a more extensive and precise determination of the whereabouts of data. This he has been doing during the academic year 1963–64 from his post at the Survey Research Center at the University of Michigan. Mr. Burnham soon found that the survey could be completed quickly, and as a result attention was turned in the fall of 1963 to the actual collection and computing of data.

At the same time the Survey Research Center at the University of Michigan expressed an increasing interest in popular election data. Established originally to collect survey data through interviewing and questionnaire techniques, the center began to collect documentary census data as well, and the extension into data on past elections seemed to be a natural evolution of its concerns. This development tied in very closely with the center's changing role in the academic world. In 1961 it took the lead in creating the Inter-

University Consortium for Political Research. It invited academic institutions to join in annual financial support of the new institution and in turn to receive political data, which it would collect in its data repository, and to participate in training seminars during the summer at the University of Michigan. Originally established as an organization of political scientists, the consortium could be developed to include those in other disciplines interested in political research.

These two developments, one growing out of the activities of the Social Science Research Council (SSRC) and the other out of the Consortium for Political Research, began to converge less than a year ago. The major problems then confronting the project to collect election data were twofold: (a) even though the existence of popular election data was now known, how could data be copied and transmitted to a central place? and (b) how could the computation and storage be financed? The consortium seemed to be an agency through which these tasks could be done, but it had neither the facilities for collection nor the funds for the technical work. Through discussions between Lee Benson, then professor of history at Wayne State University, and Warren Miller, executive director of the consortium, it was decided to enlist historians themselves for the task of collection. Other historians besides those who had presented the original request to the SSRC were drawn into the project, and meetings to elaborate it were held at the annual session of the American Historical Association in December 1963. In January 1964 the American Historical Association (AHA) established an Ad Hoc Committee to Collect the Basic Data of American Political History, composed of Profs. Lee Benson, Allan G. Bogue, Dewey Grantham, Samuel P. Hays, Morton Keller, Richard McCormick, Philip Mason, Thomas Pressly, and Charles Sellers, with Mr. Benson as chairman.

The AHA committee proposed to function through state committees, each of which, with the help of information that Mr. Burnham had already collected, would agree to undertake the task of locating and photocopying the documents containing data in its state and to send the photocopies to the consortium headquarters at Ann Arbor. Within three months committees were organized in forty-six states. Their initial task was to obtain county returns since 1824 for the elections of President, governor, U.S. senator, and U.S. representative, as well as for other statewide contests in years when these elections were not held. This project is now approximately 75 percent complete and is expected to be virtually complete by August 1, 1964, when Mr. Burnham's tour of duty under the Social Science Research Council grant will end. The response from historians who have served on the state committees has been extremely gratifying, for it reveals a considerable interest long believed to exist but now confirmed. Several hundred historians are serving on the state committees. Some political scientists have also been drawn in, and a number of state archivists and other public officials have provided considerable help. The committees have often sent in much more documentation than that originally requested. In some cases sets of returns in state archives have been microfilmed as a whole; in others minor civil division returns have been included. These will provide a good beginning for extensions of the project as the collecting moves toward the inclusion of information on other contests and minor civil divisions. From the historians' side, therefore, the entire project is off to a good start.

As the AHA committee began to function, plans emerged to request the National Science Foundation, then showing increasing interest in research in political science, to provide funds for computing and processing the data. The consortium submitted such a proposal, and it has now been approved. At the same time the National Science Foundation has provided support for a director of the project who will continue the work begun by Mr. Burnham, serving at the consortium in liaison between the consortium and the AHA committee and in general coordinating the entire project. Howard Allen, of the history faculty of Southern Illinois University, has been appointed as project director for the academic year 1964-65. It seems quite feasible, therefore, to anticipate that the county data now being collected will be computed, processed, stored, and made available for research sometime during the summer or fall of 1965.

The success thus far in its initial project, which now seems well on the way to completion, has prompted the AHA committee to define its next objectives. The first of these is to extend its collection of popular election data by covering more types of elections over a longer period of time and by preparing data for all of these elections at the smallest recorded political unit—township, ward, precinct, or other type of election district. The extended coverage of counties includes elections before 1824, primaries of all kinds, and state referenda. It will be more difficult to obtain comprehensive coverage of these elections than of those for President, governor, U.S. senator, and U.S. representative; but the data are available and can be recovered.

The collection of data for minor civil divisions is a more formidable task, not simply in the problem of recovery but more crucially in that of computing and processing. Most political historians are agreed that analysis of the distribution of and shift in votes requires the examination of votes in the minor civil divisions. Because these units are far more homogeneous in occupational, ethnic, or religious terms, analysis of them can proceed far more effectively than with county units. But while there are only several thousand counties there are tens of thousands of precincts, and the cost of computing and processing data from the precincts is far greater. Because of the enormous value of analysis at this level, however, data from minor civil divisions must be collected if the social analysis of political history is to proceed effectively. The committee, therefore, plans to start such collection on a selective basis, emphasizing those geographical areas and time periods where research is already under way.

The committee's second task is to collect and prepare the demographic data needed to interpret the election statistics. These include such data as those pertaining to national origin, race, religion, production, employment, income, communications, education, transportation, and percentage of urban or rural population. As with the election data, this information will be most useful if collected for minor civil divisions as well as for counties. The simplest part of this task will be to make available in appropriate form the printed returns of the U.S. census. The same can be done for printed state census returns, for which fairly complete bibliographies exist. But censuses conducted by municipalities and by such private groups as religious organizations will require considerable work in searching out sources before the data from them can be prepared in usable form. One of the committee's most pressing initial tasks will be to determine precisely what kinds of demographic data are needed and how the available data can be classified most appropriately for historical analysis.

The collection of data pertinent to the analysis of the legislative process constitutes a third major area of the committee's work. This includes the collection not only of roll-call votes, but also of information concerning committee assignments, bills not passed, and case histories of bills as they moved through the legislative mill. The most useful initial task will be to prepare the roll-call votes so that they can be analyzed in relation to the personal characteristics of legislators and the characteristics of their constituencies. Demographic data collected for the analysis of popular voting can also be used for the analysis of legislative voting with little change in form save the combination of smaller political units into legislative districts. But analysis in terms of biographical characteristics of legislators will require the collection and preparation of an additional kind of material. For the congressional phase of this task material already available, such as the roll-call votes of the federal Congress compiled by WPA workers in the 1930s or the lives of congressmen in biographical dictionaries, will be invaluable. Much of the committee's task will consist of preparing this material further for rapid retrieval and analysis and making the collections of data more complete. The analysis of roll calls in state legislatures and city councils will require more collection of basic data, but the task is fundamentally the same as for the federal Congress.

One of the committee's important tasks, it is hoped, will be to serve as a clearinghouse of information concerning the need for and the availability of data, and concerning research projects under way in the social analysis of political history. It is apparent that a good many historians have had access to collections of data or have spent considerable time compiling and tabulating data they no longer need. The same can be said for work done by graduate students in seminars and for M.A. theses, which are seldom published. A complete compilation exists, for example, as a doctoral dissertation, of the religious composition of each county in the United States in 1850. Availability of information about this kind of data might not only aid the individual researcher but might lead us to comparative studies of politics as related to religion, for instance, in different geographical areas—a direction in research that would be of enormous value. It is hoped that the state committees especially will take up this task of getting information about who is doing and has done what, and that such information can then be circulated by the national committee.

The possibilities that lie ahead in the collection and preparation of data for the social analysis of political history are enormous. The task obviously can occupy the AHA committee for years to come. It is so extensive that it cannot be undertaken by the consortium at Ann Arbor all at once. Most likely, a threefold approach will be adopted. For some kinds of data the collection, tabulation, and processing will be complete; this will be the case for countywide election returns in major contests and for countywide selected demographic data. The cost of compiling and processing such data is reasonable in the light of available resources. For more extensive data, such as election returns from minor civil divisions or state and municipal legislative roll calls, the cost of a complete tabulation is now prohibitive. Work on these will probably be selective and will be confined to data immediately relevant to a particular research project for which particular funds can be found. But whatever the comprehensiveness or selectivity of data storage, both the AHA committee and the consortium will faciliate research in the social analysis of history by making contact among historians possible, by encouraging the exchange of ideas and information, and by emphasizing areas of possible research.

This project to collect the basic quantitative data of American political history has special significance for archivists, because the AHA committee and the consortium are actually establishing a new type of archival collection: a repository for quantitative political data. This repository rests upon basic archival records long known to historians and archivists but now being used more extensively and systematically. Much of the success of the project depends on the degree to which the archival sources pertaining to statistical and biographical data are readily available. This, in turn, involves a sense of urgency in the preservation of manuscript records at the state and especially the local levels, an urgency not heretofore sufficiently stressed by professional historians. The AHA committee hopes that archivists will take an active part in this effort. Archivists are now members of several state committees, and some nonmembers have been invaluable in gathering county election data. Upon the active support of archivists much of the success of the entire venture will depend. For as the work moves from the printed page back to the manuscript sources the archivists' knowledge of these sources will be essential, and their efforts to preserve materials that might otherwise be destroyed will be crucial. If these vast quantities of data can be preserved, collected, computed, and stored for ready retrieval and use, research in American political history will have exciting possibilities ahead.

[13]

Quantification in History: The Implications and Challenges for Graduate Training *

THE issues which Professor Aydelotte raises have important consequences for the doctoral and postdoctoral training of historians. How much and what kind of quantitative training is essential? To what extent should graduate programs modify their curricula in order to provide students with the competence required to pursue systematic social research?

Different types of training are relevant to these objectives. First, training in *data location and development* is needed. Students should be exposed to the variety of sources of quantitative data that are available for research, and to the techniques for developing these data into categories useful for measurement and manipulation. There are vast quantities of data at hand in the historical record. Some are semideveloped; most exist in raw and original form. There are election returns, legislative roll calls, tax lists, and records of nativity, religious affiliation, real and personal property values, migration and communication, and occupation, to name only a few. Some of the data are aggregated into units of varying sizes; some are not. For those that are, the student must be made aware of the purposes for which the aggregation was developed and its limitations as well as its possibilities. In the case of data about individuals, he must be trained in techniques of classification, so that data of different kinds can be reduced to comparable units. Each type of data requires specialized knowledge and skill for manipula-

*This piece was published in the *AHA Newsletter,* 4:5 (June 1966) to complement an article by William Aydelotte, Univ. of Iowa, in the *American Historical Review* 71 (1966), entitled "Quantification in History." Reprinted by permission of the American Historical Association.

tion, some but not all of which is transferable to other types of data. A graduate training program in historical social research, then, should provide courses in data location and development.

Training is needed, secondly, in *data manipulation.* Although much can frequently be accomplished through simple counting and categorizing, far more can be achieved through statistical methods. The historian needs to be thoroughly acquainted with different methods of measurement—nominal, ordinal, and interval —and the possibilities and limitations of each. He needs to be aware of methods of describing aggregates, in such forms as distributions, central tendencies, and deviations from central tendencies, as well as the relationship of single instances to those distributions. He needs to understand techniques of establishing statistical associations between distributions of variables—techniques pertinent to each kind of measurement—to know which measure is best suited for which data and for which purpose, and to know how one can test whether or not his results are worth paying attention to. He needs to become competent in techniques, such as scaling and factor analysis, that can be used to reduce vast amounts of seemingly unrelated data to orderly categories not immediately obvious to the observer. These statistical methods greatly enhance the quality as well as the quantity of historical description and provide for the historian a greatly extended variety of observations from which he can reconstruct the past.

A quantitative approach to history also requires training in *sampling.* All too often historians do not inquire into the degree to which the cases from which they generalize are representative. Recently, for example, I came across a research proposal which sought to understand the small town in eighteenth-century America by examining one such small town. But the rationale upon which the particular instance was selected for study rested wholly upon the argument that it was distinctive. Such an atypical instance would have shed no light whatsoever upon the small town as a general phenomenon. As the massive body of quantitative data in the historical record enables the historian to describe and analyze widely pervasive phenomena, he must learn how to draw reliable conclusions about those phenomena in general from examination of only a limited number of cases. For example, Richard Merritt's study of colonial American self-conceptions, as Americans or Britishers, indicates the immense usefulness of content analysis for historical study, but it would have been impossible without sampling. Historians inevitably generalize from particular cases; they need training in sampling techniques that will render this process reliable.

Training in data location and development and in data manipulation is not enough. Far more important is training in *research design*. Research projects must be formulated in such a way that quantitative data are made directly relevant to significant historical problems. This may seem obvious, yet many historical studies are ineffective because they have not been designed to provide the opportunity for specific evidence to bear on the choice of alternative hypotheses. Consider, for example, the task of describing the characteristics of a particular group of political leaders, such as the Progressive party of 1912, or of the antislavery movement in the nineteenth century. If the research design provides only for the development of data about the particular political leaders in question, it will be of almost no value. While affording a description of one group it will in no way determine whether that group was different from or similar to other political leaders. It provides for no comparative setting and no alternative hypotheses to which evidence can be relevant. More adequate research design has yielded the fact that Progressive party leaders were essentially no different from their opponents. The same might well be found of antislavery leaders. Unless the research design itself provides for the establishment of distinctions, data gathering and manipulation will be of no avail.

All of this may seem elementary. Yet the fact remains that rarely do we train our graduate students in techniques of relating concepts and evidence. We are more inclined to ask students to plunge into the evidence and come up with some intuitive ordering of it. Such practices enslave us to the evidence and limit our historical perspective and imagination. As we utilize quantitative data more frequently this practice can no longer be tolerated, for the time, energy, and cost required are simply too great to be wasted on data development and manipulation without direction. We cannot afford to wait until after the data are developed to consider their significance; we must self-consciously utilize evidence which is relevant to alternatives in hypotheses. Quantitative data help us to choose such alternatives more precisely. For example, was the shift in voting patterns between 1894 and 1896 more closely related to economic or ethnic and religious factors? Did evangelical and conservative religious groups in the 1830s and 1840s differ with respect to economic and social characteristics? The most important single innovation in the graduate curriculum required by the use of quantitative data is training in the technique of designing research projects systematically to relate evidence to choices between alternative descriptions and analyses.

I would propose, therefore, that history departments give serious thought to incorporating into their graduate programs specific training in data location and development, in statistics, and in systematic research design. The first and third of these they will have to develop themselves. Statistical training, on the other hand, can be secured frequently from courses provided by other disciplines. But these should be used with caution, for the social sciences, with rare exceptions, are not historical and are frequently antihistorical in orientation. They are concerned with survey rather than documentary data, with indicators of contemporary phenomena rather than of change over time. A significant exception is the seminar program of the Inter-University Consortium for Political Research at Ann Arbor, Michigan, which beginning in the summer of 1966 will offer sound quantitative training for historians based upon the use of documentary as well as survey materials. Historians should utilize this resource extensively. But it is to be hoped that eventually they will develop suitable training programs in statistics at their own institutions either jointly with the social sciences or in their own departments. Only in this way can quantitative training be tailored to the varied and newly emerging analytical problems of concern to those who specialize in understanding the past.

[14]

The Use of Archives for
Historical Statistical Inquiry *

Today there is a new mood of inquiry arising within the historical profession. It is known by various names: "cliometrics," "new economic history," "political behavior," "historical sociology," or "sociological history." Perhaps the best term for it is "historical social research," since this denotes the new mood's two main elements. One is a concern for the broad structural characteristics of society and the long-term changes in those characteristics—a discontent with the narrow range of vision of limited segments of space and time, and a desire that the frame of reference be a set of articulated concepts of social change. The other is the accompanying desire to bring into the study of the past the whole range of society—the nonpeople and the nonevents, not simply the mass of people as a mass but all segments of the social order, from top to bottom, as an interacting whole. These new directions of inquiry require a broader range of historical evidence than we have been accustomed to draw upon and thus a different approach to the preservation and dissemination of historical records.

The most easily observable sign of this new mood is the use of statistics in historical inquiry. But the use of statistical data is not an end in itself. It is an instrument through which we can cope with the larger problems of historical understanding. The apparatus of statistics, the data themselves, the courses in method, the technology, the projects to develop data banks and to facilitate communication of data, the perfection of documentation—if the development of these becomes an end in itself, the promise of statistical

*This article appeared in *Prologue* 1:2 (Fall 1969).

inquiry evaporates; we wind up being technically proficient but saying nothing of any value. At the same time, those who are skeptical of the new mood often see only these outward manifestations and react sharply against their growing importance to the profession; by throwing their weight against the use of quantifiable evidence they obscure the more important questions of structure and change which are at stake no matter what kind of evidence is used. It should be remembered that in the present context we are concerned not with ends but with means to ends.

Examples of the development and use of statistical data are legion. A review of some of them will illustrate the range and variety of archival materials involved. The use of economic statistics— prices, production, wages—is so well known and well established that there is no need to do more than mention it. The availability of several types of political data—voting returns, legislative roll calls, and characteristics of political leaders—is also now well known. The joint project of the Inter-University Consortium for Political Research at Ann Arbor and the Committee on Quantitative Data of the American Historical Association has been widely advertised. Its massive amount of voting data will soon be through the final proofing stage and ready for use, and before long its county-level demographic data from the U.S. published census returns will also be available. Studies have already appeared that show the enormous value for historical inquiry of the kind of data that are in the consortium's file.[1]

But other less well-known projects illustrate more effectively the far-reaching implications of statistics for historical research and the importance of all kinds of archival collections. Several researchers, for example, are using the original manuscript federal census returns for 1850, 1860, 1870, and 1880, in addition to manuscript state census returns. Stephan Thernstrom, in his book on social mobility in Newburyport, Mass., 1850–80, makes extensive use of these data; he is now drawing upon similar material for a study of mobility in Boston.[2] Laurence A. Glasco of the State University of New

1. For a description of the ICPR project, see Inter-University Consortium for Political Research, *Annual Report*, 1963–64, 1964–65, and 1965–66, *passim*. The context of research in which the project has taken place is described fully in Allan G. Bogue, "United States: The 'New Political History,'" *Journal of Contemporary History* 3 (1968), 5–27.

2. Stephan Thernstrom, *Poverty and Progress* (Cambridge, Mass., 1964).

York at Buffalo is computerizing data for Buffalo from the manuscript New York State census, the schedules of which are more extensive than those of the federal census; moreover, the New York records are open to scholars up to the last census in 1925, while the last useful federal census is 1880.[3] Another project under way based on similar material is Jonathan Levine's doctoral dissertation at Cornell University, a study of agricultural labor in New York State in the last half of the nineteenth century.

Thus there is wide interest in data about individuals. Sam B. Warner, Jr., for example, made use of several thousand building permits in his study of Boston's suburbs.[4] Robert Doherty, using data from a variety of sources, constructed collective biographies of members of different church denominations to study religious conflicts in the 1830s and 1840s.[5] Doherty is now using a variety of statistics about individuals—federal censuses, city directories, city tax records—to reconstruct the social structure of five New England cities between 1800 and 1850. Peter Knights is using city directories to reconstruct the population of Boston in the first half of the nineteenth century; and Walter Glazer is doing the same for Cincinnati, Stuart Blumin at Skidmore College for Philadelphia, Michael Katz at the University of Toronto for Hamilton, Ontario, and Clyde Griffin at Vassar College for Poughkeepsie. Guido Dobbert at Youngstown State University is constructing a collective biography of 3,000 members of a German pioneer society in Cincinnati in the nineteenth century.

There are other examples of statistical studies: merchants in colonial Massachusetts; the location, circumstances, and leadership of slave revolts; discipline within the Presbyterian Church in Virginia during the nineteenth century; the social system of Dedham, Massachusetts, in the seventeenth and early eighteenth centuries, and of Kent and Sudbury; and the Trempeleau County study.[6] One

3. Herbert G. Gutman and Laurence A. Glasco used New York census data for their study of the nineteenth-century Negro family; see their report, "The Buffalo, New York, Negro, 1855–1875: A Study of the Family Structure of Free Negroes and Some of Its Implications," presented at the Wisconsin Conference on the History of American Political and Social Behavior, Madison, Wis., May 16–17, 1968.

4. Sam B. Warner, Jr., *Streetcar Suburbs* (Cambridge, Mass., 1962).

5. Robert Doherty, *The Hicksite Separation* (New Brunswick, 1967); "Social Bases for the Presbyterian Schism of 1837–1838," *Journal of Social History* 2 (1968), 69–79.

6. Bernard Bailyn and Lotte Bailyn, *Massachusetts Shipping, 1697–1714: A Statistical*

field of statistical inquiry less well developed is content analysis. Richard Merritt's use of newspaper content to describe the growth of a self-consciousness by Americans in the eighteenth century was a pioneering effort.[7] Louis Galambos has described the agrarian image of the large corporation between 1880 and 1920.[8]

While these examples are by no means exhaustive, they serve to illustrate the wide variety of projects and materials being used and the open-endedness of this new development. The possibilities seem enormous, and simply because of this historians are not in agreement upon precisely what kinds of statistical data can be used, or, more important, what materials not immediately in quantitative form are susceptible to quantitative treatment. We now see in progress a rush to the sources to find out what data are available and how they can be used, and we are only at the beginning stages of this process. But since we now have the necessary technical capability, the large mass of data in the record—formerly relatively untouched—are researchable. From this development two questions arise for archivists: first, what are the implications of this for records management, for the preservation of evidence produced currently for future use by historians; and second, what is available and how can it be used?

As the historian interested in social research observes the archival record, he is acutely aware of the bias that exists in the making and preserving of documentary materials and the enormous impact of that bias on historical writing. In the first place, records for the future are manifestly oriented toward what the individual or institution in the present wants to keep for his or its own use. This means that few historical records, and in this instance historical statistics, are made that can describe long-range social change. At best

---

Study (Cambridge, 1959); Marion D. deB. Kilson, "Towards Freedom: An Analysis of Slave Revolts in the United States," *Phylon* 25 (1964), 175–87; W.D. Blanks, "Corrective Church Discipline in the Presbyterian Churches of the Nineteenth Century South," *Journal of Presbyterian History* 44 (1966), 89–105; Kenneth A. Lockridge, *A New England Town: The First Hundred Years, Dedham, Massachusetts, 1636–1736* (New York, 1970); Charles S. Grant, *Democracy in the Frontier Town of Kent* (New York, 1961); Sumner Chilton Powell, *Puritan Village: the Formation of a New England Town* (Middletown, Conn., 1963); Merle C. Curti, *The Making of an American Community* (Palo Alto, 1959).

7. Richard L. Merritt, *Symbols of American Community, 1735–1775* (New Haven, 1966).

8. Louis Galambos, "The Agrarian Image of the Large Corporation, 1879–1920: A Study in Social Accommodation," *Journal of Economic History* 28 (1968), 341–62.

they may pertain to short-range social change of the kind necessary to justify to a government agency or foundation that an investment has paid off. Few such organizations are concerned about measuring yield in fifty- or one hundred-year spans. At the same time, social scientists are overwhelmingly present—let us say "now"— minded; their interest in data is in the analysis of current problems rather than social change. It is conceivable that evidence could be generated for the purpose of describing long-run social change, but it is not. And because the historical record is thus oriented toward the present, the historian himself is biased toward describing history in terms of a sequence of current-situation events rather than in terms of social change. The weight of the bias in the evidence has been too great for most historians to escape.

There is bias, secondly, in the preservation of historical records, a bias toward national visibility. The most likely candidates for survival are the records of the national leader, the national event, the national government, the nationwide business or association. At the state and local level the record of the more prominent member of the social order is more often preserved—his biography in the city or county history, his genealogy, his professional organization, his institution. At times it is the "old families" who become interested in preserving material; more frequently it is the institution, the church, the university, the government, the corporation, which has had a long life and which will continue to live beyond the life span of any one individual. It is not only a matter of what part of the record is preserved but what part is preserved more carefully, described more precisely, indexed, microfilmed, and made more readily available. These choices of the allocation of archival resources involve a crucial decision as to what is more and what is less important. They have considerable effect on what is researched in history. The weight of the record about the prominent individual or the national event and the ready accessibility of that record to the historian entice him into a subject for research built upon that record. All too often, in fact, the historian defines what he wishes to study in terms of the availability of evidence. In more than one instance a young historian has embarked upon a career because the papers of Mr. Prominent Citizen have been left at his institution and no one has yet looked at them. The greater accessibility of evidence about national events, along with the tendency of the history profession to confer more prestige upon national than local history, has steered interest toward the top level of society and politics.

Historical social research, however, starts out from a different perspective. Since it is concerned with structure and change, it involves categories of structure and change and defines historical problems as different facets of those general frameworks: economic development, social mobility, social organization, the evolution of socioeconomic levels of human relationships, migration. One then searches for evidence which will describe these patterns and changes. Often it is learned that many relevant data have been saved, even though they have not been readily developed for use; for instance, about 98 percent of all county voting returns since 1824 for the presidential, gubernatorial, and congressional elections have been found extant in one form or another. But one also finds how often similar evidence has been destroyed as being of lesser priority when a selection for preservation was made. This discovery is all the more frustrating to the social researcher because his problem is the crucial point of departure, and he does not find it inviting to shift to another topic just because the evidence is lacking. Instead he continues to search for more evidence and to find imaginative ways of using the evidence he has, hoping that patterns will emerge that are relevant to his problem.

There is still another facet of this search—the desire for greater objectivity. Many historians of the twentieth century have maintained a certain sloppy and careless attitude toward the past, often called relativism. Some have elevated this approach to the level of faith and doctrine. In such a view there may be a reluctance to look for the kind of evidence that can place some degree of limits, in the interest of greater objectivity, upon historical work. Much of the new mood in history arises from case studies in which the data used have upset prior notions based upon less complete and more traditional evidence. Studies of election returns, for example, have shown that Germans in 1860 voted not Republican, as German newspaper editors claimed, but Democratic in Iowa and according to religious affiliation in Pittsburgh.[9] Collective biographic data

9. George Daniels, "Immigrant Vote in the 1860 Election: The Case of Iowa," *Mid-*

have shown that the movement for reform in municipal government in the Progressive Era came not from the general public or the middle class but from the upper levels of the political order.[10] Statistics on the distribution of property indicate sharp inequalities throughout American history and raise doubts about conclusions based upon qualitative evidence by such authors as Matthew Josephson, Douglas Miller, or Frederick Lewis Allen.[11]

There are two important facets of the search for greater objectivity beyond the mere revision of description. One is the question of representativeness. How do individual cases relate to the larger whole? Traditionally, historians have been willing to make that jump intuitively. But now we prefer a systematic study to make sure that our case is typical. Was Andrew Carnegie, for example, typical, and are we justified in using him as representative of a group of business leaders to describe their background, their role in the economic or political order, or their ideas? A study now under way of several hundred Pittsburgh iron and steel leaders in the last half of the nineteenth century shows clearly that Carnegie was the most atypical, the least representative, of them all.[12] But to answer the question of typicality we are required to reconstruct the characteristics of the larger population from which we seek to draw a representative set of examples, and for this, in turn, we need a large amount of statistical data. But the data give our inquiry objective limits, and the vagaries of sheer intuitive and often traditional preference are avoided.

The second aspect of objectivity is the description of variation. Traditionally, historians have been prone to dichotomize historical description, to categorize in terms of mutually exclusive groups, such as political liberalism and conservatism, the rich and the poor, the blacks and the whites. Or, on the other hand, there is the tendency to think in terms of homogeneous characteristics throughout

---

America 44 (1962), 146–62; Paul J. Kleppner, "Lincoln and the Immigrant Vote: A Case of Religious Polarization," *ibid.* 48 (1966), 176–95.

10. Samuel P. Hays, "The Politics of Reform in Municipal Government in the Progressive Era," *Pacific Northwest Quarterly* 55 (1964), 157–69.

11. Matthew Josephson, *The Robber Barons* (New York, 1934); Douglas Miller, *Jacksonian Aristocracy* (New York, 1967); Frederick Lewis Allen, *The Big Change* (New York, 1952).

12. John Ingham, "Pittsburgh's Industrial Upper Class," paper presented at the first annual History Conference, Duquesne Univ., Nov. 1967.

society, of aggregate economic description, of uniformities in "national character"—those conditions or patterns of value and thought that are characteristic of the entire society. But those who work with empirical social data under a minimum of preconceptions, and who seek to discover the patterns of human characteristics in the data itself, know that neither dichotomies nor homogeneities are very widespread. Variation obtains in almost every human attribute, and historical description is woefully inadequate unless it is cast in terms of the patterns of variation. The search for an objective description of variation does not require quantitative data, but they obviously facilitate such a search and render it far more precise.

We have long suspected, for example, the close connection between political preferences and the degree of commercialization of geographic areas, but the relationship has been rough and approximate. In one recent doctoral dissertation the relationship was developed in terms of a variable, and it was thereby far more firmly established.[13] In that study an index of commercialization, from highest to lowest, was constructed for all of the more than 300 towns in Massachusetts in the 1780s. The towns were then grouped into deciles for convenience and related to percentage of votes for popular office in the 1780s, on issues in the General Court in the same decade, and on the ratification of the federal Constitution. Voting on these issues was found to vary systematically with the degree of commercialization, showing not only a relationship but a systematic ordering of the politically active impulses throughout the range of Massachusetts life in the 1780s. Such systematic variation disproves, as a simple matter of description, that Massachusetts politics then was a chaotic personal factionalism or that political parties alone brought system and order into political impulses. A description of this systematic variation would not, of course, have been possible without archival statistical data, which, fortunately, government agencies in Massachusetts have preserved.

Historical social research, therefore, requires a considerable shift in attitudes in archival management, in preserving and developing records for use. We must make available records that permit a rich variety of disaggregate description, for that alone makes pos-

13. Van Beck Hall, *Politics Without Parties; Massachusetts, 1780-1791* (Pittsburgh, 1972).

sible the reconstruction of a social system. We must not permit the prestige symbols of national life, which invade more and more of our consciousness, to exclude materials from all levels of society. In fact, since prominent institutions will probably continue to preserve much of their own record, we must make a special effort to see that data about the middle and lower levels of the social order are preserved because evidence at these levels is most frequently missing, and its absence gives the social researcher the greatest frustration. As the new mood in history grows it will undoubtedly exercise more influence in archival affairs. It is imperative that the interests of the historian, rather than of current-situation-minded institutions, produce the choices about preservation and development of archival data. And this requires that historians make known their needs more precisely to archivists.

Many types of statistical records for historical research are so well known and obvious that there is no need to stress them here. But there are several that deserve more attention than they have been given. The first concerns records of individuals. As many of the previously cited examples indicate, historical social research places a considerable emphasis on the collective characteristics of large numbers of people. In preserving information about individuals it is no longer sufficient to think about extensive manuscripts in the personal collections of a few prominent persons. We must be interested also in smaller amounts of information about large numbers of individuals at every level of society. It is instructive to note that social research has been undertaken concerning those segments of public employment for which personnel data are extensive—for example, military service. Several studies have been made of military history in the context of historical sociology. Moreover, information about individuals against whom public action is taken is equally important; in several current studies of riots information from police files is being used to determine personal characteristics of the rioters. The most extensive of these now in progress concerns riots in France in the nineteenth century, but one dissertation has been completed concerning riots against antislavery agitators in the North.[14] Records of Japanese-Americans would be an excellent ex-

14. Charles Tilly of the Dept. of Sociology at the Univ. of Toronto is undertaking a

ample of the kind of data on individuals that is needed.[15]

Federal personnel records constitute one of the most important sources of genealogical data. Genealogy has, of course, long been in disrepute among historians because it seemed to have little relevance to the serious business of understanding the past. Yet an increasing number of problems in historical social research rest upon the development of genealogical information: social mobility, the family, socioeconomic classes, intergenerational change among ethnic and racial groups, changes in leadership patterns. Much historical social research has been done for seventeenth- and eighteenth-century America, and one of the factors responsible for this is the availability of genealogical information for that period. The study of patterns of family development promises to become an increasingly important and respectable aspect of the study of history. And the ready availability of genealogical information will increasingly be at a premium. With this in mind, public personnel records—and federal records are a major part of these—will be vital. Preservation and ready availability of military records has been crucial in past genealogical research, and microfilm publication of the manuscript federal census records has become increasingly important as a source of genealogical and biographical data. Federal personnel records of all kinds should become available for genealogical research, even if they must remain in a restricted status for a period of time.

A second type of evidence that deserves special attention is original statistical data from which published materials are drawn. The purpose for which such data are gathered is peculiar to time and place; given a time interval of fifty years, perhaps even less, the kinds of categories in which data is desired drastically change. In most cases classifications and cross-classifications that can be generated from original raw data are far more numerous than those developed and published. The original manuscript federal census is an excellent case in point. Many historians are now aggregating these data by minor civil divisions to relate it to voting patterns on the same level; without the original sources this would have been

study of French riots; see also Leonard L. Richards, *Gentlemen of Property and Standing; Anti-Abolition Mobs in Jacksonian America* (New York, 1970).

15. James Paulauskas, "Statistics and Statistical Materials in the Records of the War Relocation Authority," paper presented at the Conference on the National Archives and Statistical Research, Washington, D.C., May 1968.

impossible, since most of the relevant data were published only at the county level of aggregation. The development of individual characteristics would, of course, have been impossible without the original sources.

As measurement by government agencies becomes a far more extensive practice, the amount of data accumulated becomes greater and the problem of records management compounded. One would not want to say that everything statistical should be preserved; yet it seems clear that historians should be involved more fully in such decisions than has been the case in the past. The problem of records management is primarily a matter of what historians need for future research. It makes no sense to ask people fundamentally uninterested in long-range social change to make decisions about preserving data that will eventually be used to describe such change. Unless historians can play an important role in such decisions, they will in the future be without significant statistical data that could easily have been preserved.

Third, historical social research brings into focus a shift in historical problems, and therefore of historical evidence, from the top levels of national society to the middle and grass-roots levels. But this is very difficult to achieve unless evidence—and in this case statistical data—is available that describes the characteristics of each level and the interaction among all three. Preservation of historical records has, in the past, emphasized the national personality, event, and administrative or legislative action. The new emphasis on statistics and social data requires more effort in the preservation of local —city, town, and county—records. But it also involves the preservation of local federal records. Federal administration reaches down to the grass roots, and the record of what happens there is as integral a part of the entire federal historical record as is that of what happens in Washington. Yet we are constantly faced with the fact that preservation has favored the national rather than the local context and that many records of the local operation of federal programs have been destroyed. While this is not true in all cases, it has happened often enough for this to be a major problem.

An excellent example of this is the fact that accounts of the home front during World War I have remained almost entirely on the national level. Yet two studies of changes in the popular vote between 1914 and 1920 suggest that the key to the massive shift toward the Republican party that began in 1918 lies not at the level of national politics as such but at the local level because of the adverse effect of national wartime policies.[16] The local impact of rationing programs, for example, contributed significantly to a political shift. Yet almost no records are available of the local operation of wartime agencies based in Washington, and very few are available even among records of the state councils of defense. Past records-management policies render it extremely difficult to describe this important aspect of the impact of World War I.

There is a fourth area of archival record preservation that deserves special mention: legal and judicial records—not simply those of the formal judicial branches but also those of the quasi-judicial functions of administrative agencies. The historical-social analysis of law in its application is in its infancy. Several research projects, some sponsored by the American Bar Association, are under way. The most extensive of these have concerned English legal history. But there is no reason why they will not appear rapidly in the context of American history. This material, of course, is not formally statistical, but it is susceptible to statistical treatment. Patterns of judicial decision, of juries and their decisions, of development and change in the application of law will arise out of data not about single cases but about masses of cases, and this will require quantification and statistical manipulation. Judicial records have a way of being preserved, but stress should be placed upon their importance for historical research and especially upon their ready accessibility to researchers.

Archivists can be more effective in preserving materials for historical social research, but they can also make existing records more readily available, for many extant manuscripts contain material that is statistical or susceptible to statistical treatment. The current mood of social research is drawing upon this record in a host of federal, state, and local archives, and these have only begun to be tapped. The most immediate problem is to make them more widely available and to facilitate their use by researchers. The consortium

16. John Thomas Schou, "The Decline of the Democratic Party in Iowa, 1916–1920," M.A. thesis, Univ. of Iowa, 1960; Joseph Makarewicz, "The Impact of World War I on Pennsylvania Politics," Ph.D. diss. in preparation, Univ. of Pittsburgh.

political data project will open up vast amounts of political and related data for ready use. Yet, amid all the researchable problems that historians are beginning to consider, the consortium will provide data for only a few. Most will require a far broader range of evidence, much too costly to machine-process. It is feasible, however, to improve accessibility to these materials.

Toward this end it would be very helpful if historians could be better informed of the types of statistical data available in the National Archives. Information about statistical collections in the archives is available in the preliminary inventories of the record groups, but these are often incomplete, difficult to use, and inadequate for our purposes. The same type of descriptive information is sorely needed at the state level, and it would be helpful if archivists could stimulate the dissemination of information about those sources.

These statistical collections should certainly be made more widely available, and microfilm offers the most practical method. Microfilm projects should be pressed forward rapidly. The fact that the federal manuscript census has been readily available in this form has played a major role in its use for historical research. At comparatively little cost, with such sums as are available from tight university research budgets, many institutions have purchased particular sections of the census for specific projects. Tax lists from the 1790s play an equally important role; and the current project to microfilm the Civil War tax lists will have an enormously stimulating effect on Civil War research of all kinds. It is of course important that federal records on microfilm be available at the university library, for the graduate student level of work as well as the more advanced level. The successful introduction of students to social research can come at the beginning of a graduate career, but without data readily at hand the task of demonstrating to students the possibilities of working with them is much more difficult.

The National Archives has, of course, taken the lead in microfilming historical statistical data. In the past choices as to microfilming have been made frequently in terms of pressure for use from those outside the mainstream of historical research, such as genealogists who use the manuscript census returns, elderly persons who wish to establish their age for social security purposes, or archivists who wished to prevent deterioration of the originals from intensive use. In recent years it has become clear that archivists are seeking to microfilm more in terms of the needs of historians generally. But it is not clear that those involved in historical social research have made their wants known in some systematic manner to the National Archives. This should be done. For the mood of historical social research is one of searching for data relevant to the examination of problems designed from a conceptual framework of structure and process. In this search the archivist can play an increasingly important role, but not unless the historian makes clear what kinds of records would be most useful for photoreproduction.

There is need for some kind of continuing liaison between the National Archives and historians specifically concerning historical statistics. There are, of course, committees already in existence that have established effective relationships between the historical profession and the federal government. But these committees are concerned for the most part with the older type of historical record—personal manuscripts, for example—rather than with statistical data, and cannot give sufficiently strong focus to the development of such material for historical social research. It would be logical to develop special ties between the National Archives and the North American Section of the Committee on Quantitative Data of the American Historical Association as a way of facilitating communication between the two groups.

The use of statistics in historical inquiry is undoubtedly in its infancy. We have no idea how far it can or will go. There is no need to make any claims for its role in terms of ultimate historical knowledge, to insist that it provides the only significant source of evidence for historical research, or to argue that continuing efforts should not be devoted to preserving qualitative historical records. The problem should be approached on a simpler and more pragmatic level. The important point is that there is a large part of the historical record that is either statistical or susceptible to statistical treatment and that for the most part it remains relatively untapped. We know that this evidence has added and can continue to add considerably to the range and precision of historical description. We make no pretense that it will lead to absolute or completely objective knowledge—indeed, we expect that some day when it has been extensively used we will have exhausted its possibilities. In the meantime, however, this evidence can be brought into the active life of historical research, and the description of the past will be much richer, far more varied, and more complete than is now the case.

[15]

*History and the Changing University Curriculum**

URING the past few years there has been considerable experimentation with the college and university history curriculum. Some of it has focused on the method of presentation—the use of visual media, for example. Some has stressed the debates among historians about historical problems—the Amherst Series and its successors. Some has dealt with current issues of race, poverty, and war, organizing past material to cope with current problems. Here I wish to develop an argument for a different alternative, for a curriculum based on different contexts of human life in terms of social structure, and social change. We should organize our courses, so the argument goes, in a way that will facilitate the student's understanding of systematic varieties of human experience in the past, and thereby facilitate entry into varieties of human experience in the present.

The basic problem in any history curriculum is conceptual: what are the ideas about past society which serve as the organizing principles at the core of subordinate concepts and detail? What is the conceptual context within which the student should define problems and undertake analysis? It is confusion over this conceptual context that creates confusion over the curriculum. We often seek to find answers in different methods of presentation. But this usually only confuses the issue further by ignoring it, for it fails to deal with the problem of conceptual framework, of alternatives in ideas as to

*This article is a slightly revised version of a paper read at the annual meeting of the Organization of American Historians in Chicago, Apr. 12, 1973; it was published in *The History Teacher* 8 (1974). Copyright, Society for History Education, Inc., 1974. Reprinted by permission.

what a society was like and how it changed over time. Unless we are clear about our own social theory, we will never be clear about the social theory we wish to transfer to our students and, hence, the social theory which underlies the conceptual content of our courses.

The appropriate link between social theory and the curriculum, I would argue, is the attempt to focus history courses on people in the past and their varied life-settings. In organizing what we teach we should come back to people who have particular experiences, display particular kinds of behavior, and have certain relationships with other people. We should constantly recreate for the student's entry into the past a variety of such types of human settings. We should focus on the shared patterns of experience and values of people in history and their differences in different settings. Historical questions arise out of the relationship of people in different circumstances and changes in these over time. And the relationship between students and the past, that is, the teaching process, can be considered primarily as the attempt to facilitate transfer back and forth between the experience of the present and the experience of the past.

This is quite different from the way we now organize the curriculum, for much of our history is not focused on people. Often, for example, we deal with what historians argue about. As a result the world into which we lead the student is one of historians arguing with each other. Students read different points of view about what caused the Civil War and that only transfers their imagination into the context of historians debating rather than the context of past human life. Or we frequently focus courses on the artifacts people create rather than on people themselves. Intellectual history has suffered this fate. It has often abstracted ideas from human context so as to play with the idea itself, its internal meaning and its logical implications. The people with those ideas are soon left in the background. We should focus on *people*, people who have ideas, experiences, values. Our task is to recreate the variety of experiences and perceptions of the world in the past, rather than to spin out the logical meaning of the idea as human artifact.

The most immediate and obvious implication of a curricular focus on human setting is to organize courses not around countries and time periods, as is the custom, but around thematic problems concerning the types of human contexts of life. We should start out with the different ways in which people order their lives, the different activities in which they engage, the different focal points of their experience and practice, the different ways in which they change or do not change, and use each of these as the subject matter of a course. Such courses might deal with the family, the community, the city, or the region; religion or education or legal institutions; mobility—geographical, psychological, or vertical; types of structural patterns in human relationships, such as ethnocultural, socioeconomic, local-cosmopolitan, or managerial and administrative.

There is one other principle of curricular organization which is implied by all this: courses should be comparative, that is, should compare different expressions of similar human settings. Customarily we are inclined to bring together a great number of facets of history into a single national context. A comparative approach to different aspects of human life suggests another principle of organization, that we bring into a single focus of study different expressions of a similar human context from many areas and periods. The history of the family, for example, provides comparisons and contrasts from every continent and from widely varying periods of time. The method of inquiry, and the method of teaching as well, involves the constant question: how is this phenomenon—the family —similar in all these cases and how is it different? In what way is the response to modernization in one time and place similar to that in another and how is it different?

All this is very general. Let me outline some more specific types of courses which it implies. There are several categories of concepts around which courses can be built: geographical contexts, structural settings, functional activities, and processes of change. Let me draw from each of these to illustrate possibilities.

One of the most useful courses for emphasizing a wide variety of historical phenomena is the comparative study of the community. In this context one can deal with patterns of vertical social structure and the correspondingly varied aspects of life and value; ethnic, religious, and racial relationships; family life and intergenerational relationships; and mobility of all kinds. Comparisons of rural, town, and urban communities provide a broader setting. There is even a wider opportunity for study if the comparison goes beyond a given country or period. In the study of community, students can identify with people and their daily activities in a way that facilitates teaching. Let me describe two outcomes of a course in the History of the Community in America which has been taught at the University of Pittsburgh for the past six years.

One was a spinoff course on comparative Athenian and American Democracy, which focused on the Greek and the American communities. A dozen or so upper-division students were enrolled, all of whom were interested in either a contemporary social science or twentieth-century history. By working back and forth between the American and the Greek context these students became deeply involved in history per se. One member of the seminar is now in our graduate program, working on the history of eighteenth-century French elites. Another variant was a freshman seminar in which the class as a group project studied the community of Homestead, Pennsylvania. They read the account of Homestead in the Pittsburgh Survey, interviewed elderly people living in Homestead, and carried out a survey study of students in one high school. The result was an appreciation of and concern for facets of community life— for example, the elderly—which they had not had before. They came face to face with one of those knotty aspects of urban history, that even though we as outsiders might find a community repugnant, many who have lived there for years consider it home, a "nice place to live," and without "problems." The familiar "old ways" of grass-roots life are a powerful conservative force in history; in their community interviewing the students met this head-on.

A second type of course focuses more broadly upon different contexts of social structure in general, not confined to a given community. Two of the more obvious of these are ethnocultural and socioeconomic relationships. To those who teach in urban colleges and universities the possibilities of organizing courses around the theme of evolving patterns of ethnocultural relationships should be obvious. For example, 70 percent of the students in a general survey course at the University of Pittsburgh might well be second- or third-generation migrants from Europe, and another 10 percent second- or third-generation black urban migrants from the rural South. By focusing on patterns of human relationships both within each ethnocultural group and among them, one can deal with a wide variety of historical problems and link these closely with the student's contemporary experience.

To do this most effectively the course should be organized in a particular way. First, it should compare a variety of ethnocultural groups. When one emphasizes the family, for example, changes in the number of children, or the age of birth of the last child, or the extended lives of parents after their last child is grown can be brought out far more effectively if similarities and differences among various ethnocultural groups are dealt with. Second, the internal evolution of different ethnocultural groups must be elaborated. Each one develops its own internal social structure and its own particular geographical dispersion of that structure. College students know very well where they fit in terms of degrees of cosmopolitanness or vertical mobility among the variety of individuals within their ethnocultural group. That understanding is an excellent point of departure for elaborating upon the internal structure of ethnocultural groups generally. Third, the stratification of ethnocultural groups in relation to each other should serve as a major context of course organization. In all of these a focus on change over time is essential. How does the internal pattern of a specific ethnocultural group develop under the impact of modernization, and how is this process similar or different for different groups?

Socioeconomic patterns provide an equally effective setting for course organization. Here is a curious aspect of American history writing and teaching. While our historiography has contained strong elements of economic causation in society and politics, it has placed almost no emphasis on socioeconomic inequality as a context for study. I refer not just to poverty; this is only a limited part of it. I include inequality all up and down the vertical scale as a differentiated set of conditions of life growing out of differences in occupation, income, and standard of living, with distinctions within as well as between the upper, middle, and lower levels. Such inequalities are pervasive throughout American history and history generally. Students can understand the reality of inequality no matter where they stand in the pecking order. That some have more and some have less; that my family stands in a particular position within this order; that the white-collar world I am involved in has a wide range of inequalities; that I am making choices about my life involving where I wish to rank—all this is very much a part of the student's personal experience through which that student can be conveyed into a wide variety of similar human settings throughout history. Once that reality has been laid before the student in a teaching situation and the student has entered it, then the imagination can be clued into similar human situations in the past that cannot be directly experienced.

Recently a student talked with me about a community study he was doing for my survey course in American history. His father had been a piano tuner, and as a young man he had gone with his father regularly to tune pianos in houses of a wide range of socioeconomic levels. Our discussion revealed a remarkable sensitivity on his part to those socioeconomic differences: the different kinds of music played, the different room arrangements and uses, the location of the piano within the house, the size and decor of the houses. I tried to move his thinking from this experience to both the broader contemporary world and the past in the context of the same kind of phenomenon. I think that history, for him, was a little bit different after all this. It made sense in a different way.

The various functional aspects of life provide excellent opportunities for curricular organization: religion, education, recreation, artistic creation, or legal institutions. Any one of these involves many people in many places at many times. To deal with them not as abstract institutions but as contexts of life provides an excellent curricular setting. Shift the focus of religious history, for example, from denominations and theologies to values, the orientations of people in their preferences both for larger world views and specific daily living. Once this shift is made, entry into the student's imagination is far more likely. Discovery of the ethnocultural bases of voting behavior in the nineteenth-century United States has led to some significant possibilities here. These analyses order religious characteristics not by denomination or theology, but by widely shared personal values. They provide an opportunity for entering the experience of the German Confessional Lutheran or the Swedish Baptist, for example, and of relating to those religious value orientations a host of ways of life including political party preference.

It is curious how historians have ignored the potential for dealing with many simple facets of daily life as clues to larger meaning in the past. Consider, for example, legal institutions. We have given major attention to constitutional law. But look at it from another point of view, namely, the network of legal arrangements in which the individual is involved in daily life: courts, lawyers, police authorities, property ownership and taxes, marriage and divorce proceedings. These involvements abound in many times and places. Were we to organize our curriculum around such pervasive contexts of life, were we to see people through the network of legal institutions which surround them, we could lead students into the lives of people in similar circumstances in an innumerable number of times and places. And the same could be said for the history of education, not as institution but as setting for human life, of recreation and leisure, of creative activity.

Let us take still another tack: courses based upon types of processes of social change in which human beings have been involved. The increasingly popular context of modernization, applied even to American history, provides many examples, focal points of the constant interaction of the more traditional and the more modern. Consider two examples. In seventeenth-century Massachusetts John Eliot missionized the Indians, the "praying Indians." But in larger terms this involved the impact of more modern ways brought by the Puritans upon the more traditional Indian life. Eliot taught the Indians to live in a different physical arrangement—square houses with chimneys placed in regular order; to bury their dead in rows in cemeteries, each mound with a name marker; to become artisans. And in the course of events a conflict emerged between the more traditional and the more modernized Indians. For some aspects of history this conflict within the Indian community was more significant than that between the Indian and Puritan in Massachusetts.

The student can enter into this drama of the conflict between past and present by experiencing a similar conflict in his own life. Each year I have my students write a four-generation family genealogy. Into this genealogy I urge them to bring transformations of religion, place of residence, education, vertical mobility, generational relationships, almost every aspect of human life that can be seen through the context of the family. Invariably the student is brought face to face with the interaction between the past and present. As the third-generation descendants of Polish coal-miners in

America trace the change from grandparents to parents to themselves they experience firsthand the interaction between the more traditional and the more modern. From this student experience it is easy to lead imagination into a wide variety of similar settings concerning the tension between tradition and modernity.

For both learning and teaching this kind of focus for the history curriculum has considerable imaginative potential. This is a useful and telling way of evaluating the curriculum: how much imaginative potential does it have? How much potential for taking students from where they are as human beings, in a given setting, and leading their minds out into the vicarious experience of other human beings, in other settings at other times and other places? In my experience most of our courses don't have this kind of potential. As a result they seem remote from life, from reality, and the setting provides little opportunity for leading students very far from where they are. A curricular focus on types of human settings provides far more possibility of opening up the human mind to varieties of human experience and human institutions elsewhere.

In thinking about curriculum development, therefore, we should start out with notions about the types of human settings we want to deal with and their imaginative potential for transferring human experience from the present to the past and the past to the present. The examples given above—family, community, inequality, religion, education, legal institutions, processes of modernization, and various kinds of mobility—all these are different settings which flow from such a perspective. They are not simply different subject matter, distinct and separated in terms of logical categories, but are different ways of recapturing the varied aspects of human life and experience. They come to mind readily by focusing back on people, particular people with particular experiences and particular views of the world, in particular settings of structure and process. This kind of base for the construction of a curriculum provides imaginative potential for both learning and teaching.

Let me stress again the potential of the comparative approach. We are speaking here of types of experience, setting, and behavior that recur often in many times and places, but in different expressive forms. This provides the setting for comparative history. In comparative history we take a facet of human life which has both general and particular elements; it has characteristics in common, for example, the family, about which one can form general notions, and it also has characteristics for each instance which are distinctive, about which one can inquire as to the peculiarities of that distinctiveness. The more we can place our curriculum in a comparative setting, the more we will be able to expand the significance of what is learned and taught, both in the scholarly sense of making precise generalizations and in the experiential sense of sharpening the perception and imagination of students.

This approach is no different from that used, for example, by the taxonomist who develops categories that are both general and particular. There are characteristics which are common to all cases in a genus and those that sort out cases into species. The comparative question always then enters in. How are cases alike and how are they different? That question is one of the most powerful energizers of human imagination, simply because it is difficult for an inquisitive person to take a contrasting case of anything and to be completely neutral in the face of it. The question arises naturally: why the difference? The comparative setting is a learning and teaching device built into the subject matter itself. It raises questions; it arouses the human imagination. It is a far more powerful device for honing the human mind than is a simple new audiovisual twist to an old curricular content.

All this has several further pedagogical advantages. First, it provides an effective medium of two-way communication between student and teacher in which the student's experience and what the teacher seeks to convey intersect. My own experience with teaching in this manner and bringing in such student activities as genealogies and community studies indicates the possibility of bringing together both the factor of experience and the factor of self-conscious examination of that experience in a way that most other teaching devices cannot do. For the bases of communication are concepts about human life, past and present, and the process of understanding those concepts, and not just one's affective reaction to them.

Second, this approach brings somewhat closer the different perspectives of history and some of the social sciences. The social sciences are interested primarily in very short-run change, if any at all, and historians are interested in change over long periods of time. It is clear, of course, that in interaction with the social sciences, the historian cannot give up this long-run perspective. But it is equally clear that the historian's task can be made more significant if it is possible to work back and forth between various periods so as to link many and varied settings of human life. Many linkages are possible: between past and present, between teacher and student, between student and student, between student and family, community, or institutional involvement. The approach has innumerable possibilities for imaginatively linking human experience in many contexts.

Finally, all this helps to steer the disciplinary course which we should be taking in history. As we begin to focus on varieties of human settings in the past, we begin to realize that our study is, strictly speaking, neither a social science nor a humanities subject. Notice that I have not once mentioned quantitative data or techniques, nor have I utilized an instrumentalist tone—emphasized the need to learn about the past to solve the problems of the present. But I also have not stressed the study of those things which human beings produce, such as art, literature, and philosophy, because these often tend to become divorced from the context of human life and to be considered as artifacts to be studied for their own sake. Our task is to focus on the human content of history and to develop the conceptual framework which enables us to enter into that content effectively. This has important and exciting implications for the organization of the history curriculum, implications to which we should give far more attention in the years ahead.

[16]

History and Genealogy: Patterns of Change and Prospects for Cooperation*

I

Dᴜʀɪɴɢ the past decade or so a number of significant developents have occurred in both the history and genealogy fields. For the most part these trends have remained separate. The traditional separation of their activities, often accompanied by mutual disdain, has allowed historians to pay only slight attention to genealogy and genealogical activities and has divorced genealogists from the professional work of historians. A quick review of their publications indicates the degree to which both work in separate worlds.[1] Yet developments in these fields are moving in similar directions, sufficient to give rise to the notion that closer cooperation between them would be mutually advantageous.[2] When the social historian begins to work with family history and to focus on a broader network of kinship relationships over time, and the genealogist begins to spend time and effort in indexing the same manuscript census returns that historians use, it is time for the two groups to examine their common ground.

This essay attempts to foster such a relationship. It comes from the author's long involvement in both fields. On the one hand I have devoted considerable attention to working out concepts and

---

*This article appeared in three parts in *Prologue* 7:1,2,3 (Spring, Summer, and Fall 1975).

1. See, for contrast, *The Genealogical Helper* (Logan, Utah) and the *Journal of Social History* (Pittsburgh).

2. Historians will be especially interested in Philip R. Kunz (ed.), *Selected Papers in Genealogical Research*, Institute of Genealogical Studies, Brigham Young University (ca. 1972), which are studies in social history that draw upon the archives of the Church of Jesus Christ of Latter-Day Saints.

research resources for a more grass-roots type of social history; on the other, my first interest in history, some four decades ago, was through genealogy, which became a hobby that has persisted through the years. As social history has come to focus on family-related institutions, I have found the information and insights from genealogical investigations to be very helpful in dealing with matters such as migration and vertical mobility, changes in family size and life cycle, and the impact of modernization on traditional values and practices in religion, family, and recreation. All this suggests the enormously valuable role that a more informed and imaginative genealogy could play in broadening historical inquiry and insight.

At the same time I have been involved with attempts to make usable the large quantity of historical evidence available in archives of local, state, and national governments, as well as private sources, about the ordinary everyday activities of people, in order to provide the research base for more effective social history. I have been impressed with the fact that genealogists have gone after such records to a far greater extent than have historians. The federal manuscript census returns were used effectively initially by genealogists, and their work in indexing them for more rapid use has been prodigious. The focus on the county courthouse, where the great majority of the vital materials for social history still lies, has occupied the attention of genealogists far more than that of historians. In fact, the frequently expressed disdain by historians concerning the usefulness of these records, often allowed to decay by neglect, borders on archival irresponsibility.

Here I would like to develop the argument for a closer relationship between the new social history and the new genealogy. On one side, the concerns of historians can add a wider dimension to genealogy, and on the other the work of genealogists can provide crucial evidence for social history. Both, in turn, rely on the same records and could benefit from a common approach to preserving and organizing historical sources and to making them accessible.

The new trend in social history in America has come from dissatisfaction with a narrow political history, preoccupied with the big event, the dramatic and highly publicized episode. The traditional focus has been on the presidents, the wars, the dramatic election, the prominent writer. Now there is more interest in society as a whole. Since the concern of history now encompasses everyone in the social order there is a concerted attempt to seek information about as many in the entire population and their activities as possible. Over the last decade, for example, county, township, and precinct election returns have been used extensively to analyze voting patterns at the smallest geopolitical level.[3] One township or one ward votes differently from another, and the pattern persists over the years—why? Such an approach seeks to relate variations in voting to differences in group cultural values. But even these data are not individualized, and recently there has been an effort to ferret out what information remains in poll lists, individualized records of whether people voted or how they voted.[4] All this reflects a shift in focus toward the grass-roots and day-to-day human affairs.

Other aspects of grass-roots social life also soon came under scrutiny. The most extensive recent foray into the manuscript census returns has come from historians who study geographical and vertical mobility. This research requires information about individuals, for which the manuscript census returns are the most complete source. A number of these studies examine the degree of community in- and out-migration.[5] How many people there at the beginning of the decade leave by the end, or how many there at the end of the decade are newcomers? The evidence demonstrates a high degree of moving about, far more than we had previously believed. But the studies are limited because the manuscript census does not tell how far a person moved; it might have been only into

3. A good introduction to such studies is Joel H. Silbey and Samuel T. McSeveney, *Voters, Parties, and Elections: Quantitative Essays in the History of American Popular Voting Behavior* (Lexington, Mass., 1972). A study based upon urban small-unit voting data is John L. Shover, "The Emergence of a Two-Party System in Republican Philadelphia, 1924–1936," *Journal of American History* 50 (1974), 985–1002.
4. A review of current poll-book research and a case study of Greene County, Ill., is John M. Rozette and Paul E. McAllister, "Voting Behavior in the Late Jacksonian Period: The Conceptual and Methodological Significance of Poll Book Research," a paper delivered at the sixth annual Conference on Social and Political History at the State Univ. College at Brockport, N.Y., 1974.
5. The difficulties of tracing migration within the United States are dealt with effectively in Stephan Thernstrom and Peter R. Knights, "Men in Motion: Some Data and Speculations About Urban Population Mobility in Nineteenth-Century America," *Journal of Interdisciplinary History* 1 (1970), 7–35.

the next county, or it could have been several states distant. Mere departures, if added up, might give a false notion of extensive movement or in other ways distort the conclusions.

This problem immediately raises the possibility of genealogical inquiry that focuses on the life span of individuals and generations, the mini-mini-biographies from birth to death, which implicitly rivet attention on the place of residence in between. Full genealogical information would provide just the kind of data that migration studies require. Moreover, some of the most promising approaches to the vexing problem of "Where did they go?" use genealogical materials. One such study, now under way, is based upon pension records of Civil War soldiers from Allegheny County, Pennsylvania.[6] The pension records indicate their place of birth, their moves thereafter, and their place of death. From this research project the patterns of migration—the number and distance of moves—for at least one group of people will be described. Such moves are a fact of life for the genealogist, and much effort is spent trying to fill in the data lacking in the records. How simple it would be if each individual who moved had been required to record the place to which he went or from which he came.

The new social history has brought a variety of inquiries into the history of the family.[7] What have been the changes over the years in the size of family, the spacing of children, the activities and roles of young, middle-aged, and older people? Recent interest in youth and the elderly has stimulated new historical research in those fields. We hear of "life cycle" as an important way of looking at more general social change. We focus on the social relationships among members of the family, between husband and wife, and between parents and children. We describe the long-run change from male dominance to more coordinate relationships between parents, as well as changes in patterns of child rearing from the adult-centered to the child-centered to the adult-directed. Interest in the history of the family has given rise to a variety of conferences, and

6. Doctoral dissertation under way by David Pistolessi at the Univ. of Pittsburgh.
7. See, for example, Michael Gordon (ed.), *The American Family in Social-Historical Perspective* (New York, 1973).

there is a newsletter to stimulate communication among interested researchers.[8]

Social history has focused increasingly on vertical mobility, the changing occupational and educational levels of Americans as they move up or down the ladder from one rung to the next.[9] Who moves up or down, and who doesn't? The analysis has remained for the most part on the level of broad social characteristics: what percentage of people at one occupational level have children who move up or down to another; what percentage of people at one level of education have children who reach another level? All this can be examined with more insight within the context of the family. What is the family climate for occupational or educational mobility? Is there a drive for more education for the children or not? To what extent are occupations passed on from father to son, and to what extent is there an effort to move out of old patterns into new ones? Within the same family, changes in education and occupation vary with different children. And certainly the historical trend can be visualized as a sequence of general changes within several generations of the genealogical family.

The new interest in ethnic history has also stimulated research on the individual, the family, and the close network of community and kinship relationships that are reinforced by a common ethnic or racial background.[10] The concern for ethnic or racial identity can be explored in a general and aggregate manner with evidence drawn from ethnic sources, such as newspapers and religious documents, the writings of ethnic leaders or the fortunes of ethnic institutions. One can approach ethnic and cultural history through the medium of ideology, the self-conscious expression of identity. Yet the more fundamental context is the family itself, and the process by which

8. *The Family in Historical Perspective: An International Newsletter,* edited by Tamara K. Hareven and published by the Newberry Library, Chicago. Subscriptions are available through the Department of History, Clark University, Worcester, MA 01610.

9. Two excellent examples of work on vertical mobility are Howard P. Chudacoff, *Mobile Americans: Residential and Social Mobility in Omaha, 1880–1920* (New York, 1972) and Stephan Thernstrom, *The Other Bostonians: Poverty and Progress in the American Metropolis, 1880–1970* (Cambridge, 1973).

10. A review of recent trends in one aspect of ethnic history is Robert P. Swierenga, "Ethnocultural Political Analysis: A New Approach to American Ethnic Studies," *Journal of American Studies* 5 (1971), 59–79.

cultural values are retained or modified as they are passed from one generation to the next. The impact of modernizing tendencies on traditional ethnocultural loyalties can frequently be observed most clearly in the genealogical biography. Awareness of this has prompted an increasing number of teachers to ask their students to write such genealogies, as a means of developing ideas about long-run historical processes affecting ethnicity, religion, and family.[11]

More recently the history of women has received increasing attention.[12] Historians have long neglected many aspects of this subject, assuming that the history of women was covered adequately in general histories. But younger scholars have demonstrated that this is not at all the case. As they have investigated the role of women in the family, the community, religion, work, organizations, and public affairs, such as the antislavery crusade of the pre–Civil War years, their research has opened a variety of new fields of social history. The history of women is infused with many elements of the new social history: a concern with grass-roots life rather than national events and leaders and an interest in patterns of experience, life, and thought.

Current interest in social history can be followed in ways too numerous to detail here: a shift of focus in the history of religion from theology and denominational controversy to religious values as an important reflection of human outlooks and preferences; development of a new interest in the history of youth and childhood on the one hand and the elderly on the other; a concern for the history of recreation and leisure; a marked shift in labor history from preoccupation with trade unions to a focus on work and the human setting of work; and the history of the community, of the network of personal relationships that develop within the small geographical context of the home and its related institutions. Once the perspective shifted from national events and national history to social life

11. See Allen F. Davis and Jim Watts, *Generations: Your Family in Modern American History* (New York, 1974), a manual for stimulating student research in family history; and Samuel P. Hays, "History and the Changing University Curriculum," *The History Teacher* 8 (1974), 64–72.

12. An example of the new interest in the history of women is Susan J. Kleinberg, "Technology's Stepdaughters: The Impact of Industrialization Upon Working Class Women, Pittsburgh, 1865–1890," Ph.D. diss., Univ. of Pittsburgh, 1973.

within the entire society, the appropriate subjects for historical research encompassed all its activities.

A great number of questions being posed now by social historians focus on the family, its generational sequences and its kinship networks. What is being suggested is that a wide range of historical processes can be understood if seen within the context of patterns of relationships fashioned by the individual family and the intergenerational continuities or discontinuities brought out by genealogy. Rootedness within a community or migration can best be understood as choices not of isolated individuals but of individuals with different kinds and degrees of family relationships. Continuity or discontinuity of values, of customs and traditions, and of old and new perspectives can be seen in the degree to which one generation passes on those characteristics to another or ventures into new and different paths. Involvement in the processes of modernization, including education, new occupations, and new social attachments, is a differential process in which change can be best understood within the context of family values and activities.

Insofar as improved historical understanding can proceed in this fashion, and it certainly has enormous potential, the historian is moving toward the concerns of the genealogist. In terms of common subject matter the approach logically calls for a variant of family reconstitution to include several generations, what one might term genealogical reconstitution. The format could be an extension of the family genealogical charts so familiar to the genealogist and the family reconstitution charts developed by the Cambridge Group for the History of Population and Social Structure in England.[13] The basic data as well as the method of compilation for ready use could be worked out jointly by historians and genealogists. One such effort has already been promoted by bringing together family histories written by college students under the direction of history teachers, but the success of this venture, because of its large, nationwide scale, seems questionable. A more workable

13. The reader should examine *Local Population Studies*, a periodical based on the Cambridge Group's demographic studies. It serves as a link between historians studying local demography and the research center at Cambridge; it is published twice yearly in association with the Nottingham University Department of Adult Education, Nottingham, England.

form of cooperative genealogical reconstitution might well focus on mobilizing resources for community genealogy.

All this emphasizes information about individuals rather than collections of statistics and calls for the historian to take a major interest in preserving records of individuals. Until recently the majority of such records were local, rather than state and national. They were collected daily by local agencies in carrying out the functions of government. The few that were generated by national governmental activities, such as military service records and the federal census, have been the most carefully preserved and widely used. But only recently have historians begun to use such records, especially census records for migration studies, and rarely has the concern for individual data concentrated on use of state and local records.

In this area genealogists have taken the lead and shown the way. They have spent an enormous amount of energy in making the individual records available. There is hardly a manuscript census index among the several hundred counties that have been indexed for 1850 which has not been a product of genealogical activity.[14] Only one such project, to my knowledge, has been initiated by professional historians. For a host of counties there are now indexes to marriage records, early land records and deeds, mortality schedules, wills and probate proceedings, and tombstone inscriptions. In view of what needs to be done the work so far is only a beginning. But compared with the state of affairs two decades ago, the change is remarkable. It now seems accurate to state that if one wishes to become acquainted with the world of local records and the data about individuals in them, one turns to genealogical organizations, publications, and publishers.[15]

Historians and genealogists have been working independently of each other, and most historians do not see the wisdom of a closer relationship. But the new social history could profit greatly if the energies and activities of genealogists and local historians could be coordinated with those of historians. A major requirement is that

14. Progress in indexing can be followed regularly in the *Genealogical Helper*. For example, a genealogist, Sam McDowell of Richland, Ind., is indexing surnames in the 1850 federal population census for Kentucky. Others are indexing entire states for 1800, 1810, and 1820 or counties for later years. Few go beyond 1850.

15. Two such publishers are the Genealogical Publishing Co., Inc., of Baltimore and Polyanthos, Inc., of New Orleans.

historians develop a more active interest in genealogy and community history through the medium of genealogical reconstitution. Historians should use their influence and resources to encourage the preservation and use of local and family records and the effective entry into state and national records that provide genealogical information. The efforts of genealogists could be aided by the cooperation of historians.

The expansion of higher education in the past several decades, not only through the college and university but also in the community colleges, provides an excellent opportunity for historians in those institutions to encourage community history and genealogy. To encourage their students to write family genealogies as case studies of long-run social change is one method. For the institution to use its influence to see that these records are preserved is another. The development of effective oral history programs that have a broad social context and that are not limited to the leaders of the community is still another. In varied ways an institution of higher education can work closely with genealogists in the community to mobilize the resources that are of value to genealogists and historians.

II*

IF there is a new social history, there is also a new genealogy. The most casual observation of the sharply increased level of organizational activity and publications indicates that genealogy is far more popular and pervasive now than in years past. Circulation of the *Genealogical Helper,* the most widely known of the new publications, has grown rapidly in the past decade, and numerous state and regional organizations have produced magazines.[16] These serve as communication links whereby those searching for information about individuals and families can advertise their needs in the form

*Part II, copyright © 1977 by Samuel P. Hays.

16. The *Genealogical Helper,* founded in 1947, had a paid circulation of 24,000 in November 1974. Some organizations are statewide, such as the Virginia Genealogical Society of Richmond, Va.; some are regional within a state, such as the West-Central Kentucky Family Research Association of Owensboro, Ky.; and some are county organizations, such as the Knox County (Ill.) Genealogical Society organized in 1972. Organizations and individual genealogists produce a variety of publications to foster communication among those seeking information and those who might have it; for example, *The Southern Genealogist's Exchange Quarterly* and *Michigan Heritage.*

of a query with the hope that it will be read by someone possessing the information. Query columns have become popular features of local newspapers and special magazines.[17]

This more intensive activity reflects important shifts in genealogical inquiry. Until very recently the most significant genealogical work was carried on by patriotic organizations, of which the Daughters of the American Revolution was the most important. But that activity has been eclipsed, and while the DAR still plays a significant role, its concerns and services have been superseded by a wider range of genealogical activities. If there is a center of genealogical inquiry today, it is in Utah, where a host of genealogical enterprises have grown up around efforts of the Church of Jesus Christ of Latter-Day Saints to preserve ancestral records from all over the world. The *Genealogical Helper* is published in Logan, Utah. But despite the Mormon role in genealogy, this center of activity is not nearly the dominant influence that the DAR was in the past. Genealogical work is now spread throughout the nation.

One might sketch the apparent historical sequence of genealogical activity. Originally it was confined for the most part to exclusive societies of America's past elite—those who could trace their ancestry to the *Mayflower* or the officer corps of the American Revolution or the Society of Cincinnatus. New organizations in the latter part of the nineteenth century, such as the DAR, extended the range of inquiry to the descendants of all who participated in the Revolution, even in state militias, and if only for a few days, no matter what their social position or origin. It was the DAR that brought the Scotch-Irish into the genealogical fold. Yet for the DAR the genealogical world was confined to those who were descendants of eighteenth-century immigrants before 1783, and as time went on, they constituted a more exclusive and limited group in the face of growing numbers of post-revolutionary migrants and their descendants. What had at one point in history expanded the scope of genealogical interest served in later years to limit it.

The recent burst of energy in the area of genealogy constitutes a marked change from the DAR perspective. No longer is the search for ancestors tied so strongly to their involvement in historic epi-

---

17. One of the most widely circulated is the *Tri-State Trader*, published in Knightstown, Ind.

sodes. The interest of Mormons in the ancestors of any present member or future convert of the church has expanded the range of genealogical inquiry to a far broader number of people. Genealogical work by church members has tended to stimulate research into ancestors and families of western migrants far more than those of post-1890 immigrants to the U.S. For example, there is a magazine devoted entirely to the search for ancestors and relatives in Scandinavian countries.[18] Yet there are important beginnings for the families of later immigrants. The Mormon records include materials from southern and eastern Europe, and the *Genealogical Helper* contains articles to aid in the search for ties in Poland and Italy, relations among eastern European Jews, and the ancestors of American blacks.[19] Full development of genealogical inquiry for these newer Americans is yet to come, but its beginnings have already been stimulated. The drive for identification with an exclusive and select ancestry has been replaced by an interest in ancestry as such. The search for cultural roots is dominated by the desire to find out about one's particular past no matter what that past might be.

All this has been accompanied by another subtle yet significant shift, a change in perspective from tracing one's family back to some point in the past to tracing it forward through history from more remote ancestors to the present. The search for ancestors, of course, continues; filling in gaps in the family tree remains a major objective of every genealogist. While many of the earlier searches for Revolutionary War ancestors stopped when proof of ancestry had been pinned down, today there is increasing interest in working out patterns of descent through children and grandchildren down to the present generation. There is a growing desire for the researcher to be able to visualize himself not simply as having a remotely historical family connection but as having a kinship with hundreds, even thousands, of people tied together by a common ancestry.

18. The *Scandinavian Genealogical Helper* is published by the Everton Publishers. See also Charles A. Hall (ed.), *The Atlantic Bridge to Germany*, vol. 1, "Baden-Wuerttemberg," and vol. 2, "Hessen and Rheinland Pfaltz," and Hall, *A Genealogical Guide and Atlas of Silesia* (in press), all published by Everton.

19. See, for example, Peggy J. Murrell, "Black Genealogy," *Genealogical Helper* 26 (1972), 280, 415–17; Phyllis P. Preece, "Guide to Genealogical Research in Italy," *ibid.* 27 (1973), 1, 4–9; Larry O. Jensen, "Genealogical Research in Poland," *ibid.* 28 (1974), 1, 4–6.

There is an important change in direction here that has brought the perspective of the genealogist closer to that of the historian. The historian inevitably focuses on the flow of history: on change from some point in the past moving toward the present. Much of the older genealogical thrust was contrary to this perspective. It looked backward with a limited vision that was content to stop once a remote ancestor had been found. But the new genealogy has reversed this. More and more, genealogists are shifting to a frame of mind similar to that of the historian. The flow of thought is from a previous generation to a succeeding one, from parents to children, from the past to a point closer to the present. Until this shift occurred it was difficult for the historian and the genealogist to share a similar point of view. But the change now under way in genealogical perspective makes cooperation far more feasible.

This shift in perspective has prompted the genealogist to focus on two problems familiar to the historian. The first is migration. To the historian movement in space appears to be one of the important processes in examining the continuity or discontinuity of human institutions. While one can observe outmigration, not knowing where the migrants went leads to painfully limited conclusions. For the genealogist lack of knowledge about migration is a fundamental obstacle. The task at hand is to acquire information about migrants in their new homes; without knowledge of their destinations, the family history is truncated. If this problem cannot be solved, the entire inquiry fails. No wonder that one of the many genealogical magazines is called "The Ridge Runners: A Magazine of Migration."[20] It is concerned with genealogy in the middle belt of states from Virginia and North Carolina on the east coast through Kentucky, Tennessee, southern Indiana and Illinois, Missouri, and Arkansas to the Ozark region. The area shows a coherent pattern of migration. Again, a recent genealogical publication contains an inquiry concerning the migration routes traveled by early Scotch-Irish settlers. Migration has become a subject of great interest to social historians. Genealogy, viewing history from the bottom up through

20. "The Bridge Runners" is published by William A. Yates of Sparta, Mo. Another local source is the "Emigrant Registry," a file of persons who have lived in a given locality and moved away, with information about their destinations. Such a file is maintained for New Jersey.

individual and kinship movements, provides evidence of migration as a process in human lives.

The genealogist has devoted considerable energy to overcoming this obstacle, and the U.S. manuscript census has been the main instrument for doing it. Until recent years this was confined to searching through the census for names of individuals in the county where they were thought to live. More recently, statewide census indexes and the federal soundex for 1880, though limited in coverage, have assisted in this. The statewide printed index to the 1850 Ohio manuscript census enables one to find an individual name quickly; similar indexes are available for Indiana and Illinois, though in card files rather than in printed form. If each state had its censuses indexed in this way, the facts of migration would be far more readily available.[21]

The second perspective that comes from the newer genealogical inquiry is a sense of place and of the persistence of a family in a given place. Such a perspective is salutary in an intellectual climate in which we are prone to describe only motion, continual movement of individuals through space and time. Despite the important fact of movement, many individuals put down roots and played an important role in the development of community institutions. Thus, while in many cases the genealogist searches for kin who have migrated, in many other cases the search takes the form of intensive investigation of records in one locality covering a long period of time. From this comes an understanding of the relationships among families within a given community. Within fifty, let alone a hundred, years, the kinship context of community life takes on great significance. It is greater for rural than for urban communities. One is impressed with the way in which the new burst of genealogical inquiry has been responsible for the most significant movement to preserve and make available community records in the twentieth century. A host of county histories and atlases have been reprinted; local census records have been indexed; cemeteries have been located and headstone inscriptions transcribed; and wills and deeds,

21. The opening of the 1900 census promises to be a boon for the genealogist and historian tracing the destinations of individuals. It contains a statewide soundex index for each state. One project based upon these files is being conducted now; see Charles Stephenson, "Tracing Those Who Left: Mobility Studies and the Soundex Indexes to the U.S. Census," *Journal of Urban History* 1 (1974), 73–84.

marriage records, birth and death records have been indexed.[22] Most of this has occurred through local historical undertakings that seek to promote a heightened sense of community history.

Out of these perspectives comes an awareness of a number of historical problems that professional historians have not yet emphasized and which can be illuminated considerably through genealogical inquiry. One is the selective process in horizontal and vertical mobility. Generally we describe these matters in terms of broad social categories. Those who migrate are those with fewer community ties, the younger, unmarried, non-property-owning members of the community. Those who are better off economically tend to move upward in the occupational and social order more rapidly than those less well off. Yet focusing on family genealogy brings sharply to the fore a recognition of individual differences within these social groups. Within a single family, in which individual members are apparently in the same social circumstances, some migrate and others do not; some move to the city from the rural areas for better jobs and others do not; some reach higher levels of education and others do not. Genealogy sharpens the constant differentiating process that has gone on in American history, involving both general social characteristics and individualizing characteristics.

Closely related to the patterns of individual variation is a process of sequential community formation. As a community develops, some members of the early families remain to form persisting economic, social, political, and religious institutions, while others move on to become part of a new community elsewhere. To trace a family as it moved westward from Connecticut in the 1770s, for example, might well mean tracing each generation as it set down roots in a different locality, the first in eastern New York, the next in western New York, the next in Wisconsin, and the next in North Dakota. While the individual process is one of continual movement, the family process is one of differentiation. To look only at migrants can be misleading; the process is one of the differential and sequential establishment of communities with some family members migrating and others remaining.

22. The West-Central Kentucky Family Research Association, Owensboro, Ky., for example, is publishing transcriptions and indexes to records in the nineteen counties of its territory.

Finally, genealogical inquiry gives rise to a greater sensitivity to the relationship of institutions to individual migration. In the nineteenth century, movement within the United States seems to have been confined to relatively short distances and within small-scale institutions. A sequence of short-distance rural migrations was far more common than movement over a thousand miles of terrain; movement to a town or city was far more the case when it was nearby and where the opportunities were readily perceived or known by word of mouth. For nineteenth-century rural migrants the movement was inexorably westward, rarely south or north, and even more rarely to the east. By the twentieth century, however, considerable long-distance and even reverse migration had set in, mediated by large-scale institutions. After a long sequence of westward movements, families began after World War II to move in a variety of directions. Individuals became involved in institutions of national scope that enticed or transferred them in ways that could not be predicted. For some, higher education led to more higher education elsewhere; professional training led to job opportunities elsewhere; employment in a national corporation transferred one in any of a number of directions; and service in the armed forces took one far beyond the community of origin. A series of involvements in nationwide institutions resulted in a pattern of movement far different from the regular sequence of farm to westward farm, or farm or small town to city, characteristic of the nineteenth century.

We should not overemphasize the degree to which the new genealogy has fulfilled its promise. There is much in the records and history of family and kinship that genealogists have not yet developed. It seems to me that the major contributions they have made are twofold; first, the reorientation toward the sequence of descendants rather than a given ancestor who can be clothed with importance, and second, the perspective of migration, and the differentiating processes of migration between individuals and institutions of movement and those of community development. Yet genealogists can go much further. Just as I would urge historians to reach out to work with genealogists, so I would urge genealogists to broaden the context of their family histories to make them more meaningful cases of historical inquiry. Thus far few family historians have gone beyond brief thumbnail biographies, of birth, death, marriage, children, and perhaps migration and occupation. Some facts about education are beginning to creep in, but there is little about religion, the specifics of educational or occupational institutions, recreational activities, the nature of work or community activities, or physical descriptions of housing, farm, or community. It is time for genealogists to seek from historians the kind of family and kinship information historians would like to have and to expand their bare-bones biographies into accounts in which the family members come alive as human beings.

III

FROM an archivist's point of view the intersection of the new social history and the new genealogy requires a look from the bottom up rather than from the top down. Archivists are accustomed to thinking of records in terms of the government agencies that produced them. This is the way they are ordered in the process of being created, the way they are sent to the archives, and the way they are described and controlled. The minimal approach to records is to describe their contents as administrative records, in the style of the National Archives record groups, for example, or of the WPA descriptions of state and local records. The more useful descriptions go beyond this to the details of the agency's goals and methods of operation.

From government records one can reconstruct two processes in the interaction between the agency that produced the records and the individual whose activities were recorded. First, one can visualize an administrative agency reaching out to draw people into some administrative process. Poll lists are made during every election to prevent double voting; the county orphans' court requires guardianship to take care of those whose parents have died; property owners are required to pay their taxes regularly; the individual liable for military service must report and enlist if physically fit or be put on a disability list. These records are not simply records of administrative action; they also reflect a process by which the "arm of the law" reaches out to require the individual to do something for the purposes of government. What does government reach out to? Obviously, the more individuals the government involves, the larger the number of records generated and the better their possibilities for either extensive social description or genealogical discovery.

But archival records may also give rise to another vantage point, the individual who is being drawn into some act of record by a government agency. In their daily lives individuals work, buy and sell, own property, are born, marry, die and are buried, vote, go to school, transfer property, will and inherit, migrate to a new area, town, city, or county—in short, engage in innumerable activities which altogether make up the history of their lives. And that history is played out within a kinship group of families and within a given community. Individuals are not merely the product of manipulation by government activity; they also carry on a variety of daily activities that the historian and the genealogist can reconstruct imaginatively. Evidence about these is often lacking, but since many of them involve government action, considerable evidence is available from public sources to describe much of the course of daily human life.

This is the vantage point of the genealogist. In its earlier phases genealogy was concerned primarily with the facts of birth, marriage, death, and child-parent relationships, and all this mainly of ancestors. In other words, the dominant perspective was that people were born, married, had children, and died. Since much of the earlier genealogy was concerned with proving the involvement of an ancestor in a war, war service records were crucial. As genealogy moves to an interest in descendants and the web of kinship relationships, however, the range of individuals about whom information is desired expands to the entire population. Hence the U.S. manuscript census returns have become the most important single source of evidence for genealogists, and much energy has been devoted to making those returns more readily available through indexing. From this a far wider range of records came to be exploited in order to prove the presence of an individual at a given place at a given time—poll lists, land transfers, property taxes. It may well be that in the future school records will be the most important single source of genealogical data, for they contain information about the parent-child relationships so vital to family reconstitution. Even now the school enumerations of a number of states—for example, Indiana beginning in 1843—provide not only the names of parents

but often the names of each school-age child as well. School enrollment records provide a wealth of information about parents and
children, and student records of application and admission to colleges and universities will become of increasing importance.

Because genealogists are prone to follow individuals throughout
their lives, they inevitably develop a sense of history from the individual outward and from the bottom up. Their perspective focuses
on the individual in daily life, in work and play, in religion, in
birth, marriage, and death, in place of burial, in daily movement
and movement over the years. Until recent years most of the records
about such activities were generated at the level of local government, in the township and the county, for it was there that the individual in the daily round of life came into greatest contact with
government. In the early development of a rural community, election of local officials often called out more voters than did state or
national elections. Most records about individuals in the nineteenth
century and earlier are thus at the local level, and it is no wonder
that genealogists have flocked to those records to reconstruct life
histories.

As time passed, new layers of government activity were established at the state and especially the federal level, thereby increasing the information about individuals in the archives of those
governments. Earlier federal records of this kind have long been important genealogical sources—census, war service, immigration, and
land records especially. A few additional types of records have been
added more recently, notably income tax and social security data.
Despite the increase in federal functions, however, it is significant
that many personalized records remain at the local level. As I have
indicated, perhaps the most important additional local information
for genealogical purposes will be school records, because of their
crucial information about child-parent relationships. Individualized data in local archives will probably remain the most extensive
source of information useful to both the new social history and the
new genealogy.

All this requires a new archival perspective, one that shifts from
the context of the administrative system within which the records
were created to one of individuals as they move through life and
come into contact with governmental processes. Many of the new

aids to research in public records written by genealogists and for genealogists have this perspective. From one point of view these guides merely provide genealogists with a handy form of knowing about the existence of records. But the material selected and the way in which it is presented reveal something more than just old material in a new guise. They reflect a search for information about the lives of people and a desire to facilitate the ability of the current investigator to reach and follow those lives in the form of minibiographies and with a focus not on celebrated events but on day-to-day affairs. To make their records more useful to genealogists, modern-day archivists must imaginatively reconstruct the daily lives of people and the possible ways in which they came into contact with legal processes, and then ferret through the existing records to see which human processes are reflected in them.

From this perspective the traditional organizing principles in which archivists are immersed are more of a hindrance than a help. Those principles reflect the formal processes of governmental organization and not the human processes inherent in daily life. If one is interested in the history of public administration or of law as an institution, such a perspective is adequate. But the new social history and the new genealogy require a vastly different approach. The context of history is the ebb and flow of human life and not of the administrative agency, and for this the starting point is the individual rather than the processes of government. The terminal points are not acts of the legislature but birth and death, and the in-between steps are not processes of public administration but processes of human maturation from childhood to adulthood to old age, of human movement and migration, of human affairs such as work, leisure, religion, and family. Moreover, the archival records which remain are not the comprehensive story but only pieces of it, only that small portion of the larger ebb and flow of human life which was written down as the individual came into contact with law.

The new social history is simply the new genealogy writ large, and it requires for its historical base a similar archival approach. No longer can the historical researcher justify a project on the grounds that it exploits a given body of records. This is inadequate simply because the dimensions of an historical problem are quite independent from the system which collected the historical information.

Social processes consist of the accumulation of activities in the lives of many individuals which, taken together, add up to social history. The records are not different from those required by the genealogist, but they are required in a different format which enables one to put together the happenings in the lives of many people, not just one family. And the archival perspective is the same, a shift from the context of the agency creating the records to the context of transformations in human life. The archival record is merely an artifact, a momentary product of a given act in time and space, and not a reflection of the context of life itself. It should be used as a window through which the broader ebb and flow of life may be visualized and reconstructed. Such a perspective is required for the archivist to increase the usefulness of records for both the historian and the genealogist.

The interests and activities of the social historian, the genealogist, and the archivist converge in a community of interest in the records and resources needed for research. I have provided suggestions enough about this; let me stress more explicitly several aspects of cooperative activity that are of special and immediate concern.

First is the need for much greater attention to the preservation of local records. This is an old refrain, but it requires repeating until more is done about it. Local records are in a most uneven state of preservation, with most ranging on the deplorable side. In some states during the past few years action has been taken to do something about this, but for the most part it has not led to significant tangible results. Local records remain in a chaotic state of access. Resources for effective preservation of local records simply have not been made available. I am distressed especially by the limited concern about the matter on the part of professional historians. Too many have their eye on the national event and the personal manuscripts of the prominent individual and give too little concern to the average citizen and day-to-day activities as reflected in the local records. Moreover, much local historical activity is more concerned with the preservation of buildings and the creation of museums than with the records of history. Genealogists are the most important influences for a different approach, and historians should be willing to work with them on this common objective. Certainly a major effort should be made during the bicentennial to correct this state of affairs.

A second major problem confronting both genealogists and historians is the compilation of biographical material. Genealogists are interested in family biography—that is, of family members or generations—while historians are more interested in collective biography, information about many individuals in a given category, such as schoolteacher, city councilman, social worker, iron and steel entrepreneur, or congressman. For this information both genealogists and historians have relied heavily on the biographical compilations in earlier county histories. But such compilations after 1920 are few and far between, and as a result future researchers will have previous little biographical material on which to rely for research after that time. An ongoing cooperative venture—joining historians, genealogists, and archivists—of compiling biographical information about ordinary people in communities, towns, counties, and cities across the nation is of critical importance for both genealogical and historical research.

There are several possible approaches to this. One is an extension of the clipping and filing of obituaries, undertaken by some public libraries. The task is a simple one that takes only persistent effort for a continuous program, an effort that might well capture the same volunteer energies so admirably displayed by genealogists. Another lies in oral history with a focus on short biographies of many people rather than intensive information about prominent figures. Oral history could well be focused on family biography, and genealogists might become as involved with the preparation of material by and about the living as they have been with material about the dead. Perhaps we could envisage trained volunteer groups of oral history associates who could develop this source of information. Still another might be adult education classes in writing individual and family biography as a way of getting into both genealogy and history. Certainly the leisure-time energies that have been such an important element in modern life could be focused on the task of compiling contemporary biographical information for use by later researchers.

The third task deserves more emphasis—a cooperative effort to make individualized data more accessible for both genealogical and social research. Many data of this kind are available, but considerable indexing is necessary to make them accessible. The manuscript census returns are an excellent example of the possibilities. This is the major mass data file to which computerization has been applied by both historians and genealogists. But each has gone his own way, and the work done by one is not useful to that done by the other. If it were done cooperatively, with the needs of both in mind, the result would be more effective.

The social historian has usually drawn a sample from the census for research, but a sample is meaningless to the genealogist. After all, any one individual might be just the one who is being sought. The genealogist, on the other hand, has been preoccupied with indexing the census in such a way as to limit its usefulness for the historian. Most such projects pertain to a single county, without much connection with projects for other areas. Often the information is limited to the name and the census manuscript location only, so that the researcher must then go to the manuscript record to find other data.[23] These are useful genealogical tools but hardly of the level required for historical research on a great number of individuals. Historical research requires quick access to all the data in the record, not just the surname, and a system of indexing capable of merging data in different geographical areas into one set of data.[24]

The solution to this problem is to computerize all of the manuscript census information in the same format, so that the data can be alphabetized by individual name for any one geographical unit, the data for one unit can be merged with those for another into one combined system, and all the characteristics of individuals in the census can be analyzed in the aggregate as well as individually. Such a project has been under way for some time for the cities of Pittsburgh and Allegheny in Pennsylvania. Sponsored by the History Department and the Social Science Information Center of the University of Pittsburgh, the project has already made the 1860

23. The index for the Ohio census of 1850, the largest statewide index available, cites name, county, township, and page. The reader must use the manuscript census to recover the full schedule of information.

24. Several private firms have computerized census data for given states and census years, most of them prior to 1850; for a fee they will search their files for surnames. See the *Genealogical Helper* for advertisements.

census available for both genealogical and social research; computerization of the data for 1850, 1870, and 1880 for the same cities is in process. These data are used by faculty and students at the University of Pittsburgh for social research; alphabetized printouts have also been made available to libraries in Pittsburgh and are used by genealogists.[25]

The advantages of this system are manifold. To the genealogist the information in the printout is complete; there is no need to go back to the microfilm copy except to verify the accuracy of an entry. Moreover, as other areas are computerized in the future they can be merged easily into one overall alphabetized format. For the historian the format makes possible the aggregation of data for social description of the different wards and subcommunities of the city, occupations of individuals and their geographical location, and a variety of other characteristics. Addition of other areas to the file will facilitate comparative historical research. Such a system could be applied to any county in the nation for the same census years and be equally useful to both genealogists and historians.

The census is only one of many individualized records that could be computerized for ready access, to the mutual advantage of both genealogists and historians.[26] Archivists, moreover, should be deeply involved in this venture, for the records so created will be a highly significant addition to their resources for both historical and genealogical research. It might well be time for representatives of all three groups to come together and work out a common schedule of computerization to facilitate the research tasks of both individualized and social research. Veterans' service and pension records should have a high priority. Pension records are usually sought only by genealogists and usually for one or a few individuals. The servicing of these records has been organized to respond to this type of use. The request that the National Archives assemble the records of several thousand veterans for social research—as happened in the Allegheny County, Pennsylvania, example cited earlier—sorely

25. Copies of the printout are available at the Historical Society of Western Pennsylvania, the Pennsylvania Room of the Carnegie Library of Pittsburgh, and the Archives of Industrial Society, Hillman Library, Univ. of Pittsburgh.

26. One computerized index already available is Philip W. McMullin, *Grassroots of America: A Computerized Index to the American State Papers: Land Grants and Claims (1789–1837).*

taxed its facilities. Clearly the archives are not now prepared for extensive social research into veterans' records for the nineteenth century. Yet those records contain invaluable information for both the genealogist and the social historian. Now that a program and coding system has been worked out for a group of Civil War veterans, it is feasible for projects to be undertaken to computerize more extensive amounts of the same material. These could well be undertaken concurrently by archivists, genealogists, and historians.

Genealogists and social historians have not been accustomed to thinking that their needs and objectives converge in a common set of interests. This lack of contact is becoming a liability. This is especially so as historians become more interested in building up social description through individualized information from local records while genealogists use the same records in pursuing the rapidly growing field of family history. Intergenerational reconstitution of the family is a task which both pursue but which so far has led to little cooperative effort. The possibilities are enormous and eminently worthwhile. It is to be hoped that the separate ways of the past will soon give way to joint activities of great benefit to both.

V.
EPILOGUE

In the introduction I described the development of my historical thinking during the writing of the essays reprinted here. It may be useful now, in the form of an epilogue, to outline some of the directions in which my work has proceeded since then. For some time I have been tying together varied strands into an essay-synthesis of American history since 1850 which would be organized around the theme of modernization rather than reform. That project has been taking shape slowly but persistently. The essays in this book, continually concerned with the relationships of one segment of inquiry with another, tend toward such an overall synthesis. In this short epilogue I will outline some of the more significant themes being woven into the work in progress.

I

LET me first review some of the major elements of historical inquiry implicit in the essays in this collection. First is the vast explosion in the number of subjects to be investigated which has occurred in the past twenty-five years in American history, especially social history. New realms of human life have come under investigation and have become part of the college and university curriculum. Economic history led the way in earlier years, but social history has had a more varied and creative influence, for it has drawn the historical imagination into almost every facet of human life: ethnicity, race, religion, education, family, community, popular and legislative voting, administrative politics, social class, local-cosmopolitan dimensions.

This is no mere minor addition of new evidence to old, but a major revolution in what historians must now work into their thinking. Hindsight makes one wonder how previous historians could possibly have ignored so many data in the historical record and so many subjects for description and analysis. These essays reflect the impact of this new body of information and subject matter.

A second element concerns the form of analysis used. This involves the way in which problems are defined, the kinds of questions that are posed, the relationships which are explored. Just as new facts and new subject matter come into view, so do new analytical problems. There was the problem of the impact on the wider political order of decision making implicit in science and technology, as represented by the early conservation movement; this subject continues to intrigue me as I have become convinced that it is one of the most important elements of the entire political order. Then the focus emerged on "response," the reaction to change as represented by industrialism, which defines a wide range of social phenomena in terms of the degree to which they represent participation in or reaction against the vast changes in modern society. Or there was the "situational" approach to historical analysis, which sought to define historical problems in terms of people and their context and to re-create both that context and the human perception of it as a basis for understanding. Finally, there were the questions which arose from trying to put all the pieces together into a single whole, which constantly came back to "patterns" and "structure" on the grounds that this effort at synthesis was the major task of history.

It may well be that this choice of what to ask questions about and what to explore is the most crucial aspect of these essays. I have persistently been concerned about the reasons why historians choose certain topics for investigation. All too often it seems that the rationale is simply that evidence is available. A biography is written because the individual's papers have been preserved and are at hand; a statistical analysis is made because there is a body of quantitative data available and readily manipulable; a dramatic event is examined because it generated, at the time, a considerable amount of comment. At the same time subjects are often justified on the grounds that they have not been explored before, that historians have "neglected" them, and thus "newness" becomes the rationale.

Certainly these are not satisfactory grounds for posing questions or problems for research. It makes far more sense for those questions to arise from some larger set of concepts. For the most part, these essays come from hunches as to what is important and what is not. Yet they do reflect the emergence of concepts, often half-formed, but with definite tendencies. In the writing on conservation and on municipal government is the concept that the interplay between centralization and decentralization underlie much of the political tension in modern society. Another theme is that popular voting is a peculiar and distinct form of political action which reflects the smaller context of daily life immediately surrounding the individual. Still others are that a fundamental organizing process in modern society is the construction of planned social systems through the discovery of empirical data and their centralized manipulation, and that the course of ethnic history in America entails the gradual erosion of traditional values under the impact of rapid modernizing social change. The list could be extended. Is there any connection among all these?

The process by which these ideas have evolved is very much like that of assembling a jigsaw puzzle with few parts. There is a generalized but vague notion of what the whole might be; at the same time there are some assorted pieces available, but how many is not at all clear. Gradually, in the interplay between thinking about the whole and the parts and "fiddling" with the pieces, some fall into place, imaginative bridges are built over the gaps where the pieces seem elusive if not impossible to secure, and enough of an outline of the relationship between wholes and parts emerges to develop a sensible pattern which can be verbalized, written about, and communicated. As these are translated into somewhat formal abstractions, they become a set of concepts which constitute the goal of the endeavor. One strives for a conceptual representation of the past, in terms of patterns of structure (relationships at one point of time) and patterns of change (relationships over time), which seems to take into account both the analytical problems defined for investigation and the information that has been digested.

Let us now turn to some of the conceptual tendencies implied in the essays.

II

FIRST of all, I have been persistently preoccupied with a three-tiered level of analysis. The first research venture, on conservation policy, dealt with the top level of the political system, observed happenings there, and worked out from that point. It provided an opportunity to develop a framework for organizing large political forces and, by the same token, large social forces. I have kept coming back to this perspective, as the introductory essay indicates; the introduction to *Building the Organizational Society* and parts of other essays are in the same vein. I have been continually interested in matters of broad public policy as a major context for constructing the larger synthesis of American history. But I have also come to believe that such observations should not be divorced from the wider social order, that the interconnections between society and politics should constantly be kept in mind, and that top-level analysis should be the starting rather than the ending point for probes into these larger processes and patterns. One specific aspect of the conservation policy analysis still stands out clearly—that the administrative process is an important setting for the observation of such patterns, that administrative politics is perhaps more important in the political order than legislative politics, and that insight into the larger patterns of society can best be achieved by examining the patterns of political forces surrounding the administrative system.

At the same time, however, the essays also reflect a preoccupation with changes in human life at the "grass-roots" level. The shift to this latter vantage point, which afforded a very different perspective from that of the top levels of national policy, was triggered by examination of popular voting behavior. Since that time I have frequently returned to the study of life, experience, perception, and behavior at the grass-roots level of society, within the context of primary-group relationships in the family, in the community, and at work and of transformations in such realms as religion, family, education, recreation and leisure, consumption, and residentially related institutions. As I delved into this it became clear that I would miss much if I were to concentrate mainly on national policy. At the same time, I became convinced that one vantage point was essential to the other, that no synthesis could be adequate which did not include insights and concepts derived from an investigation of both.

From the time that these two focal points of inquiry crystallized in my mind, I began deliberately to read and formulate problems in both areas in order not to become preoccupied too much with one or the other. In the course of directing graduate research there was a tendency to become heavily involved in "grass-roots" phenomena, both because they provided more manageable research problems for students and because the political climate of the 1960s constantly emphasized more personal, more "primary-group" contexts. In order to counteract this tendency I somewhat self-consciously became involved once again in the late 1960s and early 1970s in the examination of national policy through environmental issues and taught a course entitled, perhaps pretentiously, "History and Politics of Man, Technology, and Environment." As well as focusing my thoughts on the subject matter, which I continued to find appealing, this departure forced me to become reacquainted with the sources, institutions, processes, and structural patterns of national politics, and provided an excellent opportunity to observe political forces in legislative, administrative, and judicial institutions.

These two vantage points for problem definition and conceptualization soon led to a third, that of the connections between the two. How does one link what happens at the "top level" of national politics and what happens at the "grass roots"? Clearly, the vast area between the two levels should not be ignored, as it is when one remains preoccupied with only the top and the bottom. Much evidence, many types of questions, and common sense require that one work out the connections between the two. I made some attempts in "The Social Analysis of American Political History, 1880–1920," which described three levels of the political order, and in "Political Parties and the Community-Society Continuum," which associated three types of political organization with three levels of political life. Ideas about the "organizational revolution" provided the initial and persistent context in which to think about this "middle level," but the "network" theory implicit in the local-cosmopolitan analysis provided an opportunity to carry that analysis beyond formal organization to relationships in many realms of life.

These predispositions reflected in the essays continue to have a controlling influence on the definition of problems, the search for evidence, and the development of a conceptual synthesis. The reconstruction of American history, in my view, must rest on a vertical conception in which society and politics at each of the three levels described above is investigated separately of, by, and for itself, and then integrated into an interdependent whole of relationships between levels. Thus, there are two distinct sets of large problems: first, the nature of society and politics at each level and second, the connections between each level—between lower and middle, middle and upper, and upper and lower. This perspective establishes the initial major element, the structural component, of the synthesis toward which these essays are tending.

There is also the problem of social change, already noted as an important influence on my historical thinking. My early concern for the "response" to change is apparent in *The Response to Industrialism*, an initial and rudimentary foray into this large question in which I identified "reactions" to change and argued that much of American history from 1877 to 1914 could be examined around the theme of reactions to the vast changes associated with industrialization. This was a rather primitive categorization of aspects of the problem of change; further elaborations took place with time. The essay provided one critical context for inquiry by establishing a wide setting for observing change. If one were to examine "response," one had to examine also the process of change to which "response" occurred, and this logical development soon followed—opening up the theme of change and response in many varied aspects of modern society. I began to see change as all-pervasive through many areas of the economy and society, including the varied fields of social history coming into vogue. I soon dropped the term "industrialism" to describe the change in favor of the term "modernization," which included a wider range of factors. Finally, in order to avoid the notion that there was a fixed historical stage implied in the term, I now prefer to avoid "modernization" in favor of the phrase "modernizing processes" or "modernizing America."

From this initial foray into the examination of process I began to formulate a more comprehensive frame of reference. First I attempted to distinguish among three major aspects of change—its origin, diffusion, and impact. Each of these has directed a different set of inquiries. Where in the social order does change originate? If one important aspect of change is migration, in that it provides an occasion for "social discontinuity" in the lives of individuals, we need to discover who the migrants are, and what are their characteristics. Or, if social categories of analysis become exhausted, what are the individual characteristics? From such questions as these I have become interested in the general observations that arise with respect to geographical migration, vertical mobility, and psychological mobility. Second, I tried to determine the reaction to change, the response. When change occurs, many people not involved as initiators feel threatened and draw back in defense. I have continued, in the spirit of the *Response,* to identify those ideas, values, actions, and events which reflect the desire to hold on to the past in the face of change. Finally, we should study the process by which change is diffused through the social order, either in the form of directed change by large-scale institutions (such as education or corporations) or in the form of filtration through contacts among individuals (by means of cosmopolitanizing influences, for example).

There are close connections between the analysis of change and concepts of vertical layers in the social order. Each level is a locale for the examination of each phase of change. One cannot stop with outlining patterns of vertical relationships. This would freeze the analysis and result in a failure to deal with the major problem of history: change over long periods of time. Hence, one must be constantly concerned with the structural dimension of social change. One could well raise questions about the location of change within these vertical layers. The essays indicate the view that, contrary to reform theory, social changes have been initiated more in the upper (above the median) than the lower (below the median) levels of society, an observation which requires the elaboration of new ideas as to the relationships between structure and change. These are more accounted for in modernization than in reform theory. Finally, one can bring structure and change together in a larger synthesis: long-run changes in social and political structure constitute the major focus of history and thus become the major objective of historical inquiry and writing. This view was emphasized especially in "A Systematic Social History."

Finally, a belief has arisen out of my investigation into the problems of social change that one of the important characteristics of American society is the degree to which change has been so dominant and resistance to change so limited. Attempts to discover long-term resistance to change that has major staying power, that can reverse the patterns of innovation in urbanization and modernization toward less urbanization, scientific inquiry, cosmopolitan values, larger-scale systems, or centralization of social organization lead to the conclusion that such efforts have been notoriously weak amid powerful modernizing influences. America has been a radical, a revolutionary society most notable for the limited role of tradition and conservatism.

III

WE might well take the implications of the foregoing a step further. First, the widespread variation in almost every phenomenon of American history is worthy of note. I have come to place high importance on the examination of variation in values, perceptions, behavior, and action of all kinds. Theories which rest on homogeneity, whether of political power, of economic condition, of values and culture, or of perception, have little basis in fact. This is one of the most significant contributions of quantitative data to historical observation and analysis. Few characteristics of the American people are shared equally; most are distributed over a wide spectrum of intensities. This is evident everywhere, from the realm of consumer preferences examined through market research, to values associated with levels of education, to the distribution of population over space, to levels of income and consumption. Variation provides a background for asking questions and undertaking analysis; it is also a basic phenomenon of social reality which must be built into any satisfactory conceptual scheme.

Equally significant is the process by which variation has come about and the fact that it persists in dynamic fashion. Amid rapid social change one cannot assume that patterns of variation are simply rigidly built into the social structure, and that social forces are static. If by comparing county decile distributions one finds that population is distributed in 1970 in a manner similar to its distribution in 1900 but that the total population has risen sixfold, one cannot rest content with the observation that the structure is stable. If one finds that income distributions have remained the same from 1944 through 1977 or that wealth distributions in the nineteenth century are remarkably similar over time despite the rapid rise in average level of wealth, one cannot describe this structure as static. The dynamic quality of social structure which exhibits change within persistence of pattern requires an emphasis on social differentiation, on movement in and out of places, cultural perspectives, social levels, value adherence. Most critical is the focus on individuals and changes between generations. We must account for the fact that individuals who come from the same ancestral starting point do, in succeeding generations, turn out quite differently. We must account for the fact that some in the same social context migrate, move up the ladder, or become psychologically mobile, and others do not. This is the dynamic aspect of variation, the way in which differentiation between individuals, groups, communities, and institutions constantly generates variation in pattern of belief, perception, values, and behavior.

A third and more extended aspect of this line of thought is the way in which variation and differentiation become translated into patterns of inequality in terms of social description—inequality in economic condition, in cultural values, and in political resources and power. If variation and differentiation are persistent aspects of a dynamic, rapidly changing American society, then the result of that process at any one time is inequality in the distribution of resources, perspectives, and values. This inequality can be observed between individuals in terms of income and consumption; between institutions such as churches, schools, voluntary associations, and business firms in terms of resources; or between geographical areas in terms of population size. Most importantly, these inequalities can be translated into political inequalities, not simply in the "right to vote," which though elementary and fundamental is in the twentieth century a less important element of political power. Far more significant is the new context of politics in which the major elements are the acquisition, mobilization, and application of empirical information to the legislative, administrative, and judicial process. Inequalities in resources for such action translate themselves into inequalities in political power and change the terms of political controversy to differences in the possession of information.

Finally, these lines of thought, proceeding from variation to differentiation to inequality, emerge in the larger structure of inequalities of network and scale. Vertical dimensions to the social order can be effectively arranged on the basis of scale, i.e. to larger scale, with variations in scope of human relationships and communication, of information and knowledge, of tolerations of choice, of resources and perspectives. I have continued to develop this context because it brings into one format the variations in perspective and values which arise from mobility, the variations in scope of organizing processes which arise from systematization, and the variations in possession of empirical knowledge which arise from cosmopolitanization and education and form the roots of modern political inequality. This, of course, is an extended version of the local-cosmopolitan dimension which brings together patterns in perspectives, values, organizing processes, and political inequalities. It continues to have a powerful influence on my thinking about how American history should be put together.

IV

FINALLY, it might be well to mention two areas in which I am currently working out the tendencies described above. One is regional analysis. Having carried out inquiry at the level of national policy making and studied centralized-system organizing impulses, and having worked out ideas with respect to grass-roots involvements and differentiation, I have long sought to focus many questions at the level of the region. This seems to be an excellent laboratory in which to bring together all three levels of inquiry. By region I mean some system of social relationships larger than a community, beyond a single city, and smaller than the nation as a whole. This is large enough to observe centralizing and organizing tendencies and small enough to observe and integrate in a meaningful fashion changes at the grass-roots community level.

Through the region one can also work out tensions between centralization and decentralization on a level larger than the city. The region contains both dominant and subordinate elements, with the city as the organizing center, reaching out to draw the larger society, its people and resources, into its domain. Outlying areas are attracted to the center and yet fear it; they maintain a stance of independence within their subordinate role. I had begun to work out such a context in Iowa by developing materials about Iowa society and politics, but this case study of regional analysis has never been completed. I became especially intrigued with the way in which Van Beck Hall had worked out a system for describing an entire region in terms of wholes and parts for Massachusetts in the 1780s, including not only economic factors but also cultural and political factors. His analysis seemed to combine, with reference to a single state, many of the local-cosmopolitan, decentralization-centralization themes with which I was concerned.

Two recent doctoral dissertations which I directed have stimulated considerably my thinking along these lines. Both were comparative studies of regions in eastern Pennsylvania. Burton Folsom compared the development of Scranton and its region with that of Allentown-Bethlehem and their region;[1] Edward Davies compared the development of Wilkes-Barre and its region with the southern Pennsylvania anthracite field which gave rise to no single dominant city.[2] Both dealt with a single urban "field," traced the growth of a complex of towns and cities and their relationships to each other, developed a focus on the organizers, the economic entrepreneurs, of urban systems and their social and kinship relationships, and emphasized the way in which some cities drew leadership and capital from others in a migration of elites. All this made clear the possibilities of using a regional context for analysis of both social structure and social change. I was able to develop some thoughts along these lines in April 1977 at the Columbia University Seminar on urban history and to shape them further into a coherent statement.[3]

The other current context for these inquiries is environmental politics since 1960. Much of the mode of inquiry is similar to that used in the earlier conservation book, with a heavy emphasis on administrative politics. It also has many other dimensions. First, the

---

1. Burton W. Folsom, "The Economic and Social Order of the Lackawanna and Lehigh Valleys During Early Industrialization, 1850–1880," Ph.D. diss., Univ. of Pittsburgh, 1976.

2. Edward Davies, "The Dynamics of Regional Urban Growth: Elites and Urbanization in the Anthracite Coal Region, 1850–1930," Ph.D. diss., Univ. of Pittsburgh, 1977.

3. "The City and the Region," presentation before the Columbia Univ. Seminar on urban history, March 21, 1977.

environment movement represents a major change in cultural values in which a significant share of the American people have come to define their standard of living in terms of amenities, a third historic stage of consumption following earlier emphases on necessities and conveniences. Thus, it provides an opportunity to examine broad changes in cultural values in a way that was not possible with the early twentieth-century conservation movement. Second, the context of environmental decision making in all three branches of government—legislative, administrative, and judicial—is overwhelmingly concerned with the mobilization of empirical knowledge, and this provides an unusual opportunity for examining the relationships between science and technology on the one hand and politics on the other. It constitutes a case study of the way in which the technical and empirical context of modern politics generates a new and extensive form of political inequality. Third, many environmental issues involve questions of the relationships of geographical areas with a high intensity of development and low levels of quality-of-life amenities to areas with a low intensity of development and high levels of such amenities; this provides an opportunity to examine in a new context the relationship between dominant and dependent areas and central and peripheral areas, and to carry through many aspects of regional analysis.

Another related subject which has increasingly aroused my interest is the politics of planning, the process of making the political choices which are involved in the attempt to project and control the future. There are choices in the selection, acquisition, and organization of data; the projection of data into the future; the mode of analysis; the substantive questions analyzed in terms of their implied value preferences; the allocation of funds for inquiry and research—a wide range of ingredients which are involved in the technical and empirical context of decision making. I have been especially intrigued with the way in which the overlay of technical and empirical considerations in modern politics obscures values. This permits fundamental choices to be made, with the help of complex data and professional experts, in a way that hinders an understanding of the choices at stake, or even of where in the system those choices are being made.

These new concerns with environmental conservation have led

me to write two articles which are not included in this volume: "Value Premises for Planning and Public Policy—The Historical Context"[4] and "The Limits-to-Growth Issue: An Historical Perspective."[5]

From this epilogue, then, the reader may be able to sense where the ideas implicit in the essays are tending. The introduction provided some background by describing the way in which my interests arose from a variety of circumstances and experiences and then led from one inquiry to another through following their implications and ramifications. At the same time there have been tendencies toward synthesis which are not altogether clear from observing that background. In this epilogue I have indicated ways in which the ideas in the essays have led to some major conclusions that will shape the course of my future writing.

4. "Value Premises for Planning and Public Policy—The Historical Context," in *Proceedings of the Conference on Planning and Public Policy in the Regional Setting* (Akron, 1975), 12–43.

5. "The Limits-to-Growth Issue: An Historical Perspective," in Chester L. Cooper (ed.), *Growth in America* (Westport, Conn., 1976), 115–42.

Index

Swarthmore College, 4, 5
Swedes, 55, 400
Symbolic Crusade (Gusfield), 178
System, 22, 73
"Systematic Social History" (Hays),
   36, 49–50, 437
Systematization, 22–23, 72–73, 76–
   77, 81–85, 94, 125–26, 163–66;
   and municipal government, 213,
   219; and conservation politics, 240,
   243; in society generally, 244–63;
   as a political order, 312–16

Taft, William Howard, 79
Tariff, 17–18, 68, 73, 75, 113, 131,
   157, 303; as ideology, 176, 304
Taylor, Frederick W., 22
Taylor Society, 72
Teapot Dome, 234
Technical systems, 23, 245–50
Temperance politics, 90. *See also* Pro-
   hibition
Texas, 157
Thernstrom, Stephan, 27ff, 189, 381
Tönnies, Ferdinand, 129
Toronto, University of, 382
Toulmin, Harry A., 220
Township (as political unit), 77
Trade association, 9, 13, 75, 84, 108
Trade union, 9
Traditionalism in the U.S., 4, 151;
   and modernity, 33, 268–72
Transportation, 52, 75, 255–57, 315–
   16; urban, 330–31, 347
Transportation Act of 1920, 20, 57–58
Trempeleau Co., Wis., 382
Truman, Harry S, 92
Trust issue, 54
Tweed ring, 194, 336

Union Twp., Iowa, 55
United Brethren, 79
U.S. Steel Co., 213
Unsettled People (Berthoff), 190
Upper class, 148; analysis of, 31–32,
   94–95, 187–89; studies of in Pitts-
   burgh, 32, 187; in Wilkes-Barre,
   Pa., 187; in urban integration,
   341–43, 345–46

Uprooted (Handlin), 28, 53, 64
Urban government, 334–36
Urban history, 19, 25, 137, 181–200,
   326–56; research in, 24–26; quan-
   titative data for, 43; as context for
   analysis of social structure, 181–83;
   and social differentiation, 183–89.
   See also City; Municipal govern-
   ment
Urban integration, 336–46; 349–51;
   reaction against, 351ff
Urbanization, 20; size and scale in,
   193ff
Urban redevelopment, 350
"Use of Archives for Historical Statis-
   tical Inquiry" (Hays), 37
Utah, 414
Utility franchise, 226

"Value Premises for Planning and
   Public Policy—The Historical Context" (Hays), 443
Values: in modernization, 264ff;
   need to analyze variation in, 266–
   67
Variation, as focus for historical description, 32, 143–45, 167–69,
   174, 181, 196, 266–67, 273ff, 386–
   87; and description of values, 266–
   67; as establishing pattern in social
   phenomena, 438; and differentiation, 438–40; and implications for
   inequality, 439–40
Vassar College, 382
Vertical patterns, 184, 262–63, 436
Vidich, Arthur, 65, 96, 258
Virginia, 382
Vocational education, 72
Voluntary organizations, 35, 190, 191
Voting analysis, 10–12, 39, 59–63,
   77–81, 91–92, 102, 103–104, 119,
   156–57, 164, 185, 407
Voting patterns, 10, 49, 73, 95; realignments in, 12, 102, 157–58,
   160, 173, 300–301; in Iowa, 54–
   56; Republican, 1893, 78; stability
   in, 1874–1894, 78, 80; Democratic, 1904–1910, 79, 103; in precincts, 79–80; changes in North

Twentieth-Century America Series
Dewey W. Grantham, General Editor

Each volume in this series focuses on some aspect of the politics of social change in recent American history, utilizing new approaches to clarify the response of Americans to the dislocating forces of our own day—economic, technological, racial, demographic, and administrative.

VOLUMES PUBLISHED:

ALVERNO COLLEGE LIBRARY
American political history as social ana
973.072H425

2 5050 00215750 7

140021

973.072
H425

REMOVED FROM THE
ALVERNO COLLEGE LIBRARY

Alverno College
Library Media Center
Milwaukee, Wisconsin

DEMCO